Dance in the Vampire Bund

SECRET CHRONICLES

SEVEN SEAS ENTERTAINMENT PRESENTS

DANCE IN THE VAMPIRE BUND
SECRET CHRONICLES

by Nozomu Tamaki, Tikurakuran, and Gemma

TRANSLATION
Lu Huan
Jill Morita
Amber Tamosaitis
Alethea and Athena Nibley
Andrew Alfonso
Hitomi Kayama
Adrienne Beck

ADAPTATION
Janet Houck
Rebecca Scoble
Lianne Sentar
Lee Otter
Shanti Whitesides

LAYOUT AND DESIGN
Nicky Lim

PROOFREADER
Katherine Bell

MANAGING EDITOR
Adam Arnold

PUBLISHER
Jason DeAngelis

ISBN: 978-1-626920-62-0
Printed in Canada
First Printing: October 2014
10 9 8 7 6 5 4 3 2 1

FOLLOW US ONLINE: www.gomanga.com

TABLE OF CONTENTS

Dance in the Vampire Bund

NIGHT &
DARKNESS

STORY
Tikurakuran

ILLUSTRATION
Nozomu Tamaki

Late one evening, Akira left the school alone.

He rarely acted independently of Hime-san after school, but that day, a number of situations had come up. Negotiations between Mina-hime and the Japanese government in Kasumigaseki had taken longer than expected, and Vera was escorting her as her personal secretary and bodyguard. Akira himself had been asked by Yuki to stay late and help out the student council.

As he walked alone down the school route that he usually sped past in a limousine, he felt a different vibe today.

This area, located on the opposite shore from the Bund, was once a completely normal harbor region. With the completion of the Bund, however, many of the buildings were deserted, turning the area into a ghost town. While it was true that House Tepes had purchased the land, it was speculated that rumors about a local "vampire den" had been used to scare people off.

In place of harbor facilities, distribution centers tied to the Bund had been erected using House Tepes funds. Even so, the only vehicles that passed through here were trailers transporting workers to and from the Bund; the area remained largely uninhabited. Akira hadn't laid eyes on a single commuter during the entire trip from school.

He sped along at a fast pace that couldn't exactly be called walking. The damage to the sidewalk beneath his feet was extremely apparent—weeds grew wildly in the cracks and seams.

The wharf visible over the chain link fence lining the walkway was also deserted; an unused, abandoned gantry crane had since become a resting spot for seagulls. Beyond the crane, the Bund's government building stood proudly and majestically, dyed red by the setting sun.

The gantry crane stood covered in rust, while the government building shone brightly, wrapped in faultless glass.

The recession of humans, and the progression of vampires.

Years earlier, this scene never would have happened.

When House Tepes took their enormous wealth and established the Bund, they shocked not only humans, but vampires around the world. But after suffering great losses during the civil war between the Three Great Clans, was it really possible for the once-collapsed House Tepes to rally on assets alone?

Akira considered this. To him, House Tepes meant Hime-san; there were many things he still didn't know about House Tepes itself.

Maybe he should ask Vera to tell him the story sometime…

Deep in thought, Akira neared the entrance to the underground tunnel that served as the only land route to the Bund. There was a small figure loitering on the rough walkway approaching the tunnel. As he got closer, he saw that it was an elderly man sitting in a wheelchair. He was grumbling continuously in a language that Akira didn't understand.

The only people who ventured into this area were foolish humans seeking perpetual youth and longevity, or junior high students daring each other to take a peek into the tunnel. The old man didn't appear to be either.

Akira tried speaking to him in English. "Sir, are you all right?"

The man twisted his head to look over his shoulder at Akira.

The skin on top of the balding man's egg-shaped head looked like parchment glued to his skull. His skinny body and sunken blue eyes, combined with a pointed nose and stubborn-looking angled lips, reminded Akira of a predatory bird, maybe a vulture. Due to the man's strange appearance, Akira wondered if he was a vampire for a moment—but he was clearly still human; it was before sunset and the rays of the fading sun still shone brightly upon him.

The old man answered him in heavily accented English. "Oh, you came at a good time. Give me a hand, won't you?"

Akira dropped his gaze and saw that the tires on one

side of the wheelchair had gotten stuck in a crack in the pavement. Akira lifted the wheelchair easily and freed the man from his predicament.

"It's dangerous for you to be wandering around in a place like this by yourself. Where are you headed?"

With his twig-like index finger, the old man pointed in front of him. In that direction stood the Bund government building.

Akira was speechless. As it was almost nightfall, no human would wish to venture into the city center of the Bund. A tottering old man would surely be captured. Nervously, he questioned the man. "Sir, are you aware of what's there?"

"Don't insult me! How could I not know the Vampire Bund's government building? You'll do. You're young, so you must have the strength to push this thing to the other side of the tunnel. Take me to that building." He rapped his wheelchair noisily while continuing to rattle on.

Akira finally understood what the old man wanted, and was utterly amazed. "By any chance, were you waiting for someone to push you?"

"You understand now."

Without a good reason to leave the old man on the side of the road, he pushed the wheelchair into the tunnel. He knew he was going to get stopped at the security checkpoint. He could just hand the old man off to the guard at the gate, and everything would be fine.

All of the guardsmen at the gate knew Akira. One of them left the booth carrying a scanner. He looked at the old man with a suspicious expression, but didn't say anything as he proceeded to check him over.

The inspection for a first time entrant into the Bund was extremely strict. On top of comparing a hand print to the registry and undergoing a body check, entry was only allowed to those with explicit written permission from a party within the Bund.

However, the guard merely verified the old man's hand print, pulled back his scanner, and spoke easily. "Go right ahead."

Akira was taken aback. "H-how is that possible? You can't let some random person in here arbitrarily; there'll be trouble!"

Pressed by Akira for an answer, the guard panicked a little. "You said 'arbitrarily,' but this man has lifetime entry privileges granted by the government. We have no reason to stop him."

"Lifetime entry privileges?" Hearing those words for the first time, a bit of hysteria unwittingly crept into Akira's voice.

The elderly man was ignoring him with a cool expression.

Akira drew in closer to the booth and asked in a low voice, "Hey, do you know who that old man is?"

"Don't know. His hand print is registered, but there's no

ID information listed."

Irritated, the old man tapped his armrest. "Come on, let's be on our way. Don't waste the little time I have left."

When they passed through the gate, a dark downward slope stretched out before them. At the end of that slope, there was a narrow but gentle incline that extended all the way to the exit. It would have been nearly impossible for the old man to make it to the Bund by his own strength.

Akira pushed the wheelchair silently as he thought to himself.

What would be the best way to ask the old man about his background? Judging from their interactions so far, even a direct question would likely be dodged.

Right then, the old man opened his mouth as if he had read Akira's mind.

"In the past forty years, I haven't once shared my story. I haven't even claimed a name. But here in the Bund, they've allowed me that. It is all due to Her Highness' power."

Still facing forward, Akira couldn't read any emotion from the old man's narrow shoulders. He turned around to look at Akira. "You feel like listening to my story?"

Akira had no reason to turn him down.

That night, I was running for my life.

I had barely escaped my home country; I'd lost my

identity and a lifestyle that had taken twenty years to build. The only asset that remained was my own life.

I still had to walk more than a kilometer to reach the high government official's residence that acted as a safety zone. If my pursuers caught me before I passed through the gate, the only thing waiting for me would be a trial without proper legal counsel and a hangman's noose. Their tenacity exceeded that of the deceased government officials of my home country.

As a fugitive, I was grateful that there were many clouds that night and that the moon only showed its face occasionally. The few streetlights in the alleyways shone coolly on the damp stone roads. There were few people out on the street that night, possibly due to the recent left-wing guerrilla activities. Stray cats and dogs outnumbered pedestrians.

I was carefully selecting my route and making slow progress, when suddenly I heard a voice call down from above my head.

"It would be better if you didn't go that way."

I took a moment to calm my nerves, and prepared to turn back.

When I looked up, there was a young girl sitting atop a tall brick wall. I was filled with relief and anger, and called out in a voice that was louder than necessary. "Who are you?"

The girl was wearing a plain yet high quality velvet dress, and her long blond hair was tied in pigtails and secured with red ribbons. Her physique was delicate and small; she didn't look any older than ten. Youth and elegance mingled exquisitely on her round face, and even in the twilight, the eyes looking down at me glittered with innocence.

"That way is dangerous," the girl said in a thin voice, tilting her small head. "I already know where you are going, sir. If you plan to run, another way would be best."

Of all the stupid things... There was no way that a young girl I had never seen before could have that kind of information about me. Also, it was strange for such a young child to be wandering around so late at night.

I thought I must've been hallucinating from the stress of being chased, so I ignored the girl and continued walking. She said nothing more after that, nor did she chase after me. It definitely seemed like I was seeing things. And how could a little child climb a three-meter wall in the first place?

I continued on, carefully selecting a route to avoid attracting attention. I was now only a few blocks from my destination.

I heard a faint noise behind me, tickling my ear.

I stopped moving. Nervousness electrified the hairs on the back of my neck. I looked over my shoulder and realized what it was—the sound of leather shoes on stone pavement.

Preparing for the worst, I turned all the way around to see a man wearing a felt hat pulled low over his eyes and a long coat. He was standing only a few meters in front of me. Both of his hands were hidden meaningfully in his pockets.

Panicking, I turned to run—but although there hadn't been anyone standing there before, a second figure in a matching coat stood in my way. I couldn't escape.

I remembered the young girl's words. I wondered if it was a kind of prophetic dream.

Resigned, and without any resistance, I let the men lead me away. They weren't violent with me, but I could see that they'd leave me no room to disobey.

They led me to a black sedan parked at the end of a secluded cul-de-sac. There was a third man in the driver's seat...thinking back on it now, I didn't truly understand the situation I was in at the time. My head was too full of fear of our destination.

I was shoved into the back seat of the car and sandwiched between the two men; I couldn't even squirm.

The car was completely silent.

Something was wrong. The driver hadn't even tried to start the car. On top of that, none of my three assailants had uttered a single word up until that point.

Understandably feeling a little uncomfortable, I shifted in my seat.

Suddenly, the man on my left pinned my arms behind my back. I tried to resist, but the man was bizarrely strong and didn't give an inch. It felt like my body was bound to a stake with wire.

He twisted me around so I was facing the man on my right.

He slowly removed his hat. The eyes that appeared beneath the brim were a fiery deep crimson, as if they'd been infused with fresh blood; they didn't look like human eyes at all.

I finally realized what was happening. These weren't my pursuers, they were something else. And they didn't look at all like humans.

If they weren't human, what were they?

Why did they take me?

What did they plan to do with me?

Questions swirled in the back of my mind, but the man on my right did nothing to answer them as he brought his pale, bluish-white face closer to me. He pulled back his thin lips to expose canine teeth almost as large as my pinky finger— the motion warped his face into a horrifying mockery of a smile.

The man moved towards the back of my neck. His strangely cool breath blew on my face, and a scrapyard smell of rust and iron met my nose.

I realized that I was facing a much worse death than hanging.

The man's mouth was open wide, prepared to bite—when the car door behind him flew off its hinges.

Something big leapt through that opening. A thick arm shot out and seized the man on my right's head from behind, casually breaking his neck with a dry snap.

The man on my left—who was still restraining me—bared

his fangs with a menacing growl. The intruder carelessly tossed the now-dead man out of the car. At that moment, the man on my left attempted to plant his fangs in me from behind, but the intruder grabbed my head in an eagle grip and pulled me toward him.

Missing their mark, the man's teeth snapped together in vain.

I feared that my neck had also been broken, but I had only been pulled out of the way, onto the floor of the car's rear seats. The intruder and the remaining assailant wrestled above my head as I lay pressed to the floor—the body of the car swayed fiercely. Soon, the smell of feral beasts that had filled the car was replaced by the scent of fresh blood, and the cries of my last attacker turned to the moans of the dying.

Finally, even that fell silent.

The car stopped rocking. The fight was finally over.

The intruder grabbed me by the nape of my neck and pulled me up, letting me see its face clearly for the first time. I let out a shriek.

The intruder was a wolf—with a massive body that dwarfed mine, covered in waves of silver fur. I stared into the golden eyes behind its muzzle.

It was nearly impossible to believe, but this beast was my savior.

After I had calmed down, I took a moment to look around.

The man who had been sitting on my left was barely breathing. His entire jaw had been ripped off, and his body had been torn to shreds by the wolf's claws.

The man whose neck had been snapped was lying on the road. He also still lived, and squirmed restlessly on the ground. If I had doubted for a moment that they weren't human, I couldn't deny it now.

The driver was still sitting in the front. A wide metal bar had been thrust through the roof, into his brain, through his body and out his asshole. He was skewered right to his seat. But even under those conditions, he hadn't died. He was wriggling, trying to find a way to free himself.

Where had the metal pole come from?

The wolf exited the car. I followed him out and looked up at the roof.

The young girl from earlier was standing on top of the car, her arms folded. She looked down at me calmly.

"You didn't listen to my warning. And now you've had some frightening encounters."

The girl's facial expression and speech were entirely different from earlier—she didn't seem like the young child I'd seen before. She was haughty, but in a good way, overflowing with confidence.

She wasn't a hallucination.

With grace and elegance, she descended from the roof to stand before me. She was much shorter than me, but for some reason it was I who felt overpowered by her presence. She exuded a strong aura that didn't suit her childlike appearance—like an encyclopedia-sized picture book.

The wolf crouched at her side, like it was her protector.

"I'll go over the main points," the girl said without waiting for a response. "There are three forces pursuing you now. One, you are well aware of. Another was the group in the car. As you now know, they are not human. They are vampires."

Vampires.

Blood-sucking demons.

I had read Le Fanu's short stories when I was young, and saw the films starring Christopher Lee. Of course I knew what vampires were. Normally, I would have laughed it off as a joke. But, as the young girl had said, I'd experienced them first hand. I had no choice but to believe her.

"They have been ordered to kill you on sight. Without a trial, of course." She gestured to herself. "The third party is me. Unlike the others, I don't wish to harm you."

I remembered the wolf's behavior—it seemed like she was telling the truth.

At present, the wolf was keeping a keen lookout. It seemed like a regular wolf at first glance, but looking closer, the toes on its front legs were abnormally long, almost like human hands. There was something else strange about it, but I couldn't explain what it was.

"Here is what I suggest. Come with me. Serve me. If you do so, I will get you out of here alive and give you work that makes use of your experience and expertise. What do you think? Do we have a deal?"

There was a loud noise behind us. Back near the car, the

three men had turned into large piles of ash.

Is that what happens when vampires die?

All of these incidents, further and further away from the reality I had known, only served to dull my nerves; I was no longer surprised by anything. My sense of reason had shrunk to the size of a pebble. I found myself calmly listening to the girl's preposterous suggestion.

"I'm sure I don't have to tell you this, but I cannot offer you a high government office. You must be aware of what happened with Eichmann."

True, when Eichmann was arrested, he was unable to take any positions in the Argentinean government. My original pursuers didn't care one bit about national sovereignty. On the other hand, I knew exactly what would happen if I was captured by the vampires…but what about this girl?

"If one group of my pursuers is human, and the second group is vampires… Are you Mephistopheles, then?"

I was serious. If vampires were real, then it wouldn't be strange for Mephistopheles to exist as well. My situation seemed right out of a play by Goethe.

The girl laughed aloud, a dignified, refined sound.

"That would make you Doctor Faust! Though I cannot guarantee that the life I offer you will be any better than dying. Nevertheless, if you agree to come with me, I will save your life."

"And if I refuse?"

"I cannot afford to have you fall into anyone else's hands," the girl answered lightly. "If you refuse, I will have to kill you."

As if to back up her claim, the wolf at her side bared its teeth.

"That's not an offer; that's a threat."

"A threat? Not at all. I simply require your knowledge, probably as much as you wish to live. It seems like a fair exchange."

The crouching wolf suddenly got to its feet and began looking around nervously at their surroundings. The girl nodded at the wolf.

"So, we're surrounded? Rozenmann's preparations were better than I expected." She turned back to me. "We're out of time. Will you join me, or die here? Decide quickly."

There was no choice, really. I didn't want to die, and beyond that, the promise of work that used my expertise was interesting.

"All right. I'll go with you."

"Get on," she said suddenly, with easy authority in her voice.

"What?"

"Get on his back! Quickly!"

The girl was gesturing towards the wolf. As if it understood her words, it had lowered its hindquarters and was waiting for me to mount it.

As instructed, I straddled the wolf's back. When I timidly rested my hands on both of its shoulders, I could feel its stiff muscles humming beneath its thick fur. I had never ridden a horse or donkey before, let alone a wolf!

"Wolfgang, your task is to escape. I'll make an opening. Take him and head for home."

"I understand, Your Highness."

I hadn't heard that voice before—who else was here, besides me and the girl?

I was only confused for a moment before my face turned white in shock; it was the wolf. The wolf I was straddling had used human speech.

I finally understood the wolf's true identity, and the source of the uneasiness I had felt since I first laid eyes on him. There was something behind his golden eyes, a human intelligence rather than wild instinct. A werewolf. Beowulf. The words floated around in my mind.

The wolf called Wolfgang looked at me over his shoulder and muttered, "Don't let go. Remember, if you let go, you die."

Without waiting for an answer, Wolfgang took off, leaving the girl in his wake. As I had been instructed, I gripped his neck tightly. Out of the corner of my eye, I thought I saw wings sprouting from the girl's back, but I told myself that it was just my imagination. Surely, if things like this kept happening, I would lose all connection to reality.

In the blink of an eye, Wolfgang sped up and sprinted soundlessly down the stone-paved local roads. Half engulfed in darkness, the roads twisted and turned in complex patterns, but he didn't hesitate at all. Wolfgang successfully avoided parked cars and street vendor stalls with minimal effort and movement. He was even able to change our route on the fly to avoid ambushes, due to his keen ears and nose.

As for myself, I barely managed to hold on while Wolfgang skirted ambushes and sped past obstacles.

Suddenly, Wolfgang stopped.

There was a man standing in front of us. He looked a lot like the vampires from earlier, and he seemed to have trouble processing what he was seeing; he just stood there staring blankly at us. Finally, my eyes met his. With a shocked expression, he reached into his breast pocket.

Wolfgang dashed towards the man as I realized what he was doing—drawing a pistol.

Wolfgang ran even faster and kicked hard off the ground. We were suddenly floating through the air.

Compared to the wolf, the man's reaction was hopelessly slow.

Wolfgang's fangs closed like a guillotine around the man's windpipe, breaking his neck. He cried out once, then died.

The man's freshly severed head send a fount of blood everywhere. I felt it splash across my cheek.

Landing lightly on the ground, Wolfgang started sprinting again without a second glance.

I only realized it later, but of all the people I'd met that evening, he was the only human. He must have been my main pursuer.

We turned a corner.

The street ahead of us was blocked by a row of vampires. We were surrounded. The vampires who'd been chasing me earlier must have come here.

Wolfgang didn't slow down. At this rate, we'd run headfirst into the crowd of vampires. I couldn't imagine that even a werewolf would stand a chance against those odds. For a moment, I even considered jumping from Wolfgang's back and trying to run—though I had no idea what my next move would be.

Suddenly, the windows of the building beside the vampires shattered, sending shards everywhere. In the middle of the glass explosion, two dark shapes fell.

They were black wolves, both larger than Wolfgang and more sturdily built. In the midst of their rain of glass, they bared their fangs and claws and dove right into the vampires, who turned to meet the new threat.

The young girl was floating directly above the fray—just as I'd thought, she really did have wings coming out of her back. She descended quickly and joined in the attack.

At that moment, Wolfgang—who had kept running at full speed, straight ahead—took a mighty leap; he landed safely on the other side of the vampires.

"Just keep running!"

In response to the girl's yell, Wolfgang ran at full speed

away from the battlefield. I looked over my shoulder. The girl was wielding two sabers that I didn't remember seeing earlier. She swung them in every direction, brilliantly chopping up the swarming vampires.

The girl's movements were fierce, like she was doing ballet in a strong wind. But there was something so lovely about her—even when surrounded by blood and flying bits of flesh, speckled with falling ash, her beauty was never diminished. No, the chaos around her made her more beautiful.

The wolves' battles, though, relied on pure strength. They tore holes in their opponents' carotid arteries with their teeth, then grabbed their foes' bodies and swung them into the other vampires. Even outnumbered, they dominated

the battle, like the Norse gods Valkyrie and Fenrir come to life.

The beauty and power of that scene stays with me to this day.

While the battle played out, Wolfgang kept running. We were almost at the forest that bordered the town. The only thing between us and the forest was a single bridge—and I knew that we could lose our pursuers if we could just make it to the woods.

Suddenly, Wolfgang stumbled in his perfect stride—at the same moment, an intense pain stabbed through my shoulder and thigh.

A moment later, gunfire rang out.

We were being targeted.

Wolfgang and I fell to the ground, entangled in each others' legs.

My face scraped along the pavement as I tried and failed to stand. One arm and one leg were soaked in blood. I looked over at Wolfgang—multiple bullet wounds gushed on his body. If we didn't get moving, we'd be on the receiving end of another volley. Supporting each other, we managed to stumble into the cover of a nearby garbage bin.

As we looked around from our cover, we saw a tremendous number of vampires appear from out of nowhere; we were completely surrounded with nowhere to go.

"Hey, pull yourself together!" I called out to Wolfgang.

Wolfgang dragged his injury-ridden body up and stood in front of me. He planned to use his body as a shield to protect me until the very end.

The mass of vampires closed in slowly, as if to taunt us. Wolfgang stood motionless.

Suddenly, the sky cleared and the moon shone down. The vampires' red eyes and white canines glowed mysteriously in the moonlight, a swarm of two-colored fireflies.

Unexpectedly, Wolfgang's ear began to twitch. Then he smiled at me like he had all the time in the world. I had never seen a wolf smile before, but it looked just like I'd expected.

"Relax. We've won."

As soon as he said that, he lifted his head and began to howl loudly and clearly at the moon.

All of the hair on my body stood on end. It was a blood-curdling sound filled with fighting spirit and a thirst for blood; it was so ghastly, even the vampires froze.

But only for an instant. They started moving towards us again, tightening their circle.

Just when it seemed like the end, a different howl rang out from outside the circle—a reply to Wolfgang. Then there was another, and another... howls echoed all around us.

Even a human like me could understand.

"We're coming to help you."

The vampires, who'd thought their victory was guaranteed, were shaking visibly. Just like Wolfgang, I knew now that we would win.

In the end, the wolves' destruction of the vampires didn't take more than three minutes.

Once we made it into the forest, the young girl questioned me again. "I'll ask just once more. If you come with me, you will never see the sun again. Are you okay with that?"

I looked at Wolfgang. He was surrounded by his kind, lying down and resting his bloodstained body. Whatever this girl's expectations were, he had put his life on the line to save me. I wasn't conflicted anymore.

"From now on, I will live my life in the shadows. I will follow you, Your Highness."

"...And that is how I became a retainer of Her Highness. Though I didn't believe that I would literally 'never see the sun again.'" The old man laughed with a raspy voice.

Akira's head felt numb from all of this new information.

From start to finish, the old man's story was brand new to him. But this man had connections to Hime-san, and his father, Wolfgang.

Still, the old man had left out two important pieces.

Why was he a fugitive in the first place? And why did Hime-san need him so badly that she would go so far to acquire him?

Just as he was about to ask, they exited the tunnel.

They were close to the cluster of skyscrapers in the central area of the Bund. The sun had already set, and the gaudy lights of the entertainment district sparkled in the distance.

When Akira saw the group assembled ahead, he stopped.

The small figure standing in the middle could be none other than Hime-san herself. Wolfgang, Vera, Alphonse, and even the head maid, Sekiko, were present; most of her closest retainers and most senior advisers were there.

She smiled at Akira. "It took you a while to get here. Did you make any stops along the way?"

"Wh-what's the meaning of this?"

The old man left the bewildered Akira behind and rolled his chair forward, stopping in front of Hime-san. Then he bowed his head deeply, and spoke respectfully in German.

"It has been far too long, Fraulein Mephistopheles."

"It was about time you came, Doctor Faust."

"I thought to myself, I should like to see the Stigma rain once before I die, so I pushed these old bones to make the long journey."

"I thought you might. I hope that you will enjoy yourself without reservation this evening."

Hime-san neared Akira, who was still standing with a dumbfounded expression on his face, and grasped his hand. "Thank you for your hard work. That man is a very important person to House Tepes."

The old man was surrounded by the group, exchanging pleasantries and making jokes. "Vera-dono, you are still as beautiful as ever. You've lost weight, haven't you, Sekiko? Don't forget to pay your respects to me."

"Hime-san, just who is that old man?" Akira asked point-blank. He couldn't take much more of this mystery.

She smiled meaningfully at him. "We'll talk at the government building. I'll explain everything."

"I can tell from the look on your face that you won't get it." Alphonse laughed as he gripped the steering wheel of his convertible. Sitting in the passenger seat, Akira didn't say anything because he knew Alphonse was right.

As usual, the two of them were riding in Alphonse's convertible, escorting the limousine that Hime-san and the old man were riding. Traffic was slow-moving in the one lane on the main street; a large crowd was already gathering to wait for the Stigma rain. Asians, Caucasians, Hispanics, triads, goths, punks...people of every race and subculture gathered for one reason and one reason alone: a mutual thirst for blood.

Hime-san had told Akira everything. The old man's true identity was a war criminal from Nazi Germany. Originally, he was a doctor who specialized in hematology, but in the Nazi SS, he had served as a military medical officer at concentration camps. He was personally responsible for the deaths of many, many Jewish people through human experimentation. He had worked with the "Angel of Death," Dr. Mengele, at Auschwitz. After the war, he was charged with committing crimes against humanity and soon had a price on his head.

At that time, Hime-san had no physical domain, and she was fighting to maintain her influence. She needed to distribute artificial blood to her retainers scattered around the world, but there wasn't a solid way to maintain their supply lines and reach them all. Due to extreme hunger, many of them abandoned House Tepes.

Then she discovered a hematology specialist who, due to his connections with Nazi Germany, was unable to work in human hospitals. After the rescue that night, they put him to work developing a way to produce large quantities of Stigma.

The man went above and beyond their expectations, and the production of Stigma was industrialized. Having established a unifying power in Stigma, Hime-san began to work towards establishing a new domain, namely, the Vampire Bund. In recognition of his contributions in helping to restore House Tepes, he became the only human who could enter and exit the Bund at will.

"Why did it have to be him? What the hell were you thinking…?!" Akira couldn't shake the frustration and anger from his face.

"House Tepes needed him." Alphonse told him, point-blank. "That man had a wealth of medical knowledge that couldn't be obtained through normal means. And besides, any respectable doctor would have died before conducting those experiments with human subjects."

"That's my point."

"Hey, boy." Alphonse glared at him. "By human standards, he's a brute. But for vampires, we have only one standard: obeying the will of Her Highness. You'd best not forget that."

The excitement around the car rose to shouts of joyous cheering.

The blimp arrived in the sky above them and began spraying Stigma everywhere. Crimson drops began to color the windows of the car. Through the red waterfall flowing down the windshield, he could see the silhouettes of Hime-san and the old man sitting in the back of the limousine.

What was bothering him so much about this? Even he didn't know.

Was it anger at the despicable crimes the old man had committed in the past?

Was it disappointment in Hime-san for using the old man?

Was it jealousy toward a man who had forged a deep relationship with Hime-san that he knew nothing about?

It may have been all three.

The Stigma rain picked up. As if pacing their breathing with the streaks of pouring red rain, the fever of the crowd grew higher and higher. Night in the Vampire Bund had begun.

The next day at twilight, Akira escorted the old man from the entryway of the government building. Unlike the day before, Hime-san had provided a limousine to shuttle the man. Someone would be waiting to meet him on the other side.

Since the old man had said he wanted to leave as quietly as he had come, Akira had been assigned to see him off. Strangely, the old man had specifically requested him. To be honest, Akira felt uncomfortable just breathing the same air, but Hime-san had declared "Queen's orders!" and there was no way for him to oppose that.

"Thanks for taking care of me. I enjoyed talking about the past for the first time in a long while." The old man was in high spirits. "I only have a little time left, but you still have the rest of your life. Keep watching over Her Highness for me, won't you?"

Akira got caught up in his words. As he transferred the old man from his wheelchair to the back seat of the limousine, he had to ask, "Um, would be all right if I asked you a personal question?"

"What is it?"

"Why didn't you become a vampire?"

Akira hadn't been able to shake the thought. There was no doubt that this old man was human. In other words, he wasn't a part of the House Tepes hierarchy, but a retainer purely of his own will. If he had become a vampire, he would have avoided old age and death. Why didn't this old man give up being human? Why was he content to get old and die?

The old man laughed knowingly. It was almost as if he had been waiting for Akira to ask that question all along. He leaned forward and looked directly into Akira's eyes.

He opened his dry lips. "Summer will end someday. That's why playing is fun but the homework stays with you."

The old man's heavy German accent was very crisp and clear, and his words resounded sharply. As he spoke, they were carved in the back of Akira's mind with a scalpel.

At that moment, the last ray of sunshine lighting up the man's face disappeared.

Akira noticed something, something he couldn't see in the light of day.

At the base of the good-natured old man's smile was

a glimpse of gloomy darkness. Clearly, he wasn't really human, but he wasn't a vampire, either. He was an entirely different kind of beast.

"See you again, boy, if our fates align."

Akira stood there, motionless, until the tail lights of the limousine disappeared from view.

He certainly wasn't sad to see him go.

End

DEATH OF A SALARYMAN

STORY
Gemma

ILLUSTRATION
Nozomu Tamaki

One evening, a vampire died in a corner of the Bund.

It wasn't rare for vampires to die in the Bund, but there was one mysterious thing about this vampire's corpse.

He had died in a way that a vampire shouldn't be able to die.

There are more and more people trying to become vampires lately. People think that all it takes to become somebody special is a single bite—go from a regular human to an immortal, ageless creature of the night.

That's stupid, though. It's not like vampires don't die; they just don't age. A moron who drops dead at eighty is still a moron, even if he technically lives forever.

"I didn't want to be a vampire, dammit."

That day—well, at nightfall of that day—I woke up, muttered that sentence to myself as always, then slowly got up and left. I know it sounds whiny and childish, but it had become almost a ritual to me. I just couldn't seem to quit.

I drank some tasteless water in the community kitchen, then put my hands on the sink and spaced out for a while. Even in the small, dark room with only one window, I could see clearly the dirty face of a middle-aged man reflected in the stainless steel of the sink. I'd only recently broken the habit of fumbling for the light switch.

My name is Ushiki Masao, and I'm fifty-one. I was only turned into a vampire about half a year ago, so I'm actually fifty-one years old.

Before six months ago, I was a salesman for a giant electronics manufacturer whose name is known to pretty much everyone. Back when they created the blasted Bund, my company was the first to make a deal to deliver electronic products there, and I was picked to be responsible for the deliveries. Honestly, I thought it was disgusting and I didn't want to do it, but since I had been stuck as a director for years despite being over fifty, I really had no choice in my assignments. I was probably the first home electronics salesman faced with serious danger as an occupational hazard.

The accident happened about two months in. The vampire who was responsible for receiving our products at our business partner suddenly decided to bite me in the middle of a delivery. They restrained the vampire quickly, but I panicked, ran away, and apparently passed out. When I came to, I'd been retrieved by the Bund police and left asleep in a room like a business hotel. It was one whole day after I'd been bitten.

Everything after that moved with frightening efficiency. That evening, I got my termination of employment notice and severance pay from my company, a resident card from the Bund police, and my personal effects and clothing from my family. There was even a counselor. There had likely been a number of "accidents" since the Bund opened contact with the outside world, so the entire process had become standardized. I only started feeling anger and grief about half a day after I had arrived at the new apartment they had given me, and by then, it was too late to cry about it.

I had to live in this Vampire Bund.

I stared into the sink for a while, sighing. Eventually, the young man who lived next door came in. I said some pleasantries, hunched my shoulders, and quickly left the kitchen when I noticed the blood on his collar.

One of the first things I learned after entering the Bund is that vampires actually die pretty often. They don't age and their bodies are a lot stronger than the average human's, but their violent natures more than make up for that. They get into arguments over the smallest things, which turn into bloody fights, and the blood makes things turn lethal. From what I've heard, turning into a vampire changes your mind and increases both impulses and repressed desires. In particular, self-destructive urges become much stronger, and a lot of vampires turn those urges to action and end up killing themselves.

Of course, I was the same. The only reason I hadn't died yet is that I was a coward.

I'd actually thought about dying a lot. I lost my job and my family, and it's not like I had anything else to live for. Maybe it'd be okay if I were younger, but not as a fat middle-aged man with a big belly, a weak stomach, allergies and shoulders so sore that I couldn't raise my arms. Even if I could live forever, it's not like it's fun to live in a body like that. There were a few times when I'd thought about going out into the sun and turning myself into dust, but I just

didn't have the courage to go through with it.

When I returned to my room and shut the door with a massive sigh, something wiggled in the next bed, and Harvey showed his face.

"Depressed again, are ya? Hey Ushiki, if yer gonna get food, get me some too."

Harvey opened his mouth with its mismatched teeth and spat saliva into the ashtray next to the pillow. Harvey is the strangest guy in this shared apartment. He was turned into a vampire not even six months after he was born, and his body stopped growing then. Although he looks like an innocent baby, he's over a hundred years old. Since he can't stand up or walk on his own, he uses a specialized walking device and reaching tongs.

"Yer still too stiff. Why don't ya just accept it and start enjoying yer second life?"

Harvey reached up onto the shelves with his tongs to grab a cigarette, all the while speaking perfect Japanese in that casual way of his. His short fingers efficiently lit up the cigarette, then placed it between his lips. While I can laugh at a baby with a cigarette like on Van Halen's 1984 album cover, it's disturbing to actually see it. I responded with a vague smile and went out with some vouchers to get us Stigma.

Even though the country is different, this is still geographically Tokyo. The moon was blurred by the stagnant atmosphere and only faintly visible. However, there wouldn't be any problems with walking outside, even if it were completely dark. There were early-rising vampire children running around in the streets, and adults had started wandering out of their homes.

The artificial blood Stigma, which for many vampires is one of the greatest attractions of the Bund, is supplied to all residents regardless of employment status. So vampires living in the Bund have no problem obtaining food, even if they don't work. Here, Stigma is distributed in packs, but near the city center, I heard that it's sprayed from airships like rain. The younger vampires like that sort of thing.

Vampires who look young are usually pretty immature. There are vampires that look like children who are actually older than I am, but even those few still have some childishness about them. Even if you live to be hundreds of years old, I guess your physical age still has a big effect on your mind. Harvey is an extreme example. In his case, his brain isn't physically developed, so there are some unusual distortions in his mature personality. I got some Stigma packs for both of us from the distribution office, then quickly headed home.

"Hey, you're back. Gimme some food."

Harvey raised an ink-smeared hand from where he was was sprawled across an English newspaper and a bikini magazine. I cut open the pack and passed it to him, and he started licking it with obvious enjoyment.

"Hey, Ushiki. I think vampires leave behind their human mentalities. Vampires are all controlled by their obsessions, and they're motivated by self-destructiveness. So if ya don't have the mentality to resist that, then ya won't live very long. The ones that die are the ones who can't control their inner selves. All the long-lived vampires are superhuman just because they survived that long. If all humans turned into vampires, mobocracy will disappear in a hundred years. Hee hee hee."

He couldn't pronounce alveolar sounds very well because his tongue wasn't developed, so he had a slurred accent. It was also the fifth time he'd tried to start this conversation. I sipped at my own Stigma in annoyance.

"Oh yeah, Ushiki," said Harvey, as though he'd only just remembered as he licked spilled Stigma off his hands, "Do ya want a job?"

"A job?" I raised my head. "Is there any job I can actually do? There aren't any retailers in the Bund."

"It's got nothin' to do with yer old job." Harvey grinned. "Someone I know is looking for a volunteer subject fer a new drug. He needs people of different ages and races."

"Do vampires even take drugs?"

"They're drugs for people like you. For things like scars and sinus infections that people have when they're turned into vampires, so they stick around forever. This drug'll fix those problems, if it works right."

Harvey took out a pen and name card from the pocket of his walker, quickly drew a map, and handed it to me. I guess he really wanted me to go there.

It wasn't what I'd call a real job, but I knew that having nothing to do but sleep for six months had affected my mood. I gave the name card a long look.

"When does this start?"

"Tonight, if yer up for it."

The building he told me about was on a back street near the entertainment district of the Bund. The building was small, but I could see it was a classy, expensive place at first glance. A plain chrome plate labeled it the Messaby First Generation Medical Research Center. I gave Harvey's name card to the receptionist and was admitted immediately. A slightly plump man emerged. I wondered vaguely why there were so few fat vampires.

"You were sent by Mr. Harvey, right? Thank you for your help."

The head researcher was a man who looked to be in his mid-thirties, though I didn't know his real age. After going through a basic checkup and health evaluation, he gave me an explanation of the tests and the new drug. For the next six months, I would take a dose of the new drug once a week and come in for a checkup at midnight every day.

"While you may continue to live your life normally, please avoid losing blood. Also, please don't tell anyone about the details of this experiment, or the fact that you're participating."

I took the first dose of the drug after signing the contract.

It was a cool, tasteless, orange-tinged powder. I guess you could say it tasted like tissue paper.

"Will this fix scars?"

"That's what this experiment will determine. Your participation today is invaluable. Please continue to help us in the future."

That was how I became a temporary assistant employee at the Messaby First Generation Medical Research Center. My actual work was only an hour of questions and blood samples each day, but it was still a job, and I felt more confident just having a position.

The first effect of the drug appeared after about three weeks. Like I said before, I had horribly stiff shoulders, and I couldn't lift up my arms without the bones creaking and aching like I was lifting weights. But one day, I noticed that there was a lot less pain.

When I reported this, the head researcher rubbed his hands together in joy. "That's proof that the drug is working. It means your body is beginning to return to its healthy state. Please continue to help us in the future."

I wasn't sure what they meant by that, but I was glad that my body's condition had improved. In addition, I got a small stipend each week. I bought a TV and a DVD recorder with the first cash income I had received since entering the Bund. They were things I had wanted when I was human. Of course, I chose models that weren't made by the manufacturer I used to work for.

After two more weeks, the pain in my shoulders had completely disappeared. My sinus infection had also gotten a lot better. In exchange, I felt lethargic and I tired easily, but they'd warned me that these side effects might occur, so I wasn't surprised. It felt a bit like taking cold medicine.

When they heard that I had made a bit of money, the other residents in the apartment started coming to me. They said they wanted to buy clothes for their girls, or they wanted to bring their relatives from outside to visit, but didn't have the money. Oh, and there was a bar where you could drink real blood instead of Stigma; did I want to go? I wasn't sure how to deal with these people, but Harvey stepped in and rebuffed their offers.

"It's fine. I'm gettin' a commission for introducin' you, anyway." He looked at me with his grotesque toothless smile, and laughed.

"But be careful. If they'd ask a loser like me to find people for 'em, that research center is probably doing some pretty dicey things."

Like he could talk, having introduced me to the research center in the first place. When I responded with that, Harvey twisted his lips and laughed again.

Of course, I wasn't the only test subject. I sometimes saw other people entering and leaving the facility with the same special blue pass around their necks. While there were a variety of ages and nationalities, it seemed that the majority were women. Whatever the case, the checkups were always individual, and they seemed like they didn't want the test subjects exchanging information, so I never spoke to the others.

One day, after completing the examination and blood sample, I stayed a while in the bathroom. It's a habit I'd had since when I was still human; sitting on the toilet in the small bathroom stall made me feel calm. I find it important to take time for myself and contemplate my life.

A young man had entered the adjacent stall just before I came in. I didn't know who he was, but it was annoying for me; I just wanted to enjoy the quiet of the bathroom alone. So I fiddled with the toilet paper roll, wishing for him to finish his business as quickly as possible, but he showed no signs of leaving. He also didn't make a single noise. Maybe he was like me, someone who enjoyed a moment of solitary silence. As I felt a sudden kinship with the other guy, I heard the sound of something heavy falling to the floor.

Maybe sitting there too long made him anemic? Do vampires get anemia? I knocked on the wall of the adjacent stall.

"Hey, are you all right?"

There was no answer. I flushed the toilet and exited the stall, then knocked on the stall door. There was still no answer. I returned to my stall, stood on the toilet, and looked over the top of the divider. The man had fallen over and collapsed on the floor.

"Are you okay? Hello?"

He didn't answer. I jumped down from the toilet and used my pinkie finger to toggle the sliding "in use" lock and open the door. When I shook the shoulder of the fallen man, I leapt backwards in surprise.

His body was unusually light. When I'd first seen him a few minutes earlier he'd appeared to be about twenty, but now he had the face of a wrinkled old man.

I stood for a while in shock. Then I touched the man's arm—his arms and legs had also shriveled to an old man's withered limbs, limp and powerless. His lips had peeled back, showing his teeth. I checked for a pulse, but found nothing. The man was dead.

It was only then that I thought to call for help. I went into the empty hallway and yelled loudly, "Excuse me, is anyone there? I need help—someone is dead!"

After speaking, I calmed down a little and looked back at the corpse. I realized that the man was wearing the same blue pass that I had. Another test subject. Before I could think deeply about the implications, there was the sound of running in the hallway, and the familiar head researcher came in. He looked alarmed when he saw me and the fallen man, and made some sort of gesture towards the hallway behind him. I stood up and tried to explain the situation, but before I could, a security guard walked up and punched me, hard.

I lost consciousness.

When I came to, I was sleeping on a hospital bed. I saw a ceiling made of secured boards and a window with a grate over it.

"Um…hello? Is anyone there?"

I tried to call out, and a feeling of déjà vu overcame me. Footsteps came closer, and the same head researcher walked up.

"How do you feel?"

I stared at his face, and suddenly my memories flooded back. I broke into a sweat. He stared at me coldly as I tried to shuffle backwards on the bed. The head researcher in his smart white lab coat sounded like a completely different man when he said in an arrogant tone, "You'll continue to help us. Thank you."

Without saying anything else, he looked at his watch and left the room. I had been staring in shock, only remembering my anger and confusion after the door had closed. It was always like that for me.

I was in a simple and sparse hospital room that included a bath and toilet. There was only one door and no outward-facing windows, so I couldn't tell what it was like outside. The bed and chair were bolted in place, and hard objects like the walls, floor, bed and desk were covered with a layer of urethane foam—assumedly to stop the occupant from hurting himself.

Food was provided twice a day in packs. In addition, the drug I'd been taking was brought at midnight. Of course I refused to take it at first, but after being beaten so hard that I couldn't get up for half a night, I obediently drank it every time. It was a prison for lab rats.

"Hey, can't you at least tell me why you're doing this to me?" I once asked the nurse-like man who brought me my meals. "Is it because I saw that dead man? Is that why you've imprisoned me?"

The nurse—who was probably also a guard—had a chest like a lowland gorilla. He glared at me once, then snorted through his nose.

"If you want me to keep quiet about what I saw, I'll do that," I continued. "Can you at least tell me what the drug I'm taking is? No, it's okay if you don't want to tell me… Just let me go home. I only want a normal life; I didn't even want to become a vampire. Why me? I—"

The nurse got angry and hit me, and I fell into a corner in the room. I heard the sound of the white metal door closing behind me as I curled up and started to cry.

After about a month, I became completely apathetic. I tried to resist or escape during the first few days, but all I accomplished was angering my captors. I ate the food I was given, took the drugs, and answered the questions I was asked. I turned into an obedient lab rat. I was too tired to do anything else.

When I looked in the mirror, my face looked so old that

I didn't recognize myself. I didn't know if this was a side effect of the drug or just caused by my mental state.

Why did this happen to me?

Dammit, it's all because I became a vampire.

What do I have to live for?

What am I?

I kept asking myself questions and wallowing in self-pity, until one day I was brought back to reality by the sound of gunfire.

I could hear excited voices and panicked footsteps in the hall, but I felt nothing at first. I heard more gunshots, and then screams. Finally, I realized that something unusual was happening, and I raised my head from the pillow.

I first heard the noises from above. They slowly made their way down to my level, creeping closer and closer. When I focused my hearing to figure out the direction of the sounds, I suddenly heard a loud, metallic noise. White smoke poured through the lock on the door in front of me, and it suddenly blew off. The door swung open, and two men in black slinked into the room like weasels.

"...?"

"Um...huh?"

They held guns to me while I cowered, frozen in place, and one of the men said something in a deep, forceful voice. They wore black suits that looked like the clothing worn by Special Forces on TV, and their faces were entirely covered by visor-like helmets that left only their mouths exposed.

After countless repetitions, I finally realized they were speaking normal Japanese.

"Are you one of the test subjects here?"

I supported my trembling chin and nodded somehow. The men gestured upwards with their guns—they wanted me to stand. My knees couldn't support my weight, though, so it took me a while. I was terrified of the gun barrel thrust near my stomach, shaking with irritation. When I finally stood up, the deep, forceful voice spoke again.

"You were given drugs, right? Do you know where they're kept?"

There was no way I would know that. Since I was put into this room, I hadn't even been able to go out into the hallway. When I answered honestly, I saw the man's lips relax and he clicked his tongue.

"Wh-who are you? Did you come to help me?"

Neither of the men answered. The man who wasn't pointing a gun at me looked outside into the hallway and began muttering into the microphone next to his mouth. He raised his hand and beckoned us over. I tottered between them, the gun still pointed in my direction. Broken glass and pieces of drywall littered the hallway, and gunshot holes were scattered across the walls. I could still hear the sounds of gunfire and small explosions somewhere in the distance. There were piles of some powdery substance scattered randomly on the floor. When I saw the splayed white coat and empty suits in the middle of the piles, I realized that they were the ashen remains of dead vampires. A strange noise crept up in the back of my throat.

The men moved quickly down the corridor, bringing me into a small room at one end. Another man in black was in the room—he nodded in acknowledgment of our arrival, then left. There was a desk and bed, a small bookshelf, a drug cabinet, and a large freezer—the kind you'd see at a supermarket. For some reason it reminded me of a hospital examination room.

After I stared around the room for a while, I finally remembered that this was the exam room where I had been given the drugs, back when I was still a normal test subject.

"Open it."

The man with the gun used it to gesture toward the freezer. I opened it and saw a handful of familiar vials, all lined up. It was the drug I had been forced to take until just that morning. I trembled, and not only because of the cold air from the freezer.

"Put them in here." The man took out a large insulated bag and threw it at my feet. "Hurry up."

There wasn't much else I could do, so I picked up the bag and placed the vials inside. It was then that I finally started to question my situation.

It was pretty obvious that these people hadn't come to rescue me. Maybe they were assassins from a rival company, sent here to steal the drugs being developed here. But if that were the case, then why would they ask me to do this work?

It wasn't as if they were bank robbers instructing the tellers to pack money into bags.

"Hurry up!"

My thoughts had apparently slowed me down. I looked over at the man, and noticed that he'd moved even further away from me. He was clearly trying to put distance between us...no, not from me, from the drug? Was he afraid to get near the drug I'd been taking?

And that kind of man was holding me at gunpoint...what was I doing?

The rebelliousness that I had completely forgotten over the previous month took root in my chest. It wasn't something as noble as pride, just a childish stubborn streak. But whatever it came from, I finally found some motivation within myself after all that time.

As I continued to work, I loosened the cap on one of the vials, then pretended to let it slip accidentally. It fell, and the contents scattered at the man's feet.

Immediately, he squealed and jumped away from the orange powder on the ground. His face contorted as if to bite me. He clearly knew what the drug was, but not that it had to be ingested.

"Be careful, you!"

He hit me hard in the face with the butt of his pistol, and that really lit the fires of anger in my stomach. I crushed the vials in my hands as hard as I could, and they cracked immediately due to my vampire strength. I threw the orange powder and broken plastic shards into his face. The man froze with shock for a long moment, then stared at the substance now covering his body.

Then he leapt up, his entire body trembling, and started hitting the visor and his lower jaw—now coated with powder—as if he had gone mad. I took out more vials, broke them, and threw my powder grenades at the other man, who had turned around in panic at his partner's reaction. It hit his face right by the ear, and he jumped back in alarm.

"I'm a test subject. This drug is already in my bloodstream. If you shoot me, it'll splatter all over you."

I waved my arms and legs around and spat at them, and the two men retreated further. Their weapons were still aimed at me. I took some vials and shoved them into my clothing, then slowly approached the two men with my hands still covered in powder. Once I was past them, I bolted out of the room.

I hurried down the corridor as fast as I could. If I'd been in the old exam room, then I knew how to get out of there. I heard the sound of gunfire from behind me, and I felt some pain as the flesh was shot off my shin, but I didn't have time to worry about that now.

There were stairs at the end of the hall, in the direction that the men had first come from. I ran up the stairs, but when I reached the top landing, I skidded and fell.

The first floor hallway was covered in blood...or rather, covered in dust. If not for the dust, I would've called it a scene straight out of Hell. Some of the victims must have lost control of their bowels before their demise, so there were piles of what looked like stinking mud mixed in with the dust.

I tried to head towards the entrance, but I hurriedly turned back after hearing the clatter of machine guns in that direction. I recalled the layout of the research center from my fuzzy memories. I crawled down the hallway slowly on all fours, towards what I hoped was the emergency exit. When I reached a T-junction, I saw two men in suits behind a barricade firing their guns down the opposite hallway. One of them suddenly noticed me and aimed his gun, but at that moment he was hit by a bullet that blew half of his head right off.

"You, Number 68! What are you doing here?"

The other man maintained his crouching position, glaring at me with his fangs out. I felt like freezing in terror, but being called by a number made me mad. "You imprisoned me, so what do you think I'm doing? You see this drug here?"

The man's expression changed when he saw me take out the vial. "Don't take that out here, you…!" The man in the suit raised his head and tried to grab me, but he was shot in the shoulder and lumbered into the wall behind. I heard the sound of booted feet running in from the left side of the corridor, invisible to me.

"I… I'm a test subject. I have the drug. If you kill me,

you won't learn anything!" I yelled shakily. The footsteps stopped for a moment. I used that opportunity to scurry along the back of the barricade like a cockroach, cross the intersection unhindered, and then run as fast as I could to reach the iron door of the emergency exit. I didn't know when I had been hurt, but there was blood all over my hands. I struggled to turn the doorknob.

When I finally pulled the door open, I saw a man with a black face guard, waiting under the moonlight with a machine gun cocked at his waist.

"Argh!"

I stiffened, but the man in black didn't move. I guess he'd passed out.

As I crept fearfully outside, a voice addressed me from the shadows.

"Ushiki! Hey, Ushiki! Over here."

"Harvey!"

It was Harvey with his twisted, lopsided grin. He was in a large walker that he seldom used. My mind flooded with nostalgia and relief, and I felt tears welling up. I wanted to run up to him and pinch his cheeks.

"Did you come here to help me?"

"Yeah, I did. I didn't think you'd escape by yourself—it saves me a lot of trouble. Still, you look a lot older."

I was so thankful that I couldn't speak. Then, I suddenly came back to earth and looked down at the man in black lying at my feet.

"Who are these people? I managed to escape because of them, but…"

"They're the police. You've heard of VGS, right? Once I told 'em about the research they've been conducting in this building, they forced their way right in. They're fighting the researchers now, and you would've been killed if they'd found you."

Harvey took out a cigar and gave me a grin. I trembled and hurried behind his walker into the alleyway.

"Pretty impressive that you knew they had caught me."

"Well, yeah." The walker with its large tires and thick metal legs climbed nimbly over the debris and garbage, then down the alleyway. He was faster than I had expected. I had to exert a lot of effort just to keep up.

"Wait a minute. My leg's hurt."

"Oh, that's no good. We'll stop here."

Harvey slowed and turned around in a wide path between the buildings. He took out a gun and pointed it at me. "All right, gimme the drug."

I blinked two, three times, and swallowed over and over. Sweat poured out of me and dampened the front of my thin shirt. "W-wait. Wait!" My vision was flashing. "What's going on? Didn't you come to help me? But, wait… You came after me for this? From the beginning, the drug was what you wanted?"

"Ya think so, huh?" Harvey smiled grotesquely. "Go ahead. Hand over the drug. I don't wanna hurt a precious sample."

"S-sample? What, me?" That was the only conclusion. "What are you going to do with me? What's your plan?"

"Don't panic. You'll be doin' the same thing as before, just in a new place." Harvey's brow furrowed in worry. "Don't tell me ya don't have the drug."

I had the drug, and I didn't care about handing it over, but I didn't want to go back to a life of imprisonment.

"That drug is defective," I said desperately. "It's got a horrible side effect. It makes you old. You can see it if you look at me."

"Ya really don't know anything," laughed Harvey, bitterly. "That's not a side effect. The drug you were takin' is designed to make vampires age."

"What?" I gaped at him in shock. "Why would anyone need a drug like that? Not aging is a fact of life for vampires."

"There are times when that's troublesome, ya see. Look at me." Harvey's finger tightened on the trigger of the pistol.

I suddenly realized that my middle-aged shoulder aches and sinus infections hadn't really been cured. Those symptoms had just disappeared with as time passed for my body. My mind was still fuzzy with shock. I didn't want to believe it, but there'd been a lot of obvious signs along the way, now that my attention had been drawn to them.

"I get it. I'll give you the drug. I'll give you the drug, and you'll leave me alone. If you have it, then you won't need me anymore."

"I can't do that." Harvey's lips curled further, settling into a demonic expression. "I guess ya wouldn't know, but all the other test subjects died. Yer the only survivor. I don't know if it's because yer better suited to it, or if yer just plain lucky, but we need ya. Yer the only living data sample."

A sharp noise sounded in my ears and my mind cleared. Could I grab the gun away from him? Immediately, I gave up on the idea. The automatic pistol—way too large for an infant's hand—was secured to the walker, and aimed squarely at me.

"Who are you, really?" I asked, even though I didn't care. I just wanted to stall for time.

"Why do ya want to know?" Harvey probably saw through my ruse, and sneered down his nose at me. "I'm just a recruiter. I take requests and send people to work wherever they're needed."

"Requests? From whom?"

"Shut up and start behaving!" The light, fluffy eyebrows distorted into an ugly, twisted mug of a face. "I've waited thirty years for that drug. Do ya know what I've done for thirty years, just to get it? Compared to that, yer life is worthless."

Harvey glared at me with his innocent-looking face, with an edge sharp enough to match his true age. I didn't know what his life was like, nor did I want to know, but I understood clearly that my life meant nothing to him.

"Do ya know how it feels to be a baby forever, regardless of how many years ye've lived?" Harvey's tiny fingers on the trigger trembled. "I'm still a virgin."

'Vampires are all controlled by their obsessions, and they're motivated by self-destructiveness.'

Harvey's words suddenly flashed across my mind.

This man's obsession was to become an adult, to leave behind his tiny baby body. Then what was my obsession? Wanting to live? It's true that I didn't want to die, but could I live a long, long life just based on that?

Tears came to my eyes. No, that was wrong. Even if my life was meaningless and boring, it should still be mine. My life as a human being was taken away from me, and in exchange, I got a body that could no longer walk in the sun. And then, they tried to take my life as a vampire away from me, too. The only thing left was a cursed, horrible existence. It was just too much.

Harvey shook the gun up and down slightly, as if to hurry my actions. I removed a vial from my shirt, and while Harvey was distracted, I yelled, "Hey, over here! There's a runaway here!"

We weren't that far from the research building, so I figured my voice would be heard by the police. I leapt at Harvey, who had frozen in shock, but the stun gun built into his walker spat sparks at me and I collapsed on the ground. A burnt smell wafted up from my left arm.

Harvey clicked his tongue and moved the walker next to my fallen body. Since the vials were in my shirt, he couldn't get at them without lifting me up. With my ear to the ground,

I heard his approaching steps.

I grabbed the edge of the walker and pushed up with all my strength. Harvey backed the walker up a step in surprise. I grabbed the pistol in its holder and pulled the trigger, firing a shot into the mouth of the alleyway.

The bullet grazed the ear of a policeman who had just stepped into the alleyway, and bullets from their counterattack flew back at us. Two of those bullets struck Harvey in his waist and stomach. He spat up blood from his open mouth and stumbled. I retreated behind the walker, and then crawled along the ground to the back of the alleyway. I heard a few more shots behind me, then all was silent.

I fearfully looked out from my hiding spot with one eye. A policeman had fallen at the far end of the alleyway, and the walker had collapsed on its side nearby. A creature I had never seen before wriggled beside it.

The thing was mostly humanoid, with long, loose limbs and a swollen belly. Its skin was blue-gray, with dark red-purple veins visible underneath. It had protruding eyeballs and its mouth was open in a large, toothy grin. Wire-like hair grew thinly on its head, but overall, its face still resembled Harvey's.

His True Form.

It was one of the things that had been explained to me by a counselor when I first came to the Bund. Every vampire has a True Form that reflects his or her inner self. And I could see Harvey's now because he was dying.

A Gaki.

I couldn't find any other way to describe it. If that was the manifestation of his true self, then his life must have been filled with unimaginable torment and misdeeds. There were single bullet holes in the Gaki's stomach and waist, and two in its chest. Though it was only a matter of time before he turned into dust, I dragged Harvey's body with me into the back of the alleyway before more policemen arrived at the scene.

As I supported Harvey on my shoulder, he persistently reached his long fingers towards my shirt.

"I'll be using that drug."

The bulging eyes glared at me. My face was reflected in those huge, wet eyeballs. My hair had started falling out sometime in the last month without my notice, leaving me with a pathetic mop that couldn't even be called

a comb-over. My father had started going bald at sixty. If those genetics ran true, then I had aged ten years in two months.

"I've found my obsession now."

Harvey's throat gurgled, whether in agreement or in protest, I couldn't tell. I paid him no mind and kept on talking.

"I didn't want to become a vampire. I've hated everything that's happened to this body since then. So, I want to take my revenge on my body and die. I want to die as a human. I want to die of old age."

"Pointless."

Harvey's voice sounded surprisingly clearly from his throat. With that last word, his weakly trembling head fell, and the arm around my shoulder and the feet that dragged along the ground collapsed all at once and turned into white dust.

I lifted a manhole cover at one edge of the alleyway and dropped down into the sewer.

It's always the things that a person cares about the most that outsiders see as pointless. When it comes to vampires, their reasons for living must have seemed like that since the very beginning.

As I slowly climbed down the wet ladder, I counted the number of vials in my shirt with my fingers. I thought about how much of the drug there was in each vial, and recalled the quantity I had taken every day. I estimated that there was enough to reach eighty. My body wasn't all that healthy, so it was entirely possible for me to die under the average Japanese life expectancy. I briefly worried about how to obtain Stigma to keep me alive until then, but then I realized that I could go to the entertainment district and soak in the Stigma rain. It might not be all that terrible to mingle and party with the young people for a few months before my death.

As I sloshed through the rainwater mixed with waste water—as deep as my waist in some places—I slowly, carefully made my way through the sewers. I thought about the TV and the DVD recorder that I had left at my apartment.

"You've identified him?"

"Ushiki Masao. He was originally a home electronics salesman. He moved to the Bund about a year ago. Test subject number 68 at the Messaby Research Center."

One of Marquis Dermaille's sharp eyebrows raised under the dim light of the LCD panels. "We've lost the last test subject, then. I assume you're progressing with the analysis of the drug."

"We're trying, but the outlook isn't good. The individual specifications are too high."

That Harvey. A crafty man, but still just a baby's brain. Marquis Dermaille looked away from the silver console and furrowed his brows.

If he could obtain a method to make vampire bodies grow and age, he could use it to curry favor with the Three Great Clans. Still, that wasn't worth much nowadays, since Queen Mina won her bet and beat back the Three Great Clans' supporters.

"The Queen hasn't heard of this, has she?"

"No. She is only aware that we've destroyed a research facility influenced by Duke Rosenmann."

"Burn the body, but leave the investigation data. Reduce the priority of this issue. Reports are unnecessary, unless you've reached some advancement."

Marquis Dermaille closed the lid of the console without waiting for a response, and stood. He was a busy man with a lot of things to do. He could not afford to linger long on a plan that had clearly failed.

The secretary on the other end of the line was not surprised by the abrupt end of their communication. He closed each of the windows displayed on the screen, and placed them into the "low priority" folder. His fingers paused for an instant as he was adding a note to the data for Ushiki himself. It took him a moment to remember the phrase, "cremation."

The secretary tried to recall the way he used to fear dying of old age—a fear he'd lost dozens of years ago. He quickly gave up.

He shut off the display and prepared to go home.

End

Dance in the
Vampire Bund

OF ENDLESS SILENCE AND REPOSE

STORY
Gemma

ILLUSTRATION
Nozomu Tamaki

"Okay, we're done here. Do you feel any numbness in your face or lips?"

The man who rose from the cream-colored dental chair licked inside his mouth. His expression changed as though he was trying to check each of his facial muscles one by one, but finally he sat up from the chair with a nervous expression. Doctor Saji removed his gloves and mask and addressed the man calmly.

"There will be some pain once the anesthetic wears off. Your mouth will feel unfamiliar for a while, but please don't worry; you'll get used to it. You can drink Stigma normally, and you can also smoke if you want."

He gave his trademark smile, lifting only one corner of his mouth. His expression showed friendliness and the camaraderie of a shared secret.

Once again, that smile managed to calm a naive patient immediately after the surgery. The man whispered his thanks and tried to leave, but Saji called out to him and gave him another small smile.

"I hope your life will be peaceful from now on."

The man turned back and flashed a self-conscious smile of his own—showing the gaps where his upper and lower canines used to be. Before Saji removed them.

Doctor Daniel Kazuo Saji worked as a dentist in a medical center in the Vampire Bund. He took "Kazuo" as his middle name because he was a second generation Japanese-American by way of Hawaii. He appeared to be about forty years old, but he was actually more than twice that age.

Saji thought that his identity, torn between two countries during wartime, was a great advantage in his current job, removing vampires' canine teeth—the fangs—and turning them into "Fangless."

"Will that guy be okay? There's gotta be some reason he went through with it," one of Saji's newer coworkers said. Saji finished washing his hands and pulled out a pack of Stigma. "No vampire would want their teeth pulled without a good reason."

Saji sipped at his Stigma, warmed up to human body temperature, and let out a long sigh. He felt the enormous responsibility of changing a vampire's entire life spread from the palms of his hands to his brain, and he waited for it to dissipate through his whole body. The coworker who'd spoken had been scouted from medical school just a few months ago, and though his hands were skilled, his understanding was still immature. Would he come to realize what their job really meant?

The bell at the front desk rang, and Saji stood up to greet the next patient.

The only disease common to both humans and vampires is cavities. To the streptococcus mutans bacteria, the teeth and enamel of humans and vampires are the same. So the Bund had dentists, just like the human world. Though, in the case of the Bund, all dentists' offices were run directly by the government—because they could perform fang extractions.

There were a few reasons that vampires would want their fangs pulled. Some felt guilty about biting humans, and wanted that possibility taken away from them. Some never wanted to become vampires in the first place, and refused to adapt to their bodies' new form. And some vampires who'd committed a crime had their teeth pulled as a kind of penance. Whatever the reason, the dentist didn't ask questions. As long as the vampire gave permission and had the right documentation, the dentist would perform the extraction.

"Before we begin, I must inform you of several things. First, once your teeth are extracted, there is no way to restore them."

The second patient of the day was a young Japanese woman. She had come to the Bund on a training tour—she was bitten when she wandered away from her group. Her skin was beautiful and definitely tempting to bite, but Saji didn't let those thoughts show on his face. He spoke calmly and reassuringly to the red-eyed woman.

"Secondly, sometimes extracting the teeth will affect your personality. Generally, it makes you calmer and want to avoid conflict. Your relationships with your friends and significant others may change. If you find yourself unable to return to your current life, there is another option—a special area of the Bund for people who've been through this. But...be sure to think it over carefully. This is a choice that will affect you for the rest of your life, so work through any doubts beforehand.

There were three fang extraction cases that day. Two others came in for a consultation and did not actually have the surgery performed. There were still normal dental examinations as well, so his schedule was very busy. The most enjoyable part of the day was smoking a cigarette in the medical center after finishing the night's work.

"We had someone who'd lost every single molar, despite still being young."

"Seems like the cavities just keep increasing."

"Maybe they're eating too many weird things. If they stuck to Stigma, this wouldn't happen."

"I think that's even worse. The stigma drinkers think vampires can't get cavities. Their sense of taste is dulled, so they don't brush their teeth or rinse out their mouths. That kid today had awful breath."

"There was that thing in Japan, right? The 8020 Movement, to keep people's teeth healthy in old age. Should we do something like that in the Bund?"

"We'll need to think older than 80. Doctor Saji, what do you think?"

"We can show them George Romero's movies. If they saw what happens to your mouth after eating nothing but raw meat and blood, they'd get the point pretty quickly."

Saji chatted with his colleagues for a while about vampire dental health, and everyone went home when the clock struck four.

The next day, the newer dentist's comment proved more insightful than he'd realized—the patient from the day before was in the waiting room.

The man followed Saji into the exam room.

"Um… is it possible to restore fangs?" he asked with a nervous smile.

Saji had to hide a bitter grin.

"I'm sorry, but it isn't. As I said yesterday, it's impossible to restore them after they've been extracted."

"But I heard that there were people who had their teeth pulled, and they grew back."

"Some people do regrow other teeth, but fangs are different. Anyway, the operation yesterday didn't just remove the teeth, it also burned out the nerves in the gums. I'm very sorry, but there's no way to restore them."

About one vampire in every few dozen felt like that. There were a lot of cases where a person made a life-changing decision and then realized that they'd made an irreversible mistake.

"I know you're nervous, but you'll get accustomed to your new life soon. I can introduce a counselor if you'd like."

The man left, full of regret, and Saji returned to his job. The entire medical center was in a strange state of urgency that day. There had been riots in the Italian area of the Bund, and the emergency room and health divisions were working at full tilt. Saji was soon buried in a mountain of documentation and medical charts, and quickly forgot about the man.

But he returned again the next night.

"Um, are you sure there isn't any way to restore them?"

Saji turned his head to the side and coughed twice, three times to suppress his irritation, then spoke. "It's just as I said yesterday. I'm sorry."

"But I'm really in trouble."

"Mr. Marco Troigi, right?" Saji checked the medical records, coughed again, and shifted his position in the chair. "We went over all the realities of this procedure beforehand— what's making you change your mind now? Can you discuss that with me?"

The man fell silent and dropped his gaze.

Extracting a vampire's fangs without his or her permission was prohibited in the Bund. While there had been cases in the past where extremely violent vampires were subjected to the operation by their families through force, there was a famous case where a husband known for domestic violence was murdered by his wife and children after his fangs were extracted. After that, the individual's permission was always required, regardless of the circumstances. This young man had, of course, signed the affidavit for the operation.

The Troigi youth asked sullen questions for a while, but eventually he fell quiet and quickly left the office—almost like he was running away. Saji sighed loudly and returned to his work. The riots from the day before had not yet been quelled, and several of the dental staff had been mobilized to help the emergency staff. It was even busier than yesterday. From what he had heard on the news, several hundred people were confirmed dead based on clothing verification, and the origins of the situation were under investigation. Rumors about the cause spread wildly through the medical center—that it had been sparked by a mafia inheritance war, or a gunfight during daylight hours. Saji soon tired of the speculation and went home early.

When the man came on the third day, he looked extremely fragile.

"......"

"Mr. Troigi, I'd like to help you if I can. Will you tell me why you want to restore your fangs?"

"......"

"I'm sorry, but your name is Italian, right?"

The man stood up suddenly, as though he had been thrown. He stared at Saji with a terrified expression, opened and closed his mouth a few times, then ran out of the room with watery eyes.

The dental department had gotten extremely busy. Violent, bloody incidents tended to increase the number of patients for fang removal—probably because they let people see the true nature of vampires, which made them despair of that life. Besides the new patients, there was also a Fangless woman who'd had her fangs removed a year earlier and had returned to receive treatment for depression. It took Saji, who wasn't good at record-keeping, half a day to find her medical records.

But regardless of how busy he was, he couldn't forget that man's face.

The man didn't appear the next day. The incident in the Italian area had dragged on, but the government had finally had enough and forcibly pacified it by mobilizing the Special Forces squad, *Beowulf.* The medical center became less hectic, and Saji walked home in a calmer state than he had for the last three days.

He noticed the footsteps at the intersection about three blocks from the medical center. The footsteps began moving when Saji moved, and stilled when he stopped. He couldn't see anyone when he turned around to look. When he tried to hurry across a crosswalk, several men appeared around him, fencing him in.

"You're Doctor Saji, right?"

"Yes. But who are you?" Saji hid his apprehension and watched the men with a level gaze.

He thought he heard one of the men spit out the word "Cazzo!" as he struck at Saji with the stick he was carrying. Saji blocked it with his hands, but the second man kicked him in the stomach. Pain erupted in his back, across his nose, and then he couldn't tell where the pain was coming from anymore.

The sky beyond the buildings had started turning red by the time he came to. He tried to stand in a panic, but agony shot through his entire body. His arm seemed to be broken. It took him two minutes lying on the ground before he managed to crawl into a nearby building.

If he had stayed unconscious for thirty minutes longer, he would have turned into dust on the street. Saji's body trembled as he looked out at the brightening sky through the reflective glass.

The next night, Saji's colleagues were shocked when they saw him arrive at work with his right arm in a sling.

"It must have been the rioters! There's talk of some thugs who are still on the run."

Saji answered the newer doctor's smug statement with a bitter smile. A long time ago, Saji had enlisted in the army, so he had actual combat experience. He knew how to handle himself in a fight. These men had been able to beat him solidly, and they were obviously experienced fighters. Maybe there was some truth to the mafia rumors.

He awkwardly used his right arm—which couldn't move very well—to finish his work for the day. He was disappointed to have to ask his colleagues to cover the many operations he'd been scheduled to perform.

The attack the night before wouldn't leave his mind. Something about it was bothering him. Around noon, the problem finally took shape in his mind.

"One of them called me 'cazzo.'"

"Huh?" The newer doctor seemed confused by the comment—Saji ignored his reply and continued.

"He said "cazzo." It's a curse in Italian—it means something like 'fuck.'"

"If they're mafia, they would speak Italian, right?"

"But isn't that strange? Why would a mafia thug yell 'fuck' while he's beating someone up? And they didn't use guns."

Saji slowly moved his right arm and turned his head. He could feel the wound healing throughout his arm. A healthy vampire could heal completely from this kind of injury in about two days. Nothing had even been stolen. Whoever those men were, it didn't seem like they'd intended to cause much damage.

"If it were you, what would make you swear like that while you tried to punch someone?"

The newer doctor thought about it with a thoughtful expression on his face. "To vent frustration?"

"That's what I was thinking—if I knew that violence wouldn't solve the problem, but I felt compelled to hit them anyway."

In other words, Saji had done something to make them angry. Something that was an irreversible mistake to them, something that couldn't be fixed even if they killed him. He didn't need to think hard to guess what that mistake was.

After midnight, Saji decided to take a half day. He went outside and headed for the special zone inhabited by the Fangless.

Saji was greeted by the smiles of pedestrians as he walked down the road at night, his medical bag under one arm. Some of the people here had become Fangless through operations that Saji himself had performed, and many of them were thankful for the new life he'd given them. Sometimes, he'd even get special treatment when he ventured into this area—it was an advantage particular to a job that seriously affected people's lives.

"Good morning, Miss Anna. Is your mother at home?"

The girl playing with a ball outside looked him directly in the eye. She greeted him, then ran into the building. When the door opened again, a woman appeared—she had black hair in a neat, classy cut and plain but symmetrical features.

"Well, if it isn't Doctor Saji!"

"I apologize for coming to see you on your day off, but there's something I'd like to ask you."

The woman appeared to be much younger than Saji, but she was actually one of the oldest Fangless living here. She was also a living dictionary, well-informed about international affairs both inside and outside the Bund. She worked as a head nurse at the medical center, and therefore was one of Saji's colleagues. Saji was treated to chocolate cake—seldom seen in the Bund—and he asked her a few questions. He then thanked her politely and returned to the medical center at the end of the working day. He sent an email, and chose to take a route home with a lot of pedestrian traffic.

Saji chose to work overtime the next day. While he still couldn't perform actual operations, he had recovered to the point of being able to hold a pen without any problems. He slowly went through documents in the medical center after his colleagues had all left, until, eventually, the bell at the front sounded. Saji went to the reception room and found Marco Troigi standing nervously in the corner.

"Hi. How have your teeth been?"

Saji invited him into the exam room and offered him some warmed Stigma. Marco's hands were shaking as he accepted the drink.

"Um, I read your email. Your arm... That's my fault. I'm really sorry."

"If this injury is really your fault, then aren't there some other people you should be apologizing to?"

Marco's thin shoulders shook. Saji relaxed his expression and moved his healing arm. He coughed and shifted in his seat.

"I'll start with what I know. You're Marco, the eldest son of the Troigi family of Naples, right? You were supposed to become the head of your family soon."

Frightened eyes looked back at him. Saji continued.

"There were many rivals to your succession. You could have removed them by force, or even passed the succession over to one of them. But you did neither. Instead, you had your fangs removed. Can you tell me why you did that?"

Marco spun the empty cup in his hands over and over, and looked nervously at the corners of the room. Saji waited patiently, until finally Marco's face distorted.

"I hated it. I couldn't stand it anymore."

"Being part of the mafia?"

"All of it."

Marco Troigi began to speak. He described the Camorra family, a Naples mafia family entirely made up of vampires, caught up in a web of foolishness and violence.

Among vampires, there is an absolute hierarchy that doesn't exist in human society. A vampire who sucks someone's blood is known as that new vampire's "master," and the new vampire becomes the first vampire's "blood kin." No vampire can defy the commands of his master—not through duty or logic, but as a rule carved into his instincts. That dominance also passed to the "master" of the "master," or the "blood kin" of the "blood kin." Vampire society was created from innumerable pyramids based on that hierarchy. Those pyramids never change unless influenced by an outside force.

However, that doesn't mean that vampires aren't ambitious or rebellious. On the contrary, because vampires are bound by the curse of immortality and blood kinship, they are even more rebellious than humans to overcome those forces. Conflicts within vampire society are usually wrapped in violence, cruelty, and layers of intrigue.

Marco Troigi had an uncle. Though his uncle was of higher status according to the Camorra's rules, he had been human until he was elderly. Therefore, as a vampire, his rank was lower than Marco's. His uncle was a plotter with fierce ambition, and kind, young Marco couldn't stand fighting with him. He couldn't bear killing his uncle, or being woven into a new pyramid to wriggle for eternity if he lost.

"...I thought that if I became Fangless, I could be free of all those bonds."

Having no fangs meant that a vampire could not create his own blood kin. Therefore, the Fangless were expelled completely from the hierarchy of vampire society. It was one of the reasons that they were held in contempt by normal vampires, but many who became Fangless did so as an escape from that system.

"Did you find freedom?"

Marco dropped his gaze again at Saji's words. It was obvious that the Italian riots a few days ago were caused by the Troigi family succession. Marco becoming a Fangless meant that the entire family had lost prestige, and it had likely caused conflict with the uncle's faction. The people who attacked Saji yesterday were probably blood kin raised by Marco. It made sense that they would feel compelled to attack Saji.

"What should I do? What should I have done?"

Young Marco looked up at Saji with a mad, pleading expression in his eyes, and Saji let out a slow sigh. It was people like Marco who needed to have their fangs removed immediately after they were turned into vampires. He was too weak to live by his heart. That weakness had already killed several hundred people, and it would continue to kill more, so long as he existed.

Saji cast his gaze outside the window, through the open reflective curtains.

"I can only give you one piece of advice. Do you smoke?"

Marco looked surprised at the sudden question, but he nodded. "A little bit. Cigars."

"In that case, buy a good cigar and a box of matches. Then go to the highest building in town. Go out to the roof and sit down. Smoke the cigar, and close your eyes. As slowly as possible, without thinking about anything."

Blood drained from the youth's face. His gaze wandered for a while across the exam room, looking for something to cling to, then it dropped powerlessly to the floor.

Marco Troigi stood up shakily from the chair. He and Saji exchanged a few more words. Then he left without looking back.

It was just over an hour until dawn. The sky was at its darkest. Saji sat immobile for a while, but finally lifted his too-heavy body and prepared to go home.

"Doctor Saji, there's a call on line three."

"Yes, yes. I'll get it right away."

It was a bright, moonlit night, where even non-vampires could walk outside in comfort. But that made no difference to the man busy with his work behind the reflective curtains.

Since that night, Saji had walked home normally, but he was never attacked again. News of the riots in the Italian area was no longer on people's lips. The Troigi family had probably been taken over by Marco's uncle. It was something he could easily find out if he poked around, but Saji didn't want to know. Not yet, anyway.

"Yes, this is Saji. Oh, yes, you came in the other day…"

It was the Japanese girl who had come crying to the clinic. She had been invited to a clubhouse in the Bund by her "master," and she no longer wanted to become Fangless. From her voice over the phone, it was clear that she was on some sort of drug, and she hung up without warning.

Those with weak wills did not remove their fangs, but they didn't keep them, either. Saji closed his eyes briefly and let the fatigue seep across his face. Then, quickly, he put on his usual expression and returned to the exam room.

End

LIES &
SILENCE

STORY
Tikurakuran

ILLUSTRATION
Nozomu Tamaki

PROLOGUE

Night had disappeared from the eastern sky.

A form shaped like a control tower emerged at the base of the mountain, with the sky dyed red-violet as a backdrop. Sunrise was approaching rapidly.

At one corner of a large international airport, there was an enormous freight shipping yard spread out over a million square meters. There, numerous containers were gathered, and a wide assortment of freight was transported at every hour of the day and night.

Within the canopy-covered grounds, pallet transporters and cargo trailers constantly wove in and out of the piles of containers. Some of the containers were being transported outside of the airport on trucks, others were being loaded onto passenger and cargo planes to be shipped throughout the world. This was one of the largest air distribution centers in Asia.

In one corner, moving from shadow to shadow, two figures examined their surroundings.

The two shadows were a man and woman, clothed in the

jumpsuits and helmets worn by this facility's employees. The jumpsuits were stolen and didn't fit well. Still, they were better than the blood- and battle-stained clothes they'd been wearing before.

The woman was empty-handed, but the man was shouldering a fiberglass trunk. It was just under a meter long, forty centimeters wide, and thirty centimeters thick—and it was firmly fixed to the man's back, so he wouldn't drop it no matter how violently he moved.

The man and woman were in a hurry.

They had naturally expected the ambush at the airport, but the situation was even worse than they'd expected. It wasn't just that their master was at the passenger terminal, but a large number of pursuers had also been waiting in the freight shipment yard. The pair had been spotted by their pursuers while breaking into the container yard. Their pursuers had blocked off every exit, leaving them trapped.

They were supposed to use a container as a diversion and sneak onto a cargo plane. That plane had already finished loading and was headed to the runway for takeoff.

Between packing the trunk and struggling through the airport, they'd already fought their way through at least twenty-five enemies. The man had abundant combat experience, but the woman was reaching her physical limits. The facility was massive and full of hiding spots, but they had no way to escape—it was only a matter of time before they were discovered.

And sunrise was coming. They needed to act, immediately.

The man looked out a window and spotted an airplane taxiing at the end of the runway. When the plane changed its direction, the logo—written in Japanese kanji on the body—came into view. Considering the time that had passed, there was no mistaking that this was the cargo plane they had been aiming for.

When the cargo plane reached the end of the runway, it would pass right in front of them just as it begin to glide. That plane was headed for a foreign country—the land of freedom, they believed.

The man looked up. There were more blue streaks in the sky than there had been a few minutes ago, and the highest clouds were shining white, one step ahead of the earth to receive the morning's light. In mere moments, the whole runway would be illuminated by the sun.

They had few choices remaining: to surrender and return to their master, to continue fighting their ever-increasing pursuers, or to throw themselves into daylight. Their demise seemed like the only possible outcome. And that meant the trunk's contents would be lost, as well.

There was one other option. One last chance to shake off their pursuers and survive. The man tightly grasped the woman's hand, and gazed into her eyes.

That one look conveyed everything the woman needed to know. She met his gaze, and nodded firmly.

There was no time for indecision. Together, they leapt from the shade of the container, aiming for the carry-out door facing the runway. They ran, seemingly at the speed of light.

Several pursuers had already sensed the duo's movements. They slipped through the stacked containers and the spaces between conveyer belts, pursuing the pair.

The closest drew up on the man's right side, and attacked.

The man extended the fingers of his right hand. Without losing speed, he unleashed his hand in a striking motion and stabbed into his attacker's throat with a blow to the side. The attacker's carotid artery and trachea were completely severed in an instant—he toppled over as fresh blood spurted from his neck.

Another pursuer appeared in front of them, attempting to cut them off from the left.

The man pulled out a pen and a mechanical pencil from his breast pocket, and in one smooth motion threw them like shuriken.

The two writing implements pierced deep into their pursuer's eyes. He grasped at his face with both hands, ran several unsteady meters and pitched forward to collapse in a heap.

The man and woman exited the container yard through the carry-out door and ran onto the runway.

The moment they went outside, they could feel the ultraviolet rays that foretold the sunrise starting to scorch their flesh. The runway, vast and stretching beyond the horizon like the Great Plains, completely lacked any kind of shelter. There was no going back now.

At the end of the runway, the cargo plane had reached the starting point and turned to face down the runway. Any moment now, it would start accelerating right toward them.

The pair ran down the center of the runway with determination. They needed to place themselves face-to-face with the fuselage before the cargo plane reached them.

When the man glanced back, he saw that several pursuers had followed them out onto the runway. Following them this far meant there was no way for them to return to the shipping yard before daybreak. Their intentions were clear—they would put a stop to this at the cost of their own lives.

Suddenly, the woman toppled forward. The man stumbled and skidded to a stop a few steps beyond her—a small knife was imbedded in the woman's calf, thrown by one of their pursuers. She couldn't keep up with him in this state.

The man looked beyond the woman. Their pursuers were closing in on them.

And down the runway, the plane was closing in quickly.

In an instant, the man made his decision. He rushed back toward the woman.

She raised a hand, and he stopped in his tracks. Her pale palm reflected in his eyes.

Then, she gestured at the cargo plane. Her eyes told him to go. She pulled the knife from her leg, stood, and suddenly her face lit up with an impeccable smile.

She turned and faced their pursuers, brandishing the knife.

There was no time to watch her last stand. The man turned and started to run, out into the center of the runway and toward the rushing cargo plane.

Sprinting with all his might, the man locked his eyes on the wings of the cargo plane, setting the gears in his brain churning at full speed. Because the front legs under the nose of the plane were visible only briefly before take-off, they would be unusable. The main legs under the wings had four tires arranged in two rows, with shock absorbers exposed between the rows. If he made contact with those tires spinning such at high speeds, he'd be destroyed. To avoid the tires and reach the landing gear, he would have to aim for the central shock absorbers. And, if he wanted to avoid being sent flying, he'd need to jump head first at the moment of contact and grip the shock absorber with both hands.

Despite the seriousness, his excitement boiled over and pushed him to action. Reveling in danger and finding enjoyment even in death—that was one of the incorrigible traits endowed to all denizens of the night.

The plane's speed had increased in preparation for flight as it headed straight down the runway. A tremor shot through the asphalt and carried up into the man's legs. The round nose of the cargo plane aimed at the man like a ballistic missile.

The pilot of the cargo plane had spotted the human-shaped shadow running toward him, but stopping the plane at this point was almost impossible. Man and airplane were caught in a deadly game of chicken, with neither making any move to change direction.

There was nothing reflected in the man's eyes but the landing gear on the left wing of the cargo plane. He could feel the presence of his pursuers behind him, but he had no thoughts of turning back to take a look.

The deafening roar of the jet engine made the very air quake. The cargo plane filled the man's vision completely, having grown so huge and close it could easily crush him to death.

At that moment, the silver wing of the plane sliced the air above his head.

The man leapt.

His body crashed onto the landing gear with the force of a baseball bat hitting a ball at full swing.

His helmet slammed into the fulcrum of the landing gear, cracking clean into two halves and blowing away. The man received such a shock to his whole body that he lost his vision for more than a moment. Even so, he aimed for the hydraulic cylinder in front of him and held onto it with both hands. The long braid he had concealed under his helmet had come loose, and now it fluttered in the gusting winds.

A pursuer who had almost reached the man got tangled up in the tires. His crushed body flipped up, hitting the back side of the wings with a dull thud sound.

The massive tires spun violently on both sides of the man—only a few centimeters of open space separated them. The tires blew bits of asphalt violently into the air behind them.

A sharp pain penetrated his body as the headwinds raged with a thunderous roar; there was a violent vibration from the asphalt on the runway and the mind-numbing howls of the engines—his senses were assaulted from all sides. Even so, he concentrated all of his fear into his arms and legs, clinging on for dear life.

After what felt like an eternity, the vibrations suddenly disappeared.

When the man looked down, he could see the runway getting smaller and smaller below them.

The cargo plane had taken off.

As the plane left the ground, a majestic view of the freight shipping yard and the passenger terminal came into view. The man searched for the woman, but he couldn't find her.

The ear-splitting sound of the engines and the strong winds continued, but now that the vibrations had dulled, he could return to a calmer thought process. He would need to ensure he had safe footing before the landing gear was raised and stored inside the plane.

Just as he thought this, his vision exploded in white.

It was the rays of the sun. As the plane ascended into higher altitudes, the sun's light illuminated the body of the plane sooner than the surface of the earth. The light shot into the man's eyes.

Blisters broke out over the east-facing back of his hand and side of his face. As he dealt with the agony of his body being seared, he wriggled and tried to use the landing gear as a shield. The tires, still spinning, got in his way and stopped him from changing his position.

If he did not act within the next several seconds, every cell in his body would spontaneously combust and his body's decomposition would become irreversible.

Just as he resolved himself, the landing gear made a mechanical whirring sound as it began folding up to be stored in the wings. He changed his stance to avoid being caught in the moving parts.

Once the landing gear was stored and the door closed, the inside of the wing was plunged into darkness. He yanked free the fingers he had wrapped around the landing gear and fell over in exhaustion.

As he lay there, the man inspected his body. When he had jumped onto the landing gear, he had fractured bones in numerous places, but his injuries didn't seem life-threatening. The burns on his face and hand were no trivial matter, but they were healing. The blindness in his eyes also seemed temporary.

Next, he checked the trunk. There didn't appear to be any damage, and the contents seemed safe.

As the plane ascended, the temperature and atmospheric pressure dropped rapidly, but neither of these affected the man with the non-human body. Of course, it was the same for the trunk's contents.

He had about four hours before he reached his destination.

The man had no time to catch his breath; he needed to think about his next steps when he reached the ground.

He didn't even have time to reflect on that final smile the woman had left him.

On the runway, those who had remained were left to scorch in the sun. What would have been refreshing morning sunshine for most people was a ruthless executioner for them.

Flames burst throughout the pursuers' bodies, and they writhed on the ground, turning into lumps of smoldering charcoal. Those lumps soon became ash, scattered by the wind.

Even the woman whom the man had left behind was engulfed in flames now, and she had fallen to her knees on the asphalt. She suffered a burning hell of pain beyond anything she had ever experienced, choosing to devote the last moments of her life to looking up.

She saw the blue sky, and a rapidly shrinking cargo plane

with the sunlight sparkling on its wings.

At that moment, her eyeballs began to burn and her vision blinked out. But she had seen what she wished at the end.

Satisfied, the woman gingerly laid face down on the runway. As her flesh melted away in the heat and her body turned to ash, her skeleton was, for a moment, exposed.

In the woman's skull, all of the canine teeth were missing.

CHAPTER 1

A strange character had come to visit the Vampire Bund.

The only way to reach the Bund by land was through the tunnel. The security guards on duty at the entrance gate were bewildered by the vehicle entering from the sun-touched mainland side.

It was a refrigerated truck from a major food company.

It went without saying that vampires have no need for human food. A truck like that should have no business within the Bund.

The truck stopped quietly just before the gate. The driver, who still clutched the steering wheel, was a middle-aged man wearing the food company's uniform. He gazed at the security guards vacantly.

The guards, suspicious of this strange truck, simultaneously removed the safeties on their guns as the rear door to the refrigerated cargo space opened from the inside.

The cold air flowing from the freezer drifted outside. Enveloped in that arctic blast, a man stepped out.

Just one look at the man was enough to know he was Asian, but not Japanese. They thought he might be around thirty years old, but they couldn't make an accurate guess. He wore what appeared to be a high class, made-to-order suit, and held a cowhide attaché case in one hand. His charming and abundant black hair was neatly combed, and his elegant features could easily be called handsome. An all-around androgynous sense emanated from him. He didn't belong in the Bund's dark and dreary tunnel, but rather playing an active role in Shanghai as a young businessman; he could be mistaken for a heartthrob in a Chinese film.

Despite traveling in a freezer while wearing only a suit, he didn't seem to be touched by the cold. He briskly brushed off bits of frost from his shoulders and approached the driver's seat, calling to the man.

"That's far enough to return me to my work. Thank you for delivering me all this way, despite your busy schedule."

As the man spoke politely to him, the driver's expression changed completely. His eyes, which had lacked clarity up to that point, filled with light. A happy smile overwrote his relaxed face, like a dog receiving a treat from its master. If the driver had had a tail, he would've been wagging it to pieces.

"Not a problem at all! It's an honor to be of service! If you ever need anything else, please let me know."As the driver answered, he hurriedly made a U-turn and drove out of the tunnel.

The man watched the truck for a minute, then turned around to face the security guards.

The guards clutched their guns. They had listened to the exchange between the man and the driver—which lacked any hint of tension—in complete amazement. He returned their questioning gazes with a courteous smile that overflowed with carefree, disarming charm.

"That type of vehicle is the best way to move while avoiding the sunlight," he said in a bright tone. The unmistakable points of vampire fangs peeked out from the man's mouth. Then, his expression tightened.

"Forgive me for making such a fuss so early in the morning. I have urgent business and wish to request an audience with Her Highness Queen Mina at once. My name is…"

The security guards reported the man's name to Wolfgang.

Upon hearing it, Wolfgang declared a state of emergency, imposing the highest level of vigilance throughout the entire Bund—the same level that had been used when Queen Mina lost her right to the throne, or when the Bund had been invaded on a large scale.

When the alarm sounded, all of the Wolf Boys—including Akira—were called to an emergency assembly. Most of them had either just woken up or were still asleep, but once they learned the security level they shook off their sleepiness and immediately turned to war preparations.

As they gathered in the Bund's Operations Room, Hama—

who had been involved in earlier incidents—Wolfgang, Vera, and select others were observing the visitor's movements via surveillance camera.

On the display, the visitor was being escorted by the maid Nelly down the corridor that lead to the audience chamber. Remus and Romulus had nonchalantly joined the escort from behind. On both sides of the corridor, members of Beowulf were intermittently and inconspicuously lined up. The blend of hospitality and vigilance made for an odd spectacle.

The visitor spoke a few words to Nelly. Whether or not he was joking with her, Nelly returned his words with an oddly bright demeanor.

"Is that Councilor Ryuu of the Li Clan?" Kamil asked with a puzzled expression. Wolfgang had given a brief rundown of the situation, but many of the onlookers seemed just as confused.

"It is not unthinkable that you wouldn't know that name. It's only been public knowledge for fifty years, and his past activities were never confirmed. There were even rumors that he was defeated in an internal struggle among the Li Clan and involved in a political purge," Wolfgang explained.

"He has a very different vibe from those guys who came here before…is he really one of Li's people?" Heinrich asked.

Just a short time ago, the leaders of the Three Great Clans had appeared in the Bund, playing out a cowardly scheme regarding Queen Mina's chastity that was still fresh in their memories. At that time, the Li Clan members and retainers were, without exception, clothed in traditional attire from the Qing Dynasty.

"There's no mistaking Ryuu; I wouldn't forget that face," Wolfgang confirmed with a sharpness in his voice.

Looking at the monitor, Hama snorted. "Even if he's a Councilor, he doesn't resemble *ours* in the least."

"The title of Councilor means nothing," Wolfgang turned to face Hama. "From long, long ago, that man carried the darkest parts of the Li Clan. If you wish to know how he operates, ask Duke Borgiani. He'll tell you old stories until you're sick of it."

"But for a man like that to enter openly from the Bund's front entrance…" Gaute wondered aloud.

"I have already spoken with Her Highness. Until we can confirm his true intentions, we will treat him with diplomatic etiquette as our honored guest. Even if it's only temporary, it wouldn't do to treat one of the Three Great Clans' chief vassals roughly."

Leroy gave an impertinent grimace and muttered, "From what I've seen, he's unarmed and didn't even bring an escort. If she wanted, she could have us kill him."

"Leroy!" Heinrich chided his partner.

"If you all took him on at once, and it ended in a tie, I would be surprised at how well you held up," Wolfgang said coolly. "Not having an escort means he doesn't need one. The last time he visited House Tepes, he was also alone and unarmed."

"Last time?" Akira asked.

Wolfgang's eyes turned sharp, and his voice took on a harsh edge.

"The day that House Tepes fell into ruin. The day our previous ruler, Queen Lucrezia, passed."

The Wolf Boys gasped at the unexpected answer. Vera looked away, eyes locked on the floor.

On the monitor display, Ryuu was just outside the audience chamber where Queen Mina waited.

Queen Mina sat calmly on the throne. This was her second time meeting with Ryuu directly, the first time having been hundreds of years prior. Even so, the intense memories of that encounter hadn't faded in the least.

Considering Ryuu's career, this was likely not a courtesy visit. Regardless of whatever Ryuu's objective was, Queen Mina was currently in the same position as her mother, and she would need to face Ryuu on her own. Perhaps this could even be an opportunity to clear up the misunderstandings surrounding their previous meeting.

"Councilor Ryuu has arrived."

As the palace guard announced his arrival, the large wooden doors opened and Ryuu and his escort entered.

Mina could not believe her own eyes.

Something resembling a black tentacle stretched from beneath the cuff of Ryuu's dress pants and into the inside hem of Nelly's uniform dress.

She began to rise to warn Nelly. However, one look at Nelly's face made it clear that she was entirely vacant, and Remus and Romulus seemed not to have noticed the shadowy appendage. Somehow, only she could see it.

Doubtful of what she saw, she looked closer at the strange tentacle. It seemed somehow not entirely real, like a flash of light superimposed on a piece of film. She got the impression that it was part of its own reality altogether—it was probably the flow of some sort of energy. Seeing such things was the unique power of a True Blood—it would be invisible to the eyes of most others.

Mina decided to overlook it. It was unfortunate for Nelly, but she thought it would be better to hide the fact that she could see it for the time being.

Ryuu smiled at Nelly. "Thank you, Miss."

"Oh, no...you are most welcome," Nelly said breathlessly, her cheeks flushed. "Please take your time."

With that, she excused herself and rushed out of the room. As she left, the tentacle withdrew from under her dress and was sucked back up Ryuu's pant leg, leaving behind no trace. Ryuu did nothing to acknowledge that it existed.

Without wasting a step, Ryuu approached the throne, kneeling before Mina.

"It's been a while, Your Highness. Please forgive my lack of contact."

"No need for apologies. It is unusual for such a prominent vassal of Lord Li to be away from his country. Hmm, you seem more refined than last time. Did you cut off your ponytail?"

"It is a despicable concession to globalism. Our clan's traditions are all being tossed aside." Ryuu's fingers dropped to the lapel of his well-tailored suit. "Regrettably, this world can't seem to avoid caving to Western civilization."

"The head of your clan used to insist on tradition from top to bottom."

"That's still true—our lord upholds our traditions and never wavers from them. Still..." Ryuu shrugged his shoulders. "These days, with his style, he couldn't tempt a single woman."

The two of them laughed in unison.

Even as she mentally winced at the empty reply, she was impressed. True Bloods were their own masters, and joking about Lord Li was a risky act that normal vampires wouldn't dare attempt. It was clear that Ryuu had Lord Li's trust—and that he was also completely shameless.

"Let us move on to the business at hand. I'm sure you didn't come all this way after hundreds of years just to chitchat."

Ryuu gave a wry smile and bowed his head slightly. "Please forgive me. Reveling too deeply in foolishness is a weakness of mine."

When he raised his head once more, he was no longer the sociable gentleman he had been. In the charming man's place was the cunning and dangerous vampire who, since an indeterminate ancient time period, had supported the Li Clan from behind the scenes.

"I have a humble request for the one who reigns over all the vampires in this world, Her Highness Mina Tepes. Some freight that recently departed Guangzhou will be arriving soon at Narita Airport. I wish to have the vampire stowed away on that plane arrested by Beowulf."

Mina narrowed her eyes. "Let's hear the details, then."

Ryuu eyed a dining table in one corner of the vast room. "Join me at that table, and I'll show you."

Mina and Ryuu sat facing one another at opposite ends of the long table. Remus and Romulus stood protectively on either side of Mina.

Ryuu removed a low-profile laptop from the attaché case and quickly booted it up, then held it out to her. "Please have a look at this video."

Romulus walked over to Ryuu and took the computer. Concerned about the possibility of a trap, Romulus eyed Ryuu suspiciously. Ryuu slowly lifted his head to look back at Romulus.

Mina was unconcerned. "Very well. Bring it to me."

As soon as the computer was set in front of her, the video started to play.

The screen was divided into four segments, each showing some facility's corridor from different angles. According to the time stamp in the lower right corner, the video had been taken late the night before.

"This is a video from our clan's hidden data archives. Please look at the top left camera feed," Ryuu said.

In the hallway displayed in the top left portion of the screen, an automated door opened at an intersection. A man came through the door—he had a braid coiled around his neck and was cloaked in an all-black outfit. He was shouldering something that looked like a box. The man ran quickly down the corridor and disappeared off the bottom of the screen.

A moment later, he appeared on the top right feed. The man rounded a corner, not slowing a step as he turned.

He reached a new intersection, and his movements slowed as he looked around. The video had no sound, but it looked like an alarm had gone off somewhere.

Several security guards ran into frame and tried to restrain the man. With a surprising suddenness of movement, he mowed down all of the security guards in an instant. He ran off in the direction from which they had come. The felled guards didn't even twitch.

The man then appeared in the bottom left and right images. He dashed down the corridor with all his strength, exiting from the camera's view. Immediately, all four camera feeds were filled with security guards running everywhere.

"That man stole numerous important confidential documents from our clan," Ryuu explained. "Naturally, we chased him, but he killed all of his pursuers while fleeing to

Guangzhou Baiyun International Airport. And this morning, he stowed away on a Confedex cargo plane bound for Narita."

"So, you're asking to borrow Beowulf to capture him?"

Ryuu nodded. "I'm afraid we don't have the luxury of waiting until night."

"What time will that cargo plane arrive at Narita?"

Ryuu looked at his watch with an affected gesture. "In about 30 minutes."

"What will you do after he is captured?"

"We'll execute him, of course. Pilfering confidential documents is treason."

If Mina had caught wind of this incident on her own, she would have set about ensuring his protection without hesitation. Once sheltered in the Bund, she could do so still, regardless of Ryuu's wishes.

However, Ryuu had made the first move this time. Since hearing that the fugitive had done damage to the Li Clan, refusing Ryuu's request would be difficult. As head of all the clans, it was her responsibility to maintain order between vampires throughout the world, Li Clan included.

Rather than asking her permission, Ryuu had come to request aid.

"There is also another problem," Ryuu said, his face expressionless. "This man had an accomplice: a Fangless woman."

"...Continue."

"That woman died at the airport, but, according to the

pursuers, it seems that they had been aiming for Japan from the start. The confidential documents were to be a souvenir to commemorate taking refuge in the Bund."

Ryuu's tone grew harsh. "I apologize for being impolite, but we are all aware that this Bund pampers the Fangless. This incident could be seen as the result of House Tepes' political policies."

Mina sighed. "An incident caused by those unaffiliated with House Tepes is no concern of mine. This is an internal matter within the Li Clan."

"Would Duke Borgiani say the same?"

She furrowed her brows. "What was that?"

Ryuu straightened in his chair. "There should be no need for secrets from His Excellency. I am one of the longest lived background operators for House Li. There are times when vampires like us execute secret operations in the service of our clan without reporting to our lord."

"Are you saying that Borgiani sent a Fangless spy to tempt this man without my knowledge?"

"I am merely indicating the possibility."

"Does the head of the Li Clan know about this incident?"

"No. If he knew at this stage, our leader would, without a doubt, judge the document theft to be Her Highness' doing. That would cause a great fissure between the houses of Li and Tepes, and a clash between our clans could be a disaster for all vampires. That's why I decided to come here right away and request Your Highness' aid in this matter."

Now Mina was worried. She wanted to avoid having a hand in executing this man once he had finally escaped to Japan. But Ryuu had tried to lock her in by filtering his true intentions through his courteous persona.

Ryuu gazed at her with a calm expression, seeming to have all the time in the world.

"Wait for a moment," she instructed as she stood up. Speaking those words evenly took all that Mina had.

As soon as she entered the antechamber, Mina raised her voice.

"Call Alphonse!"

Ryuu was taken to a separate room to wait. Maids were inconspicuously stationed there as guards.

Everyone in the Operations Room reconvened in the antechamber.

"Figures that he's as silver-tongued as ever," Wolfgang said with uncharacteristic snideness.

"His overconfidence disgusts me, but I understand the reason. At this point, we can't flat-out refuse him. Where is Alphonse?"

One of Alphonse's subordinates—a member of the intelligence division he led—finally arrived. His expression was stiff, and the color of his face had drained.

"Why isn't Alphonse here?"

"My apologies. Duke Borgiani has stepped out to respond to a summons."

"Respond…? Where is he now?"

The intelligence division member answered like he had to squeeze out every word. "…I am truly sorry. Duke Borgiani ordered that his location remain undisclosed to everyone, including Her Highness."

Frustrated, Mina looked over the intelligence division member, his face covered in a cold sweat. For him, both Queen Mina and Alphonse were elite members of vampire hierarchy. To receive incompatible orders from both was making him collapse under the contradiction.

Even so, her orders would receive precedence in the end. If she asked him again, he could not help but respond with Alphonse's location; it was just odd, since Alphonse knew she could do that. It stood out that Alphonse would act so freely, but Mina knew that he wouldn't do anything to put House Tepes in danger. Naturally, she had to assume he had a good reason for being absent at such a bad time.

Mina carelessly waved her hand. "Very well. When Alphonse returns, inform us immediately."

The intelligence division member bowed deeply with an expression of relief, and left immediately.

"We can't deny the possibility of a spy's infiltration," Mina said, then rested her chin in her hands and lapsed into thoughtful silence. Unexpectedly, Alphonse's current activities reinforced Ryuu's story.

"How could that happen?" Wolfgang asked.

"It's not like we can choose not to cooperate. No matter

what my instincts tell me, I can't find a valid reason to refuse."

Akira approached Mina. "What's going on? Even though you know he's going to be executed, you're willing to just hand him over?"

She unclenched her hands and grabbed Akira.

"Calm down, Akira. Do you really believe I'm going to let Ryuu have his way in the Bund without a fight?"

"Well…"

"At any rate, you will find and retrieve the fugitive. While you are gone, I will think of a way to send Ryuu home empty-handed."

Everyone present was encouraged by Mina's optimistic words.

"Remus, lead the Wolf Boys to Narita at once. What's the shortest time it would take to reach Narita from here?"

"20 minutes by helicopter."

"Hmm, we won't make it in time for the landing." Mina turned to Hama. "Enlist Councilor Gotoh's cooperation. A stowaway vampire is arriving at Narita—strengthen security so he cannot leave."

"Understood." Her orders seemed to depress Hama—no doubt it was the thought of Gotoh's exasperated face at this 'request' from Mina.

"Wolfgang and Vera, keep an eye on Ryuu and don't let him do anything that seems suspicious." She clapped her hands and rubbed them together. "Now it's time for the true game to begin!"

CHAPTER 2

When the Wolf Boys' helicopter got to Narita Airport, the cargo plane had already arrived. In accordance with Councilor Gotoh's preparations, the plane was received not at the cargo terminal, but at the hangar.

As Hama was confirming the situation with airport security, a man with a braid—believed to be the fugitive—was spotted. The man shook off the security pursuit, and he was thought to have taken refuge in the basement mechanical room. With all of the routes leading above ground guarded by police officers, he was trapped like a rat.

The Wolf Boys decided to split into groups of two and enter the mechanical room from different points to search for the fugitive.

Before they separated, Remus said sternly, "He may be panicked from being chased by the police. If it becomes unavoidably necessary to subdue him, you are permitted to use weapons. However, because there is a risk of sparking a fire or causing a ricochet, firearms are forbidden."

The Wolf Boys made their way down into the basement,

and realized that finding the fugitive would not be easy.

The main airport was huge, and the mechanical room was large in its own right. It stretched down for an unfathomable number of floors, with separate sections—a mechanics facility, boiler, drainage processing, and more—intricately woven together, giving it the appearance of a subterranean labyrinth.

Within the room, there were numerous machines and pipes jumbled together along the catwalk, creating thousands of places for the fugitive to hide. And between the noise of the air conditioner and boiler and the stench of dust and transformer oil, the werewolves were unable to use their abilities to the fullest. In the end, they had no choice but to have each person walk about quietly and slowly search each area.

Gaute and Cinva checked the drainage facility's control room top to bottom, entering from the water recycling system.

The path they walked on was marked off by wire mesh running along the side. On the other side of the wire mesh was an installation for recycling surplus drainage and a rainwater purification plant.

"It stinks in here," Cinva grumbled.

"It can't be helped. Sewage has gotta go somewhere, too," Gaute responded.

Behind them, a loud clang pierced the air.

They turned to see a man wearing a jumpsuit and a braid in his hair tottering towards them. He'd staggered into a bucket and sent it flying with a loud noise.

"Are you from the Li Clan?" Gaute asked.

Without answering Gaute's question, the man clung weakly to the wire mesh. Half of his face and the back of his hand had been burned.

Gaute called out to the man once more.

"We are from House Tepes. We came to protect you."

The man staggered and collapsed, his knees hitting the floor.

Gaute rushed over to him, quickly laying his halberd on the floor and trying to help him up. Cinva followed behind.

In the next instant, the man thrust his palms up and landed a direct hit to Gaute's solar plexus. Gaute was sent flying back several meters and tumbled to the ground in agony.

"Bastard!" Cinva jumped at the man and tried to seize him.

The man threw Cinva back with one blow. Cinva's small body fell to the ground, but he rolled and sprang back up immediately.

This time, the man attacked with a strong roundhouse kick.

Cinva crossed his arms to defend his body from the blow, but the kick's power wasn't blocked and he was knocked aside, into the wire mesh.

Judging that subduing the man unarmed was impossible, Cinva pulled out his trusty janbiya dagger.

Without a hint of hesitation, the man jumped at Cinva. Avoiding his vital parts, Cinva slashed at the man's abdomen.

The man grimaced in pain, gripped his abdomen, and pitched forward to the ground—then nimbly somersaulted forward and kicked up sharply at Cinva's jaw. He hit solidly and knocked Cinva into the air all the way up to the ceiling.

An ordinary person would have broken his neck, but Cinva, who had tempered his body in spite of his small stature, was only stunned.

The man stood up straight in front of the now-crumpled Cinva and thrust his hand into the open slit on the abdomen of his jumpsuit. He pulled out a thick magazine that had been sliced in half. Anticipating the knife attack, he had placed it there as makeshift body armor.

The man threw the now useless magazine next to Cinva, then looked at Gaute.

Gaute had finally recovered from the damage of the surprise attack, and was painfully trying to sit up.

Without waiting for Gaute to recover, the man took off once more.

Kamil and Junte turned a corner and came face-to-face with the running man.

"That's him!" Gaute shouted, gasping.

At almost the same time that Kamil heard Gaute's voice, he sensed the man passing right in front of him. He felt the man's braid rustle the air.

Kamil reached out and grasped the braid—but in one fluid motion, the man swung a hand behind him and severed his braid bare-handed, leaving a fistful of hair in Kamil's grasp.

Junte also came to a quick decision.

They were at a T-intersection, with paths splitting to the left and right. The man dashed toward the impassable wall, piled high with machinery all the way to the ceiling.

Junte found a short crowbar nearby and threw it at the running man's feet. The crowbar spun like a boomerang toward the man's legs.

The crowbar should have intertwined with his legs and sent him tumbling forward when the man decelerated to turn the corner, but he unleashed an unexpected maneuver— instead of turning left or right, he continued straight and jumped.

There were four tiny crevices in the machinery, barely thirty centimeters wide. The man dove headfirst into one of them and passed straight through like a dolphin through a hoop.

The crowbar fell harmlessly to the floor with a loud clang. Even normally expressionless Junte could not hide his astonishment.

Kamil and Junte ran up to the wall of machines and

looked over, but the man was gone. Abandoning the pursuit, they returned to Gaute, who was taking care of the unconscious Cinva.

Junte picked up the magazine and mumbled in a small voice, "......"

Kamil nodded. "Yes. He was prepared to fight us from the start."

"He didn't understand what we said. He probably mistook us for his pursuers," Gaute said. "Our opponent is a worthy and experienced combatant. If we don't warn the others, we'll see who needs to be protected from whom."

Gaute called into his radio, but no one replied.

They glanced at each other.

Leroy and Heinrich searched the substation. They split up at the two ends of the room, thoroughly checking any crevices where the fugitive could hide.

Leroy had been sullen the whole time. The steady groan emitted by the row of massive transformers, and the stench of mechanical oil, were unavoidable and unpleasant.

Leroy peeked behind a charging board shaped like a big locker, then suddenly raised his head. A man was standing a small distance away, by the wall.

His hairstyle was not a braid, but disheveled like that of a fallen warrior. Still, there was no mistaking that this was the man in the video.

He had armed himself with a long-handled broom.

Leroy's mood improved at once and he flashed a daring smile.

"So, you think you can take me on with that?"

Whether or not Leroy's words were understood, the man also grinned broadly. The smile twisted his blistered face in an unsettling way.

"Interesting." Leroy stopped himself from calling for Heinrich. Propping his sword up against the charging board, he picked up a nearby iron pipe, similar in length to the man's broom.

Leroy stood in a fighting stance with the pipe in both hands. "Come on!"

They both leapt forward at the same time, the iron pipe and broom clashing.

The man was stronger than Leroy expected. High and low, Leroy unleashed a flurry of attacks, but the man dodged them easily. In turn, the man took advantage of any opening to counterattack again and again.

Leroy's defense was precise, and though the man didn't land any hits on him, he also had yet to land a direct hit on the man.

"Damn it... Who the hell...?"

The bandana around Leroy's head tore as it stretched; his face was suddenly covered in animal hair. His striking hand transformed without his grip loosening at all. When his transformation was complete, he swung the pipe again, much faster than before.

Still, the man matched Leroy, his speed increasing at the same pace, as if he had shifted up a level in his martial abilities. Even after Leroy's transformation, the two of them were still evenly matched.

As the give-and-take between them got faster, the sound of their weapons clashing resounded, combining into one long noise like a drum roll.

Just as Leroy was thinking that this stalemate would continue forever, Heinrich's voice called out from behind him.

"Leroy!"

Almost instantly, Leroy's concentration shifted in the direction of the voice.

The man wasn't about to let that chance go. He flipped up the pipe deftly and struck Leroy's nose with the tip of the broom.

The thin nerves concentrated in the skin of a werewolf's nose made it one of the most sensitive areas on his body. Having the thousands of hard, fine bristles of the broom shoved into it was unbearable. Leroy roared in agony.

The man grabbed Leroy's head and smashed it down, his knee connecting solidly with Leroy's jaw.

Leroy crumpled to the ground, unconscious.

The man immediately turned back, rounding on Heinrich.

Heinrich ran at the man, removing his sword from its scabbard mid-stride. Usually cool-headed, even he couldn't stay calm after seeing his partner so soundly defeated. He wasn't going to kill the man, but he would certainly rough him up.

Heinrich brought his sword down from above with no mercy. The man held the broom above his head in an attempt to stop the incoming slash.

In a flash, Heinrich sliced the broom handle into two. Without delay, he took a step forward, and this time, he swung up from below.

The sword was suddenly stopped.

The man crossed the boom's severed halves, halting the blade's movement where the halves intersected; he had let the handle be cut on purpose.

Shocked, Heinrich looked at the man's face. The man smiled weakly at Heinrich, then reared back and slammed his forehead into the bridge of Heinrich's nose.

"Gah!" Heinrich's glasses split into two and flew off his face. Blood spouted from his nose as he toppled backwards.

The man, no longer concerned with Heinrich, stepped over his writhing body and opened the metal door leading outside.

Akira cooperated with Hama in checking the cable rack, using a ladder that almost reached the ceiling. In Hama's opinion, the cable rack, creeping along the ceiling and walls, would be the perfect hiding place as people searched below.

When they approached the substation, the metal door opened and they saw someone come out. The halogen light placed next to the metal door served as backlighting, so they couldn't clearly make out the person's appearance.

That person glanced Akira's way and ran off quickly, rounding the corner and disappearing.

Akira chased after him to confirm his identity.

He got a glimpse of the room beyond the slowly closing metal door.

Heinrich was squatting on the floor, holding his face. Blood was dripping through the gaps in his fingers. When he noticed Akira, he shouted in a muffled voice, "That was him! Go after him!"

Akira sprinted off, chasing the man around the corner.

Suddenly, Akira's line of sight was blocked—he was covered from the head down by a big blue polyethylene bucket. Someone kicked him in the back of the knee, and he fell to the ground with a jerk. The sword he was holding flew out of his hand.

Anticipating another attack, Akira instantly transformed both hands and used his nails to slice through the bucket and tear it off. As his vision returned, he saw the man standing in front of him, already swinging a heavy piece of lumber down at him.

Just before the wood reached Akira's head, he reached up with one hand and stopped the swing. He broke through the wood with a chop like a lightning strike.

Akira then spun around and slammed the side of the staggering man's head with the tip of the wood. The man toppled to the ground, wood still in hand.

Akira tossed the beam aside and jumped for the man to try and restrain him.

The man quickly sprang up, grabbing Akira's shoulder and using his force to leapfrog over him.

The man shrank down and held the snapped lumber to Akira's throat, striking his left elbow with one edge of the board, and grabbed the back of Akira's head with the palm of his hand in a half nelson. If Akira tried to squeeze his head out like this, the man could easily strangle him.

Akira's breathing was blocked, and white lights danced before his eyes. He locked one hand on the back of the hand holding the beam. His claws dug into the man's burnt flesh, blood and serum flowing forth.

The man's expression twisted in agony, and he let out a voiceless scream. By chance, Akira saw into his open mouth, and his eyes widened in shock.

The man violently pushed Akira away, slamming him into the wall. Akira's body slumped over in a heap.

The man took an intimidating stance and looked down at Akira. Possibly due to the pain of his wounds, the color of his eyes had changed with his intent to kill; he'd realized he could actually die here. The moment that thought crossed Akira's mind, a sound like a thunderbolt roared through the room and knocked the man on his side.

Akira looked in the direction of the sound.

Hama held a handgun at the ready, smoke rising from the

barrel. Gaute and Cinva stood behind Hama.

The man quickly got to his feet and ran. The bullet had pierced his left shoulder—blood dripped off the fingertips of his limp left hand.

Hama and the others chased the man as he passed Akira. The bloodstains made a trail all the way to the stairwell. When Hama opened the door, a powerful stench overwhelmed them.

Toilet cleaning supplies had been disposed of on the stairs. Whether or not he'd actually stopped the bleeding on the landing, the blood stains were no longer visible on the stairs and the scent of blood was covered by the stench of cleaning supplies.

Unable to stand the assault on his nose, Cinva sneezed over and over. Gaute tightened his face and grabbed his nose.

"I guess he's used to fighting werewolves," Hama muttered.

Hama and the others returned to Akira as Remus and Romulus arrived. Remus' sharp eyes drifted to the gun Hama was holding.

"Didn't we say firearms were off-limits?"

Hama shrugged his shoulders. "There's no ricochet if the bullet's in his body."

Remus sighed and approached Akira, who was sitting on the floor.

"Are you okay?"

"…Yeah."

He grabbed Akira's hand and helped him stand up.

"He didn't have a tongue."

"Hm?"

"I saw inside his mouth. Where his tongue should have been, there was nothing." Akira's face was pale.

Remus, wearing a troubled expression, exchanged glances with Romulus.

After tending to each other's injuries, they regrouped. Romulus began to speak.

"It was in the middle of an operation in Laos. Remus and I were part of a small group—six people—that was attacked by only two. Despite their small numbers, they killed three of our members almost immediately, and one of them was caught in a stand-off with another of our number—both were killed. The two of us remaining managed to take our last attacker prisoner.

"He had his hair in a braid, no tongue and no voice," Remus added. "The dead one was the same. It had been cut out intentionally."

Disbelief tinged Akira's voice. "Cutting out someone's tongue... Why would anyone do that?"

"Someone whose sole purpose is fighting doesn't need a tongue." Gaute made a sour face.

Remus continued, "When we returned to camp and tried to interrogate him, he slit his own throat, empty-handed."

Hama raised his hand. "I've also heard rumors of these

mercenaries. They're terrifying men with braided hair. They never speak, so they're called the silent ones."

The group grew quiet in shock at this revelation about their opponent.

The one who broke the silence was Cinva.

"Then why is no one dead?"

They were all taken aback. In their battles with the man, not one of them had received a life-threatening injury. Not even one of them had been incapacitated.

"If he's the same as those guys from Laos, it wouldn't have been strange for him to kill Cinva and the others when he first saw them," Leroy said.

Kamil tilted his head. "I don't know how to say this, but...if he had wanted to, he could have killed us easily. He must have delayed ending us on purpose..."

"You're not kidding," Hama muttered. "Think about it, you guys. Why would someone stall for time in a fight?"

Heinrich recited some of the reasons as he counted on his fingers.

"Trying to let a friend get away, waiting for reinforcements, creating a diversion..." Heinrich's voice trailed off. "A diversion..."

Remus yelled, "No!"

There was a loud sound nearby.

Queen Mina was seated on the sofa in the anteroom, lost in thought.

Suddenly, the door opened, and Wolfgang entered briskly. Behind him, several Beowulf members filed in. They were all armed with crossbows and sabers, and they formed a row along all four walls, not leaving even a crack. This formation was to protect her from an external enemy.

"What is it, Wolfgang?"

"Your Highness, Councilor Ryuu has disappeared."

CHAPTER 3

"What in the hell were you all doing? Your job was to guard him so that something like this wouldn't happen!"

Sekiko, the head maid, was the one being reprimanded, but all of the maids lined up lowered their heads. Sekiko was angry at them—the recorded video from the security cameras showed Ryuu exiting the waiting room and calmly walking off down the hall, and the maids aimlessly watching him go without raising any alarm.

Mina folded her arms and thought for a moment.

"Nelly, explain to me what happened."

"We certainly saw when Councilor Ryuu left the room. But—and I'm not sure why—we had this feeling that there was no need to report it…"

Nella picked up from there. "I tried to stop him when he started to leave the room. However, the moment my eyes met his, I suddenly felt that it was all right to let him go"

The other maids voiced their agreement as one.

Mina looked at Wolfgang.

He nodded. "It's exactly the same as that day."

That day—the day of Councilor Ryuu's previous meeting with House Tepes.

Lucrezia's castle, which had become House Tepes' last fortress, was completely surrounded by the allied forces of the Three Clans, waiting for their chance to assassinate the queen. There was no hope of any reinforcements.

In the midst of this, a man with a magnificent ponytail, wearing Chinese armor with a flashy lightning dragon embroidered on it and a matching helmet, calmly walked into the castle.

Councilor Ryuu.

Those he passed would tense into a fighting stance, but then they'd give him a nod and suddenly lose any sign of concern. The only exceptions were the Beowulf veterans, shouldering battleaxes and javelins dirtied in blood and sweat.

Ryuu easily reached the room where Lucrezia was and requested a face-to-face meeting as a messenger urging for her surrender.

With no resistance, the palace guards opened the door and let Ryuu pass.

Inside the room, Lucrezia was bouncing young Mina on her knee in an attempt to soothe her. Facing the surprised Lucrezia, Ryuu gave the smile of a victor and made his proposition: hand over Princess Mina, and your life will be spared...

Mina stiffened at the unpleasant memory. She then quickly told them about the shadowy appendage she had seen earlier.

"A mind vampire," Vera breathed. "I've heard that such vampires exist. They suck out the emotional energy of other vampires and humans, and take control of them."

Wolfgang nodded. "If the target is a vampire, he can't go so far as to make them go against their master, but if he manipulates their thoughts enough, he can increase their apathy. For example, if Ryuu enters your line of sight and drains your animosity and suspicion, you'll lose the desire to attack or alert someone."

Nelly, on learning that Ryuu had controlled her thoughts during the time she showed him around, wore a disgusted expression on her pale face.

Vera pressed Mina, "Your Highness, at this rate, we can't help but see this incident with the fugitive as a diversionary tactic to keep the palace guards away. Even if this fugitive is real, Ryuu may piggyback on that event to make an assassination attempt against you."

"We have too little information. Not having Alphonse here at a time like this... Ah, that's right!" Mina snapped her fingers. "Vera, I want to talk to Harvey. Call him."

Mina took the phone from Vera and spoke into it quickly.

"Harvey? Oh, you... We need some help. I understand... Don't you 'but' me! You can talk to Vera about that incident later. Listen, I need you to gather any and all information you can pertaining to the person whose name I'm about to give you, ASAP."

She ended the call and returned the phone to Vera.

"The question is, Vera, where has he gone? And we still need to uncover what his true motives are."

The noise was coming from the boiler room.

From the other side of the metal door, a metallic clashing sound could be heard every few seconds.

"He's taunting us." Leroy smacked his lips.

He could guess the meaning of the sound—"If you want to catch me, come and get me!" That in order to escort the man alive, they would have to put their lives on the line—and and the man's life, too—was painfully ironic.

Remus grabbed the doorknob and opened the door slightly.

The inside of the boiler room was pitch black. Remus carefully extended his hand and groped for a light switch on the wall inside the doorway, but he found nothing.

The man was clearly trying to lure them into the darkness.

"I'll go," Kamil announced. "I'm still unharmed, and the darkness won't hinder me."

Without another word, Kamil changed into a werewolf, opened the metal door, and headed inside.

The others prepared themselves in case the man tried to leave the boiler room. They drew their swords and crowded around the doorway.

The silence continued for over a minute.

Suddenly, there was a piercing bang, followed by a sharp clatter like a cupboard being torn down and the clang of weapons clashing.

Just as suddenly, the noises fell silent.

A moment later, the metal door was torn off its hinges with a huge crash, and the man and Kamil tumbled out, intertwined and covered in blood.

The man shook Kamil off him and sprang up. In an instant, the muzzle of a gun was pushed up against his forehead.

"Sorry about your shoulder," Hama said curtly.

The Wolf Boys surrounded the man, every weapon pointed at him.

The man slowly glared at his surroundings. He hadn't completely lost the will to fight—he took a stance like he would run, if given an opening.

The tense glaring contest continued.

Suddenly, Akira tossed aside his sword. The fallen weapon made a sharp sound as it hit the steel-plated floor.

"Stop this, now!" Akira said to the man.

"Akira, stay back!" Romulus warned him.

Unarmed, Akira stepped forward and approached the man. The man's glare rested on him.

"You ran away because you want to live in the Bund in peace, right? Then why are you fighting us? What's the point of all this?"

Akira couldn't understand the man's intentions, or why

he would fight them at all. He didn't think his words were getting through, though. The battle had stirred up old memories, and he couldn't help but see a parallel between this man and one of his friends—Hiko—who he couldn't save.

"Come to the Bund with us. No matter who you are or who might oppose it, Hime-san will protect you. All you have to do is enter the Bund, and you'll be safe!"

As Akira gave his passionate plea, the man's expression changed—his blank mask melted and the atmosphere of strained tension thinned like ice.

Akira recognized the change in the man's eyes. They were no longer the eyes of the 'silent ones,' butchers and murderers. Like Akira, his eyes were those of a kind soldier who would give his life to protect those who needed him. He quietly gazed at Akira, then slowly shook his head.

Akira was relieved. "Do you understand what I'm saying?"

Suddenly, the air before his eyes swam, and he acted like he was searching for a presence. The man quickly returned his gaze to Akira.

In the next moment, the man attacked Akira with a terrifying murderous intent.

In the following several seconds, everything happened too quickly; for the Beowulf members present, they wouldn't be able to grasp the full picture until later.

The man moved so fast he hardly left an imprint. He

immediately closed in on Akira; Akira had no way to avoid him. The man grabbed the nape of Akira's neck in one hand, preparing to plunge the fingertips of his other hand into Akira's throat.

Kamil was first to react. With the sharpest hearing of all the Wolf Boys, he shouted to the others that someone or something was rapidly approaching from behind.

Kamil turned to face it just in time to get a glimpse of something passing before his eyes like wind, slipping between Kamil and Leroy, breaking into their circle.

Without losing any speed, it passed directly behind the man and slipped through Gaute and Cinva on the other side of the circle. It happened so quickly that neither of them could respond.

The man's hand—clutching Akira's neck—stopped moving.

A long gash opened on the back of the man's neck, like a horrible mouth that spewed a fount of fresh blood. The attack had sliced at least halfway through his neck.

The hand clutching Akira's collar began to shake.

Akira gazed up into the dying man's eyes.

The man's expression strangely peaceful. His eyes were not locked on Akira; instead, he was staring ahead as if watching a ghost, or a memory.

Akira had no time to call out. The man's eyes, face and hands—all of him—was turning to ash and scattering in the air.

The Wolf Boys finally caught up with what had happened. They turned toward the new threat outside their circle, and found it almost immediately.

It was shaped like a human, covered in a jet black bodysuit that resembled a combination of armor and a wetsuit. His head was protected by a tough-looking thin helmet—the face couldn't be seen at all, as it was hidden by a face mask with insect-like goggles.

The Wolf Boys' gaze was pulled to the object in his hand. The handle of the thin, straight Chinese sword was decorated with splendid ornamentation.

The person flicked the sword once, wiping away the man's lingering blood from his blade. Upon sheathing the sword in the scabbard at his hip, he slowly pulled up the goggles—two long slits for eyes appeared.

"Councilor Ryuu!"

Ryuu gave his usual courteous smile.

"That was certainly close. If my arrival had been one second later, Her Highness' precious boy would have lost his life."

The Wolf Boys had no words for this absurd turn of events. Kamil and Gaute were the most shocked. Even though Ryuu had passed right through their circle, none of them had even gotten the chance to try to touch him. They were reminded of Wolfgang's words, their truth finally revealed.

Ryuu looked around at the weapons still pointed at him.

"Is pointing a weapon at your ally proper etiquette in House Tepes?"

At Remus' signal, they put away their weapons.

"Please excuse us, but we were told you would be waiting back at the Bund."

"I admit I shouldn't butt into a matter that was left to all of you. Though my skills can't compare to yours, I thought I could be of some assistance, and so I hurried to join you." Ryuu looked at the empty clothes at Akira's feet. "It seems my decision was the right one."

It was clear that, from the beginning, he had planned to do away with the fugitive on his own. He had used the Wolf Boys—he'd let them track the man down for him.

Remus courteously lowered his head. "Thank you for assisting us. Excuse me, but what is that equipment?"

"It's UV protective armor developed by our clan. I notice House Tepes isn't using this type of armor."

Developing a way to fight freely in the daytime has been a challenge for vampires for countless years, as shade gel didn't work well on the battlefield. UV protective armor and clothing had existed since the old days. However, it's main weakness was that a single cut or tear that exposed skin during hand-to-hand combat would lead to widespread cellular breakdown radiating from that area, and the death of the wearer. That was why hardly any vampires risked that kind of armor. It could only be used by fighters with absolute confidence in their combat ability.

Remus could sense the disdain in Ryuu's polite speech. As the leader here, he was prepared to stay mostly polite and deferential. But he couldn't resist one sarcastic barb.

"There are no words sufficient to thank you for saving Akira. However, with the fugitive dead, it'll be difficult to find your precious trunk."

"I'm not worried about that; I have confidence in your abilities. After all, your kind was originally made for finding things."

Waves of anger passed over the Wolf Boys, who were now sitting in a row. Ryuu's words were true, but they were still provocative and reckless.

Remus reached the end of his patience and stepped forward to intervene with Ryuu.

"Well then, the Earth Clan will take care of the search. Councilor Ryuu, I will see you safely back to the Bund now. Romulus, I leave the rest to you."

Up until that point, Akira had been staring in astonishment at the man's jumpsuit, an empty lump on the floor. He'd felt a real connection with that man for a moment, he was sure. Having it severed so abruptly was shock. When he finally raised his head, Ryuu and Remus had already started walking away.

Akira's body burned with an anger that coursed through his body. His werewolf blood throbbed for sudden action. Akira's field of vision was dyed red, and he found himself starting to transform into a werewolf. The backs of his hands were covered with coarse hair, and his snout began extending outwards.

Akira shifted to an aggressive stance as he glared at Ryuu's back. He bent and twisted his body like a taunt bow. He tensed to jump.

His body jerked to a stop. Hama held him back by the shoulder—Akira fought against the hold, but Hama pushed down on Akira's shoulder with a strength above any other human's, forcing him to his knees.

Hama leaned forward to whisper in Akira's ear. "You're not a wolf. Fulfill your duty as a member of the Earth Clan."

At those words, Akira came to his senses, reversed his transformation and stood up, discouraged. The other Wolf Boys breathed collective sighs of relief.

Akira adjusted his collar where the man had grabbed him. When he felt around with his finger, he found something caught inside his collar. The man must have crammed something in there during his last few seconds alive. Akira tilted his head and, making sure that Ryuu and Remus were out of sight, pulled out the object.

It was a small scrap of paper.

He inspected the paper—it was torn from a diagram of the air conditioning ducts.

They all rushed to the location indicated on the map. There, a silver-colored duct ran along the walls, weaving throughout the spaces between the machines and zigzagging back and forth. With the smallest size of the group and an effective nose, Cinva was the best choice to slip into the duct and begin a search of the area.

Though the dust and mold made it difficult, Cinva discovered traces that the man had left while crawling through the ducts. He followed those traces to a trunk lying deep inside.

But why was the lid unlocked and open a crack?

Suppressing a sneeze, Cinva confirmed that there were no traps inside. He didn't see any suspicious wires or any type of timing device.

Cinva lifted the half-open lid.

CHAPTER 4

Queen Mina and Ryuu were once again seated opposite each other in the audience chamber. She was drumming her fingers rhythmically on the armrest of her chair. It was something to do to keep from strangling Ryuu to death.

"Your mischief went a little too far this time, did it not?"

"My deepest apologies. My behavior was obtrusive." Ryuu politely bowed his head.

"I would like to express my gratitude to you for saving Akira."

"I appreciate it."

"Also, I've received good news. I've been contacted by our mobile unit at Narita. It seems your trunk has been found."

Mina didn't miss the flash of surprise that crossed his face for a moment.

"What? I thought you'd be a bit happier."

"No, I am. I'd like to thank you for all this."

They spoke about harmless things for a while, until the

guard announced the trunk's arrival.

The big door opened and Romulus stuck his head in first, followed by Leroy and Heinrich lugging the trunk. They both had large pieces of gauze stuck in their noses.

They approached the table and carefully placed the trunk in front of Ryuu. Leroy glared at Ryuu with a ferocious look, but Ryuu's face was cool. The Beowulf members then departed.

The trunk was sealed up tight with tape.

"Well, open it and examine the contents."

Pressed by Mina, Ryuu smiled and shook his head. "It's nothing extravagant. It would be absurd to doubt the abilities of the illustrious Beowulf. I'll refrain from peeking and take it back with me like this."

"Now, don't say that. We must be sure all the stolen scrolls are there."

"No, no...there's no need for—"

"I'm ordering you to open it."

Mina's tone changed abruptly. Ryuu lifted his head and found himself pierced by Mina's icy stare—her voice was like a dagger suddenly thrust into his throat.

"Speak no further nonsense. The risk isn't to your reputation; it's to mine." She stared right into Ryuu's face. "If you take the trunk without confirming its contents, and then find that something is missing, it could tarnish my good name. Now, here where I can see, verify the contents of the trunk."

Vera was suddenly standing beside Ryuu, offering him the hilt of a drawn knife. The fingers on the hand not holding the knife were bent in an odd way while resting at her side. If he made even the slightest suspicious movement, Vera would immediately dispatch a dark weapon; he was certain of it.

He nodded his thanks, took the knife and began to cut the tape wrapped around the trunk. He quickly tore off the tape with his hands, exposing a lock. It was already unlocked, and pulling the lock off made the lid pop up slightly.

Ryuu slowly lifted the lid, then let it fall backwards. The trunk's contents were illuminated by the audience chamber's lights, now exposed for all to see.

The trunk was packed tightly with white packing peanuts.

Ryuu thrust both hands into the packaging, cautiously probing deeper, and immediately met an object. He lifted it gently.

It was a large paper scroll, over 30 centimeters long and bound at its center with a cord. Similar scrolls appeared one after another; once he had finished, ten of them were lined up on top of the table.

"As expected, these are Lord Li's classified documents, are they not? Nothing is missing, correct?" Mina asked.

Ryuu carefully confirmed that everything was in order.

"They're all here. It looks like the seals were not broken."

"Hmm, that's good." She nodded thoughtfully. "You

managed to punish the fugitive and retrieve the documents. With that, all of your loose ends have been cleaned up, yes?"

Something dangerous in her tone set off alarm bells in Ryuu's head.

"As you command."

"I have one request; don't worry, it's nothing complicated. I heard a very interesting legend lately, and I would like you to listen to it."

He suddenly realized that Vera and the guard had disappeared at some point. Mina and Ryuu were the only ones left in the audience chamber.

Ryuu calmed down and pondered for a moment. He was suspicious that he was being set up for something, but had no reason to refuse.

"As Her Highness wishes."

"Thank you."

Mina shifted on her seat and began to tell the tale.

"Long ago, at the beginning of the 18th century, there was a disturbance in the Sichuan province of China. The uprising was started by about three thousand Fangless and vampires who shared their sentiments. Their objective wasn't to seize political power—they wanted to appeal to the land's ruling clan for improvement of the Fangless' labor conditions."

There was no change to Ryuu's expression. He remained silent, waiting. Mina continued undaunted.

"The severity of that Great Clan's treatment of the

Fangless was widely known. Restrictions were placed on residence and migration; mingling with vampires outside of the magistrate that the Li Clan had established would lead to severe punishment. Love with vampires was particularly taboo."

Ryuu cut her off abruptly. "The Fangless are a disgrace to vampires like us."

"The outcome was this," she continued, ignoring his outburst. "The Fangless and vampires who spearheaded the riot were massacred, and the riot was officially declared not to have happened."

Mina knew that the one who took control of the riot was Ryuu himself. And Ryuu was aware that she knew. He took a shallow breath and opened his mouth.

"It was a measure to maintain the Great Clan's order and protect its subjects. The instigators involved in that incident were taken care of, so I'm surprised that the information has spread so far." Ryuu said carelessly. There was no hint of guilt or embarrassment in that tone. The anger thundering in Mina's heart couldn't be expressed in words, so she stayed her curt response.

"House Tepes is a collective of geniuses, then."

For the Bund's residential manager, Harvey, collecting information from residents born under House Li was simple.

"Well, this is the main point. After the uprising, House Li established new laws to prevent a recurrence. When vampires have relations with Fangless, not only will the person directly responsible be dealt with," Mina leaned forward and strengthened her voice, "but their master will also be punished."

Ryuu stared at Mina without twitching an eyebrow. He skillfully erased all emotion from his expression.

This was no mere legend.

"Lord Li would throw away the whole basket of eggs if one spoiled to ensure his safety and the well-being of the clan. If Lord Li knew of this incident, what do you think would happen to that man's master?"

Ryuu understood perfectly where her story was going. If this were a game of poker, any option outside of "call" or "raise" would be banned at the table. Ryuu resumed the game.

"Our leader doesn't allow much leeway, and the master would not escape responsibility. Even if the one directly involved managed to avoid punishment, that master's troops would be completely destroyed."

Mina agreed with his assessment. When she heard that the disappeared Ryuu had appeared at Narita rather than here, Mina's theory became even more certain. There was no doubt that Ryuu went to take care of the fugitive with his own hands—without reporting to Lord Li—because Ryuu was one such master himself. The fugitive was none other than Ryuu's confidant.

"That's right. If only Lord Li knew, hm?"

In the corner of her vision, something moved. The

shadow tentacle was visible at Ryuu's feet.

Mina had been waiting for this—that was why she'd kept him there for so long. If she spoke with Lord Li later, she could tell him truthfully that Ryuu had planned to use it to keep her quiet.

"The idea that I would send the Fangless woman to act as a spy and instigator is slanderous. Depending on how things go, I may need to speak with Lord Li directly."

Taking care not to look at the tentacle on the floor, Mina continued speaking despite his silence. It awkwardly crept along the bottom of the table, steadily inching closer and closer to Mina. Ryuu himself listened attentively to her words with a timid expression.

"Nevertheless…" Mina spoke conspicuously loudly, then stopped abruptly, as did the tentacle's movements. The tip of the appendage stopped, then slowly approached a spot about one meter away from her legs.

Mina suddenly rose from her chair. With elegant steps, she walked towards the throne. Left behind, Ryuu had no choice but to follow her with his eyes.

The appendage stayed at the side of the table, lingering idly.

"Lord Li has finally completed his duty of guarding me, so he can give his full attention to governing his domain at last. Having his attention thus divided cost him many vassals and caused a major obstacle for the Li Clan's domestic affairs."

As she spoke, Mina approached the throne and sat down.

"As a clan leader, I'm responsible for the safety of all vampires throughout the world. I must avoid getting involved in another clan's internal issues. Fortunately, you were able to deal with the traitor in person. The classified documents also made it safely into your hands. The problematic master will be dealt with shortly and swiftly to prevent any recurrences. Stirring things up further would benefit no one. Councilor Ryuu, what if we were to act as if none of this ever happened, as they did all those years ago at Sichuan?"

Ryuu had nothing to say in response to Mina's bitter sarcasm. At the same time, he admired the fact that she had absolutely cornered him.

In all honesty, the identity of the Fangless woman did not matter to Ryuu. His main objective, as the master of the fugitive who had betrayed him, was to erase that fugitive. If Mina had protected the fugitive or decided to keep the classified documents for herself, he knew he would have every excuse to attack House Tepes—killing two birds with one stone.

But Mina had returned the classified documents entirely untouched; this was outside his calculations. She had also realized that self-preservation had been at the root of his request this time.

Queen Mina had shown great craft and cunning in keeping quiet about Ryuu being the master in question.

If he accepted her proposition here, it would be a bitter decision to protect order in the vampire world, all for the greater good; definitely not an act to conceal his own guilt. On the contrary, if it become public that Ryuu had pushed for an explanation of the Fangless spy, the subordinates he had overseen would be snatched away and his status within House Li would fall.

Withdrawing here would be no loss, and proceeding forward would bring nothing new. Ryuu couldn't help but admire Mina's abilities—her plan was ingenious.

Ryuu's leader had tried to push his influence to the ends of this land, but he had been driven out like a dog by Queen Mina. That disgrace would absolutely have to be washed away. However, today was not that day.

"How about it?" Mina asked once more.

The appendage lying on the floor dissolved into the air.

When Ryuu stood up from his chair, he took the trunk and attaché case in both hands and knelt directly in front of Queen Mina.

"As you wish, Clan Leader."

Ryuu's answer was clear—agreeing to this plan would extend his life more than any other option.

Queen Mina nodded her head with an agreeing "mm-hmm."

"Well, I suppose this is 'case closed.'"

"I wish to express my most sincere gratitude for the aid you so generously granted our clan."

Mina could not resist the temptation to make one final push before ending things.

"Councilor Ryuu, there's just one more thing."

"Hm?"

"If that 'thing' at your feet ever touches me, you will be dead."

Ryuu knew he had lost his last card.

"I've underestimated you," Ryuu muttered with admiration, and lowered his head.

"Did you use that 'thing' on my mother?"

"I attempted to."

"When, and what happened?"

"Queen Lucrezia issued me the same command. Only that time, it wasn't with her lips, but with her eyes."

"And what did you do?"

Ryuu grinned and showed his teeth. "As you know, human nature is wicked."

Mina also smiled tightly. She once again felt admiration for Ryuu. There was a great difference between Ryuu's concession to her and the behavior he showed to Lord Li. Still, having Ryuu as a rival showed how forceful she could be.

"It's been a long and arduous journey. Give my regards to Lord Li."

"I sincerely wish you good health," Ryuu's face once more returned to that of a smiling gentleman.

Mina called out loud enough that her vassals waiting

outside could hear, "Councilor Ryuu is now departing! Please show him every courtesy, and see him out!"

After Ryuu left, she sat on her throne, completely still. About fifteen minutes later, Vera came to make a report.

"Councilor Ryuu has just exited the tunnel."

At that, all of the energy left Mina's shoulders and she slumped into her chair. Holding both cheeks in her hands, she massaged the muscles in her harshly mistreated face.

Mina took a deep breath and looked up at Vera. "It's exhausting, putting on this act with him. Next time, you take him, Vera."

Vera smiled broadly. "I must humbly decline."

Akira poked his head in through a side door.

"Hime-san, the doctor says the preparations are complete."

Mina switched gears in her mind, filing Ryuu away, and promptly stood up. "Well then, let's go."

When Mina and the others arrived at the medical center, they were quickly shown to the intensive care unit where the doctor was waiting.

Inside the room, Wolfgang, Romulus and the doctor were crowded around a bed. The doctor wore a white jacket over frilly clothes that didn't seem appropriate for a hospital.

On the bed lay an Asian girl who appeared to be no older than two or three years old. She wore a shabby red dress, and her legs were bare. She had noble looks that seemed to promise beauty in her future, and the interweaving of her long black hair and porcelain-like white skin made for an exquisite contrast. From the bag suspended at her bedside, a transparent tube stretched up her arm, injecting a red liquid into her body. She seemed incredibly small and helpless, lying on a bed meant for adults.

Mina stood with Akira next to the bed.

"How is she?"

The doctor pushed up her glasses with her fingers.

"She's receiving an intravenous infusion of Stigma right now. Through an oxygen quarantine, she's avoided death by asphyxiation. It's just a matter of time until she opens her eyes. If we use the invigoration drug, we can make her wake up sooner."

"That won't be necessary. Let's wait." Mina looked at Romulus.

"Cinva was really surprised."

Romulus nodded. "It was quite a disturbing sight."

When Cinva had opened the trunk inside the duct, he'd found several scrolls packed tightly together with a young Fangless girl.

Until Ryuu had disappeared from the waiting room, Mina had been pondering how to obtain both the trunk and the fugitive. From Narita to the Bund, there had been information on Ryuu's appearance, the fugitive's death, and the discovery of the girl. Her goals suddenly changed after the girl had been found. Protecting the girl became her top priority.

Mina ordered them to act as if the girl had never been in

the trunk in the first place. This was a measure to detach the girl's existence from this recent incident.

That was also likely the man's plan from the beginning.

"I finally understand what that man was thinking. If his master, Ryuu, had found out about the child, he would have spent the rest of their lives chasing after them. To allow this girl to live safely, there was no choice but to let himself be attacked by Ryuu and to send the girl into the Bund." Mina gave a sober sigh. "From the moment he arrived at Narita, he had already decided to give his life for her."

The battles the man had fought against the Wolf Boys had all been to stall for time so Ryuu would kill him with his own hands. He entrusted the trunk and its precious cargo to House Tepes, and kept her existence secret from Ryuu. It had been a risky plan from start to finish, but it had paid off.

They all stood there in silence for a moment, reflecting on the man's tragic heroism.

"If we hadn't given him the trunk with the documents, they would have seized both the documents and the girl eventually, wouldn't they?" Akira asked.

"To protect this girl, the case had to be wrapped up completely. If we told him the documents hadn't been found or tried to hide them, Ryuu could reopen the case someday, and not even a fortress could stop his reach from extending to the girl. And so..." Mina looked up at Akira. "If we put House Li's secrets and this girl on a scale, how would it fall?"

"That's a good point." Akira smiled.

Mina thought back to her mother's resolution on that day so long ago.

Lucrezia, with Mina still held on her knee, let out a roar that interrupted Ryuu mid-sentence.

"You think you can weigh my life against this child's?!"

With that, she chased Ryuu from the castle.

Lucrezia's death, and the fall of the castle, happened the following day.

"He could have read your thoughts and patterns. That would mean he lead you, Ryuu and all of Beowulf by the nose on his own, carrying out his secret plan beautifully," Her expression gave away her emotions. "What kind of man was he? I would have liked to meet him once."

The thought of his fearless, half-burned face surfaced in Akira's mind. The expression he displayed just before he died was one of endless kindness.

"Do you think the three of them were a family?"

"I don't know. We'll have to ask the girl."

The man, equipped with terrifying battle ability and intelligence, and the Fangless woman and child. Where did they meet? What bonds were there between them, and why did they decide to flee to the Bund? For now, there was no way to ascertain the truth.

Akira looked at the wagon in the corner of the room. The

jumpsuit the man had been wearing was folded up neatly on top of it, and the man's severed braid was coiled up beside it.

Mina gazed at Akira's profile as he looked through the things the man had left behind.

"Akira, I'm giving you a new responsibility."

"Huh?"

"Someday, you tell this girl that there was a man and a woman who loved her so much, they gave their lives for her."

"Hime-san…"

"Living isn't just having a long life. If this child bears that couple's memories and inherits their love of freedom, then they will have only changed form. Their spirit will live on, here in the Bund." Mina placed the girl's hand in Akira's.

"That man entrusted you with the trunk. He was probably entrusting you with her future as well."

Akira's expression tightened as he looked down at the girl. She continued to sleep, unaware of the exchange.

At that moment, the automatic door to the intensive care unit opened, and Alphonse appeared.

Mina flashed Alphonse a glare.

"Finally making an appearance, are you? And only after making us do all that unnecessary labor, of course."

Even as she said this, Mina understood why he had disappeared.

If Alphonse denied the incident with the spies, Mina

could have turned Ryuu away and enforced the protection of the fugitive. However, that could have served as a pretext for opening hostilities between House Li and House Tepes.

"Don't say that. It's not like I was out having fun." Alphonse was never one to shy away. "I pursued Ryuu as he left the Bund."

"Hmm? Any news?"

"The minute he left the tunnel, he caught a ride with a passing biker gang. From there, it was nothing but hitchhiking."

If he used his shadowy appendage, he would have absolutely no trouble getting humans he had never met to give him a ride. Changing cars at a dizzying pace was a countermeasure to avoid being followed.

"So, where did he finally stop off?'

"Surprisingly close by. In Azabu."

"Hmm, I see." Mina snorted.

Akira wore a puzzled expression. "Azabu?"

"The Chinese Embassy. That's probably his base. It seems House Li has deep roots in the Chinese government."

"That's his base, even though he came here from China?" Akira asked.

Alphonse shook his head. "If he had been in China, he would have stopped the cargo plane leaving Guangzhou, and it wouldn't have been able to come to the Bund. No, he was in Japan before the incident happened."

"He could have been visiting other Clan Li followers,"

Wolfgang suggested.

Vera's expression was clouded. "If that's true, then there's a chance he'll strike again while he's still in Japan."

"For now, it would be best just to investigate. Alphonse, don't take your eyes off him."

Alphonse bowed his head lightly. "As you wish."

Mina gave a bitter laugh.

"...A long road, huh? In the end, I'll be taken down in one blow."

As she looked out the window at the night scene, she could see a passenger plane taking off from Haneda Airport, gradually gaining altitude. For some reason, she couldn't look away from the navigation lights that glinted off both wings.

Until the passenger plane ascended, disappearing into the clouds, Mina's gaze followed the paired red and green lights.

EPILOGUE

The girl that the silent man had given his life to protect was in a park in the Geo Frontier, a neighborhood deep beneath the Vampire Bund. It was one of the biggest parks in the neighborhood, situated in the base of a large atrium, dotted with greenery and plenty of playground equipment. There, under lights that mimicked the faded sunbeams of dusk, many children were playing. However, a young girl who could only speak Chinese didn't join them. She lingered idly in a corner.

Once the girl woke, they had immediately conducted an interview. However, it seemed that the girl's actual age was about the same as her outer appearance, so they hadn't been able to get any sort of statement from her. In the end, the relationship between the three of them remained a secret. Mina sought to connect the girl with a Chinese Fangless— or even a Chinese Fangless family—but until such a person could be found, she was alone.

"Nihao!"

Someone called to her from behind in Chinese. The girl

turned around.

Right behind her, three kids stood in a line. They acted like siblings, but each of them was a different race. The boy who had called out to her seemed to be the oldest, with the biggest build and dark skin. The second girl had blonde hair, and the third was a short girl who appeared Japanese.

The older boy cheerfully greeted her once more. "Nihao!"

The girl stared at them without a word. She was frozen from nervousness. The four, facing each other, were stuck in an uncomfortable silence.

"Umm, ahh… Nihao."

"Ugh, Jiji! Change places with me!"

The third girl cut in impatiently. Jiji took a fleeting glance at the memo pad he held in his hand and spoke up in fluent Chinese.

"It's boring playing alone, isn't it? Wanna play with us?"

Being spoken to in her own language by children about her age was all she needed. Finally, her cautious expression opened up.

The blonde girl drew close and gently took her hand. The girl's light touch made her tense shoulders relax.

"Yeah! She smiled!" the third girl exclaimed, like part of a comedy duo.

"We know plenty of places better than this park to play in," the boy called Jiji said energetically.

"I told you, she doesn't understand what you're saying!"

"She'll get it if she comes with us."

The four children clustered together and ran out of the park.

Akira stood up from his hiding place—he had been watching them from start to finish. He ensured that the three siblings had accomplished their "mission," and quietly put the park behind him.

End

S.A.G.A
COOKING
CLASS

STORY
Gemma

ILLUSTRATION
Nozomu Tamaki

CHAPTER 1

First, collect some withered grass. You'll need a lot of it. Timothy grass dried out by the gales of Cornwall would be ideal, but you can't ask for such luxuries here in Siberia. The twisted kaya in the cracks of the rocks will do.

Then, slice open the stomach of a caribou.

It was a small, thin, old caribou, with fur falling off in places. The meat was tough and stringy and probably tasted bad. The first problem was that a whole day's hunting had resulted in only this caribou and one pika. Graham Lindgren sighed, and used his sharp claws to rip open the fascia. The intestines he pulled out were predictably red-black with disease and definitely not edible. He clicked his tongue and threw them towards a distant snow drift.

It had been two weeks since he'd started the trial, a little over ten days since they'd last been able to move as a group. He didn't think they'd been arrogant or unprepared. It was just that the land of Siberia was too severe for a group of four kids from the Earth Clan.

He opened the stomach of the pika, removed its intestines, and skinned it. He threw away the smelly bile sac and bladder, then washed the intestines carefully with snow and packed them back into the stomach. It should have been filled with herbs and nuts, but lacking that he packed the cavity full of young fir needles.

He packed the skinned pika into the stomach of the caribou, and sewed the cavity shut with tough pine needles. After placing the caribou on top of the thick mat of kaya on the rock, Graham returned to the cave to get a spark of fire.

Angie, Sanin and Akira were still sleeping soundly, and their noses didn't even twitch as he passed them by. They were exhausted from the hunt and had fallen asleep without even the energy to cook their prey, so they probably wouldn't wake until after sunrise. There was still plenty of time. Graham held a withered branch to the smoldering embers of the campfire until it caught fire, then returned to the rock. He carefully checked the moisture in the kaya and the direction of the wind, and set fire to the pile in several places. Smoke rose into the blue-violet sky.

The most important thing now was not giving up. If they started thinking that this was impossible, then everything would be over. They had to keep bolstering each other's spirits. Eating delicious food was a simple and effective method.

When the flames started to spread, he walked around the mountain of withered grass to check the state of the fire. He added more dried grass to places where the fire was weak, and snow to places where the fire was too strong. The fire needed to burn steadily for a long time. He'd been taught this cooking method by the cheerful Sir Ronald, who loved to cook.

"Not something I do very often, because it's a waste," laughed Sir Ronald as he poked at the fire with the tip of his staff. "Do you understand why we do this? Older beasts have a stronger taste to their flesh. So, if you cook it thoroughly until it's burnt, the meat juices with their tasty flavor get absorbed by the rabbit in its stomach. There isn't a single way of eating rabbit that's more luxurious or delicious than this. It's a special meal—for when something really good or something really bad happens."

The rabbit they'd pulled from the stomach of the charred deer had been steamed to a golden brown. Its meat, soaked with fat and juices, had been so delicious that he'd actually dreamed of it afterward. He'd even overcome problems at times by thinking to himself, "after this is all over, I'm going to eat that rabbit." It would certainly have the same effect on the other three.

His sensitive wolf nose soon picked up the fragrance of the old caribou's roasting flesh. Graham walked around the fire again. Maybe there wasn't enough withered grass. He had used all of the grass at hand, so he'd need to travel to the edge of the forest to collect more. He removed his boots and shook his body, and became a brown wolf by the time his paws hit their stride.

For a werewolf, traveling a distance under a mile barely counted as a stroll. As the minus forty degree winds blew in his face, Graham though about the sleeping kids behind him.

Akira Kaburagi Regendorf. Graham hadn't liked his smile when they'd first met. He still didn't like it, but he could risk his life for Akira now.

Angel Arvenanto. Physically delicate, but by far the best at making traps. Nobody could resist requests made through those teary eyes.

Sanin Humoresque, Graham's partner. Even alone, he still laughed and ran; a true wolf.

What would they think if they knew Graham's true purpose? The thoughts he had sealed deep within his mind trickled forth. Would they think they had been betrayed, if they saw Graham Lindgren's true face?

"Do that which only you can do, for our true happiness." Cheerful, talkative Uncle Ronald. His great-grandfather was said to have died in battle defending Queen Lucrezia during the rebellion of the Three Great Clans. He had described it for Graham over and over again, how everyone had died defending House Tepes. But Sir Ronald had never told him that he should defend Queen Mina the same way.

To Graham, all of that was just a brief flash of a thought deep in his heart during his one minute dash, a thought that was sealed up again once he arrived outside the forest and returned to his half-beast form. Graham was trained to not think about those things until the necessary time.

There were patches of buffalo grass in the shade of the pine forest, and he was able to quickly collect the withered grass he needed. He also peeled back the bark of the larch trees and found edible fungus underneath. It would be a perfect match for the meal. If he hurried back and stoked the fire, the pika would be steamed and ready to eat right around the time they woke up. Slightly excited, Graham hurried back. He crossed the frozen river and ran up the foothills. And once he climbed over the rock that was their landmark...

"Hey, where'd you go? We started on the food already."

"Did Graham make this? It's all burnt. You shouldn't have left when you had a fire running."

"It's hard and kind of sour, but whatever. I'll eat it because I'm hungry."

"Don't say that! It's delicious, Graham."

His carefully built campfire had been put out roughly and scattered, and remnants of the ashes littered the area. The caribou had been dragged down from the rock, and the three idiot kids who didn't understand the first thing about gourmet food were chewing on it.

"Hey, look, there's a pika in its stomach."

"Really? Do caribou eat pikas?"

"Maybe they do if they're hungry. That seems edible, can you give me some?"

"That's gross, though—it's been cooked whole. Graham, what should we do? Graham...?"

"There's no damn way I'm ever cooking for you guys again!"

Graham clenched his shaking fists and yelled at them, throwing the sheaves of grass he had carried at the others with all his might. He strode past the shocked kids and entered the cave behind them, sprawling over the furs at the back of the cave.

That's what those guys were like, anyway. They didn't have the sensitivity to get depressed about failing at hunting once or twice. It was idiotic to worry about them at all. He'd never worry about them, ever again!

When the small, weak Siberian sun finally rose into the sky, a piece of flesh from the back of the caribou and a bit of leaf bud were placed next to Graham's pillow as he slept. Graham's nose twitched in his sleep, and he muttered something in annoyance, but he didn't open his eyes. As he drifted dreamily, he heard three voices snickering, and the sound of quiet footsteps fading into the distance.

CHAPTER 2

Akira wasn't well.

Angel Arvenanto knew why. Akira's mother was ill, and he wasn't allowed to talk to her on the phone.

Akira's mother was in the hospital with a baby in her belly. Her body was weak to begin with, and giving birth was risky for her and the baby. So, for the time being, Akira lived in House Arvenanto with Angie.

Akira lived in Japan, and Angie visited sometimes with his grandfather, Lord George Scott. They were only able to meet up once or twice a year. Therefore, they were very happy to be together for even a short while. Akira used to call his mother every day and write a letter once a week, but he hadn't received any reply to the letters he'd sent that past week or the week before. Angie knew that Akira went to check the mailbox every morning—but he'd tried to keep it a secret out of kindness to Angie, who had lost his own parents.

Grandfather said that Angie and Akira were partners. They would be subjected to the trial when they were older, and after that they would serve the Queen together. That meant that Akira's torment was Angie's torment, and Akira's worries were also Angie's worries. Angie wanted to do something for him.

The secret medicine needed a lot of different types of alcohol.

Angie didn't know what alcohol was, but he knew that it was some sort of drink that only adults were allowed to have. The alcohol was placed higher than Angie could reach, and he knew Ophelia, the maid who guarded the kitchen, would yell at him if he got too near. But Angie was ten years old already, and he knew how to open the cupboard without attracting the notice of the kitchen guard.

"A bit of gin, and half of the kirsch, then we can't forget the vermouth…"

Singing the recipe that was sung in the movie softly to himself, Angie stood on his tiptoes on the chair and rummaged in the cupboard. Ten-year-old Angie was old enough to know that vermouth wasn't just the name of the whitish grass that grew on the western road, but also the alcohol made from fermenting that grass. While he didn't understand why you would put such a bitter, smelly substance into a drink, it was in Eve Horn's song. Then, a pinch of nutmeg and one lemon, and a blue ribbon from grandmother's sewing box. And finally, the last and most important thing.

Akira wasn't back yet. Angie carefully opened the bedroom door. They had played together there numerous times and even slept together, so he knew where it was. It was in the dresser in the closet, in the bottommost drawer. The lucky charm was necessary—a picture of the person you wanted to meet. It was a photo of Akira's mother, sitting in a chair and smiling gently. Angie was apprehensive about stealing a photo that was so important to Akira, but it would be okay if he returned it afterward. And anyway, Akira would certainly forgive him if he was able to see his mother again.

He carefully measured the amounts and mixed the three different types of alcohol in the glass bottle until it turned into a beautiful red liquid. He squeezed the lemon into it, added nutmeg, and finally dropped the photo wrapped in a blue ribbon into the bottom of the bottle and placed it in the refrigerator. It would be finished after sitting in the refrigerator for half a day.

After dinner that night, Angie excitedly asked Akira to come to his room. He brought out the secret medicine and two cups.

"What is this, alcohol?"

Akira was wary at first, but it seemed that he liked the drink after trying one mouthful. Angie tried drinking it too. The smell of it tickled his nose, and it was faintly sour like a lemon. It was surprisingly delicious. Was alcohol really this delicious? Or was it because it was the secret medicine's charm? He happily refilled both of their cups.

"Hey, something good will happen if we drink this."

"Really?"

Akira gulped down the contents of the cup in one go. Angie, not wanting to lose, drained his own cup. Warmth fizzled across his tongue. His face heated up, and Angie became giddy and excited.

"Yep. This is a charm."

"Charm. Hmm. Charm…?"

Akira also seemed happy, and started rocking back and forth from his seat on the floor. His cheeks were bright red. That reminded him; Eve Horn never mentioned how much they should drink. But since he made one bottle, they should drink the whole bottle, right? That was how magic worked, and anyway, it was delicious.

Their surroundings were becoming fuzzy. It looked like there was a spiral of rainbow light spinning on the edge of his vision. The magic had finally begun to work.

"Hey, Akira! Your mom will come see you soon."

"Really?"

Akira lay on the floor and started batting his arms and legs while he laughed. Angie followed suit and lay down on the floor. Shaking his head suddenly made him dizzy, and when he tried to get up he quickly lost his balance and collapsed back down. They both thought that was really funny, and took turns trying to stand and falling, laughing hard the whole time. The floor seemed to shake like it was rocked by waves, or made of some soft, bouncy material.

There was the sound of a car near the front door. It had to be Akira's mother. Hey, there were people calling out to them. Angie wanted to get up and meet them, but he couldn't stand up or even make it to the door. Akira lay on the floor and rolled around, still laughing. Opening the curtains allowed starlight to fall into the room, and it was like he'd become ticklish all over. Angie laughed, too.

When they woke up, the magic had been dispelled, and all that was left was a splitting headache and the stench of alcohol in the room.

Akira's mother had, of course, not come. The sound of the car was Mrs. Arvenanto returning from a party. With heads beating in time with their hearts, Grandfather's punch had hurt, and Ophelia's scolding had hurt, but what had hurt Angie the most was when they cleaned up the room and saw the empty glass bottle.

The photo wrapped in blue ribbon—now stuck to the bottom of the bottle—had been ruined by spending a night soaked in alcohol. It was the picture that Akira had brought with him from Japan, the only picture he had of his mother.

Akira took the soggy picture and looked it over for a while, but when he turned back towards Angie, he had a gentle smile on his face. "Don't worry about it," he said softly, but he didn't throw the picture away. Instead, he carefully placed it between the pages of a notebook and put the notebook in his desk drawer.

Angie couldn't even form an apology, and as tears dribbled down his face, he made a resolution to never forget that smile for the rest of his life.

For that smile, he would live to temper the things that Akira had to endure, and restore the things he had lost.

That was surely what it meant to be partners.

That night, Angie cleaned his desk. He moved the picture of himself and Grandfather to one side, and placed a small picture of himself and Akira in the center of the desk, at the most visible spot. Then, he offered kisses of prayer to the moon and stars, to his parents who were no longer with him, and to his most important one, Akira. Then he crawled into bed and fell asleep.

CHAPTER 3

"**I** first met her in a summer forest, when the cuckoos were calling."

And so Sanin Humoresque began his story.

"She had chestnut hair and big olive eyes. She was unbelievably beautiful."

"Hey wait, weren't we talking about food?"

"Just listen. She was gorgeous. Her hair was chestnut, with golden highlights in the light. Her legs were slender and very white."

Graham whined, seemingly bored. Akira fidgeted, as though shaking his fur, while Angie eagerly awaited the next part of the story with bright eyes.

Among the lands owned by House Humoresque, there was a forest that spread from the foot of a small, steep hill. The forest was small, but it had straight beech trees and open clearings covered in cytisus bushes, a stream that wound around stacked boulders covered in lichen, and other such features. Sanin had loved to play there.

One summer day, Sanin had journeyed to a deep part of

the forest where he didn't often go. He was unable to tell the direction due to the overcast sky, and he was lost without a familiar landmark. Sanin went into a panic and exhausted himself running around. When he sat down to rest, his gaze fell upon that girl. She stood naked at the foot of a giant oak, as through draping her body across the gnarled roots.

Sanin was surprised, of course, but he was also mentally weary due to his fatigue. He didn't have the energy to greet her or to apologize, so he simply sat there, staring at her. She stood and gazed back at him. When Sanin began to realize how beautiful her wet green eyes and chestnut hair were, she turned and disappeared into the forest. Sanin returned home to a scolding and a welcome of warm food and bed.

The next day, when he tried to return to the same location, there was nobody there. However, there was one long, straight strand of hair, chestnut with yellow highlights, caught in the branches of the tree she had stood next to.

From that day onward, Sanin went to that place in the forest every day without telling anyone else.

"I didn't know who she was, and I didn't ask. There were days when we met and days when we didn't. She was really shy, and she ran away a lot the first few times I tried to get near her. But after a while, we finally got to the point where we would nap together in the sun."

"Just that? Didn't you hold hands?"

"No way. She was shy."

"What the hell are you saying?" Graham jabbed his elbow

at Sanin, on the other side of Akira. The four of them giggled.

Sanin had sometimes brought food to the forest. He hadn't know what she liked, so he brought a variety of things: bread, honey, biscuits, apples, grapes, pears, walnuts, pine nuts and rock candy.

At first, she wouldn't approach, no matter what food he offered, but slowly she lost her wariness and began to take food from the plates that Sanin set out. When she did that, she leaned her body down and sniffed at it numerous times like a dog, and only then would she take the food and eat it.

Sometimes, when she was in a good mood, she would sit next to Sanin and chew on a biscuit. It was at those times that Sanin could gaze at her profile, with its straight nose and expressive mouth, to his heart's content.

"I built fires when it rained. Light rain didn't penetrate the forest, and it got a bit cold after nightfall, even in the summer. Then I'd get a pat of butter and a lot of chanterelles. Do you know about chanterelles? They're orange mushrooms, shaped like a trumpet. You put them in a tin cup with some butter and hang them over a campfire. You know they're done when they let off a puff of smoke.

"It got darker and darker, and only the light of the campfire was left. I heard the sound of rain overhead, and it was like there was a curtain around the forest and only me and the girl were left.

"I skewered the chanterelles on a cytisus branch and blew on them. After I gave one to the girl, I took one for myself.

When I took a bite, it tasted like well-roasted squirrel liver, dripping with juices. 'Delicious,' I thought, and when I raised my head, my eyes met hers."

There was the sound of someone gulping from Akira's direction. Then another swallowing noise from Graham's direction. Then another, emerging from Angie's throat.

"All right! I win!" Sanin made a small victory pose under the furs.

"No, that was…" Graham cleared his throat. "Over half of that story didn't have anything to do with food, so that's breaking the rules."

"The mood's part of the flavor, isn't it? If we catch another caribou, I'll fillet it," Sanin answered with a grin. Akira smiled and raised his hands, signaling surrender.

"Let's talk about delicious things."

They'd been shut in for the entire day by a blizzard. The four of them curled up in a row in the cave, and when the growling of their stomachs got strong, it was Akira who made the suggestion.

"So, the person who describes the most delicious-sounding food wins."

"What happens if you win?"

"You get the tastiest part of the next hunt. I saw a story like this in a book Mom was reading."

At that, Graham suddenly exclaimed angrily, "I have nothing to say to you about delicious food," and declared himself the judge. Akira, who made the suggestion, talked about sushi and quickly lost. He had forgotten that he was the only one of the four who ate raw fish. Angie talked about a cake he'd had at a famous restaurant in Berlin, and it sounded reasonably tasty, but neither Graham nor Sanin were fond of sweets. The last person to talk was Sanin.

"Well, what happened to the girl?"

Angie edged closer, as though wagging his tail. "Did you meet her again afterward? Did you become friends?"

"Yeah," Sanin was still grinning. "For a while after that, I brought her to my place and we lived together. She's still living in my stable now."

"Stable?"

Angie and Akira wore confused expressions. Only Graham raised his eyebrows in realization, and said, "Hey wait, Sanin. You don't mean to say that girl is...?"

"She's a horse. You've ridden her. Elvarje."

"A horse?!" The voices of the other three rang out in harmony.

"But you said she had chestnut hair, and her legs were slender and white."

"Yep. She's a chestnut, and only her feet and nose are white. Four-point white comet, it's called."

"Do horses eat butter-roasted mushrooms?"

"Elle ate them. That's pretty unusual, right?"

"And you said she was naked!"

"That's because she was a bare horse! What were you

thinking, you pervert?"

"I thought it was weird. I never heard any talk of you having a girlfriend. You tricked us into going along with your story," spat Graham in irritation.

"Shut up! Jeez, this sort of story just makes me even hungrier."

Graham muttered to himself and buried his face in the furs, while Akira punched the ground and laughed. Angie laughed as well, and Sanin followed suit and joined in the laughter himself.

There was one part of Sanin's story that was a lie. Just before Sanin had left on his trial, his entire family had died in a plane crash. Most of House Humoresque's lands had been confiscated by financial managers, and the forest where he had met Elvarje, the stables she lived in, and even Elvarje herself had been given to others. He had no way of knowing where she was now.

"That was Sanin's strategic victory." Akira stretched. "Doesn't seem like the weather's getting any better. Now what should we do? An association game?"

"Okay, I'll go first. "W" as in wolf."

"Ferret."

"...Tiger."

Now he had to think of an animal name starting with "R." He stretched his neck and looked at the narrow entrance to the cave, watching the white and gray pattern stream fiercely down.

CHAPTER 4

" **. . . R**ight, like that. Put it into the rabbit's stomach. No, no… that's fine. I'll do it."

Akira wielded the large kitchen knife deftly and separated the shoulder meat from the bones. There was a small pot of pineapple sauce bubbling next to him. Cinva was scolded by Gaute when he tried to poke his finger into the sauce to taste it. Next to the pan, a fly tried to land on the lobster waiting to be put into the pot, but it was caught and discarded by Kamil just before it succeeded.

Remus and Romulus were already sitting on a bench in one corner of the courtyard, emptying a bottle of wine between them. Leroy and Heinrich played chess at a table on the opposite side, while Junte knelt near the bushes and gazed at the swarms of butterflies in the back of the forest, Yuuhi looking on behind him. The kitchen area of the courtyard, which was not particularly large, was inhabited by Akira, busily occupied with his cooking, and Hama, who had been summoned to assist him.

The Wolf Boys had been created for emergencies, but due

to the continued state of emergency in the Bund, they had become a regular squad. This outdoor buffet was ostensibly planned as recognition of their service, but Akira knew that his comrades wanted to comfort him after losing Angie in such a terrible way. That was why he didn't voice the slightest complaint when they pressed him into being the cook—instead he happily let himself get absorbed in his tasks.

"But Akira," whispered Hama, as he licked the sauce from his fingers. "Don't you think the drinks for this meal are a little weird?"

Hama was looking at the main course of the day, the large plate containing the steamed baby rabbits and sautéed chanterelles. Next to the plate were bottles of dry gin, vermouth and cherry brandy.

"Those are usually for cocktails, aren't they? The only thing you'd be able to make with those is Kiss in the Dark."

"Hm, you know a lot about that," replied Akira as he added peeled garlic to the large plate. "It's fine, because today's beverage is actually Kiss in the Dark."

Akira glanced at Hama's surprised expression from the corner of his eye while tastefully arranging thick-sliced beef and sliced onions on the plate. Just add some parmesan cheese and dressing, and the Beef Carpaccio, Werewolf Style would be complete. Werewolf Style meant light on the spices and the meat cooked rare.

"You seem to be having fun, Akira."

"Well, yeah. It's been a long time since I've cooked for a party—Your Highness!"

When Akira raised his eyes in the direction of the amused-sounding voice, he saw Mina Tepes in a bright blue dress, smiling gently at him while twirling her parasol. The relaxed group in the courtyard all attempted to rise and straighten themselves out in a panic, but they were stopped by a wave of her hand.

"Are you okay with walking around outside during the day?"

"It is not a major concern. In this weather, the gel would be sustained if I merely walked in the shade." Her delicate fingers pointed at the sky. It was true that the overcast sky was draped in heavy cloud cover, and nothing that could be called direct sunlight reached the ground.

"That's true, but my job…"

"This party is meant to recognize the service of our knights. What kind of ruler would I be if I failed to appear?" Mina's answer was firm, but looking at the pained expression of Vera, who stood beside her, she had probably forcibly made time to appear. Akira silently shrugged his shoulders.

"Nevertheless," said Mina as she glanced over at the table, "is it now popular for meat dishes to be served with such sweet drinks? The tastes of humans are certainly fickle."

"No, that's not it—it's not that it's popular." Akira glared at Hama, who wore an expression of "I told you so," and scratched his head. "It's just that those three dishes are important to me. They...remind me of the past."

It was much later that he discovered the "secret medicine" Angie had made was almost identical to the cocktail called "Kiss in the Dark." The photo he had used was now inside of an old diary, back at home.

The morning after the blizzard had stopped, Graham told them that the real point of the meal wasn't the caribou cooked with withered grass, but the pika inside of its belly. They didn't manage to catch another old caribou after that, so they never had a chance to try it.

Akira never got the chance to verify just how much of Sanin's story was true. Maybe Tatianna would know, but based on her attitude, she certainly wasn't telling. Even now, Akira wished that he could tell Sanin that Tatianna was still alive.

"I see. Nostalgic dishes, are they?"

Mina narrowed her eyes and glanced between the dishes on the table and Akira. Finally, she passed her parasol to Vera, then rolled up her sleeves and quickly walked up to him.

"If that's the case, I will also add a dish to the meal."

"Huh?"

Mina walked past the shocked Akira, then overturned one of the nearby stacked boxes and climbed on top of it to wash her hands. Vera quickly removed a reflective sheet from her handbag and created a simple tent with the help of Hama and Akira. Ignoring the commotion around her, Mina surveyed the kitchen imperiously, then picked up a lump of ground meat that had been prepared to make scotch eggs.

"Hime-san, can you cook?"

"Can I cook? Observe."

Vampires normally couldn't cook, because they had no sense of taste. While some of the maids who served Mina were able to cook for human guests, it was merely the result of memorizing a recipe and following it exactly; it did not mean that they actually understood how the food should taste. Mina herself had never been in the kitchen, aside from the time when she made sandwiches at Yuki's house.

Ignoring how Akira and Vera watched with concern, Mina kneaded the ground meat in a bowl with a surprisingly practiced hand. Then she suddenly took an entire handful of salt from the salt pot next to her, and kneaded it into the ground meat.

"What...?"

Then she took the pepper pot and added peppercorns to the bowl whole, without grinding them; she used the handle of the knife to smash them. She then peeled about a cup of ginger and added it to the mixture. She added several whole laurel leaves, poured oyster sauce and wine into the mix, and was stopped by Akira when she tried to add mustard as well.

"Wait a minute! I have no idea what you're trying to make, but don't do something that crazy."

"Be silent. I am following the recipe. I said to observe."

After adding the mustard, she also added a bit of wasabi, then shaped the resulting spicy-smelling meat into flat patties. She placed the patties into an oiled frying pan, and put the pan over a strong fire. She cut celery, carrots and onions into large chunks, coated them with raw egg, then soaked the vegetables in olive oil and dropped them into the pan. The olive oil ignited the moment it was poured into the pan, and Mina transferred the scorched remains to a large plate. She covered the concoction evenly with rock salt, then added parsley as a garnish.

"Now it is done."

"Don't give me that! Look, Hime-san, if you can't cook, just say so."

"Do not insult me. I stated that this was done according to a recipe. Do you not remember? You taught me this."

"Don't be ridiculous! Who'd make such an outrageous... Oh."

"You finally remember."

Mina's eyes turned kind, and Akira stared at the contents of the dish in front of him.

It was on a day seven years ago, when young Akira had only been with Mina for a little while. Akira wanted to give Mina, who seemed sad all the time, something delicious to eat to cheer her up. He heard that Mina would not be able to taste anything, regardless of what she ate, so he made his own adjustments to a hamburger recipe that he had just learned from his mother. He added a mountain of spices that he disliked, and served up a strongly-flavored (or so he believed) dish with a satisfied grin on his face.

Mina said it was delicious, so very delicious, and she ate all of it. Akira thought it was around then that he started to get into cooking.

"I had forgotten it, myself. I'm amazed you remembered something like this."

He took one piece from the edge and tasted it. It was horrible, or maybe amazingly terrible. Even Mina couldn't have claimed that this was delicious if she had any taste buds.

"I'm sorry I made you eat something like this. Even if you don't have a sense of taste…"

"Regardless of the taste," Mina whispered so that only Akira could hear as she washed her hands and had Vera re-apply the gel, "Akira, you made it for me. And so, for me, it was more delicious than anything else."

"……"

Akira felt his face heating up, and he scratched the back of his neck. "I'll tell you how to make real Kaburagi-style hamburgers next time. This is my personal flavor, so it'd be pretty boring if it got spread around."

Mina giggled in delight, and Akira laughed a little too. He then gazed across the courtyard again. Romulus and Remus, Heinrich and Leroy, Kamil and Junte, Gaute and Cinva.

Akira realized then that even though the food and wine were different, the idea of cheering someone up with food was exactly the same as Angie's plan all those years ago. In the end, he and Angie were partners. Regardless of what paths they took later on, that fact would never change. The things that Angie had done for him, the things that he had done for Angie, and the things that they had done together would never disappear. That was their bond and their curse.

"Hime-san, you said that Angie's body wasn't found."

"...Yes."

"If I could meet him again..."

"Do not think of such things. Not now."

She picked up a glass and poured Stigma into it. Akira silently looked at the top of her head, then straightened his lapels and raised his voice.

"The food's ready! Everyone get your glasses and gather round!"

At last, the clinking of glasses and the sound of conversation and laughter rose into the sky over Tokyo Bay.

"By the way, I made it for you. Therefore, you must take full responsibility and eat every last bite."

"What?!"

End

Dance in the Vampire Bund

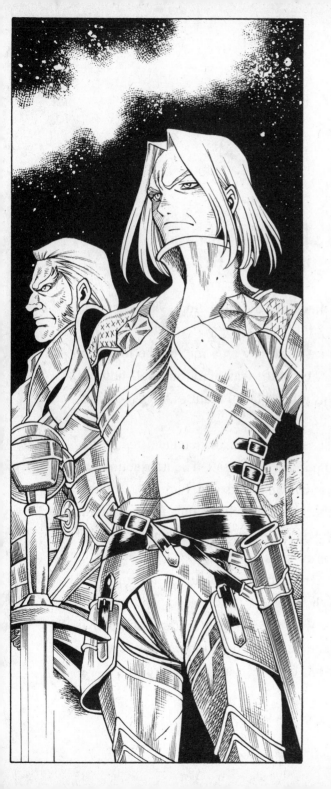

A FLAG FULL OF STARS

STORY
Tikurakuran

ILLUSTRATION
Nozomu Tamaki

1585 A.D.—Town of Bad Ishl,
Duchy of Austria

That day, very much like the day before, was coming to an end.

The young man sat aimlessly on a rock in the forest, lit by the setting sun. His outfit was plain but well-tailored, and coupled with his refined facial features, he gave off an impression of wealth.

He was the eldest son of a Venetian merchant, and he was visiting Bad Ishl to purchase rock salt. The transaction had already been completed two weeks ago, but due to another order from his father, he had trekked into the mountains alone and had been waiting from sunup to sundown in that one spot to meet someone.

His father's orders had been peculiar, through and through. All he had heard about the client for whom he was waiting was that he was 'the Lorenzo Trading Company's most important customer.' When he inquired as to where he should wait for this customer, his father's response was

"Anywhere is fine; he'll find you." When he asked how long he should wait, his father replied, "Wait for as long as you need to, until he finds you."

And, strangest of all, his father had ordered him to conceal the customer in the rock salt and bring him to Venice.

No matter how he looked at it, this was no ordinary customer. Ever since the young man had lost his mother, his father Lorenzo had been completely engrossed in expanding his business. In the process, he had acquired an increasing number of customers of unknown origin, and he had even begun arranging detour trades with the Ottoman Empire, an enemy to the Republic of Venice. More recently, there were the undoubtedly questionable customers who only came by at night to negotiate with his father. Thanks to this unnatural and sudden growth, it was not unthinkable that envious business rivals within the Republic would seek a chance to plot their downfall. However, contrary to his greedy business tactics, his father never failed to donate generously to the church, and he maintained a strong reputation as a devout Christian.

The young man rolled the tally he had received from his father around in his hand. He remembered the dire words his father had left him with.

"Do not let this tally leave your hands. It will save your life."

He didn't have the slightest idea what that meant.

The setting sun was about to touch the top of the mountains

in the distance. The shadows in the forest began to darken, and the wind brushing against the young man's cheeks gradually became cooler.

The young man put the tally back in his inner coat pocket and gathered the collar closer to his neck.

Another day had passed with no sign of the customer. His spirits sank when he thought about having to spend another meaningless day alone tomorrow, just sitting and waiting. The cost of having to keep the team of wagons, stocked with rock salt, waiting on him was accumulating, but there was no way he could go against his father's orders and head home to Venice.

Perhaps it's time I wrote to Father to release me from this order, the young man thought as he stretched with both arms in the air.

All of a sudden, the bushes in front of him trembled; he had felt no strong wind to move them.

The young man stared fixedly at the bushes, frozen, his arms still held up. The bushes moved again, and he caught a glimpse of some kind of shadow behind the thick brush. The bushes were not tall enough to cover a human being standing up. It then occurred to him that he had been extremely fortunate to spend so much time in the woods these past few days without encountering any beasts.

The shadow slowly emerged, pushing apart the leaves on the short trees.

It was a large, black wolf. The wolf, crouched low as if

ready to jump on the young man at any moment, approached him. Its eyes, glaring behind the sharp snout, were fixed on the young man.

The young man couldn't move; it was as if he was nailed to the rock. He had a short sword equipped at his waist as a means of self defense, but he had never once actually used it for that purpose. Yet his legs would not obey his command to flee.

The young man managed to bring his arms down and reach for his sword. At that moment, he felt a presence to either side. Still facing the wolf in front of him, he moved his eyes to look.

The young man broke out in a cold sweat, and the hand gripping the short sword began to tremble. Two other wolves had appeared and were inching toward him.

With the large rock behind him, the young man was hopelessly trapped. Even if he could use the short sword to its fullest potential, there was still no way he could drive off three wolves. It seemed death was coming for him.

Surprisingly, when he realized the direness of his situation, his panic slowly faded. The young man studied the three wolves once more, in detail.

When he took a good look, he noticed that all three wolves were covered in scars and wounds. Their fur was ragged and matted, but it wasn't just from dirt—there was blood caked in as well. The wolf on the right had lost one of its eyes. The wolf on the left—who was one size larger than the other two—was dragging its hind leg. Despite all that, the wolves' eyes were still brimming with will and they gleamed so bright they were almost blinding. If that glare was due to hunger, the young man only had a few more minutes to live, by the looks of it.

The wolf at the front closed in on him, stopping just an arm's length away. It opened its mouth and displayed its sharp fangs. The young man shut his eyes and prepared for those fangs to rip his throat open.

Nothing happened.

When the young man slowly opened his eyes, the wolf in front of him was sitting still with its mouth wide open. On its tongue, surrounded by vicious teeth, was a small chip of wood.

It was a tally.

It took a few seconds for the young man to realize what it meant. And even after he understood, he still couldn't believe it. *These beasts, of all things, are Father's customers?*

The young man reached into his coat to find his tally.

He couldn't feel it.

The tally was not where it was supposed to be. It appeared to have fallen deep into his inner pocket.

As the young man dawdled, the wolf's eyes emitted an evil glare, as if it saw right through an attempt to stall for time.

The young man frantically felt around in his coat like he was lit on fire, and finally, he located the tally. He would never forget what transpired next, as he presented the tally to the wolf, relieved.

The wolf accepted the young man's tally with its front right paw, and with its other paw, took its tally out of its mouth. Then, snapping together the two tallies, the wolf spoke.

"You are... Lorenzo's son?"

The young man's jaw dropped. He was still trying to come to terms with the fact that these wolves were his father's customers. That alone was hard enough to swallow, but at least he could make some sense out of it. But now *this*...

The wolf in front of him spoke up, as if reading his thoughts.

"Yes, we are werewolves. I know what you're thinking, but there's no time to discuss it now. Our lives depend upon your actions. No, not just our lives, but also the lives of many others beyond us. Please assist us, I beg of you."

The wolf bowed its head to the young man. The other two wolves followed suit, also lowering their heads.

The young man, in shock, tried very hard to think.

Conducting business with abhorrent werewolves; it truly defied God. He couldn't rid himself of the disappointment he felt for his father's anti-Christian deed. Yet still, he could not bring himself to doubt his father's love for him, when his father had trained him with hopes that he would mature into an independent merchant one day.

The wolves in front of him were completely different from the image of werewolves that circulated through society, and they didn't emit any evil or foul aura. Rather, the sincerity of the wolves humbly bowing their heads to a significantly weaker being like him, one whom they could easily overpower and threaten if the mood stuck them, touched his heart.

He could always think later. If he did not return to Venice alive, he wouldn't be able to speak about this with his father. The young man opened his mouth.

"My name is Pietro. I am Father's...no, Master Lorenzo's eldest son."

Speaking so politely to a wolf might have seemed rather strange, but it didn't feel out of place to Pietro. The wolves had an abundance of grace and dignity.

"I knew it. You have a similar scent to your father." The wolf in front of him grinned, and then turned to the wolves on both sides of him. "Rejoice, Ernest! Antonio! Our path to Venice has been opened."

The werewolves led Pietro into the depths of the forest. The already narrow path became an animal footpath, and eventually there was no path at all.

When the sun set and Pietro's steps became unsteady, the giant wolf called Antonio carried him on his back. Perhaps it was his imagination, but the wolves' pace seemed to speed up as soon as night fell. Their quick steps made it feel like they were being pursued. Pietro had to withstand being constantly struck in the face by small branches due to the low posture of the wolf he rode on.

The wolf leading the way suddenly stopped, followed closely by Ernest and Antonio. The leading wolf looked up and let out a brief howl.

Two suppressed howls returned his call. Startled, Pietro looked around, but all he could see were overgrown branches covering the night sky.

"No need to worry. They're just lookouts," Antonio mumbled to him.

As the group pressed on, the path in front of them suddenly came to an end at a towering cliff. At the bottom, there was a split in the cliff wall that served as an opening to a small cave.

Ernest and Antonio stayed at the entrance of the cave as guards, and only the leading wolf and Pietro went inside.

Inside the damp cave, a little ways from the entrance, a black piece of cloth was hung that prevented any light from leaking through to the outside. When the wolf and Pietro pushed passed the cloth, they entered a space a few square meters large, with thin candles just barely lighting up the area.

Two shadows were crouching in the darkness.

One of them was a wolf covered in silver fur, and judging from the wise look in its eyes, it had to be a werewolf. It was staring at Pietro with an obvious look of suspicion.

The other shadow was a woman wearing a filthy dress that looked like she had rolled around in it in the mud. Perhaps it used to be a rich woman's dress, as it looked like it'd had lace on its hem that'd been roughly ripped away. Her greasy black hair was unkempt, and she wore a haggard expression, but the eyes she fixed on Pietro were intense with a murderous glare. What's more, she had a thick knife clenched in her fist deliberately pointed in his direction. In her other hand, she was holding a large object bundled with a cape; it seemed she was trying to protect that bundle from Pietro.

The wolf that had led Pietro to this place gently spoke to the woman.

"It's me, Vera, Scott. This one is an ally, so be at ease."

The silver wolf sat up. "Lord Scott, you mean…"

Scott nodded and faced the woman he called Vera.

"Vera, could you please show him? There's no need to be afraid. We will be here, watching." His cautious tone sounded like he was trying to soothe a tantrum-prone child.

Vera stared at Scott silently, but eventually she put down the knife and held out the bundled object. She did not avert her eyes from Pietro for a second.

Scott accepted the bundle and gently unfolded the cape in front of Pietro.

Inside it was a young girl.

She was perhaps four or five years old. Even at such a young age, the girl had dignified facial features. Her transparently pale skin was beautiful, and almost seemed to light up the dim cave. Delicate blonde hair peeked through the cloth wrapped around her head to protect her from the cold. She was sound asleep now, but her eyelids were red and puffy; it appeared she had cried herself to sleep not too long ago.

"I present to you Princess Mina of House Tepes," the silver wolf solemnly said.

"We have traveled long and far to protect the Princess." Scott's tone was grave. "We have lost many on our journey to this place, but reaching you has made it all worth it. I must thank Alphonse once again."

Pietro jumped, hearing that name. He felt around in his coat and took out a letter. The envelope was closed with the wax seal of the Lorenzo Trading Company.

"Actually, I have a letter from my father. I was told to hand it to someone by the name of Alphonse Borgiani; is he present?"

Scott's face suddenly contorted with distress. Pietro stood there, perplexed at the unexpected reaction, not knowing what to do.

Scott spoke in a voice full of pain. "Alphonse was killed in battle," he said, complex emotions straining in his voice. "He is by our Queen Lucrezia's side now."

One Month Earlier

A new headstone gleamed white in the moonlight.

Today's burial count brought the total to twelve. There was no ritual or prayer; it was simply burying the corpses in the garden, but Scott made a point to attend them every day as the leader of the werewolves.

A prominent forehead, a stately nose, and a square chin—he was the epitome of a warrior, and there was not a shred of doubt in his gaze. However, the look in his eyes could also be due to numbness, from having witnessed so many deaths of his comrades.

Vampires leave behind only ashes when they die, but werewolves leave corpses. As he was unable to give a proper burial to the werewolves who had died in battle outside of the castle walls, it was Scott's wish to at least give one for those who died within their reach.

Her Majesty Queen Lucrezia, the lady of the castle, kindly accepted Scott's proposal and dedicated the beautiful garden, tended by the lady herself with all her heart and soul, as a burial ground. Already more than half of the garden was occupied with gravestones, but she did not express any discontent.

The rebellion started by the Great Clans of Rozenmann, Li, and Ivanovic was nearing its end. At the beginning of the war, there were a few thousand in the werewolf army of House Tepes, but now their numbers had been decimated.

When the rebellion initially broke out, hardly anyone had predicted such a one-sided ending. The Great Clans were indeed powerful, but the True Bloods who had pledged allegiance to House Tepes were also a force to be reckoned with. It was widely believed that the war would eventually reach a conclusion with talks of peace.

However, the state of the war completely changed when the head of the Bancroft family, the most influential force on the Tepes side, died a sudden and mysterious death. The other Tepes vassal families, having lost the support of Bancroft, were quickly overpowered by the Great Clans, and their remaining subjects were absorbed by the Great Clans and turned into foes of House Tepes.

After near-continuous strategic retreats, the only territory left to House Tepes was a single castle passed down for generations, and even it was now completely surrounded by the armies of the Great Clans. There was no possibility that reinforcements would arrive from outside of the siege, but they also did not have enough forces left within the castle to defeat even a portion of the enemy and force an escape route through the gathered armies. Even if they had somehow broken through the siege, the chance of reaching a future that Queen Lucrezia and her daughter, Princess Mina, could survive was very slim.

Surrender or annihilation. Everyone believed those were the only two choices left for House Tepes.

But Scott's outlook was different.

After leaving the garden, Scott returned indoors and walked along the stone floor with heavy steps. It was nighttime, and there were hardly any torches lit—there was no need for light, as vampires and werewolves could see in the dark.

Along the wall were a few Fangless who had escaped into

the castle, some crouching down with uneasy expressions, others leaning against the cold stone wall, trembling. The castle was surrounded by the ruins of the town burned down by the armies of the Great Clans in the early stages of the war. The Fangless were killed on sight, so the only choice left for them was to take shelter in the castle.

The dejected Fangless of all ages and genders directed desperate looks at House Tepes' valiant general. Scott conjured up an expression of confidence and nodded back at them, but he had long since run out of words of encouragement.

The werewolf and vampire soldiers pacing back and forth in the hallways proudly saluted Scott whenever they saw him. They still maintained high morale, yet the fatigue of constant night attacks and the ongoing siege was clearly showing.

Today is the day.

Everything Scott saw pushed him to follow through with his plan.

Scott walked up the stone steps and arrived at the overhang facing the front of the castle.

A line of ballistae stood on the passage constructed on the castle walls. Their massive bows and arrows were all pointed towards the sky. Overhead, numerous ropes were strung in all directions and countless claws hung from them— in preparation for air raids by winged vampires.

Vampires with crossbows concealed themselves within

the shadows of the arrow slits—they'd been appointed to defend the walls at night. During the day, they were replaced by werewolves, who could be exposed to sunlight. The surrounding armies used the same rotation; this tactic was only seen in Vampire warfare.

Scott looked out beyond the castle as he gave words of encouragement to the soldiers on duty.

The beautiful city that the Tepes had built over months and years was now nothing but rubble and ash. The elegant porch of the Dermaille Mansion, the belfry of the school in which Queen Lucrezia herself taught from time to time—it was hard to even see where they used to stand. Though they lay hidden in the darkness at night, the rotting corpses of werewolves and the ashes of vampires would appear along with the sunrise.

Beyond the vast ruins, the armies of the Great Clans had taken their positions. The flag that ostentatiously fluttered right in front of the castle was that of the Rozenmann Clan. The troops in charge of attacking the castle were assembling cautiously at a safe distance, where an attack from this side could not reach them. Past the well-ordered troops in their formations, masses of sun-blocking tents for the vampires were visible.

"Where is Alphonse?"

Scott turned his eyes toward where the soldier pointed, and spotted the back of a large, armored man.

When Scott approached him, the man was studying the

movement of the enemy troops through the arrow slits, his back turned to Scott. The man muttered aloud as he kept his eyes to the outside.

"There shouldn't be any night raids tonight. Instead of wasting their soldiers in an attack, it appears they're going to leisurely wait for us to surrender." The man turned around and looked at Scott. "Are you disappointed?"

"The fewer battles, the better," Scott replied seriously.

Duke Alphonse Borgiani. He was the head of one of the most influential families in House Tepes, and also essentially the commander of the castle siege army. His soft and wavy chestnut hair and his cool facial features gave off an impression of a nihilistic gentleman. However, in stark contrast to his face, his body was muscular and well-built, and he was a true warrior who belonged on the battlefield. He had headed into battle countless times, sword in hand, leading a rowdy troop of rough men.

Scott straightened his back and said stiffly, "Alphonse, I have an idea I'd like to present to you."

Alphonse grinned lazily. "Again?"

"Yes, again."

Over the past few days, Scott had repeatedly proposed that they launch a surprise attack, risking everything they had.

The Great Clans had werewolves on their side as well, but they numbered far less than their vampire soldiers. Because of this difference in numbers, their daytime forces were always shorthanded. On top of that, the enemy werewolves became less and less vigilant as they assumed daytime attacks by the Tepes side were unlikely due to the devistating losses they'd endured. Scott's idea was to use those two factors to their advantage and spring a surprise attack during the day.

He had observed the enemy's movements across several days, and he had even pinpointed the location of Rozenmann's coffin, in which he slept during the daytime. It was inside the church, which had remained undestroyed in the former castle town. The church had been erected for those who could not abandon their faith even after becoming vampires, and there was an underground temple for them.

With no intention to escape, all of the remaining werewolves would go into battle; their sole objective would be to take the life of Rozenmann himself. If Rozenmann, the heart of the Great Clans, was killed, the alliance of the Great Clans would collapse, and survival for House Tepes would become a possibility. Scott proposed this same idea to Alphonse every night for approval.

And Alphonse's answer was always the same.

They simply couldn't risk to lose their entire force of werewolves, with their ability to mobilize regardless of the state of the sun, on an all-or-nothing plan.

When Scott tried to argue his side, Alphonse waved a hand at him. "You don't need to go on; you've drilled it into my head. Here is my answer."

Alphonse gripped Scott's shoulders tightly with both hands and looked him straight in the eyes.

"We'll do it tomorrow."

"What...?" Scott, used to having his proposal rejected, was left speechless.

"But it won't be your werewolves going; I will go, along with my own Borgiani troop. If you disagree, then we'll cancel the whole plan."

"B-but, why now...?"

Alphonse leaned towards Scott. "Let's talk alone."

The two of them moved to a deserted room in the side tower. Alphonse went straight into the topic as soon as he closed the door.

"Do you remember the Lorenzo Trading Company in Venice?"

"Yes. I visited them once before when we went to pick up medicine and such."

"Actually, not long after that, we revealed our identities to Master Lorenzo."

Scott was shocked. In Venice, where the Roman Catholic Church possessed overwhelming religious power, it was impossible that any merchant would do business with the likes of them.

"He's an interesting man, that Lorenzo. When I asked if he was afraid of divine punishment for doing business with vampires and werewolves, what do you think he said? 'I don't fear punishment by a god who couldn't even save my wife.' That was it!"

To Scott, who was serious to the core, the existence of a human who would prioritize business over religious taboos was quite incomprehensible.

"Today, we received a pigeon from that same Lorenzo. Well, actually not from Lorenzo; it's from Andrea."

"From Andrea…?"

Andrea was Alphonse's only son. From a young age, he had excelled in his studies and showed great talent in communications and data analysis. However, he could not see eye to eye with his father, who deemed skills on the battlefield more worthy of praise. So he had run away, and was basically disowned by the Borgiani family.

Alphonse handed the small folded letter to Scott. When Scott opened the letter, it was filled completely on both sides, with writing so minuscule it looked like it'd been written with the point of a needle, to convey as much information as possible in the limited space.

"He is currently being sheltered by Lorenzo. He knows of others, also in hiding, who have escaped the attacks by the Great Clans."

The initial offensive by the Great Clans had been quick as lightning. Because of this, it was believed that there were still those loyal to House Tepes caught on the other side of the battle lines, unable to come back to their side.

Alphonse suddenly tightened his expression.

"Andrea's idea guarantees safe passage from Austria to Venice. We will help Her Highness and Princess Mina escape to Austria. It looks like he's also already begun preparations to secure a foundation for the resurrection of House Tepes."

Scott was awestruck with Andrea's quick thinking. Despite years of no contact, living completely displaced from the battlefield, he had so accurately grasped the situation of the war. At this point, the only way for House Tepes to survive was for Queen Lucrezia and Princess Mina to escape from the castle.

By utilizing the various escape routes in the castle, it was not impossible for them to elude the surrounding armies. However, the true problem lay after they had escaped. If they were to fight off pursuers sent by the Great Clans on their way to Austria, they would definitely need the help of werewolves, who could fight both day and night. Thus, it was wiser not to send out werewolves for the surprise attack plan.

But still, why did it have to be Alphonse leading the surprise attack?

Alphonse had already sensed what Scott wanted to ask.

"Lately, something has been troubling Her Highness. Have you noticed?"

Scott had noticed. Her Majesty Lucrezia was a kindhearted woman. The tremendous number of casualties from the rebellion was beginning to eat at her soul. The Great Clans called her "weak" and ridiculed her for her kindness, but it was because of her compassion that her loyal subjects were willing to sacrifice their lives.

"From what I can see, Her Highness is planning to surrender in a few days' time in exchange for our lives. But, of course, Rozenmann and the others would never keep their end of the deal."

Alphonse irritably pounded the stucco wall with his fist. "If Her Highness and the Princess die, House Tepes will collapse. And I don't just mean physically when I say 'die.' If they fell into the hands of the Great Clans, their leaders would undoubtedly imprison their souls. The two of them might as well be dead, then."

Scott continued Alphonse's thought for him. "On the other hand, even if all of their loyal subjects are killed, House Tepes will survive as long as the two True Bloods are free."

"You read my mind. That's my dear friend!" Alphonse beamed at him. "We need the two of them to live, even if it costs all of our lives. Their lives are that valuable. And that is the message I intend to personally deliver to them."

Alphonse was being significantly more insistent than usual, and Scott sensed that no amount of argument or persuasion could change his mind.

"I understand your intentions. I will obey your command. Now, I will let Her Majesty Lucrezia know about—"

Scott stopped mid-sentence and shut his mouth. If Queen Lucrezia found out about this plan, she would immediately figure out Alphonse's true intentions. As she was his master, a single "no" from her would suffice to thwart their entire plan.

The moonlight beaming in from the window lit up Alphonse's profile. He looked at Scott and smiled grimly.

"Ignorance is bliss, or in our case, loyalty."

Scott was at a loss for words. Alphonse would most likely not live to see the moon of another day. Yet he was going to head into battle without even bidding farewell to Her Majesty Lucrezia.

Alphonse held out a small tally to Scott.

"When you join them in Austria, you'll need this. There's a detailed plan in that letter."

As Scott accepted the tally, Alphonse gripped his hands tightly. Their gloves grated against each other and creaked.

"My troops have already begun preparations for tomorrow. It's not every day you see vampires fighting during the sunlit hours. You had better look forward to it!"

With that, Alphonse turned away and hastily left.

Alone in the room, Scott felt angry that he didn't have any words for Alphonse. Alphonse was heading into a battle of certain death, and Scott couldn't just stand around and watch him go, or he'd be a failure both as a friend and as the leader of the werewolves.

There had to be a way to answer Alphonse's enthusiasm.

Scott fell into deep thought.

The great hall was cramped with vampires, totaling around 150.

Appearance-wise, they hardly resembled one another. Among them were Normans with red hair grown out like manes, Nubians with coffee-colored skin, and Saxons with faces covered in colorful tattoos; it was like a showcase of races and cultures. Each and every one of them was a skillful warrior who Alphonse himself had scouted from battlefields throughout the ages.

This troop—supervised directly by the Borgiani family— served as the elite force of House Tepes. Their motto was "charge first, retreat last." They were always placed on the front lines and had suffered great losses already, much like the werewolf forces. The ones assembled in the room were the toughest warriors, the ones who had survived everything until now.

Alphonse was planning to commit every single one of them to the surprise attack.

There were barrels of tar in all corners of the room, with strips of linen submerged in them. The men wrapped the tarred linen cloths around every part of their bodies and wore their armor on top of them. The cloths were a way to protect themselves against the sunlight, the vampires' most treacherous foe.

Wrapping themselves in the sticky linen limited their mobility, which was a drawback in battle. On top of that, if the linens came off or were cut, their bodies would start disintegrating from where their skin was exposed. It was a dangerous mission and one misstep could easily result in their deaths.

Yet the men remained carefree. Some whipped tar at each others' faces, others rubbed tar on their armor as an extra precaution. Their excited mood made them seem more like children at play than seasoned warriors.

Alphonse watched them warmly. Slowly, he climbed on top of the table in the center of the hall. Naturally, all eyes were on him, and the rambunctious sounds of the hall turned into silence.

"Stop what you're doing and listen to me. By tomorrow, all of you are going to be completely covered in tar from head to toe. There won't be any way to tell who's who. Before that happens, will you let me take a good look at each of your faces?"

The men, understanding the meaning behind his words, stood up with their backs straight, so that their faces were in clear view.

Alphonse, hands on his hips, took his time turning in a circle to carefully look at each face. He knew that there were men among them whom he would never see again after tomorrow. Now was his last chance to carve their faces into his memory.

Once he did a full circle, he frowned and muttered, "I know I'm the one who asked to see them, but...you look so shabby!"

Laughter filled the great hall. Some playfully booed him. Alphonse, also laughing, gestured to the men to settle down.

"I take it back; you all look great."

When the men quieted down, Alphonse's smile disappeared.

"I have a favor to ask of all of you. The battle tomorrow is not under Her Highness' orders. It is a battle I *choose* to fight. Thus, this is not an order. Rather, I want all of you to fight with me because you wish it. Let's show those useless puppets of the Great Clans that Tepes warriors are in a completely different league!"

The men hesitated and looked at each other. They had always fought alongside Alphonse without a second thought. This was the first time he had formally asked them.

A man covered in scars, standing in a corner of the room, raised his hand lazily. He was an Englishman named Godfrey, one of the oldest in the troop. His meeting with Alphonse dated all the way back to the Hundred Years' War.

"I don't mind fighting the puppets along with you, Captain, but I've got one condition."

Alphonse tilted his head. "And what is that?"

"Just don't command us not to come with you."

The men stood there confused for a moment, but then shouts of agreement arose one by one. Their voices became louder and soon turned into chanting, lauding Alphonse's name.

"Captain! Captain!"

When the soldiers' excitement was about to peak, the hall doors suddenly crashed opened.

At once, all eyes turned toward the doorway.

There stood Scott, leading a group of about thirty werewolves. The werewolves had donned their complete war armor and each was toting his preferred weapons, mostly large battle axes and war hammers.

Scott and his group entered the hall and walked up to Alphonse.

Alphonse stepped down from the table and came face to face with Scott.

Scott pointed at his werewolf troop.

"Since ancient times, it's been established that the only ones who can win a fair fight against werewolves are werewolves themselves. It would hurt our pride not to have any werewolves from House Tepes at tomorrow's battle. Please take these werewolves with you."

Alphonse understood Scott's intentions. Scott spoke rationally, but Alphonse knew how much he wanted to help.

He looked over the werewolves, suppressing his soft side that wanted give in to Scott's offer, and noticed something peculiar. Most of the werewolves were injured in some way—cuts on their lips and black eyes—as if they had all just been in a fight.

Scott spoke up when he noticed Alphonse's stares.

"Truth be told, almost all of our werewolves wanted to

join you in tomorrow's battle. A fight ensued to determine who would be staying behind. Ironically, because of that fight, we can confidently say that all of the werewolves here come with a guarantee on their hot-bloodedness and the strength of their fists."

Alphonse was trying hard not to laugh at the ridiculousness of Scott's overly serious words when he recognized one of the faces of the werewolves in the group. He paled.

Among the werewolves was Scott's eldest son, Richard.

Richard stepped out in front of Alphonse. His cheek was swollen, likely from being struck during the fight, but his eyes were clear as a lake.

"Duke Alphonse, I served in Her Majesty Lucrezia's Imperial Guard, so I was never given the opportunity to avenge the deaths of my comrades. I humbly beg of you to let me join your troops."

The werewolves knew. They knew that tomorrow's battle was their last chance to fight Rozenmann head on and take his life.

Alphonse looked at Scott. Surely, this must have been something Scott did not foresee, either. If he hadn't based the werewolves "pre-fight" solely on brute force, he wouldn't have to send his only son to battle, a battle from which he would likely never return.

Contrary to Alphonse's expectations, however, Scott's eyes showed no hesitation in the least. Instead, they reflected only his complete trust in his son and a firm belief that he would return alive with Rozenmann's head in tow.

Alphonse thrust his finger at Scott.

"You are a fool."

He pointed at Richard as well. "Richard, you're a fool, too."

Alphonse went around and pointed his finger at each and every man in the entire hall. "You, and you, and you, too— all fools!"

The entire hall listened as Alphonse shouted.

"Every single man here is a hopeless, damned fool!" Then he grinned and added, "Of course, I'm the biggest fool here."

Alphonse jumped back onto the table and howled.

"Listen, all you kings of fools! Tomorrow night, all of us here are going to present Her Highness Lucrezia with Rozenmann's empty coffin! Mark my words!"

The vampires and werewolves responded with a war cry fierce enough to make the walls tremble.

As the warriors enthusiastically returned to their preparations for the coming day's battle, Alphonse called out to Scott.

"Scott, will you help me?"

Scott agreed without a moment's hesitation.

It was a sunny afternoon.

The werewolves in the besieging army kept watch on the castle for any movements.

"Keeping watch" was an overstatement, though. All they could really do was stare at the castle aimlessly, waiting for the rare times when they could catch a glimpse of the soldiers through the castle's arrow slits.

It was rumored that their master Rozenmann had already begun talks on "post-war procedures" with the other two heads of the Great Clans. To the common soldiers, there was nothing to gain if their side won the war. They were thankful that the likelihood of them being thrown into a messy siege war had significantly lessened, but it was still not easy having to stand at attention in the direct sunlight all day long.

They're surely going to lose; why don't they just hurry up and surrender?

With that thought, one of the werewolves looked up at the sky and saw a black kite leisurely flying in circles overhead. Its peaceful cry echoed in the silence.

He would be chastised if he was caught looking away from the castle, but he couldn't help following the bird's gentle flight with his eyes.

A short line crossed his vision. Leaving him no time to question it, the line multiplied in front of his eyes and flew toward the back of the besieging army.

Fire arrows, he realized too late; countless arrows were raining down on the tents under which their vampire forces rested.

Fires started all over the campsite.

The besieging army was rudely awakened by the attack. Their response was scattered and delayed, as some men correctly assessed the situation as an enemy attack and prepared to fight, while others thought it was merely a fire and ran to put out the flames.

While the werewolves ran amok, the vampires began fleeing the tents to escape the flames. Naturally, once they left the sun-blocking tents, they were exposed to the sun and burnt to ash. In their panicked state, none of them had time to think and they burned no matter what they did.

Complete chaos ensued in the Rozenmann army as the werewolves rushed to try to respond to the situation, and the vampires ran around madly in flames.

The werewolf who had watched the black kite soaring had at least drawn his sword, but he couldn't figure out the best course of action.

Suddenly, he felt an extreme pressure from behind.

Turning around, he saw a wall of pure blackness rapidly approaching him.

The werewolf instinctively swung his sword, but before it could connect, his head contorted like an empty linen bag as it was smashed down into his shoulders by a morning star.

The shadow wall was comprised of a mass of black shapes that slaughtered every soldier in its path without a single word or cry.

Eventually, after a series of death screams, the Rozenmann army finally realized that they were under attack by the enemy. The shadow at the head of the black mass issued his declaration in a resonating voice.

"I am Alphonso Borgiani of the Borgiani family, the top-ranking vassal family of House Tepes! My troops and I are here to deliver divine punishment to your master Rozenmann and his lowlife followers, who had the audacity to revolt against House Tepes, the royal house! Those who are ashamed of your deeds, come forth and offer me your heads!"

Following this pronouncement, the other shadows let out a war cry. The uniform cry of these seasoned warriors was earsplitting to the besieging army.

The soldiers who made up the shadow group were all in hardened armor painted black. Even the unarmored parts of their bodies, including their heads and arms, were seamlessly covered in black cloth; they literally looked like nothing but shadows standing and moving around. The breastplates of their armor were the only parts not painted black—they wore the emblem of House Tepes proudly.

Most of the Rozenmann army was thoroughly unprepared for the sudden warfare and death that was sprung on them, as all order and discipline in their army had loosened under their assumedly certain victory. The shadow group had already penetrated deep into enemy territory before the enemy had time to organize any sort of counterattack, and they pressed on, slaughtering, squashing and cutting down any who stood in their path.

But the officers of the Rozenmann army were experienced

warriors in their own right. First blood was spilled on the raiding team, and when they saw the soldier disintegrate into ash within his wraps and armor, the werewolves shouted to each other.

"They're vampires!"

"Cut 'em up and expose their skin!"

The enemy soldiers surrounding the raiding team all transformed their hands into beast claws and began to slice at the wraps on the soldiers' arms and heads. Any exposure of their skin meant certain death. The team was now forced to switch to defense.

At that moment, Scott's werewolf troop jumped in to support them. The werewolves, able to freely fight the enemy soldiers without heeding the sun, acted as a shield for the vampires.

Alphonse had said that once their faces were covered there would be no way to distinguish one soldier from another, but that wasn't true. To Alphonse, who was familiar with the fighting style of each and every one of his men, it was obvious at first glance who was fighting where, and with what weapon.

The former Kashmir soldier Gupta was skillfully gliding the blade of his jamadhar into the spaces between his enemy's armor, fatally wounding his opponents with minimal movement. Beside him was Dietrich, wielding a Zweihänder and cutting off three heads in one easy swing.

An enemy soldier tried to attack him from behind, but Sergei intercepted the blow by cutting off both of the man's arms with his scimitar.

Just then, Ignatio was pierced in the chest with a spear and fell to his knees. There was no time for his comrades to save him; he disappeared under a mass of enemy soldiers.

Moving forward was getting harder and harder, and gradually more of them were falling to the enemy's fierce attacks. But the Borgiani elite force—celebrated in the future as rebellious heroes through inspiring songs—continued fighting against the endless stream of attacks, pressing on towards the church where Rozenmann himself slept.

Alphonse put down his scope.

His soldiers, lying low next to him, were talking, watching the battle from afar.

"Hasim really is the best at impersonating the Captain."

"'Come forth and offer me your heads!' Yeah, that sounds like something the Captain would say."

Alphonse and the top members of their troop, numbering about ten, were hiding out in the ruins of the castle town and awaiting the opportunity to make their move.

The troop that had plunged into the Rozenmann army was merely a distraction. The man leading the raiding assault, who had claimed to be Alphonse himself, was one of his own soldiers who had a knack for impersonating him.

Among those in the troop that Alphonse was leading, half

of them possessed the ability to fly. The plan was thus: once the troop in charge of the feint had effectively drawn enough of the enemy team's attention, Alphonse and the others would fly over the battlefield and close in on Rozenmann's sleeping quarters.

Needless to say, Rozenmann's werewolf army couldn't fly, nor did their army have vampires who could counter their aerial attack. This strategy was only possible because their vampires could go out in the daytime.

The men in charge of the air assault had already transformed into their true forms and were waiting with their enormous wings folded in. The other vampires constantly painted more and more layers of tar on those wings to keep it from drying and peeling off.

"Look! The Imperial Guard is on the move!" one of his men shouted.

Alphonse looked through his scope once again.

The guards defending Rozenmann's quarters had begun to move out. They had realized that the target of the raid attack was Rozenmann himself. The Imperial Guard was made up of the most talented fighters, with battle skills far beyond those of normal soldiers. To this group of elites, the other soldiers were nothing more than disposable pawns.

Seeing the hundreds of Imperial Guard werewolves in beast form rushing forward, kicking up clouds of dirt, was just like seeing a herd of buffalo running wild across the plains.

"So, the guard dogs are finally here!" Hasim, still acting

as the head of the raiding troop, somehow sounded joyful. "This is where it really begins!"

The werewolves on the Tepes side all transformed at once and rushed to the front lines. They planned to try to fend off the enemy's attacks as they came rushing at them with a force several times larger.

The werewolves of the Imperial Guard carelessly knocked the regular soldiers out of their way as if they were merely obstacles, and crashed head-on with the raid at full speed. There was a dull sound as the muscles and bones of the two groups of werewolves collided.

Richard struck the guard that ran into him with the handle of his axe, and then swung the blade down into the back of his neck as the guard staggered from the initial hit.

He forcefully pulled out the axe that had penetrated the guard's neck bones, and, without even watching him fall as his almost-severed neck wobbled on his body, he attacked the next werewolf. However, this opponent caught his axe with a strong arm and drove him back with tremendous strength.

Richard pushed back by pressing the end of the handle of his axe to his forehead. He then let go of one hand and stabbed his opponent in the eye with the sharp claw on his thumb. The soldier, having been attacked in one of his most vulnerable areas, stepped back instinctively. Without losing a second, Richard jumped onto his opponent and ripped off his entire snout.

Another guard jumped onto Richard's back. He struggled to shake him off, but the enemy had dug his claws deep into his shoulder blades and would not budge.

Just as the guard was about to bite into Richard's neck, Hasim's mace smashed in the guard's skull.

When Richard turned to look at Hasim, his cloth wrappings had been torn and there was white smoke pouring out. Hasim's eyes, peeking through the black cloth, were smiling as if to say 'don't worry about it.'

Hasim turned away and ran back into the midst of the battle, swinging his mace wildly.

Richard broke free of the guard's corpse clinging to his back and took on another enemy with a ferocious howl.

Everyone on the raid team, each with his own versatile battle technique, was putting up a good fight. Regardless, the Imperial Guard proved to be a formidable obstacle, and the pace of their advance began to slow. The Tepes side—at a disadvantage due to the sheer number of their enemies—had to be in constant motion or they would instantly be surrounded.

The raid attack was entering its critical stage.

"Looks like it's almost time, Captain," Godfrey said to Alphonse.

The role of the raid troop was to attract the attention of the Rozenmann army and keep them from noticing Alphonse and his team of flying vampires. To do so, they needed to be as distractingly showy as possible in their fight, but still retain a level of life-risking seriousness so that the enemy would not realize that their attack was a feint. They had clearly excelled at their task, as they had even enticed the Imperial Guard, tasked with defending the church, to abandon its post and head to the battlefield.

Alphonse threw down his scope and stood up.

"Let's go."

The flying vampires already had their wings spread. The non-flying warriors mounted them with weapons in hand.

The one carrying Alphonse was Godfrey. Contrary to his usual tough look, he had transformed into an elegant bird-like creature.

"Next time, you fly with me on your back."

Alphonse prodded Godfrey on the head as he jested, and without a word raised his hand to signal the others to commence the operation.

The five or so pairs of vampires quickly and silently flew straight up.

They immediately rose to an altitude where arrows could not reach them. They had meticulously planned their timing and position to give them the greatest advantage. They had their backs to the sun so that they would not be discovered by the enemy troops on the ground.

With an overhead view, the overwhelming size difference between the Rozenmann army and their own raid team was glaringly evident—and the diminished number of raid team members still fighting was the most obvious thing of all.

Vampire warriors, who walked through life shoulder-to-shoulder with death, always exchanged vows with their comrades. They'd vow to die in the same field of battle, where their remaining ashes—stepped on by both allies and enemies—would mix together and eventually return to the earth to make a single beautiful flower blossom.

They knew now that they couldn't keep that vow with their comrades fighting below.

The sentimental moment was brief; they were fast approaching their target.

The church, built in the later periods of the Gothic Era, still retained its pure beauty despite its new master. The side walls were lined with huge, intricate stained glass windows, now boarded up with blackened wood.

Alphonse's troop fell into an almost vertical dive—strong winds blasted them in the face and howled in their ears.

Suddenly, the air was filled with arrows from all directions as Rozenmann's soldiers finally noticed their team.

The vampires swiftly dodged the arrows as they headed for the church windows.

One of the flying vampires took multiple arrows to his throat and chest. He lost control and crashed to the ground, taking his rider with him.

Godfrey's wing took an arrow as well, but he paid it no heed.

The boards on the windows rapidly grew in their vision. The flying vampires just had to hope that the windows were only blocked by that single layer of visible planks.

Each pair flew head first into one of the windows. The impact clouded their vision and sent the flying vampires tumbling to the ground.

Alphonse jumped to his feet right away, drew his sword, and looked around.

There were a number of Imperial Guard vampires inside the dark chapel, but instead of attacking, they were running around in panic.

Alphonse looked up and understood immediately. The sunlight leaking through the windows they had broken was burning the Imperial Guards, one after another.

Alphonse's team was not about to miss this unforeseen chance for victory.

No sword fight was even necessary. When they chased after the Imperial Guards with their swords, the guards stepped into the sunlight on their own and burned. Godfrey and the other winged vampires got rid of more of their enemies by grabbing them and flying up to expose them to the light.

The Imperial Guards were desperately trying to bring their werewolves inside the chapel for support. But their preparations for the raid backfired on them—the door had been locked and reinforced against invaders from outside and couldn't be opened easily.

The entrance to the underground temple where Rozenmann supposedly rested was behind the altar.

Leaving the dispatch of the guards to his subordinates, Alphonse started towards the altar. A well-built member of the Imperial Guards, probably one of its leaders, stood in his way and drove his sword against Alphonse.

"Such an arrogant plan! Is this Lucrezia's bidding?"

"This has nothing to do with Her Highness. Don't lump us in with you fools, who can't even piss without Rozenmann's orders!"

The vampire's nerves twitched in his temple and he swung his sword at Alphonse.

Alphonse easily dodged the attack and cut his opponent from his head down to his waist in one swift move. He yelled at the vampire, who was now crumbling away with ashes flying everywhere, "Never use our Queen's fair name without a title, you unmannered bastard!"

Running down the middle aisle, Alphonse at last reached the chancel in front of the altar. At that point, the Imperial Guards finally forced the church doors open behind him, and a mass of soldiers armed with crossbows came rushing in.

The ranged squad scattered along the back of the church and started firing arrows. The vampires fighting in the nave and transept of the church—both friend and foe—all fell victim to the arrows and dissolved into ash as they were hit.

"Captain!"

Godfrey flew down from overhead and shielded Alphonse with his wings. He threw Alphonse back behind a bench—and was hit by numerous arrows in his back and wings in the process.

When Alphonse looked up from the ground, Godfrey was turning into ash, still standing.

Alphonse had taken a few arrows in his left hand and right leg. He sat in the shadow of the bench and broke the arrows to push them out.

The stream of arrows continued endlessly. Many of them hit the back of the bench, and the altar in front of him was almost entirely covered.

He had no choice but to move out of his current position to reach the entrance to the underground temple. But he knew if he carelessly jumped out with his injured leg, he would immediately fall prey to the arrows.

Alphonse tightened his grip on his sword and gritted his teeth.

It was not that he feared death. But if he died here, the deaths and sacrifices of his comrades would all go to waste. He refused to give up with the chance of victory right in front of his eyes.

Just then, a giant door flew across the chapel, leapt into the air, and knocked down the row of marksmen with a thundering sound. Next came a number of benches flying across the room, one after another, that crashed down on the enemy soldiers.

The attacks suddenly stopped, and Alphonse, peeking out from behind the bench at the sudden commotion and subsequent silence, saw a towering shadow.

It was Richard.

His whole body was covered in blood, and a lot of it seemed to be his own. One of his ears had been bitten off, and a large chunk of flesh was missing from his back. There was a broken arrow and a short sword sticking out from one shoulder.

Richard was using a wooden door almost twice his height as a shield, his claws dug deep into it. Between ragged breaths, he said, "I will protect you. Please, hurry to the temple!"

Alphonse struggled to stand. Shielded by the door Richard held, he entered the underground temple.

"Richard, you come too!"

Richard shook his head. "I'm going to stay here and block these guards."

Another shower of arrows was beginning to fall.

"The battle outside's already over. The only ones left are you and me."

Alphonse was speechless. He had been prepared for this, but it nevertheless still pained him. He had always led them into battle—it was cruel irony that he was the last survivor.

"Please, go. Let's finish this up quickly and take home a tale to tell my father!"

Alphonse looked into Richard's eyes. Even after all the bloodshed and countless injuries, his eyes still shone brightly with youthful energy.

"Stay alive and wait for me. I can't carry the coffin alone."

Alphonse saw Richard nod, then he closed the entrance door.

A new troop of ranged soldiers were trying to come inside. Behind them was a mass of other Imperial Guards in beast form. The points of the arrows set on the crossbows of those marksmen gleamed sharply, different from before. They were arrows crafted from silver, made to combat werewolves.

Richard tore off the piece of armor that was barely hanging on his chest, and yanked off his chain mail. The most dependable weapons for a werewolf in his beast form were his claws, fangs, and pure brute strength. The armor and weapons were nothing but a hindrance.

Now light on his feet, Richard shouted with renewed energy, "I declare to you, men of the Rozenmann army!"

His clear, resonating voice forced the enemy soldiers to stop their movement.

"Finish me off before those arrows run out. Or else..." Richard took a breath and shouted even louder, "I will send each and every one of you to Hell!"

Richard threw down the door he had been using as a shield and leapt up with all his might. The soldiers released their arrows at once.

The stairs leading down to the underground temple were quiet and cool, a contrast to the chapel above.

Alphonse pressed his forehead against the cold wall to pull himself together and descended the steps one at a time, dragging his injured leg.

The door to the temple was at the bottom of the stairs. The

door had a lock, but it came loose easily when he stuck his sword in a crack between the door and door frame and pried it.

When the door opened, a strong chill blasted Alphonse. Perhaps it was due to Rozenmann's miasma, but the inside of the temple was as cold as ice.

Surrounded by stone walls, the temple itself was quite small; not even ten square meters in size. The ceiling was high, though, perhaps three meters. The furnishings had all been removed, and in the center lay Rozenmann's coffin.

The coffin was surprisingly plain; clad in ebony, it had a simple hexagonal shape. But the ominous aura seeping out of the coffin was anything but normal.

Even Alphonse could not help but feel a chill.

Breathing heavily, he removed the linens wrapped on his face. He had to make sure that Rozenmann could clearly see him when he finished him off, to give his enemy the pleasure of knowing the face of the man who took his life.

He glanced back—did the lid of the coffin just stir?

There was no time to delay. Rozenmann must have noticed the disturbance above.

Alphonse held his sword with the point forward and, cursing his legs for stiffening under the cold and an injury, began to rush towards the coffin.

A few meters before he reached the coffin, he jumped high in the air and brandished his sword. Gripping it overhead with both hands, he aimed the point right at the center of the coffin.

The sword was supposed to penetrate Rozenmann's chest

right through the coffin lid.

But suddenly, the lid split in half vertically, and the halves flew off to either side.

Alphonse saw it, still in midair; the indescribable thing that was inside the coffin.

The thing looked at Alphonse with eyes distorted with hatred and loathing. One second, it writhed in agony, and the next, a huge hole opened up in Alphonse's chest. His insides flew out of him, slapping against the ceiling, then sliding down.

Alphonse fell towards the coffin and felt all the cells in his body dying off at an unbelievable speed.

He had no regrets, except one.

Andrea.

In an instant, he understood the true meaning behind the letter from his son.

Leave the future of House Tepes to me, and spend your last moments on the battlefield without any regrets.

The son had a deep understanding of his father.

But the father had not understood anything about his son.

If only I could speak with Andrea just one more time.

A proud warrior shouldn't have those regrets. He had entrusted his after-death affairs to Scott, including his son. Now, he would go and listen to all the heroic deeds of his comrades waiting for him in Valhalla.

The instant Alphonse's ashes danced in the air above the coffin, his final thoughts lingered in the empty air.

Queen Lucrezia is far more beautiful than you could ever hope to be...

Clouds were beginning to form in the clear sky.

Scott, clinging to the castle walls, had watched every second of the raid.

The battle outside the castle had been over for a while. The Rozenmann army had already begun cleaning up after the battle, and the Ivanovic and Li armies were heading back to their own camps. All the Tepes vampires had dispersed into the air as ash, and the werewolves' bodies had most likely been cut up, leaving no remains to bury.

The last he had seen of Alphonse and his group was their departure towards the church; there had not been any changes since then.

Scott watched the church intently, forgetting to even blink. He heard a voice carried by the wind from the direction of the church. He listened closely.

It was not Alphonse's glorious shout of victory.

It was not Rozenmann's final cry of death.

It was the dreadful scream of a True Blood filled with wrath and rage, angered by a rude awakening.

Scott was forced to accept the outcome of the battle with the awful, gut-wrenching ringing of that scream in his ears. Alphonse and the others, who had headed out to battle with smiles on their faces, would never return.

Neither would his only son, Richard.

Scott looked down and gripped the edge of the castle wall. The stones of the wall made cracking sounds under his grip.

He stood there awhile, not moving.

"Excuse me, Lord Scott."

A woman appeared in the doorway behind Scott. She was Queen Lucrezia's maid, named Veratos. Being a vampire, she stood in the shadows of the doorway, shielding herself from the sunlight.

"Lucrezia-sama is asking for you."

With the death of Alphonse, there would be no more battle strategies. Instead, it was time for Scott to use his tactics for the survival of House Tepes.

Scott needed to explain to Her Majesty exactly what had happened that day, and have her make a decision about their future.

Scott left the castle wall and headed towards the doorway. He didn't look back.

Two Months Later

The Venetian port was entering its quietest time of the day.

The sailors who had been in the taverns until midnight

had already headed to bed, but it was still too early for the ship loaders, who started their work at daybreak.

Even the Palazzo Ducale and the Biblioteca Marciana, which had constant streams of visitors during the day, were wrapped in silence. In contrast, the grand belfry of Basilica di San Marco towered over everything with an unrivaled presence, day or night.

Countless caravels and carracks crowded the wharf, and the tremendous number of masts bristled like trees in a forest. On the coast, large galleons that could not fit in the pier floated gently with their anchors down.

Scott was standing on the deck of an anchored caravel and gazing at the quiet city, accompanied by two other men.

Scott and his group were finally able to rest for the first time after what seemed like an eternity. With Pietro's help, they had safely reached Venice, where they were taken under the wing of the Lorenzo Trading Company. After the much needed respite, the werewolves' wounds were almost fully healed, and Princess Mina and Vera had regained their inner calm.

Everyone was asleep in the main room of the ship, except for Scott and his companions.

The three on the deck remained silent for a while. The only sounds were the waves gently lapping up against the side of the ship and the mast creaking in the wind.

"We've already talked to the business in Thessaloniki. It will be an overland route to Constantinople, so there might be some danger for normal human travelers." In other words, nothing they needed to worry about. "If we had more time, we could be better prepared."

"I am in debt to you, Master Lorenzo." Scott bowed his head to the middle-aged owner of the Lorenzo Trading Company.

The thin young man with the chestnut hair spoke up.

"Soon we hope to assign someone along the Via Egnatia. That should make it much easier to contact each other."

The young man was Alphonse's son, Andrea.

Andrea did not seem especially surprised when Scott told him about the death of Alphonse. He did not fall into mourning, but instead became absorbed in rallying the survivors of House Tepes. It was like the future of House Tepes was the only thing left that interested him.

He was attempting to create an intelligence network to counter the Great Clans by having former subjects of House Tepes go undercover at various locations. Andrea believed that the most critical element to the revival of House Tepes was the collection of information.

The survivors did not consist only of loyal subjects who had served the Tepes family. One of the chief retainers of House Tepes, Marquis Dermaille—who had fortunately avoided the conflict by being in Madrid at the time—had succeeded in concealing a significant amount of House Tepes' wealth that had been saved outside of the country.

House Tepes had lost its master, its land and its authority.

However, that did not mean it had lost its people and its wealth.

And there was one factor more important than any other—the True Blood royal bloodline. The fate of Princess Mina was decided with a seemingly farfetched resolution—to hide her within the Ottoman Empire and plan for recovery.

The idea was proposed by Andrea.

Survivors of the Bancroft family had escaped Europe and were hidden away in Constantinople, the capital of the Ottoman Empire. They were building a community there. According to Andrea, they were showing an interest in joining House Tepes with Princess Mina's succession.

Scott and the others could not hide their resistance to the idea when they first heard it. For Princess Mina, who would eventually be crowned with the name of Tepes, to hide out in the Ottoman Empire of all places…!

A statement from a young werewolf named Wolfgang became the deciding factor.

"All of Europe has fallen to the Great Clans. There is no longer a safe haven for the Princess anywhere."

It was a reality they had to accept. House Tepes as they had known it no longer existed. They had little choice if they wanted to reconstruct the new House Tepes.

Scott acted fast after the decision was finalized. He persuaded Lorenzo, who had intended to let them stay with him for an unlimited time, and got his permission to board one of his ships headed to the Ottoman Empire.

In the morning, this caravel would leave Venice. Andrea and Lorenzo had paid Scott this nighttime visit to say their final goodbyes.

"Please give my regards to your son," Scott said to Lorenzo. "I can't thank him enough."

Lorenzo smiled generously.

"This was a good experience for my son. If he couldn't accept the existence of vampires and werewolves, I was going to refuse to let him inherit my company. I'm sure he'll mature well."

"Master Lorenzo…for the moment, we are unable to repay our debts to you. But one day, for certain…"

Lorenzo waved his hand and interrupted Andrea's words.

"We discussed this before. This is an investment for the Lorenzo Trading Company. You don't have to worry about compensating me. But in return, when House Tepes is revived, make sure to favor the Lorenzo Trading Company— although I don't know if that will happen in my time."

He had his own cool-headed, business driven calculations.

As trade with new lands increased, the status and prestige of countries bordering the Atlantic Ocean, such as Spain and Portugal, only rose higher. Venice, with no direct way to reach those outer waters and new markets, had already started showing signs of decline. To keep his business strong in the future, he had chosen to coexist with those who were not human.

Andrea bowed his head without a word.

Scott, watching him with sharp eyes, spoke up. "There is something I was asked to do by your father. It appears the time has come to fulfill my promise."

Andrea listened with a perplexed expression.

"I was given the task to determine whether or not you were fit to inherit the name of the Borgiani family. And if I determined that you were, I was told to say this to you."

Scott knelt down in front of Andrea. "Master Andrea. You have, from this moment, succeeded the position of your father Alphonse Borgiani as Duke, and you will now be Andrea, Duke Borgiani."

Scott looked up at Lorenzo.

"Master Lorenzo. Would you kindly act as witness?"

Lorenzo nodded gently. "I humbly comply."

In House Tepes' heyday, there would have been a magnificent celebration at the succession of the Borgiani family. Queen Lucrezia and Scott would have attended, donning their finest attire.

But that was now impossible. There was no land to inherit, let alone a ceremony to hold. There were no loyal subjects. The former Duke and his Queen Lucrezia were dead. The title of Duke Borgiani was succeeded on the deck of a wooden ship, filled with the stench of the sea and glue, witnessed by a single human merchant.

Andrea stood stiff and petrified at the sudden occurrence.

Scott slowly rose to his feet and stood in front of Andrea.

"This is a message from the former Duke Borgiani. 'I was

unable to protect House Tepes with my strength in battle; you must protect it with your resourcefulness. The most effective weapon in a long struggle of patient endurance is not the sword, but intelligence.'"

Andrea's eyes widened.

"Lord Scott, are those words from after he read my letter?"

"They are. I was given this message the night before we went into battle."

Andrea covered his face with his hands. For a moment he seemed on the brink of breaking down, but he pulled his hands down right away.

The expression he wore now on his face was cheerful, a stark contrast to the look he had held until then.

"If I could speak with my father once more..." he started, then stopped. He then straightened himself and made a declaration to Scott and Lorenzo.

"I, as Duke Borgiani, vow to give my life and body to serve Princess Mina, in order to revive House Tepes. And..." Andrea took a breath. "...One day, when I have a son of my own, I promise to name him after my father. I will raise him to be a man who will not shame the name of my father, and he will become the pillar of House Tepes."

Scott felt the weight lift off his shoulders. On the one hand, he could not help but look at Andrea, with his hardened decision to carry on his father's will, and be reminded of his late son, Richard.

I should withdraw, he thought. The era of Her Majesty

Lucrezia was over. Now it was time for House Tepes to be carried on by those of the younger generation—Andrea, and Pietro, and the young Princess Mina.

Fortunately, a young and talented werewolf named Wolfgang was among the survivors. Wolfgang believed that he could rebuild House Tepes' werewolf army from near total destruction.

Scott's mind was lighter than it had been in months. He was fully aware that their hardships were only beginning, but still, he had hope.

"It's unfortunate that we were unable to take a single Tepes flag out of the castle. If I had one with me now, I would climb to the top of the mast and raise it for all to see."

"You're so full of energy! I, on the other hand, couldn't possibly, not with this belly."

As Scott and Lorenzo chatted pleasantly, Andrea spoke as if he were trying to retrace an old memory.

"The night before I left House Tepes, my father told me this. Emblems and flags drawn by the human hand are only temporary. There is only one flag in this world that the family of the night should look up to."

"Only one, you say?" Lorenzo inquired.

Andrea pointed towards the sky.

The three men looked up. A sky filled with brilliant stars filled their vision.

"That sounds like him…" Scott whispered.

"Such a clever thing to say," Lorenzo sighed. "A sky full

of stars is certainly the flag of the night."

"Back then, I couldn't stand the thought of being tied down to my family name. I wanted nothing to do with a flag that would follow me everywhere I went. But after losing my home for good, I finally understand. It is truly wonderful to have a place that you and your comrades can depend on."

The three silently gazed at the night sky as if they had forgotten how to speak.

Lorenzo was the first to open his mouth.

"Just the other day, there was an envoy group from a country called Japan who came to sightsee in Venice. I hear that their country is on the farthest Eastern end of the world, even beyond Goa and Manila."

Lorenzo continued to speak as the other two listened, unsure of what he was talking about.

"Even in a place that far away, a country exists. This world is huge. From the eastern to the western reaches of the world, there is unlimited land on which to build a new country. And wherever that may be, this flag will undoubtedly be flying high!"

Lorenzo's face flushed with excitement as he pointed at the sky with renewed enthusiasm.

Andrea and Scott both nodded firmly in agreement, though somewhat surprised by Lorenzo's unexpectedly passionate words.

Due to the rebellion caused by the Three Great Clans, House Tepes had fallen. Yet, from the roots of that broken tree, new leaves were surely beginning to grow.

The flag of a million stars fluttered, as if watching over the three very different men.

End

TIME TO HUNT

STORY
Tikurakuran

ILLUSTRATION
Nozomu Tamaki

Vampire @3ch Forum
- This is a place to discuss vampires whose existence has been confirmed, and the Vampires-Only Zone, "Vampire Bund."
- For vampire-related topics in entertainment media such as movies, novels and anime, please post on their specific forums.
- We make no guarantees that posts where an individual claims to be a vampire, or posts with inside information about the Vampire Bund, are true or accurate. Please use that information at your discretion.

Read Before Posting | 3Channel Guide | FAQ | Chat

Forum Board Table of Contents

[1.268] Vampire Bund Tour #44

1. Name: Nameless Blood Sucker 20XX/08/10 (Tue) 23:36:26 ID:ADXPm450
   This is no. 44 of the Vampire Bund Tour discussion thread.
   Please ignore any flaming.
   Please don't claim superiority through the number of times you've experienced the tours, since it's not productive.

   Previous thread:
   http://ieyasu.3ch.net/test/read.cgi/vampire/1422673871/

   Vampire Bund Tour Official Site:
   http://www.vampirebund.go.vb/japanese/kengaku
   Safety Information Home Page of the Vampire Zone Director:
   http://www.sdsa.go.jp/info/anzen/index.html

15. Name: Nameless Blood Sucker :20XX/08/13 (Fri) 09:55:16 ID:cgWwP8K8
    >> 10
    This your first time?
    First things first, take something to cover your neck.
    Wrap a scarf around like Yon-sama or Nakao Akira.

16. Name: Nameless Blood Sucker :20XX/08/13 (Fri) 20:40:55 ID:334j7uiB
    That new product packaged Stigma strawberry jam is pretty useful.
    It's easy to spread it on bread too.
    Just don't try to suck it like a vampire. Your blood sugar levels will shoot up and you'll die.

17. Name: Nameless Blood Sucker :20XX/08/14 (Sat) 04:27:19 ID:jwUUMvUK
    Did you guys hear that they're lifting the ban on night tours?

18. Name: Nameless Blood Sucker :20XX/08/14 (Sat) 09:47:17 ID:eobbPo/n
    >> 10
    Try giving someone in Bio tomato juice. 7 out of 10 get really pissed off.

19. Name: Nameless Blood Sucker :20XX/08/14 (Sat) 21:43:16 ID:KvkX+5tP
    >> 17
    Source?

20. Name: Nameless Blood Sucker :20XX/08/14 (Sat) 22:38:02 ID:wBZMSqeT
    I went on the tour today.
    There's a guy with a really bad attitude, what's the deal? Is he gonna die?

21. Name: 17 :20XX/08/14 (Sat) 22:56:03 ID:JwUUMvUK
    Here
    http://www.seriousmoonlight.co.vb/tour/pkg/a01.asp

22. Nameless Blood Sucker :20XX/08/14 (Sat) 23:14:13 ID:LS9UssR2
    Browser crasher thx

23. Name: Nameless Blood Sucker :20XX/08/15 (Sun) 02:12:20 ID:YhSEVRsG
    > 20
    Japanese is ok

24. Name: 17 :20XX/08/15 (Sun) 03:26:48 ID:GQu0L8zc
    It's not a browser crashing site!
    Look at the domain name. It's got the vb for Vampire Bund.

25. Name: Nameless Blood Sucker :20XX/08/15 (Sun) 10:26:48 ID:yFRng7R0
    Determining the credibility of a website from the domain name? How dumb can you be lol

26. Name: Nameless Blood Sucker :20XX/08/15 (Sun) 11:52:18 ID:WyOzx2JM0
    It's illegal no matter how you look at it.

3:30 A.M.

The red light district of the Vampire Bund was lively as always.

The main strip was decorated with gaudy neon lights and LED signs. Large screen displays on the walls of the buildings were blasting advertisements at full volume for Fanasonic Home Electronics and Orinoco Online Shopping, official suppliers for the vampires-only zone.

On the streets, vampires of all appearances and fashions were waltzing in every direction. A young boy who appeared to be no older than ten years old, who looked out of place in such a district, and a couple consisting of a girl wearing 1960s psycho-fashion and an old man with an Inverness coat from the Victorian era, were strutting the streets together. It was a unique scene, only visible in vampire cities where the actual age and the appearance of the inhabitants did not quite match.

Vampires, loyal to their desires, were unstoppable when it came to pleasure-seeking. In one corner, there were groups playing risky games like Russian roulette and Spanish-style duels, and in another corner, there was a couple entangled with each other, covered in Stigma, and entirely unconcerned by whoever saw them. It was not rare for a fight to break out over an accidental bump on the shoulder, and it would take the patrolling officers of the VGS to break them up.

The daily tradition of the Stigma rain was over and the peak of their excitement had passed, but the frenzied energy of the vampires still continued. Unlike humans, who headed home after midnight regardless of how much they loved the nightlife, vampires endlessly enjoyed themselves in full force; it was in their nature.

Even so, everything must come to an end, including times of pleasure.

Suddenly, the noisy background music of the city was cut off and replaced by a heavy ringing of bells that echoed throughout the entire Bund.

It was a signal that sunrise was within the hour.

The flow of vampires changed around the time the bell rang. They began heading towards the elevator stations placed throughout the city district, which took them down to the Geo Frontier residential area. Getting caught outside at sunrise would result in immediate death. While vampires did enjoy risking their lives, being left behind to burn was a messy death they would rather not face.

As the crowds dissipated from the streets, the bars and stores quickly closed up shop. Being vampires themselves, the employees had to return underground with the customers.

The bustle of the pleasure district was replaced with silence as the sky gradually turned a light blue.

6:00 A.M.

All the vampires who'd missed the elevators and been stuck shaking in the shadows with fear had been rescued, and the streets were completely deserted. The clear sunlight beamed mercilessly down, making it a place no vampire could survive.

The elevators started moving again. They went directly to the surface floor without making any stops. The massive doors parted with a dull sound.

A strange-looking group stepped out of the elevators.

They were covered from head to toe with white protective clothing, and their faces were guarded with thick, dark shields. Since their faces were hidden, they all had large numbers stamped on their chests and backs for easy identification.

There were several large trailers waiting for them in front of the elevator station. The back door had already been opened to reveal rows of carts. Each cart contained a large vacuum cleaner and cleaning tools.

The members of the group would split up into pairs, take

a cart, and use the ramp to ride it to the ground. The carts would continue on to the streets and disperse into all areas of the district.

They were known as the Cleaners.

Their job was to clean up and organize the streets and buildings that the vampires had trashed that night, all before night fell again. There were around two hundred Cleaners on the whole island.

Of course, they were also vampires, so their protective gear was vital for blocking UV rays. If their gear or face shield was damaged at all, it would mean their death.

There were many jobs that supported the Bund, but in terms of danger, the Cleaners were second only to the VGS. And apart from cleaning, they had another important duty.

Vampires, always impulsive and living in the moment, easily lost their lives through dangerous games and senseless accidents. At times, there could be more than a hundred lives lost over the course of one night. The Cleaners were also responsible for fetching the remaining ashes and belongings of the vampires who had perished.

The residents of the Bund were required to carry an ID card with an embedded GPS tag. The government located the cards that were still on the surface and used the information from them to determine the status of the cardholders. If they were alive, Beowulf would rescue them; if not, then it was a job for the Cleaners.

However, possession of an ID card was not strictly

enforced, so many vampires who disliked the idea of being easily located refused to carry their cards. Thus, the Cleaners had to search for and collect any piles of ash, regardless of whether they had information on that particular pile.

Once they found a dead vampire, they would collect his or her belongings and suck up the ashes with the vacuum, packing them in a bag to take back. They identified the dead by their ID cards or from the occupancy status of their homes. There was no method for finding out the cause of death. The majority of deaths were caused by illegal activities, but the government had its hands full taking care of the living, so following up on dead vampires was not a priority.

Since it was such a mentally and physically demanding job, most Cleaners were able-bodied single vampires rather than the Fangless, who often had families at home. Most of them were in it for the thrill of facing death head-on, with only their protective gear standing in the way.

But there was one more reason why the government chose to employ only vampires.

3:00 P.M.

The pairs of Cleaners finished their sections and went back to the elevator station, one after another. The first team to return was Number 5 and Number 13.

For Cleaner Number 5, the most painful part of the day was about to begin. The Cleaners had another job at this point. That job was to interact with the humans visiting the Bund.

When the Bund was first established, humans held a negative image of it, labeling it a "Den for Vampires." In order to improve this image, the government, taking the advice of a major advertising company, started the "Vampire Bund Tour." The ultimate goal of the tour was to show humans that vampires aren't legendary monsters, but rather a race of flesh and blood, very much like humans. However, the reactions of the humans who had participated were not what they had expected.

Naturally, the Bund during the day was almost empty of vampires, and the only vampires with whom the tourists could interact were the Fangless who worked in the shops. However, the human tourists complained that it was pointless shaking hands and taking pictures with a vampire with no fangs. Ironically, it was the "Den of Vampires" that they wanted to see.

A tour at night—when the city would be crawling with fanged vampires—was far too dangerous and out of the question. As a compromise, the Cleaners, who were out on the surface already during the day, were appointed to interact with the tourists. The Cleaners all had fangs, and with their face shields in place there was no risk of them impulsively biting the humans. Even if they forcefully tried to, they would be the ones to end up dead, turning into ash from exposure to sunlight.

The tours were very popular. The Bund Maniacs, humans who regularly participated in the tours, nicknamed them "Biohazards." Some partook in the tours multiple times to take pictures with the various Cleaners and tracked their collections online.

Some of the Cleaners were enthusiastic and friendly. Number 5, however, wanted nothing to do with that nonsense. The only reason Number 5 had taken the job was because it meant keeping interactions with others to the bare minimum. Number 5 had once asked to be transferred to an area where there were no tourists. However, as to be expected from a former bureaucrat of the Li Clan, the commissioner-in-charge would not even consider the request, stating that they had no obligation to grant position transfers due to personal preferences.

Number 13 had a cheerful personality and was well-liked by the tourists. Even now, he was chatting happily with a regular member of the tour. A human close by seemed to want to take a picture, but Number 5 deliberately ignored it.

Then the heartwarming mingling time between the two races came to an end, and the bus carrying the humans drove off. It was time for a short break, after which they put away their tools and finally finished for the day.

When Number 5 looked up from the bench, Number 13 was casually walking away from the others, disappearing down into an alleyway in the shopping district.

Lately, Number 13 had been wandering off during their break every few days. Number 5 was usually unconcerned with others' affairs, but Number 13 was a partner and couldn't be left alone. Number 5 stood up and followed Number 13.

Number 13 left the main street and entered an area lined with modern skyscrapers.

Unbeknownst to the humans, the floors above the fifth in this area were hardly ever used. Regardless, the lights on all floors were lit up at night. They did that to keep the humans from discovering that the majority of the Bund and its population were actually underground.

Number 13 paced quickly, as if he was wary of being followed. His shadow, lengthened by the setting sun, crawled quickly across the deserted asphalt.

When Number 5 turned the corner after Number 13, Number 13 had disappeared.

Number 5 looked around the area, but he was nowhere to be found. *He must have entered one of these buildings.*

Number 5 stopped to think. Break time was almost over; Number 13 would be back by then. *I can just ask him where he went when he comes back.*

As Number 5 turned around to head back, an ear-splitting sound came from overhead.

Looking up, Number 5 saw shards of glass and two figures flying out of the side of a building.

They're falling straight toward me.

Number 5 instinctively pressed up against the wall, and at that instant, the falling objects passed by.

The glass shards shattered as they hit the pavement and sparkled in the reflected rays of the sun. Right after, two bodies bounced with a dull sound and rolled onto the ground. One of the bodies was that of Number 13.

Lying face up where he landed, Number 13's face instantly began to burn in the sunlight. White smoke poured out from all over his face like tiny geysers. He screamed and covered his face, but it was too late—the cells in his body had already begun to die. As he writhed in agony, his body shrunk as it turned into ash inside of the protective gear. The entire process was seared into Number 5's eyes.

Number 13's screams cut off when his body stopped moving.

Number 5 warily walked towards Number 13 and peeked inside of the protective gear. There was nothing but ashes left.

Number 5 looked at the other body that had fallen with Number 13. He looked like a middle-aged man wearing a plain suit. His head had cracked open and splattered brain fluids on the pavement; he was clearly dead. But the man did not seem to be turning into ash, despite being exposed to the sunlight.

This man was human.

After realizing the seriousness of the situation, Number 5 quickly ran off to notify the government, not noticing the strange thing about Number 13's remains.

The area where Number 13 and the man had fallen was immediately sealed off by Beowulf, who promptly began an investigation.

As the first one on the scene, Number 5 was excused from the rest of the shift and directed to assist the police. The officer was a man who looked Japanese and introduced himself as Inspector Hama.

Number 5 knew about the one human who resided in the Bund. Although incidents on the surface during the daytime were usually handled by Beowulf, Hama was called this time because of the human involved.

"Let's see... Che... Chak..." Hama stammered, narrowing his eyes at the memo pad in his hand.

"Connie will do," Number 5 said in a husky voice.

"Excuse me, Connie-san. You were born in Jhansi, India, in the year 1839; is this correct?"

Connie nodded slightly inside the protective gear.

"Sorry, but could you please respond aloud? It's hard to see because of the mask."

"That's right." Connie's tone was unfriendly, like bits of words being carelessly thrown on the ground.

"According to the ID we found in his belongings, the human who fell with Kincaid was named Nonomura Kouji, a physician. Do you recognize him at all?"

Number 13's name was Kincaid. Connie had forgotten

his name long ago—they hadn't used each other's names on the job.

"No, not at all."

"Did you ever hear his name from Kincaid?"

"No."

Connie continued giving terse, one-word answers. There was no obligation to give the police anything extra; the inspector wasn't a tourist.

"Inspector Hama!" One of the Beowulf members came out of the building and called over, "We found this put aside in the room that the two men fell from."

The object he brought to them was a face shield. It was inside an evidence bag, but it was obvious at first glance that it hadn't been broken.

"It was *put aside* somewhere? It wasn't on the ground?" Hama asked.

"No. It was sitting on the desk."

It finally clicked in Connie's head. Kincaid had burned to death so easily because he didn't have a shield on his face. It hadn't been broken in the fall; he'd taken it off for some reason.

Hama analyzed the shield with sharp eyes. He then directed those eyes at Connie.

"Connie-san, how long have you and Kincaid been partners at your job?"

"About three months."

"Did he ever invite you to do a side job? Anything

unrelated to your normal work?"

"No, never. What are you talking about?"

Hama did not respond, but stared into Connie's eyes.

Connie stared back at Hama. The intensity of Hama's eyes was abnormal. If he stared at suspects like that, they'd probably give up right away. Connie could sense that he wasn't just a regular policeman.

Hama's expression softened and he returned the face shield to the Beowolf member.

"Thank you. You're free to go. If you remember something, or if there's anything you want to tell me, please don't hesitate to contact me. You can reach me at any time, night or day."

Hama handed over a business card with his contact information. Of course, Connie had no intention of contacting him.

Connie promptly left the site and rode the elevator down to the underground residential area.

The Cleaners' changing room was deserted. It was two hours past their scheduled ending time, though, so that was expected.

Connie removed the face shield and tore off the hood.

Beneath the hood was a small face covered in sweat. Dark cocoa-colored skin, deep-set eyes, a sharp nose and large black pupils—typical features for an Indian woman.

Connie threw the shield and hood into the collection bin

and started taking off the protective gear. Once the heavy gloves were removed and the thick vinyl on the suit's upper body was opened up at the front, a petite but shapely pair of breasts was exposed.

As Connie slid the rustling protective gear down to her ankles, her body was finally able to breathe the outside air again. She had a flat stomach with clearly defined abdominal muscles, surprisingly full hips and thighs, and firm calves with muscles like springs.

Inside of the protective gear, she was completely naked. Sweat dripped from her body, and her smooth, dark skin gave off a luster like it was coated with oil. At first glance, her naked body was perfect in every way. But seen from the back as she headed to the shower room was a different story.

Connie's back was covered with scars of all shapes and sizes. Her back must have been pierced countless times; there were keloids from old scars in between the newer marks, running from left to right. It was as if her skin had been torn off, ripped into pieces, and then put together again like a jigsaw puzzle.

When Connie had applied for the job, the recruitment staff had explained that they had no separate changing room for women, but Connie insisted that she didn't mind sharing the room with the others. Any sense of embarrassment from being seen by the opposite gender had been lost to her over a hundred and fifty years ago.

On her first day, her male co-workers hadn't even

bothered to hide their lewd stares. Once they laid eyes on the scars on her back, though, they all averted their eyes and never looked directly at her body again. They'd found her back so disturbing that they lost any sexual interest in her.

Connie took the pin out of her hair as she walked. Her long, shimmering, black hair fanned out and slid over her back, hiding her scars.

Connie entered the shower room and leisurely took a hot shower, too hot for any normal human. This was her usual ritual at the end of the workday.

She paused from washing and looked down at her feet.

Ravi was curled up on the tiled floor.

No, "curled up" wasn't right. His body only consisted of a chest and arms—he looked like he was crawling out of a manhole with only his arms and upper body showing through the hole. He was looking down at the floor, silently letting the shower water rain down on him. Hot drops of water fell from the tips of his wet hair.

It had been almost five years since Ravi last appeared in front of Connie, and it was the first time since she'd moved into the Vampire Bund. Perhaps today's incident had led to his appearance. She had been careless. After all, she'd chosen her job because of the lack of stimulation.

They tied Ravi's body to the muzzle of a cannon and fired it.

Connie gazed at the top of Ravi's head; he remained silent. She couldn't see his expression with his face down.

The instant she saw Ravi's body explode into pieces and

scatter, her heart died.

Ravi's skin was drained of any color; it was grey like wet newspaper.

It was not too long afterward that her physical body faced death as well.

Ravi's body was torn right under his chest, and bits of his torn skin and thick blood vessels were streaming in the flowing water. The lack of blood made him seem even more unreal.

If Ravi had not died then, would they have had a family together and lived happily? No, it was more likely that they both would have died in battle. Still, they wouldn't have had to be apart for so long.

Connie's hands brushed mechanically through her hair as she became lost in her thoughts. After a long shower, she headed to her locker.

She dried her body and put on a plain pair of underwear. Then, still facing the locker, she asked, "Do you want to be charged an observation fee?"

At the end of the aisle of lockers, a man was standing with his back to the wall. The man had his hands behind him and was silently watching Connie change, from start to finish.

The man was Caucasian and looked to be about fifty, but appearances were unreliable for determining the age of a vampire. He had no tie; he wore a black turtleneck sweater under a dark brown jacket. He had silver-framed glasses and a full mustache. At first glance, he gave the impression of a mild-mannered college professor—except for the icy glare that couldn't be hidden from his eyes.

"Konkana Chakravarti, am I correct?"

It was the first time she had been called by her full name since she became a vampire. Those who had known her name had all died before her transformation.

"How do you know that?" She asked bluntly.

The man shrugged. "My position gives me access to the name of every resident of the Bund."

"And who are you?"

"I currently don't go by any special name. My master calls me the Librarian."

The Librarian waited for Connie's reaction, but she ignored him and continued putting on her clothes.

It was the Librarian who spoke first. "I have a favor to ask of you. We would like you to take over the job that Kincaid was responsible for."

Connie did not stop to look at the Librarian's face and kept on with what she was doing.

"I'm already doing that. I don't need you to tell me."

The Librarian smiled bitterly and shook his head. "I'm not talking about that garbage collection you do. This is something on a much higher level, an extremely important task, vital to House Tepes."

Connie remembered Hama's words: *a side job.* She stopped her hands.

"Does this have something to do with that dead human from today?"

"We were extremely disappointed by Kincaid. He must have been struck by extreme hunger or the desire to become a master; who knows. But trying to take something that isn't his? He needed to learn his place."

Connie, upon hearing the Librarian's words, figured out what had happened. Kincaid had tried to 'snack' on the human, and he had met with severe resistance, resulting in his death.

"So this 'important task' is kidnapping humans and making them one of us?"

"It is. Look at your co-workers. They're all just a bunch of thrill junkies seeking excitement through risking their lives. If left alone, all of them would be killed over something pointless, and the population of the Bund would only decrease. That loss must be compensated for. And that's where we come in."

The Librarian fixed his gaze on Connie and slowly stepped towards her. Connie felt some kind of strong pressure and couldn't move.

"Let me tell you something interesting. Currently, the only legal way for normal humans to step inside the Bund is that foolish sightseeing tour. Before they enter the island, there is a roll call of all participants. However, when they leave the Bund, they don't confirm the number of humans. Do you understand what that means?"

Of course Connie understood. If there were any humans who did not leave the Bund after entering, there was no way to know.

"Her Majesty strictly forbids us from attacking and forcefully turning humans into vampires, but she does not forbid humans who desire to become vampires by their own will from doing so. Rather, as you can tell from the roll call system, she endorses it."

Connie had completely stopped changing at that point. The perfect King's English accent with which the Librarian spoke was unpleasant to her ears, but somehow he possessed the ability to make her listen to him.

"Earlier, you said that we 'kidnap' humans, but we never forcefully take them. We only invite the ones that wish to become vampires by their own choice."

Connie's voice was flat. "No matter how you word it, in the end, it's still a hunt for humans."

"I'd say it's closer to 'fishing' than 'hunting.' I use the internet to disperse information that attracts vampire candidates." The Librarian did not show any reaction to Connie's words at all; rather, he seemed to enjoy her dour comments. "Eternal youth and life, superhuman strength, sexual prowess, escape from reality, curiosity... The reasons humans wish to become vampires are endless. Stimulating their latent desire to become a vampire and guiding them to the Bund is my role. Kincaid's role was to be the intermediary responsible for taking the human to the master."

"Logic aside, in the end you just want to increase the size of your forces."

"You know, we're not volunteers. Who would condemn us for acting under Her Highness' orders in a way that may ultimately result in a gain for us?"

Connie had a strange feeling. Her agitated emotions wanted to refute the Librarian, yet it did not feel right to cut him off and leave. Perhaps he was a member of the higher ranks, similar to her long-dead mistress.

"Why did you choose me? It could have been anyone."

"This job requires a high level of self control. Kincaid fell short on it and lost his life. But I believe you possess the ability to restrain yourself. Don't you agree?"

Indeed, she did have good control of herself, and that quality would definitely become necessary, sooner or later.

Without realizing it, Connie was left with only one option.

Connie sat down on her couch as soon as she returned to her room.

Her room was a standard one-person home in the underground residential area, and all of her furniture and electronics were items distributed by the government. They were adequate for their functions, but were completely generic.

Vampires who wished to add color to their lives shopped in the residential area's shopping district or online. Being in Japan, some replaced their government-issued furnishings with higher quality Japanese products, and there were even some who became huge fans of idols, influenced by the Japanese media.

Connie's room only had two items that could be called unique.

One of them was the large corkboard that hung on the wall with many printouts of images that she had found online pinned to it. Most of them were related to Jhansi, her hometown. There were pictures of the Jhansi Castle, which had now become a tourist destination, and others of the lush nature which had remained unchanged throughout the years.

In the middle of the board was the most striking picture. It was a portrait of a woman, the very woman whom Connie had served when she was still human. She was wearing a sari and armor with sword and shield in hand, and she looked straight out from the painting with a composed expression. She was a woman known as the "Joan of Arc of India."

Connie found that label revolting. Why go through the trouble of comparing her to some woman from Europe? "The Rani of Jhansi" was more fitting and sufficient to laud her name.

Connie's original reason for leaving India and moving to the Bund was this: she saw that gallant woman who had fought to her death for the pride of her country echoed in Queen Mina Tepes, who had successfully revived her homeland from utter destruction after years of struggle.

The other unique item was on the opposite wall from the board.

Connie called it her "Other Half." After becoming a vampire, she had wandered throughout India with nothing but the clothes on her back, but this item had never left her hand. She had lost her parents at a young age, so she learned how to construct and use it from her grandfather. He was the number one expert in the village. She had inherited his skills and became one of the best in all of Jhansi.

After moving to the Bund, she had tried to find materials for its maintenance, but no store carried the items she needed even though Japan was supposed to be one of the most resourceful countries in the world. In the end, she had to order online through Orinoco. The deliveryman, although used to strange and eccentric orders for vampires, could not help but inquire at her odd request.

"What are you going to use a bull's Achilles tendon for?"

The Librarian had said that her first job was tomorrow. A human he'd lured in was supposed to come to the Bund disguised as a tourist. If everything proceeded as he'd told her, she should be able to finish the job simply and easily.

Most of her thoughts were concentrated on Ravi.

If it followed the usual pattern, Ravi's illusion would appear before her every day for about two weeks. On the last day, he would pass judgment on Connie.

Since she became a vampire, Connie had been judged by Ravi over and over. She had high hopes this time. Her circumstances were different from when she had no choice but to live in the human world as an outsider. Now she was surrounded by her own race and living peacefully.

Perhaps this time.

Connie gazed at her "Other Half."

Perhaps.

The Next Day

As expected, there was a man among the tourists wearing the clothes that the Librarian had described. It appeared that he had received instructions as well; he kept glancing at Connie.

Connie casually approached him, and the man stuck his hand out for a handshake. Connie accepted his hand and used the handshake to pass along a small map.

The regular tourists in the group moaned in jealousy as they saw the man shaking hands with Number 5, notorious for her unfriendliness among the Cleaners.

The man would not be returning to the tour bus; instead, he would hide on one of the higher floors of the building indicated on the map. Connie would go to the building during her break and confirm that the man was hiding safely. At night, the Librarian's envoy would come to get the man and take him to the master.

Those were the steps for this "side job."

When Connie came to check on the man during her break, he was curled up in a corner on the empty floor.

The man noticed Connie and stood up. He hurriedly approached her and started rapidly spouting words in a one-sided conversation.

"Uh, um… Is it really true that you can attain eternal youth and life when you become a vampire? I want to live forever. You know, I'm—how do you say this?—I'm really scared of dying, like, really scared. And I was looking online, and it said that if I become a vampire, I could stop aging and I would never die, and…"

It seemed like he would keep talking forever if she didn't stop him. Even a neurotic human like this one could be of some use as a disposable pawn once taken into the vampire hierarchy. Humans like him, with strong desires and wishes, were the ones who found themselves easily caught in the Librarian's trap.

She had no intention of lending an ear to his nonsense.

"I don't know. Someone will come to get you at night, so ask them. Make sure you don't step outside this room once the sun goes down."

Her directions give, Connie quickly left without giving him any more time to speak. She had satisfied the terms of the job that the Librarian had given her. Now it was of no concern to her what happened to the man.

In the shower room, Ravi appeared as she had expected.

His body lay still with the shower water hitting him, but there were some slight changes.

Yesterday, his face had not been visible at all. Now, she could see the tip of his nose and his eyebrows.

Ravi was trying to raise his face, little by little. If it went as usual, he would slowly bring his face up toward Connie. Finally, once he was completely facing up and they could see eye to eye, he would pass his judgment.

Ravi's judgment would determine Connie's next actions.

Connie indifferently washed herself as her body quivered from hope and anxiety.

Every two days or so, a human who'd been lured to the Bund by the Librarian appeared in the tour groups.

The humans varied in gender and age, but the one thing they all had in common was the unfounded optimism that their lives would somehow improve if they just became a vampire. To Connie, who had experienced all the gains and losses of becoming a vampire, it was utterly ridiculous nonsense. However, she had no intention of dissuading them. She actually envied them for being able to make that choice themselves.

When she had become one…

Whenever she thought of it, she felt something hideous inside of her awaken. She tried her best to clear her mind and mechanically finish up her job as the middleman.

One night, Connie went back to the building where the human she had checked on earlier was hiding.

Eventually, she saw a single sedan drive up slowly and park in front of the building. All of the passenger doors opened; the driver remained in the car.

The first one to get out of the car was a large man with a bull neck whose corpulent muscles were like armor. He was apparently a bodyguard, since he looked around cautiously as soon as he exited the car, his giant body swaying.

Following him was a skinny man with tattoos covering the right side of his thin face and neck.

The last one was a red-haired man who sported stylish leather from head to toe. From his demeanor, he appeared to be the leader of the group, but he did not seem the type to have men like the Librarian serving under him. These men were most likely middlemen like Connie.

The three men entered the building together.

After a little while, the three became four and exited the building. The fourth was the woman Connie had met during the day. She seemed intimidated by the rough-looking men surrounding her.

The woman sat sandwiched between Redhead and Tattoo in the back seat of the car. Bull Neck checked the area one last time and sat in the front passenger seat, and the car drove off in the direction of the harbor area.

It seemed to Connie that their master must be very high

ranked to take all these steps for a single human.

But Connie didn't care either way.

Two weeks had passed since Ravi first appeared. Today, Connie led the sixth human to the usual hiding spot.

The man freely spoke of why he wanted to become a vampire. Apparently, he was a historian at a university; he had appeared on television and was quite well-known. He planned to become a vampire as part of his fieldwork—to interview the resident vampires in the Bund who were from various eras in history. Hearing these invaluable anecdotes directly from those who had actually lived in those times would significantly advance his research. Many parts of history had only been passed on as literature and stories passed down through the generations; the vampires could give first hand accounts.

The man had even found out somehow that he could revert back to being a human if he took a vaccine within the first forty-eight hours of becoming a vampire, and he boasted that if he had two days, he would be able to interview at least thirty people.

The man attempted to interview Connie, but she flatly refused. Of course, she did not bother to warn him that he would not be able to access the vaccine without the master's approval.

Connie headed to the shower room with a tense expression after she finished her work. Today was the day Ravi would pass his judgment. His face had already turned completely upwards. Now, she just needed to wait for his eyes to open.

Connie tried to calm her eagerness as she washed her body as usual. Then, she deliberately looked at the floor.

Ravi was there, indifferently letting the shower water fall on his upturned face. His eyes were still closed.

Connie stopped what she was doing and stared at Ravi's face.

Soon. It would start soon.

Ravi's eyelids twitched. It was not just Connie's imagination; they had definitely moved. Her eyes were glued to Ravi's face as if she was possessed.

At last, Ravi's eyes began to open. His eyelids gradually moved upwards at a frustratingly slow pace.

Connie could barely stay standing from her extreme anxiety, so she grabbed onto the showerhead for support.

Ravi's eyes, in the shape of a sideways new moon, became a crescent moon, and then a half moon, inching closer to full.

Finally, Ravi's eyes opened completely.

The eyes that had once enchanted Connie, the clear, pure black eyes that looked like ebony dissolved in water...

...were not there.

Instead, there sat in Ravi's eye sockets only the remains of his eyes, cloudy-yellow like sulfurous springs that were just about to rot and melt away.

She had failed again.

Every time Ravi's illusion appeared, Connie hoped. It made no difference to her if he was just an illusion or if his body was ripped in half. She wanted him to gaze upon her face just one more time with the eyes that had always looked at her with such love.

In the past one hundred and fifty years, her wish had never been granted.

Was he worried about the future of his homeland, India? Was he trying to look after Connie? Connie tried every method she could think of, almost to the point of insanity, to get Ravi's eyes back.

In the end, although India had regained its independence after World War II and even enjoyed great success through sudden economic growth, Ravi's eyes did not return. And now, even after Connie had found a safe place to live in the Vampire Bund, Ravi's eyes still weren't back.

Connie peeled her gaze away from Ravi.

She had been showered with shrapnel from an explosive, and she was on the verge of death from the injury.

Connie's grip on the showerhead tightened.

She woke up gasping for air, lying on the ground face up, looking at the night sky.

The showerhead broke in half with a crack under the vampire's inhumanly strong grip.

A man she did not know had pinned her down and was

biting her neck.

The hot water burst out of the broken showerhead and forcefully blasted Ravi in the face, but his eyes remained open and he did not budge.

She felt the life drain out of her through a different route than the scars on her back.

Connie tore at her head and violently bent backwards with such force that she could have broken her spine.

She gathered the last of her strength and stabbed the man in the back with the arrow in her hand.

Connie suddenly opened her eyes and mouth, and let out a silent scream.

She fell unconscious as she listened to the man's final scream of death.

Connie continued screaming with a voice that only she and Ravi could hear.

When she opened her eyes again, covered in blood and ashes, she was no longer human.

Ravi gazed at her with his rotted eyes, yellow like a maggot's underside.

She couldn't live with eyes like those staring at her. She would need to send him back to the world beyond as usual and hope for a better outcome next time.

There was only one thing left for Connie to do.

Redhead sighed as he watched the city lights go by from the car window.

Humans who wanted to be vampires were usually eccentric in some way, but this historian was particularly annoying.

When they went to retrieve him that night, the man bombarded them with questions about their origins—when and where they'd been born—as soon as they walked into the room. He had been so pushy with them that Bull Neck had to strike him. At least that had finally shut him up.

Now the man was sitting silently in the middle of the backseat with a swollen cheek. He seemed bewildered by the discrepancy between what he had expected and what was actually happening. Most humans became docile from the anxiety. *What do these humans expect of the Bund, anyway? Do they think we have some kind of welcoming ceremony prepared for them or something? Idiots...*

The car felt crowded with four vampires and one human. The massive size of Bull Neck, who took up a lot of space sitting in the passenger seat, made the already small interior feel even more cramped. Even for the vampires, who were normally able to adapt to new environments quickly, the situation was unpleasant.

I just want to drop this human off at the master's place so I can go out to the pleasure district. A new club had opened featuring young Japanese vampire girls; that sounded interesting. All of the girls' ages supposedly matched their appearance, and nothing could beat that pure innocence…

"What's that?" The driver muttered.

"Something the matter?" Redhead asked.

"Look at that…" The driver pointed ahead, so Redhead leaned forward and looked through the windshield from between the two front seats.

There was a pedestrian bridge over the road they were driving on. A shadow stood on the bridge.

More accurately, the shadow was not on the normal walkway. Rather, the slim figure's footing was firmly planted on top of the narrow railing. Without an extremely good sense of balance, it would be a nearly impossible stunt. Behind the figure, a large crescent moon shined blue, making only the figure's silhouette visible to them.

The figure had a long, thin pouch at its waist and was holding something that looked like a curved stick in its hand. The stick bent backwards on both ends, and it was shaped like a horizontally flattened version of the letter omega. It was about the size of a small harp, and the figure was holding it in one hand at the middle of the curve.

The figure pulled out one straight stick from the pouch and crossed it with the curved stick in front of its chest. Then the figure pointed the straight stick at the car.

"A bow…?"

Just as the driver murmured those words, a small hole opened up in the windshield and the long stick came flying in. The stick flew through the openings of the steering wheel and lodged in the driver's chest—it was an arrow.

The driver died instantly and immediately turned into ash. His ashes filled the interior of the small car, and the passengers fell into confusion as they were robbed of the ability to both see and breathe.

When they finally regained their vision, the car was rapidly speeding towards a thick pillar. There was no time to react; the car crashed straight into a streetlight pole at full speed.

The windshield shattered, and the four passengers in the car violently collided with the dashboard and the backs of the front seats. At the same time, the broken streetlight fell onto the car and struck the roof, which caved in and folded into a jagged M.

The passengers escaped one after another, white from the ash. They stood up to look at the bridge, but the figure was no longer there; it was now standing before them.

The figure had a piece of cloth wrapped around its entire head like a turban, obscuring its face. It wore a black tank top that exposed its dark skin and muscular shoulders and arms. The bottom half of its body was contrastingly thick, and was decked with cargo pants and high-laced shoes.

Bull Neck regained his composure first and howled at the silhouette.

"You! Who sent you?!"

The figure swiftly fixed an arrow on the bow and shot it at Bull Neck.

The arrow cut through the air with a sharp sound and hit Bull Neck right in the chest. Bull Neck looked down nonchalantly at the arrow sticking out of his body.

"You think you can kill me with some little dart?"

Bull Neck pulled out the arrow and tossed it to the ground. It seemed his unusually thick muscles had stopped the arrow.

A moment later, Bull Neck noticed the shape of the figure's chest.

"You're a woman?"

At that realization, a lewd expression spread across Bull Neck's face. He turned and looked at Redhead.

"Boss, can I?"

Redhead smiled bitterly. "Just try to finish up quickly. The master's waiting."

Tattoo shook his head with a look that said *guess it can't be helped*. Only the human stared at the figure with a serious expression.

Bull Neck started striding towards the figure confidently. He flexed his shoulders and arms.

"Hey, how about you put down that little toy of yours and play with me?"

Bull Neck's muscles suddenly swelled, somehow growing even bigger. His entire body increased in size and his clothes began to split. The skin that showed through his torn up clothes was covered in black fur.

The figure silently watched Bull Neck's transformation without making a move to attack.

Bull Neck, now in his true form, looked strangely like a grizzly bear with a human head.

"You know, it's fun tormenting women in my true form—though I go too far sometimes and end up tearing off their heads," Bull Neck laughed roughly.

The figure fixed another arrow on her bow and shot at Bull Neck. The arrow hit the exact same spot as the last one.

As before, Bull Neck was not affected in the slightest.

"I said, throw that toy away!"

Bull Neck irritably yanked the arrow out and dashed on all fours towards the figure, just like a grizzly bear. He moved unexpectedly quickly for his enormous size.

Despite Bull Neck charging towards her like a runaway train, the figure did not even twitch. She smoothly pulled a new arrow from her quiver. The shaft of the arrow was larger than the previous arrows, with a larger, sharper arrowhead; it even seemed to give off a heinous aura.

The figure fixed the arrow with confident hands and steadied her aim at Bull Neck. The tough bowstring was pulled to its limit, and the figure's powerful biceps flexed.

The eyes of the figure peeking through the turban did not move; they were fixed on Bull Neck as he ran straight for her.

Bull Neck jumped several meters before reaching the figure and flattened himself out in midair as if to smother her with his attack. Giant claws stuck out of his thick-fleshed hands. With one swipe, he could probably split her in half.

The instant that Bull Neck leapt into the air, the figure

released the arrow at his exposed chest.

The thick arrow flew through the air right toward him and hit him in the same spot for the third time.

This time, the arrow pierced deeply, digging into his chest up to the feathers on its tail end.

Bull Neck's face contorted in bewilderment, and then his massive body scattered into ashes, raining down on the figure.

To Redhead and the others, it looked like he exploded.

Once the ashes settled, the figure was standing in the same position as before. She started slowly walking towards them.

"Hyaaaaah!" Tattoo screamed in fright.

Redhead pulled the knife from his belt awkwardly, still shocked by what had happened.

"We've gotta run!"

Redhead had not forgotten about his mission. He grabbed the human's arm and began running. Staying in that open area was basically asking to be a target.

Tattoo ran after him, flustered.

The human murmured in a small voice that no one could hear, "That bow…"

The group ran into an alleyway, trying to elude the figure. The slow human was a hindrance, but they couldn't forget their master's orders and abandon him.

The district they were in was one of the areas disguised to deceive humans, so it remained empty throughout the day.

If the figure had purposely attacked them here, then she was quite a formidable opponent. *There must be a great force backing her,* he thought.

Tattoo had passed Redhead, running wildly in a panic. He was free to run at his own pace, since he didn't have to tow a human along. He kept running further and further ahead of them out of fear, his own life being prioritized over the mission.

Tattoo turned a corner and disappeared from sight.

Redhead followed, turned the corner, and almost crashed right into Tattoo, who had stopped dead in his tracks.

Tattoo looked as if he was about to break down crying, and a gurgling sound came from his throat.

There was an arrowhead poking out about fifteen centimeters from Tattoo's Adam's apple. On the opposite site of his neck, the other end of the arrow stuck straight out. With every breath her took, a small amount of blood squirted out like a thin thread.

He reached out at Redhead with both arms as if asking for help as he staggered towards him. The blood inside his lungs made a splashing sound with every step he took.

All of a sudden, a sharp sound cut through the air, and an arrow penetrated the middle of Tattoo's chest. He fell to his knees as he was pushed down by the arrow's momentum, turning to ash while still kneeling.

Beyond the cloud of Tattoo's ashes, the figure stood at the end of the alley with her bow still ready.

The figure just stood there and didn't fire, as if mocking him.

"Come on!" Redhead dragged the human and turned back the way he came.

They reached the corner of a large container berth. There were containers of all sizes stacked everywhere; it was the ideal hiding place. Redhead thought to lose the attacker in this area, so he proceeded carefully, keeping an eye out for a good hiding spot.

Just then, an arrow crossed Redhead's vision and struck the side of the container right next to him. The arrowhead had penetrated the metal wall of the container and stuck straight out.

Redhead finally lost his cool, staring at the swaying arrow in front of his face. He purposely jumped out into an open area and pressed his knife against the human's throat. The human stiffened without a word.

"I know it's the human you're after! If you do anything else, he's dead! Put down that bow and come out!"

He had no idea why they had been attacked. The only way he could think of to get out of this situation alive was to use the human as a hostage. Redhead turned in circles searching for the woman, the human held against him as a shield.

There was no response. However, he was certain that she was watching him from somewhere nearby.

"Come out! I know you can hear me, damn it! If you don't

come out—"

Suddenly, a shrill sound like a whistle came from overhead.

When Redhead looked up, he saw a single arrow pierce the night sky.

He was nothing more than a thug; it was no surprise that he was unable to recognize the *kaburaya* whistling arrow when he saw it.

When Redhead looked back, the figure was standing right beside him. She had already readied the next arrow and aimed it directly at him.

He had no chance to react. The arrow barely brushed the human's throat and stabbed Redhead's hand that gripped the knife.

"Ahh!" Redhead and the human let out a scream together.

Redhead's right arm stretched out as the arrow pulled it, and the knife slipped out of his hand and hit the ground. He let go of the human's collar and reached for the knife with his other hand.

A moment later, another arrow flew through the air. It penetrated Redhead's left arm and dove into the ground.

Redhead screamed and tried to pull his left hand up, but the arrowhead had lodged itself deeply into the ground and wouldn't budge. Unable to pull out the arrow with his already-injured right hand, Redhead was pinned to the ground.

The figure calmly walked towards Redhead, who was struggling desperately on all fours. The figure stopped a few meters from him and produced an arrow from her quiver.

"Who in the world are you?! Why are you doing this?!"

The figure did not answer Redhead's cries, but instead silently pulled back the bowstring.

The arrow pierced his right thigh. It must have hit an artery; blood gushed out with surprising force. Redhead screamed again and began sobbing from extreme pain and fear.

"It hurts… Stop it, please! What's the point of all this…?"

The figure readied another arrow and pointed it at Redhead's chest.

He stared at the arrowhead with glazed eyes and sensed that his death was near.

"It's probably all pointless to you," Connie muttered as she released the arrow. There was no way she'd miss at that range.

Before Redhead's scattered ashes had even touched the ground, Connie turned her head and yelled, "Come out! If you don't, I'll kill you too!"

From behind one of the stacked containers, the human peered out.

"Come over here," Connie ordered in a hoarse voice.

Connie's mind was at peace, having easily killed four vampires. *I can still fight as a skilled warrior. Ravi must be at peace now, too.*

Since becoming a vampire, every time Ravi passed his judgment Connie would choose her prey and hunt them down with her beloved bow, her "Other Half." This was the only way to soothe her lover's soul and erase his illusion.

At first, she mainly targeted British officials stationed in the Indian government, but her prey changed along with the times. The bandits of Bihar, Pakistani soldiers who had invaded Kashmir, Soviet troops and Mujahideen in Afghanistan, the mafia in the city of Mumbai, the guerillas of the Taliban…

This was her first time hunting vampires, but the result was better than she had expected. There should be no need to go after the human as well.

The man, trembling, approached Connie slowly.

Connie noticed that the man's eyes were transfixed; not on her, but on her bow.

When the man reached Connie, he crouched down and observed the bow closely.

"This shape… that power… No doubt about it, this is a composite bow from the Mughal Empire!"

Connie looked at the man dubiously at his unanticipated words.

"There's some animal's—maybe a bull?—Achilles tendon and horns pasted onto both ends of the wood. Amazing, it's just like I've read about! I can't believe such a small bow could outdo that huge monster."

The man's perspective was certainly different. That was only to be expected, since his desire to become a vampire stemmed from his obsession with history. He had just witnessed the merciless slaughter of four vampires, yet he was completely consumed by Connie's bow.

"The construction technique was never passed down, and it's supposed to be impossible to recreate one of these... So, this is the Vampire Bund..."

The man finally looked up at Connie.

"You're from the Mughal Empire, right? Whose era were you born in? Aurangzeb? Akbar? Or maybe even the first Babur!"

Connie was offended by the man's arrogance as he disrespectfully named those honorable rulers without their proper titles.

Connie pressed her face against the man and bared her fangs.

"Eeeek!" The man let out a pathetic cry. He jumped backwards about two meters and fell on his behind.

"You still want to become a vampire?"

The man shook his head hastily at Connie's question.

"Then stand up." Connie's voice was as sharp as her arrows. "Stand up!"

The man awkwardly stood as if he were a marionette being pulled on its strings. Connie handed Hama's business card to the man.

"There's a human police officer at this address. Have him help you. Don't let any vampires spot you before dawn. Vampires don't attack humans just to increase our numbers; the majority will only see you as food. If you understand, go now."

The man hesitated, holding the card with both hands.

"Um… you're not going to take me there?"

"Why would I do that? Hurry up and go! I have things to do!"

The man hurriedly turned his back on Connie and hesitantly started walking. He disappeared into the darkness with unsteady feet, looking back at her from time to time.

There was less than a fifty percent chance of the man reaching Hama in his unstable state. Yet even that was of no concern to Connie. If the man spoke to Hama about her, she could simply deny whatever he said. After all, she was about to purge the evidence.

The moment the man disappeared from view, Connie set out on her mission.

She revisited the areas where she had killed the vampires and retrieved her arrows. She also collected any of their clothing that the arrows had pierced. As she had predicted, none of them were carrying an ID card. The windshield of the abandoned car was completely shattered, leaving no trace of where the arrow had broken through the glass.

All of the evidence was now gone. In the morning, the Cleaners for this area would discover the ashes and clean them up as one of the many unidentifiable deaths, just like they did every day.

The sky in the east was beginning to lighten.

The hunt was over; now it was time for her to return to

being a Cleaner.

If she headed back to the residential area and disposed of the evidence, she would make it just in time for work.

Connie left the hunting site behind with leisurely steps and headed towards the nearest elevator station.

The next day, Connie finished her job as a Cleaner nonchalantly. She was in a good mood and even agreed to pose for a picture with the tourists three times.

Ravi did not appear in the shower room. He was nowhere to be found on the tiles at her feet, and she purified her body in solitude for the first time in weeks.

When she returned to the locker room, the Librarian was waiting for her.

As before, she began changing without acknowledging the man. He began speaking to her without being asked.

"The human we had you escort yesterday has disappeared." The Librarian's expression was concerned, but there was no telling how he truly felt inside. "The intermediaries who were dealing with him vanished as well. Most likely, they're all dead."

Connie looked at the Librarian unconcernedly. She had nothing to fear. If the Librarian had realized that she was the culprit, he would not have come to see her all alone.

"I did what I was told to do," Connie said.

"Of course you did. I didn't come here to punish you. There's a force in the Bund that opposes our master. It interferes with our work occasionally."

The Librarian shook his head and sighed.

"What a pointless thing to do. We have unlimited replacements for men like them. Of course, for you and I as well. The only irreplaceable person in the Bund is Queen Mina."

"So, what do you want?" Connie's good mood did not mean she wanted to sit here and listen to him babble.

The Librarian shrugged. "I just came here to warn you. That's all. It would be troublesome if you were killed, too. Who knows what would happen if you were caught off guard, even if you are a survivor of the attacks by our British troops."

"What did you say?" Connie asked without thinking. She had never revealed her history to anyone in the Bund, let alone to the Librarian.

"You were in the mercenary army under Lakshmibai, correct? I knew the instant I found out your birth date and origins." The Librarian smiled at Connie. Two fangs peeked through his thick mustache. "What a coincidence. I witnessed Bahadur Shah and the second surrender at Delhi with my own eyes."

Connie understood. She and the Librarian were of the same era. And considering he was an Englishman present at the extinction of the Mughal Empire, his identity was obvious. He was a member of the East India Company, the very company that had robbed her country of independence.

"After the Indian Rebellion, the East India Company was forced to disband. We may have been enemies back then, but you and I are comrades who lost our place in the world around the same time. It's only natural that I am concerned about your safety."

His speech was full of the same presumptuousness as the former suzerain state.

Connie came to a decision.

Kill the Librarian.

He had let Rani Lakshmibai's name past his filthy lips, which was reason enough to kill him. However, to top it off, he had the audacity to say that the two of them were *comrades*. In his book, the extinction of the Mughal Empire and the disbandment of the East India Company were equal in the pain that those involved had experienced.

It would not be sufficient to end his life with her usual bow. *I'm going to torment him. I'll kill him slowly, in such a cruel way that no weak human could withstand it.*

Of course, she had no intention of doing so here and now. She would never break her own personal law, not after all this time. She was not like Kincaid.

Next time, when Ravi appears…

She had killed many Englishmen over the course of a hundred years, but it had been a long time since she'd targeted one who was directly involved in the deaths of Rani Lakshmibai and Ravi. She had no idea when Ravi would appear next—perhaps in one month, perhaps in ten years—but just imagining mercilessly killing the Librarian was enough to make her go weak at the knees from sheer pleasure.

Up until now, her manhunt had been only an inevitable ritual to send Ravi's illusion away. However, she now eagerly awaited the day when she could see Ravi again with his half-obliterated body.

She did not yet realize that her purpose and her means had switched places.

"Are you listening?"

Connie snapped out of her thoughts when she heard the Librarian's voice. He was unaware that he had just signed his own execution papers. Much like Connie, who still remained a warrior of the Mughal Empire, he too was still an Englishman of the nineteenth century. He had the arrogance to assume he understood the natives of the lands his country had enslaved.

Connie smiled—a gentle smile that she had never shown on her face before—and looked at the Librarian.

"Thank you for caring about me. So, when's the next job?"

End

THE SUN BEYOND THE WINDOW

STORY
Gemma

ILLUSTRATION
Nozomu Tamaki

When he heard that Noma Eriko had died, Daniel Kazuo Saji wasn't surprised. He didn't think it was impossible, based on her personality. But if she'd been *killed*... Well, that was a different matter.

The two policemen who visited him were visibly nervous. Saji doubted it was because of the murder case, but rather that this was probably the first time they had entered the Vampire Bund. The dental office—illuminated from corner to corner by white light panels and relaxing mood music, mixed with the high-pitched whine of the dental drills—was probably the most familiar place in the Bund for a human, but that didn't seem to reassure the visitors. It was four o'clock in the morning, an unthinkable hour for such a visit by human standards. The policemen would have been more nervous had it not been so close to dawn.

After the officers introduced themselves, the younger of the two wiped away his sweat and began to speak. "Ms. Eriko had the operation to become Fangless here, approximately six months ago. Is that correct?"

"That is correct. I was responsible for the operation." As he answered the question, Saji recalled his memories of the incident. "It was at the beginning of March. I can give you an exact date if I look at the medical records."

"Did you know that Ms. Eriko attended a school outside of the Bund?"

"Yes, she discussed it with me, and I advised her to do so."

"When was that?"

"Approximately one or two weeks after her fangs were removed."

"Did you hear anything about how she was doing at school?"

Next to the young policeman who quickly proceeded with his questions, the older policeman flicked his gaze across the room with an expressionless face. He probably thought that the pace of the questioning was too fast, but didn't want to linger here for longer than necessary, so he didn't stop his younger colleague.

After answering several of their questions, Saji asked one of his own.

"How did she die?"

The policemen taking notes stilled their hands for a moment and looked at each other. They gave off an aura of rapid, silent communication through their eyes. The younger one coughed slightly.

"She was exposed to the sun during the day, in the school

principal's office. The window was broken."

The school had a proper name, but most of the Fangless simply called it "the school." There had never been a school in the world where vampires could go to classes without hiding their natures, so it was a place that could be designated as "the school" without any further description.

The evening after the police had come to visit, Saji walked along the hallways of the school by himself. The beautiful checkered floorboards were made not from linoleum, but from real white oak and ebony. That sort of thing was to be expected, given that it was the school that Her Highness had attended. Another student formally welcomed Saji as he passed by.

It was already past midnight, but there were scattered presences around the campus. The school was open twenty-four hours a day to cater to vampire nighttime activities. *The teachers certainly have it rough,* Saji thought detachedly as he stopped in front of his destination. He straightened out his lapels slightly, then knocked and pulled open the door.

"Excuse me, Ms. Brussel. Hello."

"Doctor Saji, I've been waiting for you. It's been a long time."

The smell of antiseptics irritated his nose. An old woman spun her chair around and rose up to greet him. She wore a white coat draped over her small body, and her bound hair was as white as snow. She was the very picture of gentleness.

Although the school accepted Fangless students, the majority of the student population was still human, so it was important for a healthcare professional specializing in vampires to keep a tidy appearance and upright bearing. Ms. Brussel was a carefully selected individual who had also written books on child psychology; she was currently the only vampire allowed by the government to work outside of the Bund.

"The dentures you made for me fit extremely well and are very helpful. You came to ask about Miss Noma, correct?"

Saji sat in the chair she gestured to. Ms. Brussel drew over a teacart with a carafe of hot water and spoke in a gentle voice.

"Yes. I apologize for interrupting you while you're busy."

"Not a problem. I found the matter extremely suspicious."

She explained that two days earlier, during the daytime, multiple students had heard the sound of breaking glass from the direction of the principal's office. A group of students, led by the student council, had quickly gathered outside of the office to find the principal absent and the office door locked. A student had circled around to the central courtyard and found broken glass and a vampire who had turned to dust inside the room. Based on the remaining school uniform and student ID, it was determined that the remains were of second-year student Noma Eriko. The student who had discovered the remains "thought" he had seen her face while it disintegrated.

Nobody knew who threw the rock. The corner of the school that contained the principal's office had a certain level of security, and there was no place for an outsider to enter. While it was likely that the perpetrator was someone related to the school itself, it was still unclear whether this was a tragedy caused by a prank, or someone had performed the act with murderous intent.

"That's all I heard. I don't understand at all why Miss Noma was in the principal's office, or why she was killed." Ms. Brussel picked up a small cup with her thin, wrinkled fingers, added a bit of salt, and sipped at the water.

"How was Miss Eriko doing at school?"

"I think she was the same as before, when she attended school as a human. She was a very kind, sensitive girl and had some self-blaming tendencies." The old woman continued to look down at the cup and blew softly across the surface of the liquid. "It seems that she only became that way after her fangs were removed, though?"

"Well," Saji explained, "she was violent when she came to me; that's *why* her fangs were removed. It was a rare case to see nowadays."

Noma Eriko was one of the victims of a tragedy that had occurred at the school soon after establishment of the Bund, when a group of students turned into vampires lost control of themselves and attempted to gain control of the school. After the incident, the Bund had taken her in, as not even the vaccine would have worked by then, and her family had disowned her. It was, sadly, a common situation.

She hadn't exactly been a model student while alive, but nothing bad enough to make her parents cry—she'd exhibited the behavior of an ordinary delinquent acting out for attention. But, perhaps predictably, Eriko had turned violent after her family's sudden abandonment. Instead of going to the apartment she'd been given, she'd chosen to hang around amusement centers and pick fights with everyone. And on the rare instances she *had* returned, she had tried to bite her neighbors.

The frustrated neighbors had forcibly dragged her to the medical center, and her fangs had been removed as a result of her counseling. It was a very rare case because such violent vampires usually came to physical blows and got themselves killed before arousing any concern. In Eriko's case, several other classmates had all become vampires at the same time, so their collective emotional support had changed her future.

"There were other children from that incident who had their fangs removed, but none of them came here?" Saji asked.

"The only one who came back to school was Miss Eriko. We could have provided advice if they'd come."

"I see. Did she have any friends at school, or was she alone?"

Ms. Brussel frowned. "I think she'd grown apart from her old friends. But she tried to proactively seek out others, and was even a member of the photography club."

"Photography? I heard that she did swimming when she was alive."

"Yes, but the swimming club does not admit vampires."

Saji took a mouthful of the water that Ms. Brussel poured for him. The tongues of vampires could slightly taste salt, but he no longer remembered whether the taste was the same as when he'd been human.

"At a time like this, we wish we had Her Highness around," sighed Ms. Brussel. "She hasn't been here since the incident; she hasn't visited at all for over a month now. Maybe she's extremely busy?"

"The Bund has been in constant commotion recently. I assume that's been keeping Her Highness occupied."

"I suppose so," said Ms. Brussel sadly. She sipped another mouthful of water.

Saji drank up his own cup. He stared at the white porcelain at the bottom of the cup until his eyes hurt. He thought he saw a reflection of Noma Eriko's face in it, so he set it down on the table.

"Thank you for the drink. Ms. Brussel, the principal's office is currently empty, is that right?"

"I think there's one policeman," answered Ms. Brussel as she stood up and smiled softly.

Saji said his farewells and left the infirmary.

The door to the principal's office was made of solid

mahogany. It looked heavy, as though a metal slab stood inside the door, beyond the facade.

Saji pulled back the yellow tape and pushed opened the door slightly. He greeted the person inside.

"Hello. It must be hard to work this late."

"Oh, hey." The older policeman who had come to Saji's office the day before looked up. His surprised expression turned into a tired smile.

"There are some people you can't talk to unless it's nighttime," the officer explained. Saji remembered his name was Morita. "What's up?"

"I'm still thinking about the case. Can I see something?"

"Nn... Yeah." While Officer Morita seemed reluctant, he still waved Saji into the room without making an issue of it.

The office was luxurious and calm, with a deep red carpet. There was a sofa and table to the right of the entrance, a huge desk in the middle, and an empty, black leather chair behind the desk. A window behind the chair took up the entire wall opposite the entrance. Saji could see the well-tended bushes and ornamental fountain in the courtyard.

Someone had carefully covered the cracked window with a black, reflective sheet. The carpet underfoot had been cleaned, but Saji heard the tiny crinkling sound of powdered glass being ground into the carpet after each step. Tape cordoned off an irregular shape in a corner of the room; after a moment's thought, Saji realized that it indicated the location of the body. The place where the vampire had died was clean—no hint of blood or death. There would have only been a small pile of dust.

"What happened to the victim's remains?"

"I don't really know; they took them for identification. Maybe we need the help of your hospitals." The policeman gestured with his slightly crooked chin. "It seems as though she didn't have any family, so I'm not sure what will happen in the end..."

"There's a communal graveyard in the Bund. She'll be buried there." Noma Eriko's parents and siblings were still living on the mainland, but they wouldn't come to retrieve her dust.

"Even in our world, there's seldom anything you can determine from examining dust. But why was she in the principal's office in the first place?"

"That's a question I want answered, too. It just might lead to more answers."

Saji saw dark circles under the eyes of the stoically smiling man. It had only been three days since the beginning of this investigation, but he seemed to be extremely tired.

Saji could imagine how politically awkward a vampire death was in this particular location. He could easily see the Bund dispatching its own investigators, but that didn't seem to be the case. The Japanese government had sent detectives who were jumpy just visiting the Bund, so it didn't seem like *they* were honestly trying to resolve the situation, either.

In other words, no one had the time or the drive to

investigate this. Perhaps Saji and Ms. Brussel were the only ones who thought Noma Eriko's mysterious death should be resolved for the peace of the girl's own soul.

"A stone was thrown, and it broke the glass. Is that correct?"

"It landed somewhere around there." The policeman pointed to a depression—slightly smaller than a clenched fist—in one corner of the carpet. The rock itself had probably been taken by the police, but there were traces where it had pressed down into the carpet.

"This room is usually locked, right? Who has the keys?"

"The secretary, the vice-principal, and the student council... You really are curious." Officer Morita gave him a slightly wary smile.

Saji lifted a corner of his lips and showed the man his fangless mouth as he grinned. "That's because she was a patient of mine."

"You're very enthusiastic. Well, I'm leaving now."

"Thank you." Following his example, Saji exited the principal's office and closed the school gate.

He couldn't see the moon, but Saji could feel it setting in the west; he was very sleepy. Saji felt an indescribable sensation akin to irritation in his heart, and he resolved to help settle the girl's puzzling demise.

Perhaps it was fortunate that he'd noticed that the stock of anti-vampire vaccines in Ms. Brussel's infirmary was old.

He used the task of replacing it as an excuse to visit the school again.

How many years had it been since he'd gone outside during the day? Saji could feel the heat waves from the summer evening, even when walking through the air-conditioned, underground passageway. He was very conscious of the bright sun beyond the ceiling.

He could see the yellow sunlight slanting down on the turnaround on the stairwell to the first floor. Saji went up the stairs and stepped into the sunlight.

All of the windows in the school had reflective glass, rendering the sunlight harmless to vampires, even if they emerged in bright places. Even though he knew this, Saji was still uncomfortable. Looking at the school directory again, it seemed that he could reach his destination without having to go up another level. Saji turned around and went back down the stairs, then proceeded down the corridor while looking around at his surroundings.

He hadn't realized something the day before—despite the campus' many windows, not a lot of sunlight came through to the inside. More accurately, he saw clear divisions between the places where external light was present and where it was not. Thus a person could do most of his everyday school activities while staying within the latter zones. The building had been built with care.

There were two pools; the underground pool was larger and more extravagant than the one aboveground. He suspected it was not designed this way to increase the property value, but to make it convenient for vampires.

"There are still club members who resent this," the young head of the swimming club explained to him. Saji heard a mocking edge to the boy's tone over the echoes of splashing water and voices around them. "They refuse to participate in training sessions in the underground pool.

"I think it's ridiculous, though. But in the end, there weren't any other vampires who wanted to join the club."

The boy had loose, long hair and wore a jacket over his swimming trunks. He looked very shifty, but his answers were serious. Saji's visit as a doctor from the Bund didn't seem to faze the boy. It seemed there was good reason that this boy was also the student council vice-president.

"I heard that you were the first person to discover Miss Eriko," Saji said.

"Yes." The boy flashed a pained expression. His speech and actions seemed fake or overly exaggerated. *Maybe he's a narcissist or suffering from some other personality disorder,* thought Saji.

"I'd appreciate it if you could tell me what happened. There are things that her family must be notified of." The family had given no answer when told of her death. There was nothing that Saji could tell them, but it was the least he could do for the deceased.

"I see... But I don't have much to say. I've already repeated it a lot."

He proceeded to tell a story similar to Ms. Brussel's—he'd been chatting during lunch break with his friends about improving the student body, and then had heard the sound of breaking glass from the principal's office. When he'd circled around to the courtyard, he'd seen the broken glass and Noma Eriko dissolving into dust...

"You were able to clearly determine that it was Miss Eriko?"

"Well, I wasn't able to see her clearly. Maybe I was mistaken." He scratched his head. "Maybe I thought it was her because that's what I heard afterwards. She used to be a club member, after all."

"Hm. When she was a club member...in other words, when she was still human, what was Miss Eriko like?"

"She tried very hard. She was a little short-tempered, maybe. She cut class a lot, but she was serious about swimming." He gazed at the surface of the water.

Saji could feel a number of suspicious looks cast in their direction from the pool. It was probably time to wrap this up.

"When Miss Eriko returned to school, did you associate with her?"

"No, I didn't see her much. Um... We're about to start our training exercises, so..."

"I apologize. One last question: Do you know why Miss Eriko was in the principal's office in the first place?"

"No, not at all. Not many people have keys, and anyway, it's not a place people would really want to go... Well, good luck."

The boy bowed his head before rushing to the poolside where the rest of the club members had already gathered. There were several students among them who looked at Saji with obvious fear and revulsion.

Although he wanted to remain by the water for a bit longer, considering the steamy heat outside, Saji rose slowly to avoid antagonizing them. He left the underground pool.

Saji's next destination was the student club building, located off campus.

When Saji had been a student himself, the literature-oriented clubs had operated in a garage near an empty classroom—but this campus had a proper building dedicated to these activities. Looking at the directory at the entrance, it seemed that there was even a shower room, a nap room, and a mini hostel. However, the behavioral precautions on the recruitment flyers and posters in the corridor remained the same.

As Saji walked down the hallway, reading the nameplates on each door, he was suddenly addressed by a young voice from farther down the hall.

"Hey, Doctor Saji!"

A door opened, and the face of a young girl looked out as though she was clutching the doorknob. She quickly trotted toward him.

"Anna! It's been a while. Did you join a club?"

When Saji met her eyes, Anna Evers smiled, revealing a

fangless mouth with neat rows of teeth. While she definitely looked like she was in grade school, she was actually a proper high school student. She was the daughter of the head nurse at the medical center that Saji worked at, and he had seen her numerous times before.

"I'm in the English Speaking Club."

"English Speaking Club? Oh, I see..." There were many multilingual people among the Fangless. That was because they did not settle down in one place, but wandered from location to location. In Anna's case, her English was actually more fluent—Saji knew she had only spoken Japanese when she'd actually been a child, so her Japanese speech patterns matched her appearance.

"Are you here for work?" she asked him.

"Something like that. Where's the club room for the photography club?"

She gripped his hand and climbed the stairs with him, eventually gesturing to a door with the label *Photography Club*. "Right there."

On a piece of paper shoved under the nameplate, someone had written in large letters: *We might be working in the dark room, so knock loudly before entering!*

"Is it about Eriko-senpai?" Anna asked, tilting her head as Saji considered his words for this visit.

"How well did you know Miss Eriko, Anna?"

"A little bit." Anna smiled. "She was very nice."

As Saji started to ask her more questions, the door in front of them opened and a female student emerged. She nearly bumped into Saji, then froze in surprise. Saji hesitated for an instant.

"Hello," he offered. "I'm Doctor Saji, a dentist at the Vampire Bund Medical Center. I was responsible for Miss Noma Eriko."

It was fortunate that he had Anna with him. He was also correct in predicting that a student who remained at the school until nearly dusk would be more accepting of vampires. The student seemed slightly dazed, but invited him into the room and answered the questions he asked without any sign of suspicion.

"Yes, Miss Noma was one of our club members. I'm really sorry that something like that happened. She didn't talk very much, but she was good at looking after other people and worked hard for everyone's benefit. The number of Fangless has been increasing little by little, and she used to be one of the students here, so I think a lot of people depended on her. She was the contact person for the student council.

"But there was something a little strange... While I don't know that much about other Fangless, they seem to not like walking in the aboveground hallways during the daytime. They say it makes them 'feel bad.' But Miss Noma was the opposite—she liked walking in the bright hallways during the day. Well, maybe not really 'liked'... It was more something she would do, some sort of stoic resolution."

"What are your club's plans now?" Saji asked.

"Now...? We're preparing to photograph the stars. We'd planned to take pictures of the stars *tonight,* along with Miss Noma. She had good eyes and could see well in the dark; she didn't need any lights when working in the dark room."

The last comment was perhaps the girl's attempt to lift the mood. Saji thanked her politely and left the room. He then asked Anna, next to him, in a quiet voice: "Are there any places near here where you can smoke?"

"It's forbidden to smoke on campus," answered Anna firmly.

There was no way around it, so Saji sat at a steel desk downstairs and spent some time thinking.

The personality that the girl had described matched the Noma Eriko that Saji knew. She was stoic and self-blaming, and she seemed unable to relax unless she put pressure on herself.

But he felt that something was off. Something was missing here.

"Anna, is there a group for only Fangless students in the school? A liaison group, or something like that?"

Anna nodded. "Sometimes we get together."

"What was Eriko like during those times? Were there any people she was especially close to?"

"Hmm..." Anna tilted her head in thought.

For the next several hours, Saji investigated the school with Anna in tow, but he was unable to obtain any results.

He found and questioned a number of Fangless who were still at school, but he didn't get any new information. It seemed that Noma Eriko didn't have any particularly close friends or partners. He couldn't find any humans *or* Fangless who were able to truly explain her behavior.

He became aware that the night was almost over, and so was his search for answers. There were, after all, limits to an investigation carried out by an amateur. He needed to return to the Bund, and he had to see Anna home first.

But before leaving, Saji decided to walk around the courtyard he'd seen from the principal's office. It was a small garden enclosed by its groundwork and the wings of the buildings around it. A narra tree had been planted in a slightly raised area near the center, beyond a pond with a fountain and surrounded by neatly trimmed bushes. Stones in the pond allowed people to walk over the water or between the bushes.

While there had been blinds in the windows of the principal's office, it was obvious to Saji's eyes that the place had been designed to prioritize the view from the office itself.

He and Anna crossed over the stones and went all the way to the roots of the narra tree, looking for suspicious footprints, but they were unable to find anything. If the police barrier to entry had been removed, they would have already investigated that sort of thing.

When Saji touched the dark, wrinkled bark of the

branches and looked up at the moon, he noticed that the thick branch over his head had a new wound in it. The bark in one spot was peeled, as though a strong force had been applied.

"Excuse me. You shouldn't be going in there yet."

Saji turned around at the warning voice; Officer Morita rounded the corner of the school building and climbed toward them. He circled around to meet Saji with a frown on his face. When Saji pointed at the branch over his head, Officer Morita shrugged his shoulders in disinterest.

"That's a bit strange, isn't it? If you added some tools, you could shoot a rock from there. Though I suppose it could be unrelated."

Of course, the police had naturally noticed something that obvious. Saji felt discouraged and scratched his head. "I'm sorry," he offered. "I'll return home."

"You've been asking a lot of questions." Officer Morita stepped onto the pond's stepping stones as though blocking their path. He and Saji glared at each other for a moment.

"I was concerned about a number of things. I apologize if I got in your way."

"Well, you're troublesome," said the policeman, but suddenly, he changed his attitude. "That's what I want to say, but it's not like my situation is any better." He waved at Anna, who glared at him from behind Saji.

"If it's all right with you, how about we exchange information? I'll get it approved."

"Well, okay... But are you even allowed to talk about this with a civilian?"

"Not at all," Officer Morita answered with a shrug. "But I'm willing to bend the rules a little. I'm out of my depth here, in this investigation."

Saji examined the policeman in front of him as though seeing him for the first time. It was obvious when he thought about it. Maybe Officer Morita had been sent by people who didn't want to deal with the case, but the policeman had his own opinions. The corners of Saji's mouth relaxed unconsciously, and he bowed his head.

"Please give us your help."

Saji then told Officer Morita all the things that he had learned. Morita also informed him of the current state of the investigation, but it didn't seem as though the policeman had any major leads. Noma Eriko had been too much of a loner.

"I think she just never really got especially close with anyone."

"Hmm. But..." Saji felt some objection to that conclusion. He started to think about it, but then a hand tugged at his shirt.

"Oh, Anna! Sorry, sorry. I'll take you home now."

"I think Eriko had a boyfriend," Anna said.

"What?" Saji twitched in surprise and turned toward her. "Really? Did you just remember?"

Anna shook her head. "I don't know if it's someone from

school, so I didn't say it before. But I really think she did."

"You *think?*" Officer Morita crouched down next to Saji. "Why do you think that?"

"It's a gut feeling."

The officer's shoulders fell in disappointment, but Saji thought differently. "Officer, I think what she's saying is probably true."

"Why?"

"Because it fits the pattern. I finally realized what wasn't sitting right with me—Miss Eriko liked to put pressure on herself, but that wasn't the only thing. Her personality was such that she needed someone to *escape* to after stressing herself out."

When Saji had counseled her, he'd almost become that person himself. It was why he'd been relieved when she'd returned to school.

"She must have had a boyfriend or a close friend. She couldn't have lived without one."

"I see..." A thoughtful expression settled on Officer Morita's face.

"Anyway, you can't ignore Anna's intuition. She's twenty years old, even though she looks like this." Saji was nearly knocked over when he was hit in the face by Anna's school bag.

"Well, I'll take a look. If you find anything in the Bund, tell me." Officer Morita adjusted the edges of his suit and stood up. "But are all Fangless this helpful? It seems weird that a dentist would go to such lengths."

"A vampire's personality changes when you remove her fangs."

Saji stood up and rubbed his nose. "Removing a vampire's fangs means changing her life. Our work is a fork in the road—like changing tracks. To keep doing this sort of work, I feel like we have a responsibility toward the people we treat."

"It's like that, huh?"

"It is like that. For example, imagine that you'd gotten a vasectomy. At sixteen." Saji gestured to the man's crotch.

Officer Morita jumped, then laughed sheepishly. "Yes, well... That *is* scary and life-changing!"

For two or three days after that, Saji didn't do any real work. He couldn't stop exploring those questions.

Why had Noma Eriko been in the principal's office alone that day?

Why had the glass broken?

Who was her boyfriend?

Why had she been killed?

Saji asked questions in the Bund whenever he had time, but he only came to the conclusion that—never mind the boyfriend—she had more acquaintances in the school than in the Bund. Most of the Fangless who went to school changed their habits to be diurnal, so they had little association with most people in the Bund.

Yet he still felt that he was missing something obvious. Saji eventually received an email from Officer Morita while he was drinking his afternoon Stigma. DNA testing had verified that the dust was from Noma Eriko.

And if that was so...

A sudden idea flashed across his mind. Saji straightened his back and added a note to his thank-you message to Officer Morita.

"...If you haven't checked that yet, please investigate it immediately."

He himself thought it was a stupid guess, but it was a possibility. Saji completed the day's work feeling calmer, but with a sense of purpose, as though he had discovered what he had to do.

He received another email from Officer Morita the next evening. Saji read it and called Ms. Brussel immediately.

"I apologize for interrupting you again, but has the window in the principal's office been broken before?"

While she seemed surprised at Saji's earnestness, Ms. Brussel still answered in her usual, calm way. "Of course not. Any glass breaking at this school would be a major issue. But I heard that a long time ago, there were some people in a bike gang or something who played a prank like that. I wasn't here, so I don't know the details."

"I see. Is the principal's office cleaned every day?"

"Yes. We have professionals come in to clean the office

every day after noon."

"Thank you. One more thing... If there are any students who know a lot about who's dating whom, could you direct me to one?"

Saji thanked her and hung up, then requested vacation time. He made arrangements to go to the school again near dawn, after he had completed his work for the day. He knew he would be exhausted by the next night, with him up and moving around during the day as well, but he couldn't complain about it.

He found Ms. Brussel's suggested student immediately. Saji asked two or three questions, and the girl's eyes widened.

"Yes, there was a rumor like that. You're well-informed, aren't you?"

Saji thanked her and left the campus, then called Officer Morita.

"I don't know the motivation, and I don't even know what caused it, but I definitely know who did it. Please ask him about it."

Saijo Takashi, student council vice-president and captain of the swimming club, was arrested the next day.

"When we interrogated him, he didn't hold back very much; he told us what we wanted to know. Saijo was meeting with Noma Eriko in secret in the principal's office after school. It would be a bit archaic to say that they were on a date, but that's what it was. It seems he had two or three girlfriends on the side, though the others were human." Officer Morita put out his cigarette, and poured the flat beer into his glass. "But how did you notice that something was wrong with the glass?"

"It was just an idea." Saji lit his second cigarette. While there were almost no restaurants in the city that permitted smoking, the rules were looser in the common district near the suburbs of the Bund. Grubby cheap bars, fogged by cigarette smoke, had made a big comeback there.

"The only evidence we had of Noma Eriko dying at that time and place was his testimony. I thought it was too convenient. But even if it was a lie or a misleading truth, we had the place and the remains confirmed, and at the time, everyone heard the glass breaking. So I started to wonder if the glass breaking was actually her time of death. There was the possibility that she'd been exposed to sunlight *without* the glass breaking."

"The glass in that room was apparently a special UV-transparent glass. But then a plastic film was applied to make it prevent ultraviolet rays. I thought it was odd that nobody noticed that."

*But there was no **reason** to notice it,* thought Saji. A transparent film applied to transparent glass wouldn't be particularly noticeable to humans, and most vampires wouldn't approach a window to examine it closely during the day. It was unfortunate that Noma Eriko had happened to see it.

"The person who removed the film was Miss Eriko herself?"

"That's what Saijo said. It was probably curiosity. Saijo must have panicked—he would be seen as the perpetrator if he left it like that. If he left her and ran, she would still be discovered the next day by the cleaners. So he set up a slingshot that night on the branches of the tree, using a signal from his cellphone to activate it. Everything has become so convenient these days..."

And the next day, he'd pretended to be the first person to discover her and had removed the slingshot. It had been a pretty smart decision on the fly.

"What I don't understand is why the window glass became that way."

"About that... Well, keep this a secret between you and me." Officer Morita gulped down the flat beer. "I guess that Saijo kid had joined an anti-vampire extremist group. That glass might've been set up by them for an assassination later."

"Set up? That's crazy...!" Saji almost began to yell, but then calmed himself. "It's a location that Her Highness frequently visits. To do that so easily..."

"There was a big commotion there earlier, right? Maybe based on that incident, they investigated the location to see if it could be used for a bombing or something." He poured more beer into his empty glass. "I don't know much more than that. It's been blocked by the higher-ups."

Officer Morita spat out saliva that stank of beer. "We've gotten no real reaction from the Queen, either, even after reporting this to the principal. I guess once you become someone important, you don't get bothered by one or two death threats."

"Really? But that's so..." Saji trailed off, unsure of what to say.

The school was supposed to be a location where Her Highness could mingle with the Fangless; in other words, it was a relaxing garden for her. Wouldn't she be angry that it had been sullied like this?

But it had been a month since she'd last visited, when the previous incident had occurred. Saji thought about Ms. Brussel's words.

Perhaps among those in charge...something unimaginably awful had occurred with the distant upper levels of the Bund. Saji trembled, then poured the tasteless beer into his glass and drank it down in one gulp.

"So is this murder, then? Not destroying a body or hiding evidence?"

"Well, I don't know. He seemed to know about the glass... We'll sort this out. Otherwise it wouldn't be fair to the victim."

"Thank you." Saji bowed.

"Hey, Saji." Officer Morita looked at Saji with drunken eyes. "What does it feel like to have your fangs removed? Why do vampires have their fangs removed, anyway? Do they want to become human again?"

"Well, there are a variety of reasons. But vampires can't become human again, no matter what you do."

Had Noma Eriko wanted to become human again? Removing her fangs, going to school, walking during the day, having a human boyfriend... Had she tried to get closer to humanity by doing those things?

"It would be tragic if we didn't understand that."

"Was Noma Eriko unhappy?"

"I don't know."

Saji adjusted his glasses and looked over the oily atmosphere of the dive bar. He poured the cheap beer into their glasses before raising his hand to pay their tab.

Fast-flowing clouds crossed the face of the moon high in the sky, swirling and ripping the moonlight apart.

End

Dance in the Vampire Bund

APPLES
FROM A TREE

STORY
Gemma

ILLUSTRATION
Picture Bride
by Yoshiko Uchida

PROLOGUE

A woman wrapped in a red stole sat on a covered bench at the bus stop, protected from the rain that sprinkled from the sky.

She appeared to be about forty years old, although she wore the weathered stole in an old-fashioned way. It was probably obvious to any observers that her true age was not as she appeared. She sometimes raised her eyes and gazed at the other side of the street, clearly waiting for someone.

Another woman of approximately the same age emerged from the hospital. She had similar features, but instead of a red stole, she wore a red scarf wrapped around her neck. The way she wore it was *also* old-fashioned, somehow.

The woman with the scarf raised her hand to ward off the rain as she walked under the roof of the bus stop. The woman with the stole smiled slightly and said something to her. After observing the other woman for a while, the woman with the scarf returned her smile.

Together, they disappeared into the hazy drizzle, chatting as they went.

CHAPTER 1

1931, Honolulu, Hawaii

"My mother was an awful woman."

When drinking with Sonia Takahashi, her mother always became the final topic of conversation—so all her friends knew to stay silent or leave before the topic came up. Daniel Kazuo Saji was no exception, but he stayed because she was beautiful.

"Are you even listening, Daniel?"

"Yes, yes…"

Then someone made a toast, and the clinking of shot glasses filled the room. After the weeklong finals, the diner was filled with exhausted but relieved students. Before Sonia had caught him an hour earlier, Daniel had been one of those people.

He heard ominous sounds and cries from the radio. It seemed to be a vampire drama, based on the story of Bela Lugosi's *Dracula*. The group at the next table over collapsed into laughter at the drama's cheap screams.

"They say you're rewarded for having a tough life when

you're young, but that's a lie. If you have weird difficulties when you're young, it twists your mind and you aren't raised properly. She was like that. If I had kids, I wouldn't make their lives hard."

Sonia's expressive eyebrows were beautiful, and she blurted the words with enough force to nearly blow bubbles from the Primo beer at her lips. She had surprisingly pale skin for an Asian, and it contrasted well against her trademark red scarf.

Sonia Takahashi had come to Hawaii from San Francisco several years earlier. She was a strange woman; she said she was saving up money to take a trip to Japan. While there were many Japanese people who moved to Hawaii with the intention of eventually moving to the American mainland, few people tried to do the reverse.

Although everyone was wary when a young, single woman began looking for work without any introductions, the friendly Japanese community in Hawaii had easily accepted Sonia's aggressive, honest personality. She worked a number of jobs, from restaurant hostess to babysitter, and sometimes even did physical labor, while often associating with Japanese students like Daniel at the University of Hawaii.

It was said that she had even begun to sneak into lectures at the college. Her peculiar, hard-to-resist charisma made her an idol among the students, but her drinking habits were a big problem.

"Hey, Danny! You came."

Matthew Ninomiya, who shared classes with Daniel, approached with a bottle of Primo. He'd clearly started celebrating the end of exams early on; his feet wavered.

He pulled back when he saw Sonia at the table already—her eyes glazed by alcohol, a number of empty beer bottles scattered on and under the table. But Daniel grabbed him by the collar and yanked him down to sit.

"Hey, stop it! I stayed up all night and haven't slept yet."

"Me, too. Think of it as your bad luck."

Sonia looked amused as she watched them mutter to each other. Then her smile disappeared.

"Did I tell you? Mom was a picture bride."

Daniel and Matthew stopped arguing and looked at each other in silence. They'd heard the same story several weeks earlier. Sonia never talked about her family when she was sober, but all bets were off when she was drunk. All of her drinking buddies, including Daniel, were more or less aware of her past life.

Her mother had apparently been a "photo bride"—she'd come all the way from Shinshu to marry a Japanese immigrant who ran a convenience store in San Francisco, based on an arranged introduction photo.

At the turn of the century, hard-working Japanese immigrants who made their money quietly had unnerved white Americans, who then created various laws and unspoken pressures to restrict Japanese immigration. Thus the Japanese community came up with the idea of "calling over family from Japan." Since strangers would become family after marriage, marrying a first-generation Japanese person became one of the easiest and most effective methods of crossing over to America for the next decade or so. When a strict anti-Japanese immigration law was implemented in 1924, the method stopped working.

For the brides, marriage had simply been a convenient way to achieve their dream of living in America, but it had also been true in a different sense for their grooms. There had been many unhappy marriages and lives. Sonia's mother had been no exception: after a series of nasty complications, she had run away from her husband to elope with another man, abandoning Sonia.

Daniel knew that that night's version of the story would probably reiterate the same, but he also knew that pointing that out wouldn't stop her. He and Matthew nodded wordlessly, signaling her to continue.

"She was on welfare in Japan, so it seemed like she was happy to come here. They were told that all the first-generation Japanese in America were rich, and once here, they would live like princesses. But when they arrived here, they saw the truth—the poverty. Of course they did. Nobody rich or even *normal* would choose a bride like that... Wow, that's loud!"

Someone at the next table had turned up the radio. Sonia spat out her words in irritation and nursed her beer.

Daniel thought that it couldn't be that simple, but he himself was a student who had problems with his parents. He watched silently as a trickle of beer dribbled down from the corner of Sonia's mouth and soaked into her scarf.

"She chased a naive dream. She kept saying that she'd been betrayed and it was all his fault. And what did she do when she ran away from her husband? She giggled a lot while pouring drinks for whites. She wasn't much different from a prostitute. Saying that it was only her own life that was hard… That's ridiculous."

"Didn't your mother have a hard life, though? She had to raise you, too," Matthew interrupted needlessly. One of Matthew's flaws was poking holes in logic even when that wasn't called for. As expected, Sonia's pretty eyebrows lifted.

"What do you know? Yeah, she worked hard to raise me, but only for the first few years. When I was five, she already had another man, and when I was seven, she was gone more than half the time. Do you understand what it's like for a kid to wake up in the middle of the night and find herself home alone? Do you know what it's like to have a woman like that come home and complain at you that she sacrificed her lifestyle for you?!"

Sonia grabbed Matthew's collar and jerked him close. Her eyes bulged unusually large as she spoke with breath that stank of beer. She seemed more annoyed than usual.

"That's why I'm going to Japan. I'm going to go to Japan

and have a family, where I can raise my children carefully and lead a good life. In Japan, the place that she ran away from," said Sonia in a single breath before emptying her glass. "That woman ran away from Japan. She ran away from a lot of things…including being human. Do you believe it? That woman wasn't *human*."

Daniel frowned. Sonia had said a lot of things about her mother before, but this was something that he couldn't let pass without comment. He grasped the arm that was holding onto Matthew, but her arm suddenly dropped. Sonia's body pitched forward and collapsed, her pale face hitting the table.

"She's pretty excited today," sighed Matthew as he adjusted his collar.

"Is that something we should be talking about now? Don't let her drink anymore."

Daniel stood up, trying to bring Sonia with him by supporting her with his shoulder. She was unable to put forth any strength, but she still tried to get away from him. When he finally managed to lift her with Matthew's help, she looked up at Daniel and fixed him with a serious stare.

"It's true," she whispered with her beer breath. "That woman isn't human. She's not human anymore…"

It wasn't simple antagonism. Daniel raised his head at the feelings embedded in Sonia's voice and its strange nuances. Sonia's gaze wavered from him to Matthew and back…then dropped to the floor as her eyes slowly closed.

Daniel had never seen a woman that drunk.

Matthew settled the tab. While they took turns carrying her toward their apartment building, Sonia kept talking, her eyes still closed.

"I'll live in Japan. I'll live in Japan, even if she ran away from it. I'll live the life she abandoned…"

It ended up being the first time Daniel and Matthew heard about vampires. *Real* vampires.

But at the time, they had no idea.

CHAPTER 2

1956, Portsmouth, England

"Are you new? Hm… Better do this right, then."

The first time they met, he thought he'd found Sonia Takahashi again.

The woman was about forty years old, as Sonia would have been. Her neat, well-shaped eyebrows and the way the edges of her mouth turned up when she smiled hadn't changed in twenty years.

"Did you become a vampire, too, Sonia?"

When Saji spoke to her casually, she stared back at him in clear surprise. After a long moment, she giggled.

"Sonia! I didn't expect to hear my daughter's name here."

It was *Fuji* Takahashi—the mother Sonia had always complained about.

"You came on a mail boat, right?" she asked. "You must be hungry."

"Well, a little." He was actually starving. Saji hadn't eaten a single thing during the daylong trip, lying hidden in the bottom of a ship crossing the Dover Straits.

"I don't have any virgin blood, but I do have chicken blood. Do you want some?"

"Yes, please."

"Okay… Let's go hunting."

"Huh?"

As he learned later, when she offered food to someone, she actually meant, "If you want to eat, then help me find food." So Saji, who had only just arrived in England, spent the next three hours with Fuji, stealing a chicken from a farm outside of the city.

"So you were a military doctor," she clarified on their little hunt. "A deserter? I see, I see. Nobody really cares about what you were when you were human. I guess you were bitten recently?"

"Yes. About a month ago."

"Is that girl doing well?"

"The last letter I received from her said she got married in Japan. It was twenty years ago, and I don't know how she's doing now…"

Based on what he'd heard from Sonia in the past, Saji had imagined a snake-like, selfish, and cold woman—but Fuji Takahashi seemed cheerful and straightforward once he'd talked to her. She was one of the representatives of the small vampire community he'd arrived at.

"That country has finally entered a period of good fortune. I suppose it would be easier to live there now." As Fuji parted the heather bushes, she stretched and let out a long sigh that didn't turn white in the air.

It was nearly dawn by the time they returned. The others at the hidden house fell into a panic; because Fuji stole chickens so often, most of the nearby farms had grown wary. And she'd been warned about it.

In front of the enraged community elders, Fuji smiled apologetically but still wrung the chicken's neck. She poured its blood into a porcelain cup and passed it to Saji.

Their small vampire community existed because it could hide within the diverse populations passing through Portsmouth, one of the busiest port cities in England.

It didn't take much time for Saji to realize that for the vampires there, Fuji was a troublemaker, but also a Madonna. She was vivacious and quick-witted, and good at taking care of people—even if there were times when she was uncontrollably enthusiastic or entirely self-absorbed, when she would prioritize her desires over everything else.

She was like that in her relationships with men as well. The leader of the Portsmouth vampire community was an aging Englishman named William, and Fuji was considered his common-law wife, but there had apparently been a lot of complications leading up to that. Many people had left the community for romantic issues. Rumor said that William held his position as a result of winning a fight with the former leader over Fuji.

"It's not like you can do anything about falling in love," said Fuji with an apologetic smile, although she didn't appear to regret her actions. When Saji asked what had happened to the man she had eloped with when she abandoned Sonia, she said briefly, "I don't remember anymore."

Saji later discovered that *that* man had turned her into a vampire and caused her to come to England. She'd eventually left him, too. Fuji was attracted to older, well-built white men, and Saji secretly thanked God that he was completely outside of her interest zone.

Later, Saji saw the one incident when Fuji honestly regretted her actions.

Like Saji, Fuji wasn't particularly interested in attacking humans, so she didn't have her own "blood kin" followers—which was generally a good thing, since their community frowned upon randomly adding to their numbers. But she supposedly had given birth to *one* vampire by sucking on his blood: Joseph, the second son of a Portsmouth merchant. He was a fat, well-built young man. He was unassuming, and he had a strong sense of self-control—a rarity among vampires. He helped teach Saji how to live in Portsmouth in those early days.

Fuji had brought Joseph in a rare case where she was interested in a younger man, and they had apparently been affectionate for the first year. But then Fuji's attention had turned to William, leaving no time for Joseph. Even so, rather than flying into a rage, Joseph had retreated to live quietly in a corner of the community.

Unfortunately for Joseph, he'd been enamored with a

different lover while human—a love that had been repressed by the power of blood kinship. And after Fuji's attention had wandered elsewhere, he recalled his old lover in steadily building frustration. One day in early summer, two years after Saji had joined the community, Joseph ran away.

It was the same day that his lover, who had given up on Joseph when he'd vanished, was marrying another man. Saji heard that Joseph crashed the wedding—wrapped head-to-toe in reflective cloth—bit the bride's neck, and was then restrained by the guests. They tore the cloth from his head.

If William had not appeared in his True Form—that of a frightening black horse with sulfurous flames emitting from its eyes and mouth—and taken Joseph away immediately, he would have turned into dust in the public eye. As it was, Joseph was still exposed to too much sunlight. When William, his own body covered with burns, finally returned to the secret house, the only thing in his hands was a pile of dust wrapped in reflective cloth.

A few nights later, two vampires were selected from the community and sent to the home of the newlyweds. The bride seemed to understand what had happened to her body, and she came to the house without any resistance. While she agreed to abandon her life as a human, she stubbornly refused to adopt the life of a vampire.

"In that case, your fangs will have to be removed. Do you agree?" announced William in a grave voice. It was the first time Saji learned of the existence of the Fangless.

The Fangless bride, having shed all her tears, left Portmouth in quiet despair. She never spoke a word to Fuji, blaming her or otherwise. The others were unable to verify whether Joseph's sudden romantic obsession had been an effect of the blood kin bond or not.

After the incident, Fuji didn't leave the house for over a month. She spent her time staring blankly through the window.

"Maybe I should get my fangs removed, too," she murmured, surprising everyone.

When autumn came, she returned to her normal, carefree self. But from then on, there were times when she could be seen standing at the edge of a pier, silently gazing out to sea.

Saji thought that her back resembled Sonia's, but didn't tell her that.

CHAPTER 3

1982, Tokyo, Japan

For fifty years, she had labored like a workhorse. She'd literally given up sleep and meals to work day and night.

And what was she left with in the end?

Takahashi Sonia Tokiko stared at her hands in frustration.

With the birth of her daughter Akane, she had thought she'd finally become a true Japanese woman. She took to writing her name in the Japanese style. After the hardship she had endured as a woman coming from the enemy nation during the Pacific War, she thought of Akane's birth as her reward.

Her husband had died in the war, leaving Sonia to work desperately to make money for Akane; money was their only support in the harsh environment after the war. It felt like fate to meet the young cabaret manager, Robert Yamaoka—another foreign Japanese descendant living in Japan. They understood each other and quickly fell in love.

When she discovered that he was a vampire, she thought that entering his world of darkness would be a good thing for Akane's well-being. She hesitated at following the path of her mother, but convinced herself that it was all for her daughter's sake; it wasn't the same situation at all. She managed to convince Akane—who didn't want to live apart—that it was for the best, while crying tears of her own.

A large vampire society was hidden within Japan. There were many dangers, but also many opportunities. She began to work as a construction broker, using the financial knowledge she had acquired years before at the University of Hawaii. She worked even harder than before, sending more and more money to the daughter who now lived apart from her.

Akane ran away from home when she was sixteen.

Sonia felt her vision darken.

She had given her daughter all kinds of love and had worked to provide her with a comfortable life. She couldn't understand why the girl would run away.

After dazedly cleaning her house for half a day in her shock, she searched for her daughter using her information network. Sonia didn't like sucking human blood, so she only had a few blood kin—but she had built up a position within vampire society that allowed her to move a certain number of people.

Two months later, Akane was taken into custody, along with a gangster wannabe in a cheap hotel in Izu.

"Why did you do this?"

When Sonia asked, her daughter turned away and wouldn't meet her eyes. She sent her daughter home, and continued to send her money—along with observers—but she felt that a sudden wall had grown between them.

As a distraction from her cold relationship with her child, Sonia threw herself into her work even more than she had before. She became distant from her lover Robert, but she didn't care. There was an opportunity to make a lot of money, since a wave of urban reconstruction was sweeping across Japan.

And then she heard rumors of her mother.

"I saw a vampire who looked very much like Ms. Tokiko in London."

Even when she heard the rumors, Sonia only recalled painful memories, and she didn't feel any longing. Her heart grew even harder when she heard that the vampire was Fangless.

Her mother had run away from Japan, run away from being human, and now she had finally run away from being a vampire as well? She was a degenerate, through and through.

When Sonia thought about it, she wanted to work even harder. She wanted to become a proper vampire—one of the wires that manipulated her country from the shadows. Akane would live happily on the soil of the country that they built.

She wanted her daughter to have the happy life that she and her mother had lost.

One week earlier, Akane had come to the apartment Sonia lived in.

It had been several years since her daughter's last visit. As Sonia prepared tea and snacks, two fangs shone in her daughter's mouth as she gave a bland smile.

It was then that Sonia's vision turned truly dark.

"Why?"

Sonia grabbed her daughter, furious. "What wasn't *good* enough? Why do you have to make so much trouble for me?"

The daughter, who looked almost the same age as Sonia herself, didn't change her expression as she violently shook her mother off.

"You're not the only one who gets to become immortal."

Sonia's voice trembled with her rage and disappointment. "How much hardship do you think I endured for you?"

"Don't act like you're the only one who's had a hard life!" Akane stared right back at her with antagonistic, cold eyes.

"I never asked you to keep making money, to the point where you gave up on being human. I don't want to hear how much you've sacrificed for me, from a woman who hasn't even bothered to see her daughter in twenty years. I'm going to be living on my own now, so leave me alone." After spitting the words, Akane left, slamming the door behind her.

According to Sonia's investigation, Akane had sold her home in Yokohama that day. She had taken only the bare necessities, leaving her sizeable bank account untouched.

A single opened envelope and letter lay on the desk in

front of Sonia. Sonia, racked with despair, hadn't sent her subordinates after her daughter's whereabouts—she wanted the identity of the vampire who had bitten her. She couldn't forgive the person who had destroyed Akane's life, because Akane was everything to Sonia—the symbol of all her hopes and dreams.

Sonia gripped the letter and looked at the name once again. A single name written in crisp, plain script with a ballpoint pen.

Robert Yamaoka.

The same man who had turned Sonia.

CHAPTER 4

2010, Vampire Bund

"Ms. Takahashi! Ms. Takahashi Sonia Tokiko!"

Sonia heard someone call her name. She slowly stood up, returning the magazine she'd been reading to its rack.

She presented her ID to the nurse at the reception desk, verified her identity, and sat down in the treatment room. It had been more than half a century since she'd last visited a dentist; compared to back then, this room was brightly lit and clean, the chairs were covered with comfortable, cream-colored leather, and the decor was tasteful. It seemed almost like a well-appointed hotel, but...

"The smells and sounds are still the same."

As she frowned at the scent of antiseptic and the high-pitched whine of drills, the dentist who emerged from the adjacent booth smiled sardonically.

"Both the medicine and the techniques have improved a lot, though."

"It's been a long time, Daniel."

"It's good to see you. I'm sorry, but can you please call me Doctor?"

He'd grown a beard in the seventy years since she'd seen him, and he looked slightly more mature. He appeared to be forty years old, meaning he'd probably become a vampire around the same time as Sonia.

"Should I take this off, Doctor?" Sonia gave a small laugh as she touched the scarf at her neck.

Doctor Saji grinned back at her, then took an apron from the basket next to him. "You can leave it. Would you wear this and read the pre-operation instructions, please?"

She went through an examination and an explanation, then a simple test. While they were careful with the informed process, it was still quick. It didn't feel much different from removing ordinary human teeth.

"It's that easy to change someone's life."

"It's actually a very small operation and doesn't take much time. You can stop here and think about it again, if you'd like."

"No, I'd like to do it today." Maybe her nervousness had shown on her face. Sonia took a deep breath and lay back on the headrest. "Daniel... Doctor Saji. You said you knew my mother?"

"She helped me out a lot when I was a new vampire." Doctor Saji nodded and placed the electronic medical charts next to him. "Ms. Fuji is also in the Bund. Have you seen her?"

"No, but I told her I was getting the operation today, so maybe she'll come and meet me."

As she sucked the mint-flavored antiseptic into her mouth, Sonia tried to recall the face of her mother from a distant memory. She had hated her mother so much, yet felt nothing when she saw her mother's name on the list of immigrants. But through a faintly nostalgic fog wrapped around her memories, she had seen her path share so much in common with her mother's. Then she'd found herself writing a short letter.

A short while later, she had received a similar letter back from her mother.

"Hey, Doctor. I had a daughter."

She winced at the painful needle that delivered the anesthetic. While she waited for the drug to take effect, she massaged her chin and moved her tongue, thinking about her daughter. They sometimes exchanged emails; they weren't much closer than Sonia was with her own mother. They hadn't met up in over a decade.

"She's like me—she develops crushes on people a lot. And has no taste in men." The master of Sonia and her daughter, Robert Yamaoka, had been looking for business opportunities in Cambodia when he was dragged into a coup and turned into dust. Sonia didn't understand why Akane would pine after a man like that her whole life, but she herself had been like that in the past, so she couldn't really say anything. Apples never fell far from the tree.

"I bet that girl will remove her fangs someday. Please take care of her then, Doctor Saji."

"I see…"

The anesthetic had begun to take effect, and she found it harder and harder to think. Doctor Saji checked his rubber gloves, then gripped a tool like a curved drill and a small hammer.

She suddenly wondered what her mother's mother—her grandmother—had been like. She realized that her mother had never spoken a single word about her family in Japan.

Had her grandmother *also* ruined her family due to a man?

Probably, Sonia thought as she felt the faint sensation of cold metal entering her mouth.

End

THE MANCHURIAN CANDIDATE

STORY
Tikurakuran

ILLUSTRATION
Nozomu Tamaki

Present Day—Tokyo, Japan

When I finally stepped off of the long escalator and exited to the street, the sun had nearly set. As I stood in the subway station exit, the freeway overpass towered directly over Roppongi Avenue like an enormous gate.

I still had more than forty minutes before my appointment, and my destination was only a ten-minute walk away. I saw a large, chain coffee shop just past the front of the Asanuno police station, so I decided to go there to wait.

The front of the café had an outdoor seating area with several tables lined up on artificial grass. Whether or not it was because the evening temperature had dropped, the outdoor tables were all empty. To contain my growing excitement, I chose a seat outside and settled down with my coffee.

When I gazed at Roppongi Avenue in front of me, I saw a never-ending line of women heading toward Roppongi Hills. In a reflection of the current prospering economy, the women all wore cheerful expressions. Most office ladies shopped on their way home from work or ate out for dinner.

As I sipped terribly overpriced coffee, I thought back to how I had ended up here in the first place.

Nearly six months had passed since the girl called Mina Tepes made her startling speech on the existence of vampires, and even more shockingly, established a special district for vampires.

The transition of Japanese public opinion was very interesting. At first, everyone laughed at what they thought was nothing more than a series of rumors started by the media. Then, when the special district for vampires was formally established along with proof of vampire existence, the dismissive laughter turned into chirps of fear.

Then things got *really* interesting. When the public learned that Japan had escaped its dire economic crisis with the aid of House Tepes, they forgot about their fear of these monsters of myth and began to merrily enjoy the new "vampire business state." It was a repeat of the same flexibility that had allowed the Japanese to successfully adapt to paradigm shifts caused by external pressure—such as the Meiji Restoration and the country post-World War II.

The publishing world, which I was a part of, benefitted a great deal. People's interest in vampires soared, and publications related to vampires of all ages and origins began flying off the shelves.

Publishing houses released book after book in the

boom. They covered a lot of ground, from the legend of the Romanian Vlad Tepes the Impaler—the historical source of the Dracula story—to romance and mystery short stories featuring vampire and human interactions. On top of that, there were even miscellaneous articles, like the sensationalist exposé, "Freemasonry: A Vampire Cover-up!" Soon the bestsellers list was comprised of nothing but trashy rehashes, like *If Dracula Read Hagakure.*

As a small-time historical writer, I'd made a meager living by contributing to books related to the popular Taiga dramas or miscellaneous publications that included historical material. But the aftereffects of the boom even reached me; I constantly came across historical commentary jobs that were related to vampires. I had never imagined that a four-hundred-year-old girl would bring stability to my life.

With the emergence of an economic surplus, I felt my previously suppressed desires resurface. Although I'd been content with writing for various literary publications, I had majored in history in university, and had once dreamed of becoming a famous historical author like Izawa Motohiko or Chin Shunshin. One day, I decided that instead of working just to put food on the table, I would analyze history in my own unique way and try to make the world stop and consider history in a new light. I felt like I had a new chance with the sudden public revelation of the existence of vampires.

I had my eye on the Three Great Clans that stood alongside House Tepes. Although it was hard to track down information about them, the general consensus was that they had ancient roots in America, Russia, and China.

The strangest part was that those three countries' governments still wouldn't admit that vampires existed. In official presentations, they denoted the Vampire Bund as the "Tokyo Bay Special District" without one reference to the vampires who surely resided there. They also remained absolutely silent on information regarding the Three Great Clans. Even so, American and Russian civilian media reported vampire-related news, and the Internet was active with vigorous information exchanges.

Of the three, China's control of information was exceptionally strict. Of course, official government press releases and mass media were regulated, but even on the Internet, information concerning vampires was completely censored. They eliminated the presence of vampire-related literature on bookstore shelves. It was almost proof that the Great Clan in China—the Li Clan—held major influence over the Chinese Communist Party. In other words, there was a strong possibility that vampires had been involved in Chinese history since ancient times.

It was an interesting intellectual experiment to insert vampires to explain different aspects of Chinese history, which was already puzzling enough—even without vampires. And I knew that if I exposed the fact that the Li Clan had performed a role behind the scenes of Chinese history, it would no doubt create a worldwide sensation.

I began researching Chinese vampires through any way I could think of, beginning with public organizations such as the Japan-China Friendship Association and the United Association of Chinese and Japanese-Chinese in Japan. I even joined a tour of the Vampire Bund and attempted to speak directly with a Chinese vampire, working there as a cleaner.

I ended up with pages and pages of notes, but when I summarized my findings, it didn't even fill five pages. Although no one refuted my assumption that there were indeed vampires in China, no one would speak of it or even hint at any concrete relationship between the Li Clan and the government. Public opinion had lined up with the government's official stance.

I assumed there were mountains of journalists chasing the same information, and there was no way that a nameless history buff like me could unlock the mystery of the Li Clan that had evaded so many others.

Literally blocked at all turns, I was about to give up when an unexpected breakthrough occurred: I received a letter from none other than the Chinese Embassy in Japan. It said that they would honor my request and wanted me to come to the embassy. The time was set for seven o'clock in the evening.

Inviting a human who was currently researching vampires after sunset was suggestive. As a human, of course I could see the inherent danger of the situation—but as a historical writer, I still couldn't turn the invitation down.

I accepted the offer immediately.

I left the coffee shop and arrived at the Chinese Embassy right on time.

The main gate facing TV Asahi Street was locked up tight. Several fences laced across the front of the gate, behind which numerous Japanese policemen stood as security detail. During the day, one might catch a glimpse of Falun Gong devotees gathering support on the opposite sidewalk of the main street, but they were gone that night. I attempted to slip through the fence, and one of the officers approached me.

"Do you have an appointment?"

I was at a loss for words. I hadn't been told whom I would be meeting there.

When I stated my business to the embassy official in the booth beside the main gate, he seemed aware of the situation; he let me through right away as the police officer returned to his post.

I passed through the door on the side of the booth to find another door inside. *That* door was surprisingly heavy—I couldn't open it without using my entire body weight.

On the opposite side of the heavy door, I stepped into a land separate from Japan.

I could see my destination—the embassy—at the end of a driveway lined on both sides with tall trees. It was a plain building with a turnaround in front of the entranceway, like a mid-scale corporation headquarters in the suburbs. It didn't look at all like the branch office of a world superpower, where its impressive influence toyed with the rest of the world.

With every step I took toward the building, I felt as if the protection of Japanese laws faded away, little by little. I wondered what was waiting for me in there, but it was also too late to turn back.

When I passed through the automatic front door and entered the building, the lobby felt like it belonged in an ordinary, private business. The walls and ceiling gave visitors a sense of history, but there was no gaudiness or opulence. A reception desk sat to the left of the entrance, but no one was behind it.

Since I'd been invited, I assumed that someone would come out to greet me. I mentally prepared myself and sat down on one of the chairs arranged in the waiting area.

The lobby was dotted with Chinese ornaments, such as an exquisitely carved wooden folding screen. Beside the waiting area, a magazine rack held tourist guidebooks for China and Japan, mostly written in Chinese. I picked up a pamphlet about the Tibet Autonomous Region and flipped through its pages. It beautifully depicted features like the Qinghai-Tibet Railway connecting Beijing and Lhasa, and the Potala Palace—the UNESCO World Heritage Site—but there was absolutely nothing written about the oppression of the Tibetan independence movement or their exploitation by the Han Chinese.

"I recommend Lhasa at this time of year. In the summertime, there are too many tourists; it's not enjoyable at all."

Startled, I looked up at the voice above my head.

A man stood before me, smiling affably. I hadn't sensed his approach.

He seemed to be in his thirties and was extremely handsome. I could tell he wasn't Japanese. The man's almond eyes squinted when he smiled, so unlike a shady spokesman merely delivering a government's official statement to me. His well-tailored suit fit him perfectly from his necktie to his shoes, and even a layman like me could see how high-class the clothing was.

Panicking slightly, I stood up and returned the pamphlet to the rack. The man stuck his hand out expectantly.

"It's a pleasure to meet you. I'm Councilor Ryuu."

That title meant he held a position directly below the ambassador. In other words, he was one of the top-ranking embassy officials.

After shaking his hand, I held out my business card and introduced myself. Councilor Ryuu glanced at my card and smiled.

"Of course I know who you are. After all, I invited you here. Right this way."

As I followed the councilor, I silently wondered if the man was actually a vampire. I had seen his teeth when he'd laughed. They were large for canines, yes, but they seemed a little too small for me to call them fangs.

The reception room he led me to had no door—it was simply a round opening in the wall. A large couch lined three sides of the room, with no table in the center. I'd seen a similar arrangement in a summit meeting in China featured on the news.

As I sat down, a female employee of the embassy came and served us tea. At the councilor's urging, I lifted off the lid of the white teacup; the fragrant scent of jasmine wafted into the air. The glass next to the councilor contained ordinary water.

He noticed my gaze and smiled. "Did you think I would drink blood?"

At that point, I thought I could ask him directly. "Um, forgive my audacity, but you mean you actually are..."

"Yes, I am a vampire," Councilor Ryuu admitted lightly. "This is quite embarrassing to say, but as a vampire, I have one defect—my body has trouble when I ingest blood. Take a look at my fangs." He opened his mouth and showed me his teeth again.

"Instead, I have a special ability that allows me to obtain energy in a different way. It's an extremely useful ability, and it brought me the position I hold now."

"And that ability is...?"

Councilor Ryuu raised his hand and stopped me mid-question. "Before that, let's broach the main topic for today.

The reason I asked you here is that I would like to offer you some profitable information. You want to know more about the role played by the Li Clan in Chinese history, is that correct?"

"That's right. But why—"

"Let's stop asking 'why,' shall we?" Councilor Ryuu quickly cut me off. For just an instant, his eyes glinted. "For now, let's just say that I have extremely keen mental perception. As for providing you with information, it's something I will also benefit from."

Having stumbled upon a dry spell of information, the proposal was welcome rain in a drought. Even if I had wished for it, speaking with a Chinese vampire in the Chinese Embassy was not something easily granted; there had to be a catch. Something deep inside of me warned me against the man's offer.

"If my offer doesn't appeal to you, you're welcome to leave now. I will bestow my offer on someone else." Councilor Ryuu leaned against the back of the chair, casually waiting for my answer.

The councilor clearly had the initiative. If I refused, he would summon another journalist who would publicize the information to the world. That journalist would bathe in the spotlight and I would regret it for the rest of my life.

Without this opportunity, I had no future.

I took a sip of my jasmine tea.

"Please tell me your story."

Satisfied, Councilor Ryuu smiled. His smile reminded me of the wolf's expression in "The Three Little Pigs," just before eating the pigs. But my swelling expectations for his story extinguished my uneasiness.

"Wonderful. Let's begin right away." He bent toward me. "I've prepared for many subjects, but do you have any preferences?"

I thought for a little while. Older stories would mainly appeal to history buffs like me. I would have a larger impact if I focused on a time when readers were alive. "An event as close as you can get to the present day, please."

"Hmm. Let's see... How does September 13, 1971 sound?"

I swallowed my breath. Anyone who knew *anything* about modern Chinese history knew that date.

The Lin Biao Incident.

A coup d'état staged by one of the leaders of the Chinese government. Marshal Lin Biao had suddenly plotted the assassination of his direct superior, Mao Zedong.

Apart from the government's official statement, information concerning the incident was scarce, and many mysteries remained unsolved. Initially, Lin Biao had been named Mao Zedong's successor. Why had he led a coup? Why had the relationship between the two suddenly deteriorated? And why had it all ended that way?

If it had been caused by *vampire intervention*, it would have resulted in censorship and controversy. It would have uprooted the very foundation of the Chinese government.

"Please begin." Trembling in anticipation, I pulled out my notebook.

September 12, 1971—Beijing, China

The Li Clan suffered for the first half of the twentieth century. Having misread the tendencies of the Xinhai Revolution that had begun in 1911, the Qing Dynasty collapsed, leading to the eventual fall of the ruling classes.

The Ivanovic Clan, having participated in the Russian Revolution, continued to preserve its interests, even after the establishment of the Soviet Union. The Rozenmann Clan had been fortifying its position at the top of American capitalism since the United States had just been a collection of British colonies.

In comparison, the Li Clan had put too much support behind the Manchurians who controlled the Qing Dynasty, and failed to build relations with the political powers behind the Nationalist Party of the newly born Republic of China. In the following period of upheaval that continued with the military defending local authority and the formation of Manchukuo, the Li Clan was unable to manifest any influence, and thus its presence further declined.

Then Mao Zedong appeared.

Mao Zedong faced the Li Clan and asked for their support.

He wished to single-handedly take control of the Chinese Communist Party while exterminating the Nationalist Party and all foreign influences, eventually unifying China. When asked about what they would receive in return, Mao answered, "The vampire world is the ultimate communist society. Regardless of a citizen's class or where he is born and raised, he eats the same thing as the others and lives forever at their sides."

Mao wanted to build the ideal communist society in China, and the Li Clan hoped to restore China as an imperial vampire state—which meant their interests aligned. They began negotiations.

Following that, Mao successfully purged all of his political opponents within the party in one single blow. While the Nationalist Party Army was winnowing away— bearing the brunt of the Second Sino-Japanese War—the Communist Party Army was steadily expanding its influence. In 1949, after pushing the Nationalist Party Army back to Taiwan, Mao formally declared the establishment of the People's Republic of China and completed his vision of a communist China.

The Li Clan provided a lot of behind-the-scenes assistance for those movements. It was finally the Li Clan's turn to enjoy the benefits of the deal.

Although Mao claimed it would increase national power, his "Great Leap Forward" campaign implemented in the 1950s ended in resounding failure, and the entire country struggled with severe famine and crop failure. Following that, China's Cultural Revolution began in the 1960s, but suspicion and violence related to the Revolution invaded Chinese society. The result was said to be nearly one hundred million people dead from either starvation or state execution.

Among the dead, a fair number were changed into vampires and contributed greatly to the growth of the Li Clan's influence. Even in ancient times, famine and mayhem had been sources of vampire reserves. Mao Zedong was repaying the Li Clan in an extremely cruel and cold-blooded way.

Then the honeymoon ended.

The Li Clan had expanded its numbers in the new China, but they hadn't recovered any economic strength. Although the Li Clan had flourished up until the Qing Dynasty, their wealth was exhausted by the overbearing reformation led by Mao Zedong, nearly paralyzing the country's economy.

Also, traditional art and culture had been dismissed altogether; the majority of precious art objects—including those from the Qing Dynasty—had been destroyed. The only paintings and songs allowed were government propaganda or things that Mao appreciated.

The Li Clan finally understood—Mao didn't want a vampire-led communist state, but a feudal state where he himself ruled. Realizing that they'd been used as a mere stepping stool, the Li Clan was furious and ordered Ryuu to kill Mao.

Ryuu offered counsel to the Li Clan, prepared to incur their anger. If Mao disappeared, China would fall into political disarray with no government, and there would be no possible way to repair their devastated territory. And Mao's demise wouldn't instantly guarantee the clan's revival, either; before they eliminated him, they needed to have a suitable successor ready to assume leadership.

That wasn't the only problem. Mao Zedong was a "Mediator."

Although human, Mediators stood between humans and vampires, a position wisely designed by both species to prevent the humans from being devoured to extinction. In matters concerning humans, the Li Clan couldn't ignore the will of the Mediators.

Killing a Mediator was a taboo in the vampire world. The fact that Mao Zedong had conspired from the beginning with True Blood vampires to usurp China itself would result in a huge scandal, and if the Li Clan killed Mao, the vampires behind the deed would likely face execution themselves.

At the very least, they needed to have a successor arrange a coup and assassinate Mao Zedong. Ryuu was granted one year for preparations.

Ryuu easily selected his candidate, Mao's successor at the time: Marshal Lin Biao. He was the Minister of National Defense—the same ministry that directed the People's Liberation Army. While the previous Defense Minister Peng Dehuai and Head of State Liu Shaoqi had lost their party standing and suffered miserable deaths, Lin Biao had acquired his rank through earnestly supporting Mao. Lin Biao was the most suitable candidate to handle the transition of political power after a coup, since he already held fundamental political power.

Ryuu intermittently entered and manipulated the minds of Lin Biao and his family. Since Lin Biao already bore a deep resentment for Mao Zedong, he only needed a small push to naturally elicit the growing desire to stage a coup. On the other hand, Mao felt uncomfortable with Lin's growing rebellious behavior and strengthened criticism of him.

While confrontations between Mao Zedong and Lin Biao grew more heated, it was Lin's eldest son, Lin Liguo—the Deputy Director of Military Strategy at the Air Force Command—who finally set the coup d'état in motion.

The plan was to attack Mao Zedong's private train as he made a tour south, beginning in August. With no military troops, however, Lin Liguo couldn't follow through with his plan, and Mao returned safely to Beijing at the end of his journey.

September 12th. With all assassination plans on hold, Lin and his retainers gathered in a villa located in the Beidaihe District to discuss counter-strategies. They solidified a plan for their escape to Guangzhou, taking advantage of Lin's strong influence in the Zhongnan military province in order to use the People's Liberation Army to lead an armed uprising.

Upon hearing of their strategy from a vampire on

surveillance, Ryuu was worried. If this plan were put into action, the country would fall into a state of civil war, just as he had feared. There was only one way to prevent this inevitable unrest and still attempt to re-establish the Li Clan.

Before Lin started an uprising, Ryuu needed to assassinate Mao Zedong with his own hands.

Ryuu stared out the vehicle's window at the cityscape moving past.

Running from east to west through the heart of Beijing, Chang'an Avenue was fading into the darkness of night. There were almost no cars in sight, except for buses and military vehicles. During the Cultural Revolution, only high government officials owned family-use cars. Instead, citizens rode the vast number of bicycles continually traversing the streets.

These roads had been much narrower during the Qing Dynasty. In 1952, with the outbreak of war, the roads had been widened and paved for use as runways that could withstand tanks. Many of the surrounding buildings had been demolished to accommodate this construction. He guessed that the ancient observatory beside the Jianguomen intersection was the only structure that remained from the previous era.

Ryuu was in heavy spirits. That night's plan, although simple enough, felt rash. There were too few ways to assassinate Mao Zedong. If anything unforeseen happened, the plan would fail completely. He knew it was necessary for the Li Clan, but he couldn't shake off his uncertainty about a plan that lay outside of his usual style.

Eight soldiers rode in the large van with Ryuu—dressed in civilian uniforms, but all Air Force officers under Lin Liguo. They sat in silence as well, staring ahead with backs straight, as though they had swallowed sticks. Ryuu had already erased their egos, essentially making them marionettes. He planned to have the men directly assassinate Mao Zedong and arrange for Lin Biao's coup.

While vampire soldiers boasted superior combat skills, he hadn't allowed any vampires (save himself) to participate in this operation. When a vampire lost his life in battle, he left behind ashes. Well aware of the vampire world, Mao would see the ashes and know that the Li Clan was involved.

The van passed the nearly deserted Dong'an Market and Beijing Hotel as it neared Tiananmen Square.

A banner hung ostentatiously from the top of the Forbidden City's main gate, bearing the slogan: "Wei da de ling xiu mao zhu xi wan sui." *Long live the great Chairman Mao.* Next to the slogan was a realistic portrait of Mao Zedong, the man who had pushed the Li Clan aside to form his own personal cult. Ryuu wondered how that slogan would change if Lin became the new ruler.

To the west of Tiananmen was a large area surrounded by a tall wall. The Zhongnanhai was the central headquarters of the Chinese government, and it also housed many important government officials. According to Ryuu's intelligence, Mao Zedong had disembarked from his private locomotive at Fengtai Station and should have returned upon nightfall.

This Zhongnanhai would be their battlefield.

The van drove past the Xinhuamen that faced Chang'an Avenue and turned right onto Fuyou Street. Rows of trees and the long wall ran alongside the street, and then the substantial main gate—facing the west—came into view. The van stopped right in front of it.

The main security detail guarding the government facility quickly neared and surrounded the vehicle. All of the heavily armed men of the Central Security Bureau had their guns out and aimed, ready to fire at any moment. It was the most secure facility in all of China.

Ryuu opened the passenger seat window and removed a scrap of paper from his breast pocket.

"We are a group of executive members from the Shanghai Revolutionary Committee. We have humbly come to meet with the Central Committee member, Wang Hongwen. These are our orders."

Ryuu prattled on in Cantonese and went to hand the paper to the guard.

The sentry stretched out his hand. At the same time Ryuu handed over the paper, he extended his mental "feeler" into the guard's arm. The guard clearly didn't notice anything unusual. He inspected the paper closely, then returned it to Ryuu.

"Let them through."

The scrap of paper was blank; Ryuu had used his invisible "feeler" to show the guard's mind some imaginary official orders. Even as he manipulated the guard's feelings, he didn't let his guard down.

Ryuu had been able to put the entire garrison under his influence using his "feeler," but since forced mind control left lasting effects on the deeper human psyche, he only utilized it when necessary. The guards retreated and the van entered the Forbidden City without any further interruptions.

With his power, Ryuu could go anywhere. For him, it was only natural that in most cases, he didn't worry about being vigilant. It was because of this special power that he had been respected as the leader of the Li Clan's Special Intelligence and Security Division for such a long time.

In order to avoid attracting the attention of the palace guards, the van proceeded slowly to Mao Zedong's residence in the Imperial Garden built during the Qing Dynasty—a building called the Pavilion of Fragrant Chrysanthemums that had come to serve as the Chairman's office and living quarters.

Ryuu stopped the van a short way from their final destination.

All the soldiers in the van checked their concealed pistols. Ryuu himself wasn't carrying a weapon; if his opponent was human, there was no need for him to resort to violence.

They exited the van and began walking toward the

Pavilion of Fragrant Chrysanthemums. A large security presence loomed here as well. Ryuu walked closer and glanced at them.

All at once, the guards shouldered their weapons and stood frozen at attention. They all just shut their eyes and stopped moving.

If Ryuu withdrew his "feeler" at any time, they would regain consciousness, so he didn't plan to show them *anything* to prevent any later disturbances after they passed.

Ryuu and his soldiers arrived at the entrance to the Pavilion of Fragrant Chrysanthemums without having to fight at all.

A door waited at the end of the hallway.

On the opposite side of that door lay the secretary's antechamber. Beyond that was Mao Zedong's study. He had brought a large bed into the room and on it, surrounded by books, it was said that he rebuked his executive officials and fooled around with his lover, among other things.

A single guard stood at the door that led to the antechamber. With practiced skill, Ryuu stretched his "feeler" toward the lone sentry's spirit.

Suddenly, Ryuu froze. He stared hard at the guard.

"You... What are you?"

When Ryuu probed at this enemy's soul with his "feeler," it felt entirely different from the same attempt on a human. He recalled having encountered this feeling before...

The guard cracked his neck and casually returned Ryuu's gaze.

"Of all the stupid things!" Ryuu's sense of calm vanished as he started to tremble.

The guard reached his hand up toward his helmet. His sleeve ripped, exposing his arm muscle as it swelled and burst yellow bristles. He removed his helmet with a hand that had stretched out like a glove. His eyes beneath the helmet glittered gold.

His entire body grew and split the seams of his uniform. Like his arm, the exposed, indomitable figure was completely covered in yellow fur with black stripes.

He was a weretiger.

The guard curled his lips into a smile, as if to say to Ryuu, "So you finally figured it out?"

Weretigers had been developed by the Li Clan to oppose the werewolves created by the vampires of the west; they were a half-human, half-beast race built for combat. Substantially stronger than werewolves, they had been expected to contribute to the spread of the clan's influence.

However, there was a defect: weretigers and werewolves had completely different mental dispositions. Werewolves acted within the defined organization of a pack and valued teamwork when executing battle strategies. In direct contrast, weretigers favored individual action and could never dedicate themselves to a team; they always followed their own instincts rather than the orders of a lead vampire.

Furthermore, weretigers were entirely immune to Ryuu's extrasensory mind abilities. He could manipulate a human's mind and behavior; with a vampire, he couldn't penetrate deeply enough to negate a master's orders, but he could influence the vampire's feelings and his will to fight. Ryuu was even able to affect the minds of werewolves, although their resistance to his mental abilities was stronger than that of humans.

He just couldn't force *weretigers* to follow his orders. Aside from them, there was only one other species he couldn't control, and that was a single man: Mao Zedong.

The weretigers were a formidable presence because they hadn't become faithful retainers of the Li Clan—and in certain circumstances, they couldn't be trusted. The Li Clan had decided to abandon the weretigers. Ryuu and other subordinate vampires had commanded werewolves to hunt down every last weretiger. The weretigers had resisted fiercely, and although they had caused more than a few casualties in the fight, the Li Clan had supposedly eradicated them.

And now one of those weretigers was here, protecting Mao Zedong.

For the first time, Ryuu was in awe of Mao's abilities as a Mediator. However, he didn't have time to spare for admiration; Mao lay just beyond the weretiger.

Ryuu sprang at his opponent. Mid-leap, he revealed a sword from his sleeve and swung at the weretiger's throat.

Already fully transformed, the guard flung out his left hand and successfully slapped Ryuu away. The sword broke into pieces that clattered to the ground.

Without wasting a moment, the weretiger swung his right arm. His fist was nearly the size of Ryuu's head, and he scored a direct hit to the face. The force threw Ryuu backwards over the heads of his men before he slammed into the floor.

The weretiger advanced and swiped his claws at the soldier closest to him. The attack sliced the soldier's torso almost all the way through; his stomach looked like a swinging hinge, the floor around him dotted with blood and shredded intestines.

Ryuu applied pressure to his bleeding nose and managed to wobble back to his feet. He was concussed and dazed, so his influence via his "feeler" didn't respond; his soldiers simply stood there, unblinking.

The weretiger grabbed the next soldier's head and crushed it.

Ryuu couldn't let all his soldiers die; if a human didn't kill Mao, all was lost.

Ryuu shook his head, adjusted his posture, and leapt a second time. He took a second step off of the wall near the ceiling and attacked the weretiger with a drop kick.

The weretiger grabbed Ryuu's ankle, swung him around by the leg, and sent him crashing into the wall.

Ryuu's mangled body slid to the floor. He felt the blood

trickling down his lips and realized he'd broken several ribs, and they had punctured either his lungs or stomach.

The weretiger still gripped his ankle; he dragged Ryuu up and swung him all the way around, sending him flying toward his still-motionless soldiers.

Ryuu slammed into the soldiers. They hit the wall as a group and crumpled to the ground.

Ryuu struggled to get up, but his dislocated ankle folded under him. Ignoring the immense pain, he reset it and managed to stand. The soldiers lay immobile against the wall where they'd landed, their necks twisted in unnatural directions.

Ryuu looked up to see the weretiger leap toward another soldier; this time he sliced off the top of the soldier's head and tossed it aside.

Only four soldiers remained. Ryuu couldn't lose any more.

He picked up the Jingdezhen flower vase nearby and threw it at the weretiger. The weretiger abruptly destroyed it.

Bending down to avoid the flying, shattered fragments, Ryuu pushed off of the wall and closed the gap between him and the weretiger in an instant.

The weretiger quickly swung his arm and struck Ryuu in the stomach. His claws caught in the side of Ryuu's uniform, their momentum ripping across Ryuu's abdomen. Just like the first soldier, Ryuu's internal organs tried to spill from his abdomen.

Instead of stopping, Ryuu rushed the weretiger and threw an uppercut into his jaw. The sleeve of Ryuu's civilian uniform burst into pieces and scattered.

Both Ryuu and the weretiger stood stock still, entangled with one another.

Ryuu's arm had grown to one and a half times its original length; his wrist had become a sword that resembled the scythe of a praying mantis. The transformed portion of his arm had embedded deeply into the soft chin muscle of the weretiger, allowing the blade to pierce through his brain and stick out of the back of his head. Blood gushed from the weretiger and stained Ryuu's clothes.

On the other hand, Ryuu's stomach—sliced open by the weretiger's claws—wasn't bleeding at all. Beneath the torn fabric of his uniform, Ryuu's skin was completely covered by strong armor, resembling the abdomen of a beetle. Four shallow scratches were left across the surface of his stomach.

Ryuu removed his hand-sword from the weretiger's chin. Without any support, the large body fell back and shook the floor when it landed.

It had been about a century since Ryuu had been forced to transform in battle. Thinking back on it, his opponent that last time had been a weretiger, too.

Ryuu reversed his transformation. He had to hurry—there was no way security had missed that ruckus.

Ryuu marched the remaining soldiers forward. The first of the soldiers approached the antechamber, held his gun, and turned the doorknob.

The door blew off of its hinges and fell on the soldier, flattening him. A large pair of feet walked across the fallen door; Ryuu could hear the sound of bones snapping underneath the wood.

The newcomer was another weretiger. This one was large enough to nearly fill the doorway. Behind him stood a third weretiger.

Just how many weretigers did Mao Zedong keep?

Ryuu was at his limit. He didn't want to admit that it was an impossible situation, but he had to—there was no way for him to protect the remaining soldiers while taking down two weretigers and still successfully assassinate Mao Zedong.

If there had been werewolves around, he would have had a more or less equal chance in crossing swords with the opposition. But after the Warsaw political purge, many werewolves were estranged from the Li Clan, and they wouldn't willingly come to his aid.

Ryuu quickly settled on a course of action. He ordered all of the remaining soldiers to fire their weapons at the weretigers.

The soldiers, without any fear or remorse, turned toward the weretigers. The weretigers' howls for blood echoed through the hallway.

It only took ten seconds for them to slaughter the soldiers, but those ten seconds were enough for Ryuu to escape.

Officials swarmed throughout the building to investigate the commotion.

Ryuu's clothing was shredded and streaked with blood—both the weretiger's and his own. He concealed himself in the shadowy corners of a hallway and watched the busy stream of people, looking for someone he could use.

An officer of the People's Liberation Army, similar in build to Ryuu, happened to walk by. Ryuu extended his "feeler" immediately. He stopped the officer and guided him into an empty room.

As Ryuu changed into the military officer's uniform, he shook his head irritably, trying to decide on his next course of action.

The plan to assassinate Mao Zedong was a failure. After what had happened, it was imperative they get Lin Biao out of the country as quickly as possible. Mao would soon discover the identity of the soldiers killed by the weretigers; if Lin Biao and his retainers were arrested and questioned, Mao would realize that Ryuu had used his mental abilities to infiltrate the Zhongnanhai. In addition, if Mao realized that Ryuu had participated in an assassination attempt, the Li Clan would lose face for breaking a taboo.

As long as Lin Biao stayed alive and healthy—even if he fled the country—there was still a chance for him to be reinstated and make a comeback. He was fourteen years younger than Mao Zedong, after all.

The military officer stood in his underwear with a

dumbfounded look on his face. Ryuu dressed the officer in his own discarded clothes. It was a risky and reckless plan, but it would save him time.

Once the officer wore the tattered clothing, Ryuu made him stand on top of a chair, hook his belt on an overhead beam, and wrap it into a loop. After that, Ryuu had him put his head through the belt loop. Although the officer had indifferently prepared for his own hanging, he was now sweating profusely. The officer's feelings of misery and terror flowed into Ryuu and rejuvenated him, replenishing the energy he'd spent in the battle with the weretigers.

Ryuu looked on as the military man knocked over the stepstool, and then left the room behind.

He feigned a look of complete innocence as he fled the Zhongnanhai in a party-owned vehicle. Fully aware that he could get trapped in narrow streets, he headed north, using the main truck lanes. He wasn't stopped at any checkpoints and reached Ditan Park in several minutes. He abandoned the car near the edge of the park and ran toward the grassy clearing.

Ryuu dashed into the darkness at speeds beyond human comprehension. With his excellent night vision, he successfully skirted the line of trees in front of him. He heard the sound of flapping wings right behind him.

Suddenly, something that resembled a leather mantle covered him, and thin, stick-like arms wrapped around his torso. Without dropping any speed, they took off, climbing higher and higher until they could look down at the tops of the trees.

The vampire who whisked Ryuu away into the night sky was one of his subordinates—a vampire who could sprout wings to transport him to Lin Biao's location. He'd been prepared for the assassination getaway.

"What's the situation?" Ryuu asked.

"Lin Liheng, Lin Biao's eldest daughter, betrayed her father," the bat-like vampire replied.

Ryuu looked over his shoulder without thinking. "What did you say?"

"She leaked information of his escape plans to the Central Security Bureau. Not long ago, Prime Minister Zhou Enlai issued an official prohibition, banning Lin Biao's private aircraft from taking off. We're racing against time."

Ryuu sucked his teeth. He'd thought that he had spent enough time planting the seeds of rebellion within the Lin family, but it seemed as though Lin Liheng had been reverse-brainwashed by Mao Zedong. Certainly Mao Zedong was one of the greatest human brainwashers throughout history. If he hadn't been, the six hundred million people in China would not have been swept up by the hype of the Cultural Revolution.

"So where is Lin Biao now?"

"According to our most recent intelligence, the Lin family has assembled and will depart from their vacation home momentarily. They plan to take off by force, if necessary."

"Then let's head directly to the airfield. Quickly."

The vampire flapped his wings and soared higher into the night sky. Below them, the Beijing cityscape faded into the distance.

Lin Biao's private plane, a large, British-made jetliner called the Hawker Siddeley Trident, stood on the People's Liberation Army Air Force Shanhaiguan Airfield on the coast of the Yellow Sea. Moving faster than had they taken the land route, Ryuu and the other vampire arrived in the airspace above the airfield in less than an hour.

Ryuu looked out over the surrounding area; he could barely make out headlights on a connecting road, approaching the airport at a remarkable speed. It had to be the car carrying Lin Biao.

The headlights slowed, then abruptly stopped.

The headlights illuminated shadowy figures spread out on the road, blocking the car's path. Apparently, members of the Central Security Bureau stationed at the airport were expecting them.

"Drop me over there!" Ryuu shouted.

The bat-like vampire flew directly above the location and released Ryuu from the sky with the precision of a dive bomber. As he fell, Ryuu selected the soldier on the very edge of the assembled group.

The soldier slowly changed the direction he was facing and fired wildly at his comrades. Taken by surprise, the other soldiers fell to the gunfire, one after another.

Ryuu landed on the ground in front of the Lin vehicle and dropped to his knees. Without wasting a second, he bounced to his feet and stared at the single remaining soldier.

The soldier placed the barrel of his gun on his own temple and stoically pulled the trigger.

When Ryuu looked over at the car, Lin Biao and the others stared at him in disbelief.

Behind them, several more sets of headlights appeared and flickered in the distance. Their pursuers were catching up.

He didn't have enough time to put on a show for the humans. He just took control of them as group, using his "feeler," and then jumped into their car.

The car soon entered the airfield and screeched to a halt next to the parked Trident. Their pursuers were now only a few hundred meters away.

The party exited the car all at once. Lin Liguo waved a rifle around, and Lin Biao's wife ranted hysterically. Lin Biao himself was in poor health and was unable to walk; the driver and a friend of Lin Liguo supported him on either side.

There was no time to pull over a stairway to reach the main cabin's entrance, so they used the rope ladder hanging from the door to the cockpit.

Keeping one eye on them as the entire Lin party struggled to push Lin Biao up the ladder, Ryuu ran over to the mechanics refueling the Trident.

"Get the refueling truck out of the way! We're taking off now!"

"What? But we're still—"

"Move it!" Ryuu boomed angrily as he flung his "feeler" at them.

One of the mechanics bent backwards as if he had been struck by lightning. "Yes, sir!" he cried out before quickly removing the fuel hose.

Ryuu climbed the ladder with the mechanics and boarded the cockpit. There was only a pilot—no co-pilot or navigator—but that couldn't be helped. He sat down in the co-pilot's chair and ordered the pilot to take off.

The control tower strictly stated that they were to stand down, but Ryuu ignored it.

Equipped with three engines and designed to ferry one hundred and fifty passengers, the Trident took off from the Shanhaiguan Airfield with a sparse ten people.

Before Ryuu knew it, the date changed—and it was September 13th.

Completely disregarding Lin Biao's anti-American and anti-Soviet stance, Ryuu was prepared to escape with the man to the Soviet Union in an emergency. If he passed outside of Mongolia, he could escape Chinese airspace in less than an hour.

In order to seek asylum in the Soviet Union, Ryuu—on behalf of Lin Biao—would be forced to make some very risky deals with the Ivanovic Clan, but at that point in time, their safety was of the utmost importance. He fastened his seat belt.

The Trident flew northwest at a low altitude to avoid being detected by radar, and they successfully entered Mongolian territory.

Still sitting in the co-pilot's seat, Ryuu considered just how to negotiate with Ivanovic. He lifted his head casually and noticed several small demons illuminated by moonlight in the sky before them. The pilot, with weaker eyesight than vampires, hadn't noticed them yet.

The creatures hurtled toward the plane. Ryuu locked his eyes on them. They weren't demons; it was a swarm of vampires.

The winged vampires were about to crash headfirst into the Trident. As far as Ryuu could tell, it was on purpose.

The Mongolian Prime Minister Tsedenbal was a supporter of the Soviet Union, so it wasn't strange for vampires belonging to the Ivanovic Clan to be in Mongolian territory. It was, however, unthinkable that the Chinese and Soviet governments would cooperate at all, given their purely antagonistic relationship from their military conflicts two years earlier.

If it wasn't the two governments, but actually Mao Zedong and the Ivanovic Clan, conspiring behind the scenes...

"*Qu si ba, chou shan yang lao tou!* Drop dead, you decrepit, senile goats!"

Ryuu's angry roar reverberated in the cockpit.

At the speed of nearly one thousand kilometers per hour, the gap between the Trident and the horde of vampires closed in an instant. All of the vampires were armed with guns.

Ryuu forced his seat all the way back.

The windscreen shattered into tiny pieces with the battery of bullets. Ricocheting bullets zoomed past each other and embedded themselves in the dashboard instrument panel, the wind screaming around them.

The sudden attack ended just as abruptly as the vampires flew past the Trident.

Even buried in his chair, Ryuu was shot several times. Luckily, each and every bullet had missed his vital organs. He struggled to lift his head up in the rushing wind and looked over at the pilot's seat.

The pilot was covered in blood and slumped against the back of his seat. Blood flowed from his mouth, and his right hand hung limply at an awkward angle.

While avoiding transferring the pilot's pain to himself, Ryuu increased the control level of his "feeler" and forced the pilot to keep operating the plane. Ryuu glanced back and saw that the three mechanics were all dead.

Suddenly, he felt someone's eyes on him.

He turned back around; a suspicious face was hanging upside down from the empty frame of the windscreen. A vampire clinging to the roof of the plane above the cockpit had poked his head inside for a look. A malicious smile stretched across his wrinkled face as he threw something toward the pilot's seat.

"Yób tvoyú mať!" he spat. *Motherfucker.*

The vampire disappeared as his gift rolled by the pilot's feet.

A hand grenade.

Ryuu ripped off his seatbelt and leapt for the back.

The grenade detonated, splattering pieces of the pilot's body across the cockpit. Ryuu barely managed to shield himself with a mechanic's corpse.

He dropped the body, moved toward the pilot's seat, and cleared away the lump of meat that had once been the pilot.

The control panel had become a tangled scrap pile of metal, plastic, and wires. Without its operator, the Trident began to hurtle toward the ground at a steep pitch.

Ryuu flopped into the co-pilot's seat. The howling, cold wind tore past his face.

When the Trident exited the clouds, he could already recognize some things on the ground. They were only a few minutes from a crash.

The entire Lin family would die. The only silver lining was that the Li Clan would no longer be tied to this incident.

The remaining problem was what would happen to Ryuu.

He wasn't going to die with a clichéd last line, such as "Glory to the Li Clan!" A dead retainer was worth nothing. If he lived, he could offer his allegiance to the Great Clan and earn their favor. Regardless of whether the plan succeeded or failed, whatever happened, his life came first and foremost.

His trickery had awarded him his long life in the vampire world.

So in that moment as well, he resolved to stay alive as long as possible.

The skin on Ryuu's face and hands turned green as it began to harden. Before long, a beetle-like outer shell covered his entire body.

Halfway through his transformation, Ryuu tried grabbing the throttle in front of the co-pilot's seat, although he knew it was probably a waste of time. It didn't make things worse; it made him feel like he was actually controlling the plane, if only a little.

A strange thought suddenly struck him—in Russian, the word "goat" meant "man whose spouse was taken from him." Ryuu used the time he had left to think up a bitter joke involving two True Bloods: an older figure and a young girl. It was a surprisingly good joke, so Ryuu began chuckling.

By the time his quiet chuckle turned into loud laughter, the Trident crashed into Mongolian soil.

Local policemen from the nearby village were the first to arrive on the scene. Many scattered pieces of the plane had caught fire around the dark plains. The officers found dead male and female bodies, one after the other. All of the bodies were burnt and blackened; most of their clothing had been destroyed. One of the men still wore a gun belt.

When one of the police officers searched through the

rubble, he thought he noticed a large fragment moving next to him. He attempted to lift up the curved fragment, which looked like a piece from the cockpit.

A burnt body lay beneath it, face down.

When he was about to get up and inform his colleague, the dead body's hand suddenly caught the back of his neck. Before the shocked, struggling officer's eyes, the corpse slowly lifted its head.

The blackened skin around its neck began to peel off and flutter to the ground. One eye popped open in the middle of the burnt, cracked face and focused on the officer.

"At dawn, take me away from here," it rasped. The voice sounded like scraping glass.

The officer opened his mouth to cry out, but the shriek got caught on something and returned to the back of his throat.

All nine plane crash victims found at the scene were buried at the site. When the Mongolian government contacted the Chinese, the Chinese replied that they didn't want the bodies returned.

The following day, the KGB-commissioned officers, dispatched by the Soviet Union, dug up the buried bodies and confirmed that Lin Biao was among the dead. Was the Kremlin really concerned with only *his* death? That wasn't clear.

The Chinese government didn't formally report the incident to the public until the following July. And it took them more than two decades to reveal more details—in 1993.

Present Day—Tokyo, Japan

"In the end, the confrontation in the Zhongnanhai was never publicized. As one would expect, Mao Zedong did not want to set up the Li Clan without any proof." Councilor Ryuu finished his story and took a sip from his glass of water.

My initial question had nothing to do with the Lin Biao Incident.

"So then, your ability is..."

If I believed his story to be true, his ability was *mind control.* He could manipulate human minds while absorbing their feelings as energy. A "mind vampire."

"Do you think that you're being controlled?" Councilor Ryuu preempted my question with one of his own. "Stop and think about it. Did anyone make you come here? Did anyone force you to stay here and listen to my story? Did anyone make you take notes in that notebook?"

I thought about it. True, I hadn't been forced to do anything. All of the things he had mentioned were things that I had wanted to do in the first place.

"I don't use my abilities except when it is absolutely necessary. Using it all the time would literally waste my energy."

It made sense. After that, I asked a general question about the Lin Biao Incident, but he was very courteous and continued to provide detailed answers until I was satisfied.

"Allow me to ask just one more question," I said at last. "If I may. Why did you decide to go public with such sensitive information?"

The councilor touched his chin, seemingly lost in thought.

"To put it simply, I want to revolutionize the Li Clan." Compared to when we had first met, the councilor made no attempt to avoid answering the question.

"House Tepes establishing the Vampire Bund drastically changed the relationship between humans and vampires. My wish is to create a new way of life in this changed world. Just as House Tepes did in Japan, I would very much like for us, the Li Clan, to start off on a new foot in China.

"In China now, it's extremely difficult to present this kind of information. It would make me very glad if I could borrow the power of someone like you to expose this information in modern-day Japan, where such freedom is enjoyed by all."

As soon as I was escorted out of the embassy building by the councilor, a plan began to form in the back of my head.

Submitting a story of this level to a magazine would be a waste. After a little more research, I could write a book that would redefine Chinese history, all the way from its roots. In the short time it took to walk to the main gate, my excitement grew and grew.

My goal was no longer just to be a writer like Izawa Motohiko—I would even surpass Jung Chang's book that had exposed Mao Zedong's darker side to the entire world. My book could even revolutionize the world of humans and vampires.

The iron door I had struggled with on my arrival now opened easily for me. My body was full of energy; if I wrote for three days straight, I would have a manuscript ready in hand. Passing though the side entrance, I skipped past the guards and waved at them cheerfully.

"Thanks for your hard work!"

Triumphantly, I stepped out onto the street, where I triumphantly stood in the way of a truck barreling down the road, whereupon I was triumphantly rolled up by the front wheels.

As I imagined myself standing triumphantly at the Pulitzer Prize award ceremony, the giant tires crushed my head.

Councilor Ryuu sat leisurely in the desk chair in his basement room at the embassy, cocking his ear toward the nearing sirens. Since he had left his "feeler" connected even after he and the writer had parted ways, he was fully aware of the writer's death. Just before the writer had died, Ryuu had absorbed all of his emotional energy—without sparing a drop—and was completely full now.

He had no intention of releasing a human who had learned that many secrets. At least he had shown compassion by amplifying the writer's delight and allowing him to die with extreme happiness.

As the controller of the Li Clan's underground network, Ryuu lived in a world full of secrets and lies. Every once in a while, he enjoyed inviting someone in and confessing all of his secrets as a change of pace. If he picked a docile, insignificant human, there was very little—if any— consequence afterward.

He hadn't told the writer a single lie. He *had* omitted one thing, however.

He had one shame in his countless years of dirty, underhanded work. Even if he had planned to silence the writer, he couldn't bring himself to admit it to a human stranger.

The real motive for assassinating Mao Zedong had been the Li Clan's hatred of the citizens' clothing. At the time, Mao had been seventy-eight years old. They had known that if they failed to assassinate him, he still didn't have long to live. As it was, Mao's life ended a mere five years after the Lin Biao Incident.

For a vampire who lived forever, waiting five years was equivalent to a human waiting a single day. However, the Li Clan had refused to wait. They had been impatient to eradicate the dull-colored, shabby, woven civilian uniform from their previously brilliant and gaudy Qing territory, colored by the pleasure industry.

The Li Clan's political and economic issues with the Mediator Mao had only been secondary.

And the assassination plot—set into motion by the ruling head of the Li Clan to restore a fashion aesthetic—had ended in failure. At the time, Ryuu nearly died from his injuries; he was locked in a buried coffin for more than forty years for both punishment and recuperation.

When Mao Zedong died, Ryuu heard the obituary announcement from within the confines of his coffin. He thought about the Li Clan and the world after Mao, who had restricted free thought.

If Mao had been assassinated, the Li Clan would have been under Lin Biao's control and thus protected from a political purging—that round-faced, small-statured man had wielded true political power. Mao had wagered his life on the Cultural Revolution, and that had been his undoing.

Ryuu knew that Mao's natural death would change the very foundation of China. It had to accept outside influences in order to exist, such as from the Soviet Union, Mongolia, India, and even Japan.

Amidst all of that, could the Li Clan still exist without changing as well?

No, the Li Clan had to change; Ryuu had believed it then and he believed it now. Everything he had told that writer was the honest truth.

House Tepes had recovered from their downfall, changing

in a big way; Queen Mina had become a force to be reckoned with. On the other hand, the Li Clan idly sat on the benefits of the developing Chinese economy, obsessing over a lost Manchurian culture. They held unwavering power as one of the Great Clans, but it was obvious that their True Blood line was weakening.

When he'd emerged from his coffin several years earlier, Ryuu stopped wearing his hair in a braid and started dressing in modern, Western clothing.

The Li Clan had to change like he had.

Ryuu opened the desk drawer and removed a single, candid photograph. He gazed at the raven-haired young girl smiling brightly in the photo.

I'm protecting the future of the Li Clan, he told himself. *Not anyone in particular.*

End

Dance in the

Vampire Bund

LES ENFANTS
TERRIBLES

STORY
Tikurakuran

ILLUSTRATION
Nozomu Tamaki

It is said that in the Vampire Bund even the poorest can live free of poverty.

It is said that in the Vampire Bund there are no laws; residents are free to live as they choose.

The humans on the mainland often said things like that about the Bund. Though neither of those popular rumors was incorrect, the actual circumstances in the Bund were a little more complicated.

While it was true that vampires in the Bund were able to live without spending any money because they received furnished housing and the artificial blood Stigma as a free food source, the government only provided them with the barest necessities for survival. Installed appliances and clothing were plain and utilitarian; items appealing to individual tastes or indulgences were never included. Most vampires were hedonistic pleasure-seekers who could never be satisfied by such a conformist lifestyle.

The only way to obtain new items was to purchase them.

If a vampire wanted an item, a seller of that item would make contact, and a mutually beneficial transaction would take place.

Although the Bund lacked its own currency, most vampires used cash to make purchases at shops and bars. Money-exchange businesses that traded Japanese yen for US dollars and Chinese yuan—brought by vampires from their homelands—did exceptionally well.

With any economy comes a disparity of wealth. Prior to entering the Bund, the economic situations of vampires were as varied as those of ordinary humans—some had amassed fortunes from businesses started under false human identities, others had lived like stray dogs with only the clothes on their backs. This disparity endured, even after entering the Bund.

Eventually, all vampires without fortunes had to work to earn money. The more serious vampires found steady work and began earning an honest income. Others, only interested in quick and easy money, would take on more questionable tasks, creating a new type of transaction between vampires.

The rumor about the Bund having no laws was not entirely accurate, either. Certainly, there were very few—if any—clearly established and documented laws, but that was only because of a decree stricter than any human law: everyone submits to Queen Mina's will.

If Queen Mina said to do something, then it was done.

If she forbade it, then her orders were followed without exception.

For all affiliated with House Tepes, there was no higher law to obey.

That being said, Queen Mina's orders were basically a list of prohibitions, so as long as her subjects avoided a few specific things they could do whatever they pleased.

Giving them that much freedom was risky, however—life in the Bund was based on a careful equilibrium of forces, forces which could destabilize if crime went unchecked. Queen Mina could not account for every one of her subjects' future indiscretions with her words alone. She knew they needed a more tangible way to maintain order within the Bund.

The VGS and Beowulf were extremely effective as defenders against foreign enemies, but as an internal police force they were insufficient. There was a plan in place to resolve this oversight, known as General Public Outsourcing.

The government selected several individuals who excelled in organization and had plenty of personal connections. They became members of the Public Welfare Committee, tasked with resolving problems involving civilians, settling conflicts of interest, and assuming the role of arbiter when necessary. As they began handling conflicts between individuals, the VGS and Beowulf took over those involving humans or any large-scale disturbances, and a clear division of labor was established.

Unexpectedly, the general public accepted this system without any resistance. Compared to the VGS, who would pass swift judgment on offenders and sentence them to death without any kind of trial, the Public Welfare Committee members were much more reasonable overseers of the street.

As compensation for their time and assistance, the vampires appointed by each region were allowed to use their position for financial gain. In short, a committee member held the same position as a local mafia boss, or the head of a yakuza clan who ruled a specific region.

Among the Public Welfare Committee members, there was one vampire who had been personally appointed to his position by Queen Mina. He had been alive for more than one hundred years, longer than any other committee member. Even Queen Mina acknowledged his outstanding organizational skills. His practice of taking newcomers under his protection regardless of their legality and teaching them about local customs and vampire life essentials was partially accepted as standard procedure.

Individuals seeking conflict mediation or work referrals constantly requested an audience. It was just another day…

"Please, help me. If this keeps up, I'll be humiliated."

An elderly man stood in front of a big desk and pleaded. His large, portly frame quivered as he mopped the sweat dripping steadily from his forehead with a worn-out, wrinkled handkerchief.

The inside of the small room was dim, and slowly filled with thick cigar smoke. The only pieces of furniture were a desk and an old sofa in the corner. A thin man sat on the sofa, holding a thick notebook. To one side of the desk, a hulking man who resembled a gorilla stood with his arms folded, assuming a daunting pose. He glared intensely at the petitioning man, never dropping his gaze for an instant.

The owner of the desk had turned his head to listen to what the corpulent man had to say. Blowing cigar smoke, he responded in a high-pitched voice.

"First of all, go apologize for yer joke. I know yer little one already tried to interfere."

"But, those Fangless…"

The desk owner lifted his pointer finger and stabbed the air, cutting him off before he could argue. "At times like these, ya bow yer head before ya do anything else. Then, if they don't forgive ya, it means they're the unreasonable ones. Also…" The desk owner bent forward to stare at the man. "Yer aware of Her Highness' kindness toward the Fangless, right? Say ya shared yer joke directly with Her Highness. Chances are, she wouldn't appreciate it. And ya'd lose something worse than a little pride."

Crestfallen, the man hung his head.

"As for yer joke, I'll tell ya; if ya don't settle this here and now, it'll only get worse fer the both of ya." The desk owner drew back, signaling that this was his final word to the man.

Perhaps finally understanding, the man put his handkerchief away in his pocket and bowed his head. "Thank you, Harvey-san."

Seeing that the conversation was over, the skinny man got up from the sofa and opened the door.

Harvey watched as the man left the room, then pulled over the ashtray and put out his cigar. Even though the desktop was at least a meter squared, the lamp, cigar case and everything else were arranged rather unnaturally, concentrated around the chair. This was because Harvey's physical age was roughly six months old; he couldn't reach anything if it was placed normally. Even in his chair, which was actually a child seat placed on an office chair, he could barely place his elbows on the desk.

Harvey pulled a new cigar from its case and placed it between his lips. Without a moment's delay, his gorilla-like subordinate produced a lighter and lit the cigar.

"Next!" Harvey ordered.

The skinny man opened the door a second time.

He ushered in three young vampires.

The first was a young boy with darkish skin; of the three, he had the largest build. For some reason, he seemed extremely fired up; his mouth was open and his shoulders were squared.

The second was a blond, Caucasian girl who seemed awed by the atmosphere. An uneasy expression grew on her face.

The third and smallest was a black-haired girl with a short haircut. She looked around the room in curiosity. Just what was so interesting?

The three looked nothing alike, but somehow they resembled an older brother and his younger sisters regardless.

The boy stood at attention and greeted Harvey.

"How do you do? I'm Jiji Evers!"

"I'm Clara…" the blonde girl said in a small voice.

"And I'm Anna!" The black-haired girl cheerfully added.

"What do I care about yer names?" Harvey was curt. "This is not a place fer children."

"Even though you're a baby?" The girl who called herself Anna asked.

A vein appeared with a pop from Harvey's temple. He screamed at the vampire who escorted the children.

"Miguel! I keep tellin' ya not to let anyone in without an appointment. Ya know that!"

"That's because… Boss, they had this."

Miguel handed Harvey a small envelope. When Harvey took the envelope, he saw it was made of a higher quality paper than he'd expected.

Harvey calmly turned the envelope over.

On the reverse side was the crest of House Tepes in deep crimson sealing wax. There was only one person in the Bund who could use that crest.

After staring at the seal for a good ten seconds, he opened the envelope cautiously and removed the letter inside. The contents was only a few short lines.

Though your body is small, your dedication to this family

is admirable. That is why I am entrusting you with these siblings; please resolve this situation with the utmost care.

Furthermore, they are not to be put in any danger. In the event that they sustain injury or die, know that your own flesh and blood will be held responsible. You have been warned of the consequences.

It was signed just below the body of the letter in perfect calligraphy: *Mina Tepes.*

Harvey didn't stir an inch, even after he finished reading. He peeled his eyes from the page and looked at the children anew.

The children returned his gaze with shining eyes.

Queen Mina didn't make idle threats. He knew exactly where he stood with that letter. Though the House Tepes hierarchy could be unclear or faulty at times, a direct order could not be ignored, and the children couldn't be sent away.

"You said ya wanted to work for the sake of yer family?" Harvey asked quietly.

"Yes. We want to give a present to our Mama and Papa, but our allowance isn't enough," Jiji replied.

"No, actually it was enough, but Jiji spent it!" Anna interjected. "He said he was going to buy exploration supplies, but he bought a bunch of expensive things—a flashlight and a rope! So, the money ran out too fast."

"The flashlight wasn't that expensive!" Jiji pouted.

"Yes, it was." This time, Clara responded. "They had one that was about half as expensive, but you said we should get the one you can wear on your head, and—"

"Shut up! Enough already!" Harvey waved his short arms and interrupted the siblings' endless chatter. "Just what kind of work can ya do?"

The three siblings raised their hands immediately.

"A bookstore clerk!" Anna said.

"A florist!" Clara blurted out.

"A member of Beowulf!" Jiji declared.

"I didn't ask ya what you wanted to be! And being part of Beowulf isn't a job!" Harvey retorted in disgust. "I'm asking what work ya *can* do!"

The three thought for a moment before replying again in order.

"Reading books."

"Making flower arrangements."

"Taking out bad guys."

Harvey slumped over his desk and held his head.

"I…I got it. It was my fault for askin'."

The reality was that of all the work Harvey could possibly arrange, there were absolutely no jobs for a Fangless child. Positions like daytime cleaners, black market transaction lookouts, and participants in drug trials either risked bodily harm or couldn't be made public.

Harvey scratched at the peach fuzz on his head and put out his cigar. "Hey, gimme my phone!"

A scantily-clad female vampire rushed into the room and respectfully handed Harvey a cell phone. Harvey deftly operated the large phone with his tiny hands and held it to his ear. "Gregor? It's me. Didn't ya have a Fangless working for ya as an arbiter or somethin'? Money's not an issue… Do ya have a safe job that even a Fangless kid could do? Translating the archives? Nah, they haven't lived that long. They look and act like the real deal. Kids these days…"

After exchanging a few more words, he hung up the phone. He let out a small sigh and looked at the children. "I'm gonna take ya to the arbiter offices. They said they would find ya some work to do before we arrive."

After he rattled off instructions, he called his subordinate over from the sofa, who drew a large red "X" in the notebook he had been holding.

"Cancel the rest of my meetings fer today. Let's head out."

"Wow!"

"I've never seen a car like this before!"

"This must be what it feels like to be… What's it called again?"

"Rich?"

"Yeah, that's it!"

Harvey's beloved car was a snow white Cadillac DTS limousine. Its glossy body reflected the glittering neon signs of the bustling business district like a mirror. There were two tiny chandeliers installed beneath the headlights that jangled as the car rocked back and forth.

In the back of the car, Harvey sat enshrined in a child's car seat between two grim bodyguards. Jiji and his sisters sat in a row, facing Harvey.

The interior of the car was magnificent. Both the floor and seats were lined with plush fur and rows of colorful LEDs that illuminated the area. Wine bottles filled with a red liquid—assumedly Stigma—were held in the champagne cooler. A TV showed an anime character flying around in the sky.

The children couldn't help but gawk at the inside of the car. Every time one of the children—especially Anna—attempted to touch something, Harvey scolded them.

"I told ya, don't touch that! Just don't do anything! Don't even breathe!"

Irritated, Harvey smoked a cigar as he observed the children. He didn't think that Queen Mina would write an introduction letter for them out of pure kindness. Perhaps the children had received orders from Queen Mina to investigate the secret business ventures he kept up on the side. As far as he could tell by their behavior, all three were as innocent as their physical age suggested, but he couldn't be sure that it wasn't an act to get him to drop his guard.

Harvey decided to drop a few crumbs and see how they reacted.

He picked up the telephone receiver in the car and relayed a message to the driver. "Take us to Adolfo's first."

The limousine pulled away from the city limits and drove for a short time before stopping in front of a building. The façade looked classic European and there was a large wooden door at its entrance.

Harvey disembarked with both of his bodyguards. He held up his hand to stop the three siblings, who had begun to follow.

"Stay here, all of ya. Don't ya dare touch nothing!"

"Okay!" The children readily returned to the car.

Harvey was disappointed. They really were just children.

Adolfo looked about fifty years old, with a perfectly groomed mustache and black hair smoothed down with pomade. He looked like an Italian vampire out of a painting.

"Harvey, if you had just given me a little warning that you were coming, I would have prepared…"

"If ya have to prepare every single time I show up, ya should prepare ahead of time so it doesn't matter when I visit," Harvey said calmly from the lap of his bodyguard. "Do ya have this month's order together? I'm sure yer aware that tomorrow is the deadline."

Adolfo signaled to his lackey, and a large cooler was brought into the room and placed on the floor. Harvey's other bodyguard lifted the cover of the box to reveal its contents.

Inside the box, there were ten or so plastic packages. All of them were covered with frost and filled with a frozen, dark red liquid.

"Not much here." Harvey snorted as he picked up one of the packages. "I know I told ya to have at least thirty."

Adolfo paced nervously by the window. "As you well know, Harvey, more and more blood banks are closing down across Japan. The nearby Red Cross blood centers are also about to be consolidated. Our supply routes keep getting cut off..."

"Don't repeat what everyone already knows and make excuses for yerself," Harvey said coldly. "'Lorenzo Blood' distribution didn't start yesterday. Surely ya've had more than enough time to prepare some countermeasures."

'Lorenzo Blood' was another name for Stigma. The umbrella corporation for House Tepes, Lorenzo Pharmaceuticals, supplied all-purpose blood products for human use to countries all around the world. Due to Stigma's popularity and abundance, Red Cross blood donation operations had been greatly reduced everywhere. For humans, a product called Stigma would carry bad connotations, so 'Lorenzo Blood' was the brand name often attached to Stigma made specifically for them.

"You say that, Harvey, but the black market—"

Without warning, the window behind Adolfo shattered into tiny pieces, and the top half of his head exploded.

Left behind in the limousine, Jiji and his sisters were absentmindedly watching TV. Outside the car, Harvey's subordinate, who had been riding in the passenger seat, was keeping a vigilant watch of the premises.

Suddenly, there was a noise that sounded like a firecracker.

The lookout searched for the source with a puzzled expression.

The noise continued intermittently, and then it got louder and louder. Gunfire.

He removed his own gun from its holster.

All of a sudden, one of Harvey's bodyguards burst through the front door; he was clutching Harvey tightly to his chest. Harvey was still gripping the frozen pack of blood.

"Open the door!" the bodyguard shouted.

The lookout threw the limousine's back door open. As the bodyguard turned to jump into the car, more gunfire rang out behind them.

The bodyguard and lookout took the brunt of the attack and turned to ashes, which scattered in all directions.

Dropped from his late bodyguard's hands, Harvey tumbled through the air and into the car. The plastic pouch he was holding fell right in front of Anna's eyes.

From where he had landed face up on the floor, Harvey turned to Jiji and yelled, "Shut it! Shut it! Shut the damn door!" He could see a number of vampires armed with guns running out of the house.

Jiji frantically swung his body outside to close the car door.

As the door shut, bullets rang against the windows. They didn't have enough power to pierce the bulletproof glass, but

Clara and Anna froze at the sound of the relentless gunfire.

"Go! Go!" Harvey yelled, and the driver floored the gas pedal. It felt like the rear wheels were spinning in midair and making smoke when the car peeled off.

The attackers aimed at the rear of the limousine and began firing anew; a number of bullets hit the rear window.

The limousine swung away at a fierce pace and started weaving through side streets.

After he confirmed that they were no longer being followed, Harvey climbed back into his car seat.

"He wasn't targeting Adolfo; he was trying to kill me! That bastard…who the hell does he think he is?!" Harvey was spitting mad. "Oh, he wants to make me an enemy? Well, he screwed up, that bastard…"

The tires creaked as the limousine turned left onto the road that ran alongside Tokyo Bay's drainage channels. On the right, beyond an expansive chain link fence, there was a steep slanted concrete embankment. Below the bank, there was almost no water in the drains.

"Hey, boy! Gimme the phone!" Harvey shouted angrily at Jiji. The boy took the car phone and was about to hand it to Harvey when a blinding beam shone through the windows, illuminating the inside of the car. When Harvey and the children looked to the left, they saw two bright lights on either side of a grate, coming right toward them.

It was a large truck, which barrelled down a side road and rammed right into the side of the car.

Harvey's small body was thrown by the attack, and the car flipped on its side.

The limousine slid toward the fence, pushed by the large truck. The four tires scraped against the asphalt with a terrible noise. The truck kept moving even after it had buried its front end in the body of the limousine.

With no way to resist, the limousine flew past the fence and into the drainage canal.

"Waaaah!"

Inside the car, everyone shrieked at once as the limousine slid on its side down the slope of the embankment.

It seemed that the limousine would continue tumbling until it reached the bottom of the drainage ditch, but halfway down the slope, it stopped abruptly. Harvey, Jiji and the two girls had all been pushed up against the right side door from the force of the fall.

The limousine was caught on the mouth of a drainage pipe jutting out from the side of the slope.

Harvey and the children were lying in a heap on the door, along with all the furnishings from the inside of the car. They struggled to untangle themselves.

A group of vampires appeared at the ledge of the slope and began firing down at the car. Bullet after bullet struck the bulletproof glass, leaving white graze marks behind.

The driver desperately returned fire from a crack in the window.

"You! Take the boss and run away!" the driver shouted.

"Run away? To where?!" Jiji, finally managing to stand, called back.

"Down!" It seemed that he meant for them to open the downward-facing door and escape to the sewers.

Jiji picked up Harvey. The man in the baby's body was only semi-conscious, possibly from hitting his head.

Clara grasped the door handle and pulled, but the door only opened a tiny crack. "It's stuck!"

The three children worked together and jumped up and down on the door in unison. "One, two! One, two!"

The sound of sporadic gunfire was suddenly joined by a steady rain of bullets on the roof of the car; their attackers had brought a submachine gun into the fight.

At last, the driver's side window succumbed to the gunfire. With the barrier gone, the driver was filled with bullet holes in an instant.

"One! TWO!"

With one exceptionally hard kick, the door finally opened. The children lost their footing and tumbled to the bottom of the canal. Harvey's car seat and a few cushions also landed nearby.

Jiji and the others got up quickly and scrambled up the slope toward the open sewer pipe, but the incessant rain of bullets prevented them from leaving the shelter of the limousine.

"What do we do, Jiji?" Anna asked.

Harvey opened his eyes. He quickly grasped the situation

and offered a suggestion.

"Use my car seat as a shield."

The siblings grabbed the seat and huddled together, holding the it above them like an umbrella. As they ran out from beneath the limousine, a number of bullets hit the car seat, but the attached metal plate protected the children.

The group ran into the dark, damp, cave-like sewer pipe.

As they headed in deeper, they could hear the sound of gunshots echoing behind them. Turning back, they saw the shell of the limousine, engulfed in flames, slide down past the mouth of the pipe.

"Hurry! They'll be after us soon," Harvey urged.

The four kicked up dirty water as they determinedly ran further and further into the sewer system.

Drainage systems don't usually have lights built into . them. But these children were vampires with sharp night vision, so they were able to keep moving forward quickly.

"Do you know where we are?" Clara asked Jiji.

"Yep! If we keep going this way for a little longer, there'll be a shortcut back to Harvey's place."

Jiji—still carrying Harvey—stopped when they came to the aforementioned shortcut. It was a fork in the tunnel, with three larger pipes and a fourth smaller one that they could enter on all fours.

"This way." Jiji pointed at the narrow pipe.

"Hold it! We ain't going in that tiny deathtrap. Stop

kidding around," Harvey protested, raising his voice.

"But this is the best shortcut…" Jiji pouted.

"Stop saying such irresponsible things. Kids like ya don't know anything!"

"But Jiji really does know everything about the underground," Clara said, trying to smooth things over. "Also, if it's this narrow, adults can't chase us."

"We should do as Jiji says," Anna said, agreeing with Clara.

Harvey's expression grew suspicious.

"You kids aren't gonna tell me what to do! I will decide where we run! I'm the leader!"

Jiji, who had been deep in thought, suddenly looked up in shock. Voices could be heard from behind them; it had to be their pursuers.

"Harvey-san, where are we going?" Jiji gave up arguing for the moment.

The usually confident Harvey was suddenly at a loss for words. "Er, this way…"

The group ran into the pipe that Harvey had indicated.

For about thirty minutes, they followed Harvey's instructions and ran through the darkness. They couldn't shake their pursuers, perhaps due to the fact that Harvey selected only easy-to-enter larger sewer pipes.

Naturally, their fatigue got to be too much, so they decided to take a short rest in a storehouse for raw materials that they'd stumbled upon. Jiji and his sisters huddled together in a corner. Unable to relax, Harvey crawled around with unsteady movements.

"Jiji, do you know where we are now?" Clara asked in a small voice.

He shook his head. "I don't know anymore. I've never been around here before."

"Dammit, someone gimme a cigar!" Harvey looked like he was about to scream, but he suddenly gave up and hung his head. "Of course, ya don't have any…"

"Do you think Harvey-san knows?" Anna was suspicious.

"Who knows?" Jiji had no other answer.

Suddenly, Harvey was alert and on guard.

"Hey, did ya hear something?"

Jiji and the girls jumped up halfway. "A sound…? You mean the people chasing us?"

"No. A rustling sound…" Harvey's voice began to tremble slightly. "There, look! There's definitely something here!"

Where Harvey was pointing, there was a single rat.

"Was that all? You scared me." Jiji said.

"O-Over there." Clara pointed in a different direction.

This time, there were several rats, all larger than the first one.

"Hey, wait a minute…" Anna backed away slowly.

More rats started to appear. As the children watched, the rats multiplied and filled the floor and walls, looking at them with glowing eyes.

Before they knew it, the children were completely surrounded by a large swarm of rats.

"W-what's happening?" Jiji picked up Harvey.

"We're about to become breakfast, lunch and dinner," said Harvey grimly. "In the Bund, there aren't enough leftovers, you know. They must be starving."

"We're going to be eaten?" asked Clara.

"That's right." Harvey's voice was full of conviction. "Still, there's a way out. We can probably get away if we make it over there, since rats don't swim."

Harvey pointed at the waterway ten or so meters ahead. Of course, the rats were completely blocking their way.

"It's only scary because yer thinking of them as a group. One at a time, though, they'll be easy to handle. Just calm down and exterminate the rats in front of ya, one by one, and push toward that waterway." Harvey nodded at Jiji and the girls. "Believe me. I have experience."

They all wanted to ask what it was exactly that Harvey had experienced, but there was no time to waste.

Jiji and the girls each grabbed a nearby lead pipe and stood back-to-back, forming a circle. This way, they could concentrate on the rats in front of them without worrying about their exposed backs.

Harvey was hoisted onto Jiji's back, fully protected within the circular formation.

"You all set? I won't be able to support you, so hold on tight, okay?"

"I'm fine. Hurry!" Harvey stretched his arms as far as he could and clung to Jiji's neck.

The children moved forward slowly, inching their way into the crowd of rats.

The rats bared their teeth and began pushing toward the children.

Jiji aimed for the rat directly in front of him and swung the lead pipe down. The rat took a direct hit and let out a shrill cry.

Clara and Anna copied Jiji and began hitting rats, one by one.

Maintaining their formation, Jiji and his sisters broke through into the middle of the swarm. However, the rats were angry now, and their attacks kept getting stronger and fiercer.

"Aah!" Jiji was bitten on the neck.

"Kyaa!" A rat crawled under Anna's skirt.

"It's no good! There are too many!" Clara yelled, almost in tears.

"Don't give up! If ya stop here, we'll die!" Harvey yelled.

Suddenly, Jiji began singing in a loud voice. It was the first Japanese song he had learned when he came to the Bund.

Moshi jishin o nakushite, kujikesou ni nattara
ii koto dake, ii koto dake, omoidase...

If you lose confidence, if you get discouraged,

Remember only the good, only the good...

No matter how off-key his singing was, it helped to calm him down. His movements grew stronger and surer.

Sou sa, sora to umi wo koete, kaze no you ni hashire...

That's right, hurdle the sky and sea, run like the wind...

Clara and Anna began singing along. Even as they were singing, they never stopped striking at the rats.

Yume to ai wo tsurete, chikyuu o hitottobi.

With dreams and love, jump the earth in one leap.

They were only two meters away from the waterway.
"That's enough! Run!"
On Harvey's signal, the children took off, kicking rats every which way as they ran. They quickly sprinted the remaining distance and leaped into the waterway.
The water was deeper than they had expected, and none of the children could reach the bottom.
Jiji and the others struggled for dear life. Eventually, they managed to pull themselves up on the other side.
There was a large pair of shoes in front of them.
Coming from the shoes were two thick legs. Harvey

snuck a quick glance up.

A huge man was staring down at them, his head so high above them that it seemed to scrape the sky. He was pointing the barrel of a gun right at them.

"I guess someone was bound to hear yer singing," Harvey muttered to himself.

The room was completely empty. Harvey and the children were huddled together, sitting directly on the chilled floor.

"Sorry, kid," Harvey said to Jiji. "It would've been better if I listened to ya, but I'm really bad with sewers. I just lost it in there."

"Why don't you like sewers? Because they're dirty?"

"Remember only the good," Harvey responded, echoing Jiji's song in a subdued whisper. "Thanks to ya, I remembered a lot from a long, long time ago. When I was about yer age, I lived in sewers a lot like these ones. I was stark naked, I couldn't speak, and the only food was rats."

"Rats?" Jiji asked, incredulous.

"That's right. Even though I was a vampire, I was still a baby—powerless and stupid. There was no way I could catch and bite an adult. Not many humans deliberately entered sewers in the first place. So, I would catch rats in the pipes and sink my teeth into their heads." Harvey mimed the process of catching a rat and gnawing on it. "Soon, the rats began to see me as their enemy. Near the end, every time I was about to bite one, it'd bite me back, until my entire body was covered with wounds."

Jiji and his sisters were stunned into silence by the intense recollection.

"A human infant would've died a hundred times, but vampire bodies are tougher—no matter how many times I was bitten, I never got sick. That continued fer a long time, ten, maybe twenty years—I didn't have a good feel for the passage of time back then, so I don't really know fer sure."

"But you can speak properly now, can't you?" Anna asked.

"There's more to the story," Harvey gave her a broad smile. "A while later, the number of humans underground suddenly started to increase. With humans wanderin' around, the rats sounded the alarm and stopped coming out. All of my food had disappeared and I was on the verge of starving to death…when I met Mack."

"Who's Mack?" Clara asked.

"Mack was the first human I bit." Harvey folded his hands behind his head and lay back, face up. "He was homeless. Lost his home in the Great Depression and tumbled into the sewers after his family got split up. He was a good caretaker, and he gave me the name Harvey. I also learned to speak and dress myself from him."

Harvey got a distant look in his eyes and trailed off into silence.

"Ya know," he continued, "if I was told to go back to that time, I'd say I'd rather die. But thinkin' about it now, they weren't all bad memories."

"Is Mack—" Jiji's question was cut short when the room's iron door swung open with a creak.

Clara swept Harvey up in her arms.

There were three vampires standing in the doorway. The first vampire—who had to duck to enter the room—was the large man who had first found Harvey and the children. He appeared to be the leader.

"Ya don't look like a criminal mastermind type at all. Ya lack the proper qualifications," Harvey declared confidently from his spot on Clara's knees. "Is it finally time to meet the master?"

"No. It seems that won't be necessary," the large man said indifferently with a sullen expression. "I received orders to kill you here."

"W-wait! Wait just a minute!" Harvey waved his small arms around. "Ya can't kill me in a place like this! If I could see my island one more time, I'd forgive ya. Won't ya just let me walk around a little?"

"What's this? The great Harvey-sama doesn't value his own life?" the large man sneered.

"All lives are valuable. I just don't think much of dying in a filthy cellar. If you're gonna kill me anyway, why can't ya give me this one little thing?"

"You're a talkative one. There's no way you're the big shot who runs so much of the underworld." The large man's tone went beyond scorn; he seemed genuinely astounded.

"It doesn't matter if yer a big shot or small potatoes; it's all the same if ya die," Harvey argued. "I'm begging ya, it's like this. It doesn't matter what ya do to me, just help these kids. They have absolutely nothin' to do with my business. Look at 'em; they're just kids who don't know anything... Hey, Mack, what're you waiting for, there's nothing else to see! Hurry and clean up this mess!"

Confused by Harvey's last words, the men turned around at once.

Suddenly, the door behind the men flew open with a bang. The men spun around and fired their guns at the doorway, but hit nothing.

A small silhouette stood roughly ten centimeters below their line of fire.

Taking advantage of the second it took for them to lower their aim, the shadowed figure curled into a ball and hurled itself toward the men's feet. With inhumanly fast speed, it wove patterns around their legs while emitting several sharp flashes of light.

A moment later, all three of the men cried out in pain and crumpled to the ground. One of them had flung away his gun and was clutching his legs.

Every one of them had had his Achilles' tendons or hamstrings completely severed.

The small shadowy figure got up quickly and stabbed the largest attacker in the chest with a combat knife.

As the dead one went up in flames and dust, the small

silhouette dealt unceremoniously with the remaining two. It had only taken about five seconds from start to finish; Jiji and the others could only stare in awe at the small shadow's skill.

It returned the combat knife to its sheath and turned to face Harvey and the children.

The shadow revealed itself to be a young, male, Caucasian teenager. He looked about 14 or 15 years old.

The boy's innocent facial features seemed out of place above the completely black SWAT armor protecting his entire body—jacket, gloves and boots. The only feature that stood out was the battered New York Yankees baseball cap that he wore on his head.

At first glance, he looked like a kid dressed up as an action star for Halloween. But the cool-headed gaze he gave Harvey and the children—and the sinewy, muscular arms peeking from beneath his rolled-up sleeves—showed that he was indeed an experienced veteran soldier.

"Fine performance, Harvey." The boy's voice cracked—like a young man going through puberty.

Harvey jumped down from Clara's arms and sat cross-legged on the floor.

"Ya sure took your time today, Mack."

"Mack? You mean, him?" Jiji muttered.

The boy called Mack walked over to the four and produced a cigar from one of the many pockets on his tactical vest.

"If you wanted me to arrive sooner, you shouldn't have left while I was out," Mack answered in the sticky pronunciation of a Bronx accent. He stuck the cigar between Harvey's lips and lit it. "If you hadn't, I wouldn't have had to cancel two business deals."

Clearly enjoying his cigar, Harvey narrowed his eyes and glared at Mack uneasily.

"Two? Which two?"

Mack took a black helmet hanging from his shoulder and put it on Harvey. Made to order, it fit perfectly on his small head. As Mack fastened the chinstrap, he answered.

"Wells and Shimazaki."

"Ya idiot!" Harvey's face turned bright red as he screamed. "If ya cancel on a pigheaded guy like Wells at the last minute, he'll tack on a cancellation fee next time!"

Undaunted, Mack yelled right back at him, "Which is more important, a cancellation fee or your life?!" He removed a harness from a pouch at his hip and quickly began securing it to Harvey's body.

"Money, of course! Ya've served me for more than a hundred years, and ya still don't know that?"

"It's only been eighty-five! And I don't serve you because I like you; I felt sorry for you, and when I tried to help, you bit me! Talk about ungrateful!"

Although Mack continued arguing in a loud voice, his hands kept moving; he picked up Harvey and secured him to his own back with the harness' metal fittings. Harvey's mouth cursed back at him while his body was obediently strapped to Mack.

"That's my line! If I didn't bite ya, an idiot like ya would be six feet under, getting gnawed on by rats!"

"And where do you think you'd be without this idiot looking after you for all those years? Plus, you always act like *I'm* the idiot for falling for your trap, but anyone would try to help a naked, crying baby! You didn't have to do anything!"

Jiji and his two sisters were dumbfounded; they watched silently as the pair's endless argument continued. They didn't seem anything like a typical vampire master and servant.

Finally, Mack pulled out a folded black sheet from the rope bag by his shin. Unfolding it revealed two sleeves attached. With Harvey still on his back, he covered the small body with the sheet and put his arms through the sleeves—it was some kind of body armor to protect Harvey from bullets. With only his head poking out, Harvey looked like a child who'd been tucked into bed.

Finally, they both stopped yelling. Mack muttered, "All right, let's go home."

He headed toward the door without even a glance at Jiji, Clara and Anna.

"Wait," said Harvey. "Take 'em with us."

Mack spun around and glared at the three siblings as if he'd only just noticed them.

"Stop screwing with me, asshole," Mack muttered

threateningly from the corner of his mouth. There weren't many vampires alive who spoke to their masters like that.

"These three were left in my care by Her Highness. And…" Harvey reluctantly said, "I owe 'em a debt."

Mack glared at the children again, but clicked his tongue and shook his head.

"If you fall, I'll leave you behind. I don't care if you cry."

Mack exited the room with a brisk stride. Jiji and his sisters scrambled to their feet and followed him.

When they were in the hallway, Mack looked up at the ceiling; the grating of a vent had been cut and was hanging loosely.

"If I didn't have extra baggage, we could have just gone back the way I came in, and that would be that," he muttered.

The five "children" formed a line and continued down the hall, led by Mack, who was still carrying Harvey.

"So, who started this mess?" Harvey asked over Mack's shoulder.

"Gregor," Mack answered curtly. "You said you were going to meet him today, didn't you? That was a mistake."

Usually, Harvey never told anyone his schedule. When he wanted to meet someone, he either summoned the other party to him or called on them without warning. He did that to prevent ambushes set by his enemies. He'd broken his own rule this time, and his enemies had taken advantage.

"Stupid. If you were going to discontinue Adolfo's route,

shouldn't my stand-in have gone? Senseless bastard…
Speaking of Agari, what's he up to now?"

"Resting in bed. I'm never gonna mess with ya again."

"That's fine by me."

The party rounded a corner only to see a lookout waiting down the hall. Mack motioned for Jiji and his sisters to back up around the corner, and he hid his own body by pressing up against the wall on the opposite side.

Mack removed a lighter from his vest pocket and threw it at Jiji's feet. The dropped light clattered on the floor.

Hearing the noise, the lookout came walking down the hallway and saw the three children.

"What are you doing here…?"

"Hey," Mack called out from behind the lookout; he turned around reflexively.

Mack slammed his fist into the lookout's throat. With his Adam's apple crushed, the lookout groaned and toppled over backwards.

Picking up the lighter, Mac paid no more attention to the lookout as he stood and turned to retreat.

"Wait a minute!" Jiji called out suddenly to Mack.

Up against the wall, Jiji checked the serial number of a wide gas pipe.

"All right! I know where this is; I even know the way to Harvey-san's place!" Jiji nearly jumped for joy.

"You… you're familiar with this area?" Mack asked, puzzled.

"Jiji knows everything about the underground," said Clara.

"That's right!" Anna chimed in.

Mack walked up to Jiji and stared into his eyes. "Is this true?"

Without hesitation, Jiji nodded.

"If that's the case, tell me the shortest route from here to the ocean."

Jiji looked doubtful. "Harvey-san's place is in the opposite direction from the ocean, right? Why do you want to go the wrong way?"

"I'll tell you, boy." Mack brought his face down to Jiji's. "Side streets and back roads aren't just for running away. They can also be used to crush your pursuers."

Harvey stirred from his position on Mack's back.

"Hey, what are ya scheming? If ya know the road, let's go home already."

"You promised to leave the fighting to me, didn't you? Keep your mouth shut."

At that moment, the lookout Mack had felled raised his gun and fired a single shot into the air.

The group could sense their pursuers heading toward the sound of the gunshot.

"We'll be fine. Lead the way."

Under Jiji's guidance, the group of five headed toward the sea through various underground facilities. They didn't move at full speed, however—Mack stopped intermittently to track the movements of their pursuers. They were definitely still being followed.

When they finally crawled through a manhole and out onto the street, they were surprisingly near to the towering embankment that surrounded the Bund.

Mack grasped Jiji's shoulder and looked down at him.

"Listen up. Follow me without leaving a gap of more than two meters. When I give the signal, duck, turn ninety degrees to the left and run at full speed. Can you do that?"

Jiji nodded vigorously. "Yes!"

"You've got guts, kid." Satisfied, Mack smiled and patted Jiji's head. His sweet smile was the only thing about him that suited his physical appearance.

Mack picked up Clara and Anna in either arm and took off running. Jiji followed carefully behind.

They could hear the footsteps of their pursuers close behind them. Mack and Jiji kept running on the dark asphalt, not looking back.

"Now!" Mack yelled, and quickly bent down.

Without a moment's delay, Jiji imitated Mack's position.

At nearly the same instant, a blue flash exploded over their heads. If they hadn't have ducked down, they would have been caught right in that light.

Without standing, Mack and Jiji adjusted their heading and continued running. Blue spotlights appeared on the streets around them, meant to flush out non-permitted persons. Mack and the others just barely avoided being caught by the lights and ran to shelter.

Their pursuers weren't so lucky. As they came up behind Mack and Jiji, they ran right into the blue light.

The men caught in the light screamed, and their skin started to smoke. They stood still in the light, unable to move.

The blue lights were infrared searchlights.

"Freeze!" A distorted voice echoed from a speaker. "This is your final warning! You are trespassing in the coastal embankment area! Turn around immediately!"

Multiple figures appeared on top of the enormous building. All of them were brandishing weapons.

They were members of the VGS Border Patrol. Guards were positioned around the coastal areas of the Bund twenty-four hours a day to prevent smuggling and escape attempts.

Once the commander saw that they were holding weapons, the tone of his voice changed completely.

"Drop your weapons! If you do not drop them immediately, it will be considered an act of resistance, and you will be shot!"

"W-w-wait a minute!" The pursuers' leader raised his voice and waved both arms. "We have no intention of resisting! We're going to drop our weapons, so don't shoot!"

The group of pursuers put their weapons on the ground, one by one. They were defeated.

Harvey and the others watched this unfold from their shelter.

"You knew this would happen?" asked Jiji.

Mack nodded.

"Our work is one big game of hide-and-seek with the VGS. How many lookouts in each area, where the searchlights are located, how to avoid them and which ones will react…I've memorized most of it."

"Now what? The VGS isn't going to help—"

"Quiet!" Harvey shushed Jiji.

Mack carefully aimed and fired several shots.

Several of the infrared searchlights shattered, and one of the VGS members leapt backwards in surprise.

"They're resisting!" shouted the VGS commander.

The VGS began shooting, all at once. The pursuers scrambled to pick up their discarded weapons, scattered to find cover, and returned fire.

Mack's actions were the spark to the figurative powder keg; the unstoppable gunfight quelled any concern that they'd be pursued. With excess numbers and firepower, the VGS overwhelmed their opponents; one by one, their pursuers were shot down and turned to white ashes.

Jiji and his sisters watched, shocked at the unexpected outcome.

"Boy, let me explain." Peeking out from the gap between the sheet and helmet, Harvey's eyes were laughing. "In our trade, there are only three choices if ya happen to encounter the VGS."

Harvey stuck out his tiny fist and counted off on his short

fingers. "One, ya run away. Two, ya get arrested. Three, ya get killed. We chose number one, and they chose number three. Ya see? Now, let's get home."

Without staying to watch the inevitable conclusion of the gunfight, the five children disappeared into the darkness.

Upon returning to his base of operations, Harvey began making phone calls and sending out his subordinates in all directions. Now that Gregor and Adolfo were out of the picture, the balance of power in the Bund was quickly changing, and Harvey wasn't about to let an opportunity to expand his influence pass him by. He was already formulating plans to acquire their territories.

Jiji and his sisters had been taken by Harvey's female underlings and given a royal welcome.

The clothes that had been soiled while running around in the sewers were laundered, and any injuries they had sustained were carefully treated. Fortunately, though the children's lives had been on the line, they had escaped with only bruises and scrapes. They watched intently as the cigar-smoking Harvey worked frantically, and occasionally exchanged looks.

At last, when Harvey's phone war had calmed down, the three siblings readied themselves and approached his desk.

"What do ya want?" Harvey asked as he raised his head from some accounting ledgers.

"Um…" Jiji hesitatantly opened his mouth. "We have

something we need to apologize for."

"Apologize? What are ya talking about?"

"Anna," Jiji prompted her. She removed something from the pouch hanging on her shoulder.

It was the vinyl pack of pharmaceutically-produced blood for transfusions that Harvey had been holding.

"I tried some without telling anyone," Anna whispered in a tiny voice. "I wondered what Swiss-made Stigma tasted like, and…"

At first, Harvey didn't understand what she meant, but then he saw the Red Cross markings on the front of the package. Anna had mistaken it for the Swiss flag, even though the Red Cross symbol used the opposite colors.

"We couldn't get any work, and we don't have an allowance, so we don't have any money to pay you back." Jiji pleaded with a desperate look on his face. "But we'll do anything! Please don't tell our mother and father! Please?"

The three siblings bowed their heads in unison.

Harvey put out his cigar and folded his arms. He glared at the children with a stern expression. "Ya did a serious thing," Harvey said in a solemn voice. "That was a very important trade item. If ya cannot repay me, then yer parents must shoulder the debt. That's how the world works."

Jiji and his sisters began to tremble visibly. Anna looked like she was about to cry.

"But I'm not a demon. It was my responsibility to find ya

work. So let's say ya don't own me nothin'." Harvey raised his voice. "In return, ya won't tell anyone about the events of today. Not yer father, not yer mother…not even Her Highness. Do ya understand?"

The three nodded in agreement.

Harvey was relieved. He had been wondering how he could get them to keep their mouths shut.

Regardless of Queen Mina's strict orders, the children had been put in some extremely dangerous situations and had even been injured. He didn't know what kind of punishment he would have to endure if Queen Mina got word of his indiscretion.

"When are you going to repay your debt?" A voice called out suddenly from the corner of the room.

Mack was lying sprawled out on the sofa, his hands folded behind his head. Since his cap was pulled down low over his eyes—in place of an eye mask—they'd all assumed he was sleeping.

"They did a fine job as bodyguards, didn't they?"

Even though they obviously didn't have any military expertise, the fact that they had risked their lives to protect him could not be discounted. That was why he'd insisted that Mack protect them in turn.

Harvey sighed and beckoned the brother and sisters forward with his pointer finger. He opened his desk drawer, removed a single ten thousand yen note from a small cashbox, and handed it to Jiji.

"Good work today."

"Huh. Harvey's life really is cheap, isn't it?" Mack said. Even with the cap still covering his eyes, he had somehow guessed the amount.

Harvey glared at Mack out of the corner of his eyes and pulled out a narrow roll of banknotes. He took back the ten thousand yen note from the hand of a confused Jiji and presented him with the roll of money in its place. Jiji seemed to struggle for a moment between politeness and shock.

"This is too much," he said after a moment. "We don't need this much."

"If ya have extra, save it or something. Tell yer parents it was a reward for saving a child."

Jiji, Clara and Anna all stared at the bundle of money for a moment; then, as one, they raised their heads.

"Thank you very much, Harvey-san!"

Harvey looked at the three shining, smiling faces before him. He had met with many vampires in that room over the years, but it was the first time he'd seen such pure expressions. He felt an emotion stirring within him that he had never experienced before. Sensing that he would change forever if he accepted it, Harvey responded curtly.

"With that, yer business with me should be complete. Get on home, now."

The three children turned to face Mack and bowed.

"Mack-san, thank you!"

Without raising his cap, he waved at them.

They formed a line and headed toward the door. With his hand on the door handle, Jiji turned around and spoke.

"When we run out of spending money, we'll come back!"

"Bye bye!" Anna waved.

Harvey was speechless. No matter how hard he tried, the words, "Don't ya ever come back again!" wouldn't come out. In the end, he just saw them off in silence.

"Are ya satisfied?" Harvey muttered, still staring at the door.

"You're satisfied too, aren't you?" Mack responded from the sofa.

Harvey pulled out a new cigar from the case and lit the end.

"Jeez, those kids are only going to get worse from now on."

Mack snorted. "What you mean, 'from now on?'"

There would be no "from now on" for the three siblings. They would remain children forever. Both Harvey and Mack knew that very well.

Harvey angrily tried to come up with a retort, but instead, in a strangely kind voice, he muttered, "...Shut up. It was just a figure of speech."

Harvey dragged deeply on his cigar and let out a grand puff of smoke.

"I'm so sorry that my children caused you an inconvenience."

"No, not at all. The store was on my way home from school."

Kaburagi Akira took a bite of the shortcake in front of him, then sipped at his coffee. Human food was rare in the Bund, but as far as mementos for one's human life were concerned, there weren't any better tasting ones.

Jiji, Clara and Anna's mother had invited Akira to the Evers house.

A few days earlier, Jiji and his sisters had asked him to purchase the latest video game console from an electronics store outside of the Bund. It included several games that the whole family could play.

When Akira had asked about the reason for the purchase, they told him that it was a birthday present for their parents. But it wasn't really their parents' birthdays; they were all Fangless with equal status. The five orphaned Fangless had joined together to become the Evers family, and exactly a year had passed since that family had been created.

Akira happily accepted the shopping request—he was impressed that the children had taken on a part-time babysitting job to save up the money. But after he'd though his part in the gift was over, their mother invited him over unexpectedly to talk about the children.

"Actually…"

She told him that the children had lost interest in the game console and were now completely engrossed in something else.

"What are they doing?'" Akira asked.

"Whenever they have free time, they pull out a large

stuffed bear and all three of them gang up on it, treating it like a punching bag."

"Huh?"

"If I ask them what they're doing, they just tell me that it's secret special training. They're also asking for a baseball cap; I have no idea why…"

Akira thought about it for a minute, but he couldn't think of a reason, either.

"Maybe something interesting happened to them at their part-time job." Their mother seemed sincerely worried about them, so he tried to reassure her with a story he thought up on the spot. "My brother Yuuhi is the same way. When anything new and exciting happens, he tries to imitate it. But it's kind of like catching the measles—after three days, it passes."

"Even so…" Their mother looked doubtful. "I wonder what training like that has to do with babysitting."

End

HEMATOLOGIE
DU GOUT

STORY
Gemma

ILLUSTRATION
Nozomu Tamaki

Tell me what kind of blood you have consumed, and I will guess what kind of vampire you are.

"One, plasma. White female, twenty years old. B+, virgin.

"One, blood platelets. Black female, twenty-four years old. AB+, non-virgin.

"One, thick red blood cells. Asian male, thirty years old. O-, virgin.

"One, thick red blood cells. Mixed-race male, parents are white and black, seven years old. AB+, virgin.

"One, whole blood. White female, eighty-two years old. B+, not a virgin.

"Mix these types of blood in the ratio of 7:4:3:3:1."

"Yes, master."

"One, red bone marrow and urethral stromal cells. Black female, twenty years old, virgin. Do you understand? These last parts are the key—they're what will determine the freshness."

"Yes, master."

Thick blood, fresh blood, dark, clotted blood, blood with

white bubbles, reddish-pink blood, all mixed together in one beaker. Two new red objects were carefully dropped into the beaker, where they swirled together with the rest.

"As you know, the cells that form erythroblast colonies are incorporated into the blood-producing structures of the bone marrow, which then become erythroblast cells under the effects of the erythropoietin produced by the stromal cells. These cells undergo cellular division up to five times and are then released into the bloodstream and become red blood cells. In other words, the erythroblasts are extremely fresh cells, the freshly-laid eggs of red blood cells."

"Yes, master."

The automatic stirrer in the beaker let out a tone like a clear bell.

One drop, two drops, transparent liquid dripped from the edge of the trembling dropper.

"This reaction takes seven hours in vivo, but it is possible to speed the reaction with a temperature adjustment and a suitable catalyst. Two minutes at 35 degrees Celsius, fifteen seconds at 38 degrees Celsius, and one minute thirty seconds at 32 degrees Celsius; a total of three cycles. You weren't lazy with the temperature control, were you?"

"No, master."

Long, slender fingers wrapped in white gloves moved nimbly over the information displays on the incubator. There were no abnormalities in its light green numbers.

"It is easy to forget, but make sure you match it to the

Duffy blood types. Make a note of it."

"Yes, master."

One minute. Two minutes. As I watched with bated breath, a soft electronic sound announced the end of the cycles. Securing the stirrer with a magnet, I poured the contents of the beaker into two suitably warmed cups. As I carefully poured the last drop, I announced, "It's done! Perfect!"

A perfect blend of sweet aroma and deep iron flavor, the raw taste of fresh blood paired with the smoothness of mature blood. All vampires would savor this ideal taste, and the name of Baronet Vittorio Spallanzani would be carved into the pages of vampire cultural history. It might even be placed next to names like Karem and Escorfie in the annals of innovators of world cuisine.

"Master, it failed."

"Yes, I failed—what?"

"It failed, master. Try to drink it and you will see."

When I was turned around, Bartro had already drunk half of his own cup, and he was wiping his mouth with a wrinkled handkerchief that resembled his own face. I was struck by uncertainty. I took the cup and sipped it.

There was no taste. Or rather, there was no taste any better than that of ordinary human blood. There was only the stench of clotted red blood cells and the bitterness of bone marrow that struck the tongue. I threw the cup to the floor and ground the remnants with my foot, ignoring the blood splattered on my white coat.

"One of the pioneers of the baroque art style, Laurentiis, was a vampire. His art was called 'the art of darkness' because his sight could actually pierce the dark. It has been said that Caravaggio would never have become successful without his praise."

"Yes, master."

"Oscar Wilde had dealings with the vampire society of England in his time. It's been famously said that *The Picture of Dorian Grey* was based on Count Dorian of the Tepes family, who he had idolized in his youth."

"I see."

"Artists, writers, musicians, architects, sculptors, playwrights and poets. Vampires have been involved in almost every kind of art since the beginning. Our patronage *produced* the art of human society. Art history could be called the history of vampires. This is the truth!

"Only in the field of gourmet cuisine is that not the case. There has never been a vampire who found fame as a cook, a food critic, or a gourmet. Why is this?"

"Vampires have a different sense of taste from humans."

"That is no excuse! Taste is merely a biological function that makes the food people ingest seem desirable. This is true for both humans and vampires. Humans have raised this biological function to a highly aesthetic place, and built a broad, deep world of culture through the culinary arts. But what have we vampires done?

"Laurentiis, Lord Ruthven, Lady Dieudonné, the literary

giant Bierce, and even greater geniuses! They have grace and intellect far surpassing that of humans, yet their attitudes towards food have not progressed for a thousand years; they still drink only raw blood. If asked about the taste of blood, their sole reply is that the blood of young virgins is delicious. Even a seven-year-old human brat can tell you that food tastes better if it's new and fresh!

"Beasts eat. Humans eat. Any civilized person knows how to eat. This lack must be a sign of laziness and poverty in our vampire culture. Ah, that vampires do not have a concept of gourmet cuisine!"

"We have Stigma."

"How can you call that powdered swill *cuisine?!* The world of the vampire gourmet is empty and tragic. I have dedicated my life to repairing this flaw—a flaw that can only be called a blemish on the face of the world—by creating a Gourmet of Blood. I swear it upon the name of Vittorio Spallanzani, grandson of the great Lazalo Spallanzani!"

I, Vittorio Spallanzani, pulled back the sleeves of my white coat and spread my arms to the sky. In my enthusiasm, I lost my balance and fell. Bartro, who had been quietly cleaning the laboratory during my speech, quickly approached with a wet towel and a replacement coat.

"Please change, master."

"Ah, thank you. I apologize for getting you involved yet again."

On the nights when the experiments failed, I always

gave a speech to encourage myself in the face of despair. The audience was only Bartro, and I know not how many times I'd repeated the same words, yet he always nodded in agreement without interruption. He was a man with an expressionless face that looked like a pork shoulder that had been boiled and then dried in the sun, but he was sensitive to things like this.

"But why? The mixture should have been perfect."

In truth, this was not the first time that this experiment had failed; I had yet to succeed. The blending and seasoning of blood was an extremely precise and deep world of study. Even using all of the hundreds of years of collected knowledge in the Spallanzani clan—founded by the great biologist and hematologist Lazalo—it was still like touching an elephant in the dark and trying to describe it. I had not yet progressed beyond the realm of trial and error.

"I was thinking, perhaps the problem is in using blood alone in the mixture. What about including other ingredients?"

"That would be deviating from pure blood cuisine. And anyway, it is difficult to find substances other than blood that we can taste."

"I see…"

I raised a hand to stop Bartro—who had begun to say something else—and took a moment to think in the quiet. His suggestion was reasonable, honestly. Unlike human cuisine, vampire cuisine could only use one type of ingredient. No matter the race or age of the person, blood is blood. It was like trying create a full-course meal while using only beef—there was a limit to how varied the meal could be.

"Ha! Ah ha ha ha... Don't worry about it, Bartro."

It wasn't as if that limitation was unexpected. After formulating a plan, I smiled slyly and struck the table, rising to my feet.

"I thought we might have to attempt this at some point... perhaps now is the time. Bartro, make an order with the usual supplier. I want the blood of the sick."

"The sick? But..."

"Yes, the sick. You said the problem was with the ingredients. If normal blood doesn't work, then we will use abnormal blood. If our scope is too narrow, we will broaden it. Ha ha ha... I feel so *inspired*. Hurry, Bartro! Hemophilia, leukemia, malignant lymphocytes, any sort of sickness of the blood. Tell them to have it here by tomorrow at sunset."

"That's impossible."

My excitement suddenly cooled. I glared at Bartro with annoyance all over my face, but he did not budge.

"What's impossible? Tell me why. Why!"

"Adolfo died last night in a fight against a competitor. His killer is controlling his old smuggling routes, so we won't be able to obtain any blood for a while."

"Why didn't you tell me something that important earlier?!"

"I thought to wait until your usual speech was over, but I

missed on the timing. I'm looking for a new supplier, but the anti-smuggling system has become stricter both inside and outside the Bund. It will not be easy to find a supplier who can fulfill your requests."

"What about our current stock?"

"We used everything in the previous experiment."

"Why didn't you tell me that either?! I would have saved some if I had known!"

"You said that this was the grand experiment of the century, and you didn't want to spare any expense."

"...How can this be?" I fell into a chair, deflated.

"Would you like some Stigma?"

"Yes. With extra salt, please."

Several days had passed.

I walked along Tatsumi Pier, avoiding the sunlight that penetrated the air like punches.

I didn't have a specific objective. I clung to the possibility that maybe I could obtain human blood if I spent some time in the outside world. Being a baronet was convenient at times like this, because while I could get a pass for leaving the island by applying pressure to the authorities, I was not important enough to cause a political problem if something happened to me.

And besides, there was nothing weaker than a vampire in summer. It was extremely hot, yet we had to wear heavy clothing to avoid exposing our skin, which drained our stamina. We had to stay in the shade and reapply protective shade gel once every fifteen minutes. Even if we avoided exposure to direct sunlight, most vampires would fall ill just from being outside during daylight hours. Since vampires were weaker than normal humans during summer, inspections for those leaving the island were relaxed during the season. After I first came to the Bund, I had secretly snuck out to wander around Tsukishima and the edges of the Shinkiba area. I was, of course, seeking out new tastes.

Japanese cooking placed a lot of importance on the flavors of the ingredients, and I had high hopes for their raw food. Unfortunately, the thing they called sashimi smelled fishy and tasted of nothing. I heard that they took care to remove all of the blood, which was a wasted effort from my point of view. The shish kebabs that I ate in a back alley in Tsukishima were a delicacy, but since they were made from beast organs, the blood had also been removed. In the end, I had to accept that there was nothing as delicious as blood among human cuisine.

The Tatsumi district that I walked through that day was made up of park land, buildings and highways, with no restaurants in sight. There were makeshift tents made out of blue tarps set in the shadows of the park's trees. I'd heard about the refugees waiting outside the Bund, hoping to become vampires—this must be where they lived. I thought that people who lived in a place like that might be more likely to be sick, so I considered taking a taste. But adding to my Blood Clan while outside the Bund would cause political problems.

"Hmm…"

As I walked along and glanced at the park out of the corner of my eye, I passed someone strange.

He looked like a normal young man without any particularly conspicuous characteristics, but he was dressed like a college student or at least someone who shouldn't have been walking around in that neighborhood in the middle of a weekday. When I realized this and looked around me, I noticed a few more people dressed similarly. They all seemed to be heading in the same direction. It piqued my interest, so I decided to follow them.

The youths did not look around at their surroundings, but sometimes they took out their phones to check a map while walking briskly towards their destination. Finally, we stopped in front of a familiar building. The front was entirely covered in glass, divided into a narrow grid in a clean, simple pattern. A small red cross was carved on the duralumin plate facing the street.

"Isn't this a blood center?"

It was the Tokyo Red Cross Blood Center, a strange place that collected hundreds of gallons of blood daily. When I first saw it upon my arrival at the Bund, I was struck with such envy and desire.

The young people gathered in groups of three or five, seemingly drawn toward the center point. I reapplied the gel under the shade of a tree, then approached the entrance.

"Thank you all for your help today!"

There was a space in the hallway, just next to the entrance, where a human girl with a conspicuous outfit was speaking cheerfully. She was quite pretty, with long brown hair and a clear voice, and the people who'd entered were gathered around her.

Some listened to her quietly, others took candid photos with their phones. There were even people who looked like reporters with actual video cameras.

"I'm only here for one day, but I'll do my best to teach you all about blood donation. There's a tour of the facility after this, so please enjoy yourselves!"

The board next to the enthusiastic girl was marked 'Department Head for a Day,' and I suddenly understood her purpose.

"I see, she's trying to attract customers."

I had heard that the rate of blood donations had dropped significantly once Stigma was supplied to the human world. Blood serum could be created from Stigma, so there were much fewer people willing to go to the trouble of acquiring real blood when such a convenient substitute was readily available.

Since both supply and demand had dropped, the operation of blood centers had probably been threatened. Once that idea occurred to me, I looked closer at the room around me and noticed that the inside of the building was slightly dirty, and the whole place felt lonely. The center must have hired this singer to drum up publicity.

Although their purpose was shallow, I was lucky to have encountered this event. It seemed that they were letting people inside to tour the building, and perhaps I would be inspired by seeing some human research. After waiting for a few minutes, I saw some young people who did not look particularly interested walk in the direction of the stairs. I followed them past the reception area.

When I climbed to the second floor, I found a long corridor of bland, cream-colored walls and floor tiles, much more utilitarian than the downstairs area designed for outside visitors. I lagged behind the group of youths following the signs for the "tour route" and quietly slipped into the opposite corridor. No proud vampire would follow a predetermined route.

From the signs on the walls, it seemed that the second floor was where they tested blood and created blood serum. Their security was robust; there were many areas that I could not enter, but I could guess the activities taking place in those rooms by simply peering into the occasional open door. They didn't seem to be engaging in any particularly high-level activities.

The underground research center that Her Highness had built at Bergamo forty or fifty years ago had been involved in much more advanced research, even that long ago.

The faces of the researchers working in those rooms

were slack and spiritless. One could tell the liveliness of an organization through such things; their listlessness was only to be expected, though, for an organization that called in entertainers to make itself more popular.

As I walked along the medicine-scented hallway, I recalled the old Bergamo research center. The research laboratory itself was called 'Bergamasque' after Debussy's famous piece. It had been created as a bastion of knowledge by Her Highness, dedicated to finding the vampires' long-awaited solution: a food substance that could be substituted for human blood. It was a place where select doctors, therapists and biologists (most of them vampires, naturally) gathered, and I, a young scion of the sciences, learned about the depths and charms of blood. The result of that research was the Stigma that now flows throughout the world.

"I could be considered a business competitor to these guys," I laughed quietly to myself as I began to climb the stairs.

Suddenly, a loud alarm bell sounded throughout the building.

I hid in the shadow of the stairs and held my breath. It seemed that my intrusion had been discovered. Well, I had seen most of what I came here to see, so I wouldn't have any regrets about leaving so soon.

"There is an intruder in the building who has stolen blood. The perpetrator is thought to be a vampire. Guests and staff, please evacuate immediately."

"What?"

I couldn't help but raise my voice. I did intrude, yes, but why was I being called a thief? I heard many footsteps stomping down the hallway outside, and anger overrode caution. I stepped out into the hallway and announced, "You! Listen to me! I apologize for my intrusion, but I did not—"

A hole opened in my shoulder with a small, dry sound.

The security guards jogged toward me with their guns drawn. One gun had smoke coming from the barrel. The small cylinders on their belts were familiar to me, as well: portable ultraviolet torches.

Agony radiated from my shoulder and into my brain. I didn't even have time to scream as I ran back into the stairwell I had emerged from. Footsteps approached from below. I was already on the highest floor; there was nothing but the roof above. I headed upwards without hesitation. As I rushed up the stairs two at a time, I removed the shade gel bottle with my right hand—my left hand wouldn't move. I bit off the cap with my teeth, slathered the contents all over my face, and opened the door to the roof.

I was hit by the light of the summer evening, just beginning to turn orange at the horizon. The roof of the blood center might have been subject to environmental protection, as a large part of the roof had been turned into flowerbeds with yellow flowers—buttercups, perhaps—blooming. My eyes were blinded by the light, but I saw a single door across the rooftop, and I rushed towards it with all my might. Bullets hit the ground at my feet and kicked up dirt into my face.

When I poked my head into the room, I was hit by hot air and the sound of running machinery. It was some kind of utility room; the machines lined up neatly in front of me looked like some kind of generators. A section of wall to the right was half open like a hidden door, and I ran in without thinking and shut it solidly behind me. At the same moment, the outer door slammed open and I heard the sound of footsteps running into the utility room.

But the footsteps stopped right there. I heard some whispered conversations, but it didn't seem like they were about to break down the door that I was hiding behind.

"Ah..."

I didn't understand what was happening, but I heaved a sigh of relief. At the same time, my mind began to work again.

It seemed that I, a baronet, had been framed for blood robbery. But there was something even stranger about the day's events. Even against a vampire, would security guards at a public facility shoot at people without warning? And the ultraviolet torches that hung from their belts were more the realm of an organization like the VGS. Were those men really security for a charitable organization?

Come to think of it, the door I'd hidden behind was strange as well. It was unusually thick, and it seemed to be camouflaged so it would be inconspicuous from the outside.

Why did a utility room have a door like this? What was this room, anyway? It seemed strangely cool compared to the outside.

"Um…"

As I started to turn around, I heard someone address me and leapt up in surprise. I made a half-turn with the momentum of my jump to face the rest of the room.

The room was light green all over, floor and walls alike. It was about the size of a small cottage. There was a table in one corner, and some machinery lined up next to it. There was another strong-looking door on the other side, and a woman had appeared from beyond that door.

She was probably in her late teens, with a very pretty face. Her long brown hair was beautiful, and she had a slightly troubled gaze as she looked at me; it contained both a softness of character and strength of determination. In our world, she would be described as "a woman you'd want to bite," although I didn't want to bite her at that moment, considering the circumstances.

"You're a vampire."

Before I said anything, the girl scanned the room and entered. She wore a plain jacket with a red cross on it and a miniskirt and high heels underneath. Her appearance, clothing and location—none of it matched.

"Are you being chased?"

"As you've probably seen."

"You're the thief?"

"How rude!" I involuntarily raised my voice. It was not an attitude I should have taken with a lady, but considering that I had been running for my life and being shot at only moments before...

"I am Baronet Vittorio Spallanzani. I am being chased due to some misunderstanding. I am most certainly not a thief!"

"I'm sorry," the girl apologized unexpectedly. "I think that's probably my fault."

"What?"

It was then that I noticed the package the girl was holding against her chest. It was wrapped in a towel, but I could see a clear vinyl bag with frost on it and the reddish-black contents within. There was no mistaking that color.

"*You're* the blood thief?"

The girl nodded. "I'm sorry."

"Apologizing won't help." All of this was beyond my comprehension. I shook my head and attempted to gather my thoughts.

First, I put my ear to the door and attempted to listen for sounds of pursuit. I could still sense the presence of the men in the outer room, but they appeared to be discussing something, and they didn't seem like they were about to break the door down. I twisted the handle as hard as I could so that the door could not be easily opened. Satisfied, I left the doorway and walked over to the girl.

"Let me ask you some questions. Who are you?"

"Um..." The girl scratched her head in disappointment for

some reason. I saw that her clothing under the jacket looked like a cross between a lab coat and a nurse's uniform, but it was strangely revealing. I suddenly realized that I had seen that clothing before.

"Wait, you were the director for a day downstairs..."

"Um, yes!" The girl's face lit up, and she bowed again. "I'm Makihara Ruli. I'm a singer. Pleased to meet you."

"Ah, yes, pleased to meet you." I had no interest in the arts of the human world, and I unfortunately didn't recognize her name. The girl had probably deduced that from my response, and her expression clouded over slightly.

"Why would you steal, anyway? Even if you're the director, you shouldn't take blood."

"That's true. Well..." The girl trailed off vaguely.

I pushed her aside and peered into the room behind her.

Cold air hit my skin. Although the previous room was unusually cool, this room felt like a freezer. Perhaps it actually was a freezer. Shelves were constructed to the left and right of the narrow room, and frozen packs of blood were lined up on the shelves.

"There's a blood storage area here? This is a very strange design."

As I looked over the shelves, I noticed something strange. If this blood was meant for transfusion, the packs should be marked with blood type and the date they were drawn, but there were no official labels on these packs. Instead, they were marked with what looked like handwritten notes.

"Initials and dates?"

Were they records of when the blood was obtained? No, that wasn't it. There were identical initials and dates on four or five packs, but if a single person gave five 400 milliliter packs of blood at once, he or she would be dead.

Besides, it was the height of insanity for there to be a blood storage room here. What sort of idiot would store valuable blood packs in an inconvenient, out-of-the-way room on the roof?

Suspicious blood. Suspicious labeling. Suspicious thief. *Really* suspicious storage area. All of these things combined to form one conclusion in my mind.

"Miss Ruli. Are these…smuggled blood?"

There was no answer, but I saw that her shoulders had tightened.

"Um, Mr. Vittorio, was it…? Do you serve Queen Mina?"

"Of course. Would someone who was not a subject of Her Highness be wandering around here?"

"Oh…" The girl lowered her eyes as though considering something. After a long minute of deliberation, Miss Ruli raised her head and determinedly looked me in the eye.

"Please, will you help me? For Queen Mina's sake?"

Stigma had become too common—that was the source of the problem.

Now that Stigma was available everywhere, blood donations were far less necessary and blood centers had become largely obsolete. The Red Cross itself was being reviewed to determine its necessity. That was when the blood center administrators came up with the idea of smuggling blood to vampires.

While Stigma was the source of life for vampires living in the Bund, it was merely a well-made substitute food. There were always vampires who sought real food—that is, real blood. The blood centers in the Kanto area—the ones closest to the Bund—became ideal locations for smuggling operations. However, once they had successfully started their smuggling businesses, there was too much demand for the blood, and their supply could not keep pace. The administrators tried to increase the supply by letting humans *sell* their own blood.

"This only happened before I was born, so I don't know too much about it, but apparently blood centers used to buy people's blood from them sometimes."

"There are countries that still do that, even now. But the problem is that some people fake their blood credentials because they want the money. It can lower the quality of the blood, or even lead to contaminated blood entering the supply, which could make our blood into an incubating system for contagious diseases on a large scale."

"Yes, and it seems that something like that has happened here."

Miss Ruli had discussed this issue with a vampire acquaintance, and had decided to infiltrate the blood center through the "Director for a Day" event to search for evidence.

"So it was coincidence that you raised the alarm with your theft while I was walking around the facility. I suppose assuming a vampire was responsible made sense."

I cut open the corner of one of the packs she had brought out and licked a drop of blood. The taste was mild with a hint of a bitter caramel flavor.

"It's hepatitis."

"You can tell?" Miss Ruli's eyes went wide.

"Of course. Who do you think I am?"

"I see. Um…why did you come here, Mr. Vittorio?"

"To seek gourmet cuisine."

"Huh?"

Whatever the case, I finally understood the situation. I also understood why the people outside didn't seem to be normal security guards. They were probably the smugglers' hired enforcers. I assumed they hadn't followed me into the hidden room because it was the heart of their operation.

"But he must be an awful man to make a simple singer like you investigate such a dangerous situation! It is inappropriate behavior for a vampire."

"Oh, no! Akira just said to tell him if I noticed anything; I did this on my own. I just wanted to help!"

The look on her face gave away even more than she intended. I pretended not to notice her face turning pink as she shook her head frantically.

"Except raising such a commotion isn't particularly helpful."

"Sorry…"

Miss Ruli bowed her head. She was an honest girl. She was brave to go to such lengths to help the man she loved, and I wanted to help her. But in reality, it was my life at risk. The people outside would not hesitate forever.

As I considered this, a commotion could be heard on the other side of the door. There was no more time to wait. To fulfill my great calling, I could not die in a place like this.

"Miss Ruli. I apologize, but you will have to be a sacrifice."

"Huh…?"

I ignored the stiff look of shock on her face, grasped her wrist to pull her towards me, and bit down on her pale neck.

The light of the ultraviolet torches illuminated the room from corner to corner as the door was forced inward.

"H-help me!"

The security guards who tromped into the room with their heads covered with full helmets and visors saw a girl trembling against the wall, covered in blood from head to toe.

One of the security guards recognized her face and raised his visor in surprise.

"…Miss Ruli?"

"A v-vampire! He attacked me. I…I was bitten!"

She approached the man, who retreated half a step with his gun still cocked.

"Please, calm down. Can you explain what happened?"

"Blood... The blood that was here, it splashed all over me..." Her blood-covered body shook as spoke. "He said this was sick blood! AIDS and hepatitis B and stuff! That's not true, right? I'll be okay?!"

A commotion went up from the security guards. The man with the raised visor retreated two more steps and raised his gun again.

"Please calm down. Don't panic. It's okay." Even as he said that, he lowered his visor. The circle of men around her retreated with each step she took.

"Where did that vampire go?" another man, who seemed like their leader, asked as he put careful distance between himself and the girl.

"There. He went into that vent just before you arrived."

She pointed at a ventilation shaft positioned at approximately head height. The cover had been torn open. All of the guns and torches pointed towards the opening.

I took advantage of that moment to fly out of the freezer room. Miss Ruli made a dash for the entrance as well. As she ran, she waved her hands around and splashed blood everywhere, and the men in her way flinched away from the liquid. Not even fully-armed guards could withstand being tackled by two vampires.

The orange light of dusk slanted into the door to the roof. Yells, bullets and the light of the ultraviolet torches pursued us, and I felt pain run along my neck and left leg. Just before jumping out of the room, Miss Ruli leapt onto my back and used her whole upper body to cover my head.

"Turn right. Then go left, then straight!"

If I put my hands in my pockets, I could avoid revealing any of my skin, but the tradeoff was that my eyes were covered and I was blind. I ran as fast as I could, following Miss Ruli's instructions.

"Careful, there's a pipe near your feet! Jump in about ten steps. Three, two, one... Now!"

I kicked off the concrete with all of my strength. The wind from the shore blew up beneath me. In the dark, I felt myself fall for longer than I'd expected, then a great shock went up through my legs, and I heard a horrible cracking sound in the back of my ears.

I fought down the urge to scream, hid my face in the collar of my coat, and hunched over. The moment before I closed my eyes, I verified that the situation was the same as I'd seen from the room; we were in the parking lot behind the building, and there were blood donation and emergency rescue vans lined up in the lot.

Miss Ruli dragged me along by the arm—my legs had broken in the fall and I could not walk—and into an emergency rescue van nearby. I ignored the pain and broke the dashboard, then fiddled with the wires and easily started the engine. Miss Ruli sat in the driver's seat, and I sank under the passenger seat. We crashed into the adjacent vans numerous times, but we were able to drive over the bushes and emerge onto the road.

The sound of sirens chased us from behind. While it was not possible for a vehicle this obvious to escape for long with an amateur driver at the wheel, we didn't need to run far. We sped straight along the road to the east, crossed the intersection, turned into the empty field, then continued straight on and drove into the blue canal that spread out before our eyes.

It was several hours later.

Miss Ruli and I waited for the sky to turn completely dark before swimming to shore and climbing out near the lumberyard.

"Are you injured?"

"I'm fine. But Mr. Vittorio, are your legs all right?"

"What, this is merely a scratch! This is too minor to be considered a wound for a vampire such as I."

While I spoke with confidence, in actuality my legs were unstable and wouldn't hold my weight. It was pathetic that I had to be carried on her back.

While there was still a guard perimeter around the blood center, the edge directly opposite the Bund was only lightly guarded, as I had suspected. If the contents of the theft was illegally sold blood, they could not make too much of a fuss.

"I will take responsibility for you and make sure you are given the vaccine tomorrow. I know that you are uneasy, but please bear with me for a while."

"I'm fine; I've dealt with this before. But is it true that

vampires cannot get human diseases?"

"Do not worry about that. The only disease common to both vampires and humans is dental decay. Although I suppose it would be for the best if you burned all of your clothing."

While her clothing had been washed to some extent by her swim in the canal, it was probably difficult for a young girl to bear being drenched from head to toe in contagious blood. I'd done what I had to, but I regretted putting her through something so unpleasant.

"These clothes belong to the company, though." While I couldn't see her face, I could hear her resigned smile. "How did you know, anyway? That I'd been bitten before?"

"It's called a boomerang case. I could tell from the atmosphere around you."

Humans bitten by vampires were generally dazed for a while afterward and couldn't do anything but rest. But humans who were bitten by vampires and then given the anti-vampire vaccine—these so-called 'boomerangs'— either recovered much faster from their second bite, or sometimes were not affected at all.

Under those tight circumstances, it was fortunate that she was a boomerang. I remembered thinking that she was a girl any vampire would want to bite…and it seemed someone had already tried it once.

As we turned along the intersection, we could see the husks of abandoned buildings in the light of the streetlights.

Miss Ruli straightened her stance and adjusted my position on her back.

"That's the building. I heard that if you wait in the bathroom on the first floor until nearly dawn, someone from the Bund will come and get you."

"Understood. Thank you for your help with everything."

"No, no... I was the one who got you caught up in this mess. If this attracts a lot of attention, I think this will be the end of the smuggling. Aki—my friend—was happy, too. I want to thank you."

"Hm." I felt around in my pocket as I was carried along. The frozen pack of blood that I had stolen during our escape had largely melted. It was evidence of the smuggling—if I gave it to the appropriate authorities, the blood center would be censured by the Bund and the smuggling organization would be destroyed. The wealth of blood stored there would be confiscated as evidence, and then probably destroyed as well. I coughed once, then asked in a calm voice, "Miss Ruli. If you truly want to thank me, may I ask you to relay a favor?"

"So, this is the "blood of ultimate flavor," Lord Spallanzani?"

"Yes. Please have a drink, Your Highness."

I bowed deeply in front of the Queen in the reception room of the palace, filled with pride as I answered her questions.

"I have mixed twenty-seven types of blood—from the old and young, males and females, over the course of many, many experiments. I do not believe that there is any blood more delicious than this; none that I can declare suitable for the Queen's consumption as a palace delicacy."

"Twenty-seven types of blood? Surely it could not have been easy to obtain that many different types."

"It required supreme effort. But I swear to Your Highness that I have not done anything that would damage the honor of a vampire."

As I predicted, the secret of the taste lay in the blood of the sick. The bitterness of hepatitis, the sour taste of methemoglobinemia, the lightly sweet taste of anemia... The tastes that were missing or exaggerated due to sickness were what I required as seasoning in my pièce de résistance.

The large cache of ingredients that I had obtained thanks to Miss Ruli allowed me to create a blend that combined the light flavor of rabbit garnished with shallots, the smooth texture of porcino mushroom potage, the robust sweetness of grunts at the end of spring, the rich oily flavor of rare veal steak, the tender sweetness of gooseberry pie, and the intoxicating flavor of the best Toscana wine. This blend was a complex pyramid of artistry in the world of vampire gourmet. When I'd first tasted it the night before, I was moved to tears and hugged Bartro.

She lifted the glass in her small, delicate hand, and touched the rim of the glass with her pink lips. She drank one, two mouthfuls, then drained the glass. She placed the glass down and wiped a small trace of blood from her lips with a napkin.

"It is sweet."

"Yes."

"Also bitter."

"Yes!"

"There is also a sour taste. It is a complicated flavor, very different from normal blood."

"Yes! All my hard work has been to depart from the taste of common blood! The strange flavor that Your Highness has detected is—"

"Lord Spallanzani."

I raised my eyes and met Her Highness's gaze. Or rather, she glared at me with the gaze of a lion.

"You imbecile! Blood is most delectable when it tastes like *blood!* Why would you think that something this bizarre would be enjoyable to the palate? Try again!"

After Lord Spallanzani stumbled out of the room, Mina sipped the blood in the glass one more time, then frowned in distaste and offered it to Vera, who stood at her side. Vera smiled in resignation and shook her head. Mina sighed in exasperation.

"It is because of people like *him* that they say vampires have no culinary culture."

End

AN AFTERNOON WITH THE WOLVES

STORY
Tikurakuran

ILLUSTRATION
Nozomu Tamaki

They call themselves the Wolf Boys: a pack of young werewolves who protect the Vampire Queen, Mina Tepes, and claim to have that duty in mind at all times. All the Wolf Boys play their part, but the whole thing wouldn't exist without Kaburagi Akira, however he may deny it. It'd be ridiculous to hold Akira responsible for everything, but his very existence is the reason things turned out the way they did.

It all started at a school festival. The Kaburagi Akira Fan Club stands out from the rest of the school clubs as the only one that features a particular person, however unnoteworthy. Though actually, Akira does have his admirers, and his appearance at Mina-hime's Vampire Bund conference only added to them. It seems that people appreciate a kind-hearted guy, even if he's a little rough around the edges.

"If you love Akira, now's the time to make your move!" called out Mina-hime, special adviser to the group, at the school festival in the Beowulf Café. Mina was sharing her usual monopoly of Akira's attention as a goodwill gesture towards the club's members. Meanwhile, the Wolf Boys served as maids at the Beowulf Café, bringing out tasty sweets and drinks for a very appreciative female clientele.

"Looks like you guys are popular with the Japanese ladies," said Leroy. While Akira and Cinva were still in their teens, the other Wolf Boys were already in their twenties and had had their share of experiences with the fairer sex. Kamil was already married, having tied the knot before coming to the Bund. Since their arrival in Japan, there had been almost no chance for romance; the Hysterica incident and all of the subsequent attacks had kept them far too busy. In response, the Young Wolf Boys Association for Happiness in Japan club was created, comprising of Leroy, Heinrich (armed with his extensive knowledge of the fairer sex), Cinva, and Akira, who brought his knowledge of Japan and Japanese customs to the table.

First, the group set out for the Bund police station to seek advice from a man who had seen a lot of action.

"Okay, enough about our combat duties. How should we go about looking for love here?" Leroy asked Hama flat out, not mincing words.

"Why are you asking me? I'm just a mercenary who roams the world. If you're looking for love, there's tons of women around here."

"Hm. I think Gotoh-san has you locked down," quipped Akira.

"Can we stay on topic here?"

Hama's advice was clear: meeting as many women as

possible was the top priority. Once they had some more experience, everyone decided that they'd set out for their homelands and try their luck at landing Mrs. Right.

The next day, the Boys learned their numbers had grown by two.

"Why the hell is Kamil here?" grumbled Leroy.

"I didn't have anything to do today, so I figured I'd tag along."

"But you're married!"

"Well, you see, you can never have enough. You can't let that desire for something fresh and new eat you up from the inside. And besides..." Kamil pointed to Junte, who was standing by himself, "he really wanted to come along."

"Huh. Doesn't look like it to me," Akira said, shooting Junte a dubious glance.

"Nope, he's pretty serious about it. He was talking about how the Korean boom made this a prime opportunity."

Everyone gave Junte a second glance. He wore a depressingly bored look on his face.

"I guess it'll be all right," Leroy finally said with a shrug.

LEROY

"Takeshita Street doesn't suit me at all. Look at it; it's criminal!"

"Huh. No matter how I look at it, those eyes seem like they're searching for prey, not ladies."

"Well, this is the face of a killer."

"What the hell are you talking about?"

"……"

"I suppose you're trying…"

"Provoking reactions from women isn't bad, but it won't get you anywhere either."

"You're just not focusing enough. Just now, you were looking at that store."

"Seriously, did you come here to find women or to shop?"

"Here we go, into the store again…"

"Looks like every time they leave the store, they come out with even more stuff."

"Hey, did you pick Harajuku because you're more interested in clothing than women?"

"What are you talking about?! Let's head to the next one!"

HEINRICH

"I know he likes to visit Jimbocho, but do you really think we can pick up girls here?"

"You're as bad as Leroy; you're more interested in collecting old books than women!"

"What the hell are you talking about?! I'm serious…"

"If that's the case, then what's with the stuffed animal you're holding?"

"What? Th-this is just something to shut down a girl's defenses. That's all."

"Very cute, although at least you're starting to take this seriously."

"Well, I was hoping you'd do better, but you're getting nowhere fast."

"Of course not. Someone's standing around here reading and causing a scene."

"Oh, wait! It looks like he's striking up a conversation!"

"No, that's just a salesperson for some English learning course."

"My ears can tell the difference between chit-chat and a sales pitch, thank you."

"That was the fifteenth building."

"......"

"Junte, my time is running out, so let's hurry up."

"Guess we're out of time."

JUNTE

"Oh yeah, if you're in Shin-Okubo, the hot-looking Korean guys are the ones with the power. You can't expect to get anything done if you just stand there without saying a word."

"He's not silent. He's been talking the entire time."

"Huh?"

"Junte never stops talking, you know. It's just that his voice is so soft, you guys can't hear what he's saying."

"Are you serious?"

"Huh. I had no idea."

"Man, I thought he wasn't even opening his mouth."

"So he's talking, even now?"

"Of course! 'Her feet are beautiful. Her breasts are huge. Her skirt is so short, just a little higher and…' He's constantly talking. But of course, the girls can't hear him either, so they just ignore him."

"……"

"……"

"……"

"……"

"That's totally disgusting."

CINVA

"Odaiba really suits you, Cinva."

"Yep, a very childish place, that's for sure."

"And it's for brutes who like their festivals."

"It's a great spot, especially since TV stations hold their events here."

"Yup, a great place to let yourself go."

"Sports attractions, huh? That's got some appeal."

"You can take off your personal limiter here."

"Oh look, those girls are checking us out!"

"Ah, no… Just a wild pitch."

"They're hitting that ball very oddly."

"I think they're asking if everything's okay."

"Oh, someone said 'baby'…"

"Are they looking over here…?"

"This doesn't look good…"

"Crap, they got a sword!"

"Oh god, we're gonna get murdered!"

"Stop!"

"STOP!"

The boys held an urgent meeting at the coffee shop.

"Japanese women are not to be trifled with…" Leroy muttered.

Akira thought about pointing out that maybe the women weren't the problem, but he said nothing.

"Well, we definitely can't carry out these missions individually," Cinva despaired, as he slammed the table and buried his face in his arms.

Akira searched his pockets and took out a crumpled piece of paper.

"What's that?" asked Junte through hand signs and Kamil's interpretation skills.

"Hama-san said that if we completely struck out, we should call this number."

"Of course the legendary mercenary would have a back-up plan," said Kamil admiringly.

Huh. This number looks oddly familiar... Akira thought, as he dialed.

"Hello, this is Saegusa."

The voice on the other end of the phone sent an electric shiver down Akira's spine.

"Yuki?!"

She had heard everything.

"Hama-san told me that if those guys couldn't get the job done, then he wanted me to set up a group blind date for them."

"That sneaky old bastard..." Akira said.

"There's a couple of real cuties in my class that love guys who aren't shy about their intentions. They've already agreed to the date. I also talked to some of my friends in my university group."

"Guys who aren't shy with their intentions, huh." Akira looked at the guys. Well, wolves definitely weren't shy.

"Oh, and Akira..." Yuki said in a different tone. "You're coming along, too."

Akira let out a sigh, a silent cry of anguish that only a young werewolf could hear. If he didn't come up with a really good answer, he'd be in deep trouble.

He took a deep breath and answered with an extremely upbeat voice. "I seriously don't care about group dates, but it's the master's orders. I'll go keep an eye on everyone and make sure that they don't get into trouble."

"Okay... That's fine."

Yuki's tone sent another shiver down Akira's back.

When Akira arrived at the designated pub, six university women were already waiting for them. The Wolf Boys' drinking cheers were loud and crude, thanks to their trampled pride. Heinrich used a kitchen knife and his Iai techniques to impress the girls by dissecting a chicken thigh, while Cinva ate an entire serving of pork kimchi in one gulp.

Because the girls were underage, they focused on the food. Leroy hit it off with a girl from Kyushu, and taught her a drinking technique involving mixing shochu with hot water and chili powder. Junte, with his cool looks and his apparent brooding silence, had girls all over him; while Kamil, showing the reserve of a married man, silently feasted on stewed giblets and salted tongues. It was evident that the Wolf Boys were getting very excited over the promising state of affairs.

Now, werewolves can definitely hold their liquor. Despite some individual differences in tolerance levels, they usually never get drunk, no matter how much they drink. However, they aren't very fond of spicy foods. Mustard, wasabi, and other spices with strong aromas have a powerful effect on their senses. So the sandwiches at this pub, heavily doused in chili peppers, sent them into a tumble. Werewolves have the unique ability to become "drunk" from exposure to heavy, pungent spices. This causes their sense of smell to decline, and with it, their judgment.

Akira took a look around and surveyed the dangerous situation. Heinrich didn't notice that his precious glasses had been severely bent; Cinva was already on his fourth plate of pork kimchi, having downed the third one in mere minutes. Leroy was drinking glass after glass of spiced shochu, while Junte was writing the character "no" on the table with his fingertip.

Just as he was about to ask Kamil what they should do, a voice derailed his thoughts.

"Hey, aren't you the kids from Odaiba?"

In the hallway near their table stood a group of young men—the ones Cinva had been screwing with during the afternoon. Akira hadn't expected to see them again, especially in a place like this. At the sound of their voices, the spice-drunk Wolf Boys slowly turned around and looked up at the young men. All eyes were locked on them.

"You guys ran away in a hurry. How 'bout we finish what we started? Doesn't look like you'd put up much of a fight now, though…" said the apparent leader of the group. The guys behind him laughed.

"Yeah, we're not looking for a fight," said Heinrich, with

a sense of purpose in his voice.

This isn't looking good, thought Akira. "Hey, Kamil."

No answer. Akira turned his gaze to Kamil's face. He was in a deep sleep, despite still sitting upright at the table.

"Fine, we'll see you outside." Leroy said with a crazed grin.

The Wolf Boys, save for Akira and Kamil, all stood up together.

Akira noted with alarm the coarse hair that sprouted from the back of their hands as they rose from the table. He closed his eyes, so he had to depend on eyewitnesses to learn about what happened next.

WITNESS TESTIMONY 1
Electric Company Worker
Odawara Jiro (65 years old)

I was driving my car when, all of a sudden, someone burst out from the inside of the pub and landed right in front of me, maybe five centimeters away. I got out of the car to see what had happened, and I heard another noise, and then—from the wall or the window; I don't know which— seven or eight other kids flew right out of there and landed on the hood of my car. This is a company car, so I'm gonna have to come up with a good explanation eventually…

WITNESS TESTIMONY 2
Bunroku Women's University 3rd year student
Miura Marika (20 years old)

The guy in the bandana grabbed the other guy's neck and literally tossed him at the window. Just tossed him, like he was nothing. Then that guy just jumped through the window and headed outside. While everyone else was still getting their bearings, those wolf guys grabbed the other boys one by one and threw them through the walls like they were playing rugby.

They kept yelling, "This is a shortcut!" I was thinking it was all a joke, right? But then they all burst through the wall.

There was a loud boom. When I looked outside, they had hit a car. Everyone was lying on the ground, not twitching a muscle. They were making such a ruckus that Kazumi and I ran away right after that.

Money…? Of course I didn't pay. I didn't exchange any email addresses with them, either. They were all so cute and so fun to talk to; I was thinking it was such a waste that I didn't get anywhere with them, but if they're going to get that pissed off so quickly, I don't even want to be friends.

WITNESS TESTIMONY 3
Sakeha Torihei Aomono Yokocho Branch Manager
Yamazaki Shingo (36 years old)

I thought a gas line had exploded or something. But there was nothing wrong in the kitchen, and then when I checked the tables, the windows and an entire wall were gone, and there were a ton of customers just lying out in the street. So I told the staff to take care of the customers, and I called 119. But what happened next—that's what shocked me.

I wasn't sure if the ambulance would arrive soon or not, but then this huge, military-looking car showed up with all these people who looked like they were straight out of the army, and they picked everyone up. This super cute foreign girl came up to me and told me, "We'll be back later. We'll pay for all the damages. Regardless of the amount, we'll pay you immediately."

When I looked at the business card she gave me, it said the Vampire Special District. Does that mean those people were vampires? But they were just eating and drinking like regular people, you know?

WITNESS TESTIMONY 4
Head of the Tepes Household
Mina Tepes (approx. 400 years old)

My observation tour was going exactly as planned. It appeared that the Bund's image was finally improving, until this incident undid all of our progress. Reprehensible! That this debacle was recorded and uploaded to the internet is simply rubbing salt in the wounds! Because of this, we'll be subjected to unending lectures from Councilor Gotoh! Aside from missions, you are all expressly forbidden from setting a foot outside!

Naturally, the consequences didn't stop with Mina-hime's decree. Wolfgang gave orders to split up all of Beowulf's work shifts, aside from sleep and meal times. It'd be another two weeks before any of them had any private time; and even then, private time did not include personal freedom. In what free time the Wolf Boys had, they were only allowed to meet up in the common space in their residential quarters. That said, whenever they did meet up, they simply scattered, with one other person at most, and rested quietly.

Unexpectedly, someone's cellphone sounded off with "Zigeunerweisen." Only one of the Wolf Boys would use a song like that as their alert. Heinrich excitedly took out his cellphone and checked his email. His face lit up at what he saw.

Leroy peeked over to see. "What the hell? Isn't that an email from a girl?"

"Yeah, one of the girls from Jimbocho. We had a lot in common, so we exchanged email addresses."

"Hey, when the hell did you...?!" exclaimed Leroy.

"Ooh, she read the book I recommended!" Heinrich smiled as he read the email, ignoring Leroy. "I know we're going back to Germany, but I guess when our punishment is over, I'll go and see her again."

"Hey, Heinrich, introduce me to some of her friends! You're gonna give me a chance to use my considerable skills, right?"

Leroy draped himself over Heinrich, who gave him an insincere smile. The others around them seemed to be on the verge of tears.

"Hmm... I don't know. You haven't read Thomas Mann or Kafka yet, have you?" Heinrich's answer was blunt and devastating. "Yeah, I don't think I'd want a guy like you near her or her friends. Sorry."

Heinrich lifted his glasses with his hand. Suddenly, Leroy's bandana split with a resounding crack. None of the onlookers could stop them from exploding into balls of fur and teeth and launching at each other.

It took Veratos herself to finally break up the two of them.

End

EVER AFTER

STORY
Gemma

ILLUSTRATION
Nozomu Tamaki

CHAPTER 1

He didn't know where to start, so he introduced himself.

"Um... I'm Desmond Evers, the Director of Urban Planning for the Bund."

Two Japanese women sat on the other side of the table. One was approximately thirty years old, and the other was only a child. She might not have understood the words, as she gazed at him with a calm expression that was neither wariness nor a smile.

"I was born in Mississippi, and I'm good at football. I studied sociology at Alcorn, and majored in modern urban planning. I wrote a thesis on the road policies of Tokyo. I have come to Japan many times, and I like a sweet called *kaminari-okoshi*."

He tried to put project a friendly air, but neither woman so much as smiled. He coughed awkwardly. When he thought about it, just because they were Japanese didn't mean that they had actually lived in Japan. That was often the case with the Fangless.

"Ms. Miyagawa, you're a nurse. Is that correct?"

"Yes. I'm working at a medical center."

"That's a very good profession."

"It's not that impressive."

"……"

"……"

Desmond began to think that it wouldn't work.

It wasn't as if he had been confident that it would go smoothly. When he was a human, when he became a vampire, even when he became Fangless, he had never been able to make many friends, never mind find a girlfriend. Her Highness had arranged this for them, so he decided to join the Fangless to be matched up, but it wasn't possible to spark a close family relationship with someone he had just met.

"I heard that there was a custom for arranged meetings like this in Japan."

"It is an old custom. It's not done very often anymore."

"I see…"

He only knew that the woman's name was Miyagawa Hiroko and that she was a nurse. She was an attractive woman with beautiful straight black hair and eyes with large dark irises. However, she had only given him a vague smile since the start of this meeting, and her responses were short and to the point. She had also decided on this match voluntarily, so he didn't think that she would take a strong dislike to him.

"Um…"

"……"

The silence stretched uncomfortably on.

"Um."

It was the child who broke the silence. Desmond realized that he had been focusing on Miss Miyagawa, who looked like an adult, and his face flushed. Vampire ages were, of course, impossible to tell from their appearance alone. The persistence of this human attitude was also one of the failings of the Fangless.

"When did you become a vampire?"

As he expected, the girl spoke fluent English. He felt slightly relieved as he switched to English.

"It wasn't that long ago, around the time the Olympics were held in Japan."

"When did you remove your fangs?"

"I did it myself, immediately after I became a vampire."

The child had an innocent expression, but she asked some fairly hard questions. Her name was Anna, and she had probably lived for quite some time.

"Did it hurt?"

"It hurt so much I wanted to cry. Pulling out your teeth without anesthetic hurts more than being shot."

"Shot? You mean, as in a war?"

"Yeah… Well, no…"

Anna fell silent. Something must have shown in his expression. Desmond hurriedly manufactured a smile and continued on.

"I was involved in the black liberation movement. It was around then."

He tried to say it as casually as possible, but both Anna and Miss Miyagawa looked down at the table uncomfortably.

"Um, that must have been really hard for you."

"It wasn't that bad."

As Desmond answered, he thought that his response was very similar to Miss Miyagawa's terse replies, so he chose his words carefully and began to talk a little about himself.

Once the war was over, Desmond, who had been deployed to Europe, returned to his home and found it unchanged. Even though they had risked their lives for their country and for peace, black people were still treated as second-class citizens and did not even have full voting rights. Overcome with deep disappointment and fury, Desmond threw himself into the extremist black liberation movement. As a result, he was assassinated by a right-wing white supremacist group.

He was turned into a vampire just before the end of his life and managed to survive, but what awaited him was only more disappointment. In the vampire world, there were the Fangless, another group of people who were discriminated against. Desmond pulled out his own fangs and tried to join another liberation movement, but the barrier of prejudice in vampire society was much stronger than in human society. His movement was completely crushed without gaining any real supporters. In despair, Desmond entered a life of exile and hiding.

Then he met Her Highness Mina Tepes and heard her idea of creating a Vampire Bund.

"Mr. Evers…"

It was Miss Miyagawa's voice that broke the silence that resumed after he finished his story.

She lifted and opened the tote bag at her feet, removed a small basket, and placed it in the center of the table.

"Um… I baked a cake. Would you like to try it?"

Desmond sat for a long minute, his mouth open like a fool.

A small cheesecake sat in the basket, and Miss Miyagawa was looking up at him through her eyelashes in embarrassment.

Desmond suddenly felt amused and laughed loudly. Miss Miyagawa and Anna looked surprised, but then they both began to giggle.

"I don't know how many years it's been since I last had cake. Thank you, Miss Miyagawa."

"You're welcome."

"May I call you Hiroko?"

"Y-yes!"

He felt like he could make a good family with this woman. With that thought, Desmond took the first piece of cheesecake.

CHAPTER 2

Miyagawa Hiroko was nervous. She was stuck in the conversation.

(Weather? Baseball? Drama? Politics? The economy? What should I talk about? Oh, I have no idea!)

She had liked black actors when she was little. She had half-jokingly written "someone like Don Cheadle" in the request field of the matchmaking form. When she met him, she was excited to see that Mr. Evers was a handsome, intellectual black man with heavy-lidded eyes, just as she'd requested.

But Hiroko had never been very social to begin with. She knew that he was trying his best to start a conversation, and she tried to answer him, but it just wouldn't flow.

(What sort of answer is "It's not that impressive"? I'm a moron! Say something! Don't stay silent! Just keep talking and take it one step further!)

The man in front of her had joined the black liberation movement when he was human, and he had joined a movement to fight prejudice even after he became Fangless.

It was not something she was proud of, but she had never thought about racism her entire life. She had led a normal life—was born, got a job, got married—and only became aware of the truth of the world after she had been bitten by her husband one day. She had been terrified of her husband, who even tried to bite his own child, and decided to remove her fangs. But after that, she had simply gone with the flow for the rest of her life. She had even become a nurse merely because her mother had suggested it as a good profession that would support her.

He had participated in politics; just knowing that made him seem all the more serious. She didn't think that she could talk about the subject. After all, Hiroko was a woman of her generation. Her thoughts became more and more confused as she listened, and she could not keep up with the conversation. It took all her effort to keep her smile, and she began to think that marriage didn't matter—she only wanted to apologize and go home. Suddenly, she remembered the contents of her bag.

"Mr. Evers…"

Mr. Evers raised his eyebrows in surprise. Thinking about it, maybe that was the first time she had talked to him first. She took out the basket sitting at the bottom of her bag.

"Um… I baked a cake. Would you like to try it?"

As expected, both he and the girl, Anna, looked surprised.

When she was human, she hadn't had any particular interests or hobbies, but she did like baking cakes. Even after she stopped being human, there were times when she wanted some cake, and she would either import it from Japan or make it herself. Of course, she could not actually taste it, but she felt that eating connected her to her feelings and the world she had lived in when she was human.

The cake she had brought today was a cheesecake with sliced almonds scattered on top. She was confident in her skill at baking cakes. It was only a cake, but it was the one thing that she could share that was uniquely hers.

Mr. Evers gazed silently at the cake. Hiroko held her breath and waited.

Finally, dimples appeared on the thin face with the heavy-lidded eyes, and he began to laugh cheerfully.

"I don't know how many years it's been since I last had some cake. Thank you, Miss Miyagawa."

"You're welcome."

"May I call you Hiroko?"

"Y-yes!"

The man lifted a piece of cake in his large fingers and brought it into his mouth. He should not be able to taste anything, yet Mr. Evers savored each bite as though it were delicious. As she looked at his face, a feeling of "Yes, I'm going to live with this man from now on" welled up slowly inside of Hiroko's chest and spread throughout her body.

The dream family that she had lost back then... She thought that maybe she could find it again.

"Mr. Desmond, would you tell me more about your time

with liberation movements sometime?"

"I would be glad to."

The man stretched his wide mouth into a smile. Looking at his face, she thought that he was most definitely handsome.

CHAPTER 3

Watching the two adults grin at each other and begin to eat the cake, Anna finally felt a sense of relief. It seemed that they had managed to avoid the worst-case scenario, abandoning the date.

When she'd first heard about the government's project for gathering together the Fangless who had lost their families in order to create new families, she didn't think it would work. Honestly, she thought it was a bit tasteless.

But Jiji and Clara needed parents. There could live like strays for only so long, and Anna herself was tired of trying to live alone in her current form. She had desperately clung to the idea and felt uneasy when the people she came to meet turned out to be a serious black man and a seemingly weak-willed Japanese woman. But once the conversation began, she felt a greater sense of relief than she could have imagined.

"Anna-chan, would you like some?"

"Thank you."

She ate some of the cheesecake. While she couldn't taste

it, she still enjoyed the smooth feel of the cheese against her tongue, the firm texture of the graham crackers, and the crunchiness of the almonds.

She was more of a child than she thought, although she was actually over twenty years old. While taking care of Jiji and Clara, who appeared to be the same age as herself, made her feel like an adult, perhaps her true self was still a seven-year-old child. She thought she had read in a book somewhere that the mental age of a vampire was constrained by their body's physical age.

She took a second piece of cheesecake. As she ate, Anna remembered the taste of cake that she had eaten a very long time ago and felt something warm on her face.

"Anna-chan?"

Hiroko peered down at her in concern. "Are you all right? Is something wrong? Do you not like it?"

Anna shook her head desperately and tried to indicate that she was okay. Crying had blocked her sinuses, and her mouth was full, so she could not breathe very well. She thought of how childish it was to cry, and new tears welled forth.

She finally calmed down after she swallowed the cake and Hiroko wiped away her tears with a handkerchief. Desmond had moved forward and was peering gently into her face.

"Anna-chan... can I call you that?"

"Yes."

"Can you speak Japanese?"

"Um, yes, just a little."

"I can speak a little too. Well, in that case, how about we speak Japanese as much as we can from now on? Both of you are Japanese, and we're in Japan. Is that all right, Ms. Hiroko?"

Hiroko nodded, but Anna hesitated to answer.

"No?"

"No. Not that I don't like it, just… umm…"

Anna's gaze flickered between their faces. She coughed slightly to clear her throat, then said, "I can only speak children's Japanese. I only used it when I was young."

Desmond and Hiroko looked at each other, then looked back at her and began to laugh. Anna began to laugh too.

As she laughed, Anna felt a hard, dry lump in the back of her heart slowly begin to melt, as though it had been turned to water.

Anna Evers. Anna Evers? It was a good name.

She could go back to being a child. She could be a child again with her mom and dad.

For the first time in a long while, Anna smiled genuinely.

"Mom, Dad, please take care of me from now on."

End

Dance in the Vampire Bund

WALKING THE BEAT

STORY
Tikurakuran

ILLUSTRATION
Nozomu Tamaki

An excerpt from the duty log of the acting Police Chief of the Metropolitan Police Department's Special District Division.

XX Month, XX Day, 6:30 P.M.

Escorted two illegal immigrants who had come to the island via the area of the south coastal gate. They were handed over to the Tokyo Bay Coastal Division.

Hama was waiting.

On one corner of the beach that surrounded the Vampire Bund, he waited alone. In a few minutes, the sun would set. Before the vampires began to walk around outside, he had something to settle.

While the Coast Guard was securing the ocean, the VGS insisted upon being there with tranquilizer guns trained on any vessel about to disembark, but Hama avoided them both.

From the other side of the fence surrounding the beach came a dull clanging sound. Moving quietly, Hama climbed swiftly up and over the fence. To ensure that he couldn't be seen from the ocean side, he flattened himself against the fence. Rustling sounds and hushed conversation could be heard from the ocean side. Then a hand appeared on the edge of the fence. Someone was trying to climb over.

Hama straightened up. He crept around in hopes of finding a clue and almost stepped on a hand. He grabbed the hand, and with great force, pulled it up.

The hand belonged to a middle school boy wearing glasses.

When Hama yanked on his hand, the slender boy lost his balance and pitched forward, landing on all fours.

Hama looked to the base of the fence and called out, "I'll lend you a hand, so hurry and climb up!"

A small boat bobbed in the water at the base of the fence. On top of it stood a second boy. This boy, sporting a crew cut, stared up at Hama in amazement.

"Hurry up! You're keeping a lot of people waiting!"

The boy with the crew cut was hoisted over the wall, and he sat down next to the other boy.

"Who are you, mister? A vampire?" the boy with the glasses inquired.

"Nah, just a cop." Hama pulled out a cell phone from his jacket and made a call. "Yeah, this is Hama. I've secured two middle school boys at the 4-B area of the South Coastal Wall... Yes, please do."

Hama closed his cell phone and crouched down, peering into the boys' faces. "So what's the story? A dare, or were you hoping to become vampires?"

"……"

Shrugging, Hama lowered himself to sit cross-legged next to the boys.

"You do realize, don't you, that I have to return you to the mainland?"

"……"

"Crossing the ocean in a stolen boat is quite a feat, but you've stirred up a lot of trouble here."

The two boys' faces tightened and they persisted in their silence.

Finally, a Beowulf Humvee arrived. Hama and the boys climbed into the Humvee, and it began to roll.

Hama and the Beowulf Humvee driver were completely silent. Unable to endure the silence any longer, the boy with glasses opened his mouth.

"…I don't see why it's forbidden to become a vampire."

The driver glanced at Hama.

"I researched it on the internet. There's no law forbidding it, and it wouldn't really hurt anyone if we became vampires…"

"As I said before, I'm just a cop. I don't care about your reasons for wanting to become a vampire," he rejected the argument flatly. "I just have something to show you first."

"…What?" The boy with the crew cut asked, with worry in his voice.

"Today is Tuesday, isn't it?"

With those enigmatic words, silence once again overtook the Humvee's interior.

The Humvee entered a tunnel connecting to the mainland. As they continued through the suffocating, dark tunnel, the boys noticed something strange.

Countless people were walking the footpath flanking the tunnel towards the mainland. From the elderly to young children, a wide range of races and genders. Naturally, they were all vampires.

"What's that?" The boy with glasses inquired.

"You'll know soon enough." Hama said curtly.

The Humvee stopped in front of the gate guarding the entrance to the Bund. Several patrol cars were parked on the other side of the gate.

A spectacle unfurling at the parking space in front of the gate had caught the eyes of the boys, who had stepped down from the Humvee.

Several vampires were crowded around a truck. They were inspecting piles of vegetables and fruits on the truck's flatbed, while an older man took money from the vampires in exchange for the goods. The owner of the truck seemed to be a human. The fact that a thick scarf was wrapped around his neck, despite the warm weather, made his fear of being bitten unmistakably obvious.

Though the truck already had attracted a huge crowd, the stream of vampires walking up the tunnel continued to increase.

"It's a mobile market for vampires," Hama said. "Held every Tuesday and Friday."

In fact, the market had been Hama's idea. Since there were no stores selling human food within the Bund, Hama had asked the head of a supermarket, with whom he was familiar, to deliver produce to the gate. Hama spread the word, and all the Fangless who longed for food from their human days would come and place orders, and the market grew and thrived.

"But don't vampires only drink blood?"

"That's right. Anything else they eat provides no nutrition. It doesn't even have a taste. But still, they yearn for human food."

Hama turned to face the two boys.

"It seems you understand what can be gained by becoming a vampire," Hama said calmly. "Next time, think about what you stand to lose."

The two boys were led into a police car, and in exchange, an older man whose clothes sat uneasily with his overall appearance stepped out. He drew back the gate and approached Hama.

"Good evening, Morita-san," Hama gave a slight bow.

"Officer Hama." The detective from the Tokyo Bay Coastal Division returned the gesture.

Previously, Morita had investigated the "Vampire Murders Case" at a school in his jurisdiction. His guidance in solving that case had proved highly valuable, and before long, he was elevated to a position in charge of services regarding the Vampire Bund.

"Thanks for your hard work. I'll take it from here. Those two hoping to become vampires?" Morita asked.

"Yes. I thought it'd do them some good to see the consequences firsthand."

"I spoke with the Juvenile Affairs Department and it seems the number of middle and high school students wanting to become vampires is on the rise." Morita heaved a sigh. "About a decade ago, there was a drug for folks wanting to 'quit being a human; quit humanity.'"

"Think it's about time to make a PSA?" Hama said jokingly.

Morita laughed effortlessly, handing a large envelope to Hama.

"We've begun pulling out names from this week's missing persons reports. From computer databases and family testimony, the only thing we can confirm is that the victims wanted to pursue vampirification."

Among Hama's professional duties within the Bund, the most common was searching for missing persons. He would safeguard those who snuck into the Bund, or who had gotten lost on a whim, and return them back to the mainland. Though the half-hearted dares were a category of their own, Hama knew from experience that the amount of people seriously seeking to become vampires was increasing.

"They will be saved. Especially those with the greatest need…"

Suddenly, he felt a sharp gaze on him.

Hama whipped around, his eyes landing on the truck.

On the other side of the crowd, a man wearing a worn-out black yacht parka was leaning against a pillar. He wore his hood low, throwing his face into shadow. He was clutching an apple, most likely just bought at the market.

His eyes were downcast now, but he was definitely the one who had been looking their way.

"Officer Hama?" Morita called to him.

Hama returned his gaze to Morita, still glancing over his shoulder.

In the moment that Hama looked away, the hooded man disappeared into the shadows.

XX Month, XX Day, 4:00 P.M.

Arrested a visitor who become belligerent during a field trip tour of the Bund and began to obstruct business.

"You can't take him back until tomorrow?" Hama's voice was more on edge than he realized.

"The President of the United States is visiting," Morita sounded exhausted. "That escort is already taking up all our manpower; we absolutely can't handle any more shuffling. On top of that, there was an incident with an attacker in

Odaiba yesterday. Our station has to do the reception, and it's just… too much…"

"To do the reception" was jargon that meant "to establish headquarters for an investigation." Hama knew about the President's visit and the attacker incident, and under these circumstances, he doubted he had enough influence to change anything.

One of the visitors participating in that day's tour of the Bund had suddenly flown out of control. Not only did he damage a storefront, he also injured the store's Fangless employee. In order to expedite the extradition of the suspect to the mainland, the Bund police had focused on the riotous activity and arrested the perpetrator, but there was nothing the mainland could do about the situation.

"I'll come get him first thing in the morning. Just deal with him until then." Morita had gotten another call, so he hurried to end the conversation.

As if on cue, the moment Hama hung up, a piercing scream began to echo out from one of the inner rooms.

Hama heaved a sigh and walked towards the sound.

The man Hama had arrested was clinging to the bars of his holding cell, letting out screams to his heart's content. He was fairly articulate for someone so heavily under the influence of alcohol.

"I think you've made enough of a fuss for one night," Hama said.

"I demand justice! This is the bloodsuckers' country,

right? Does a human cop even have the authority to arrest me? Get your station chief!"

In order for the Vampire Bund to maintain its autonomy, the criminal laws of Japan were not applicable within the Bund. However, in the event that either a victim or a perpetrator of a crime was human, Hama had the authority to act on behalf of the police.

Hama had explained this immediately after making the arrest, but this man clearly had no interest in listening to reason.

"You should be grateful they let me arrest you. If the Bund's Public Safety Division had stepped in, you'd probably have been shot to death on the spot."

"So instead of being shot to death, I'm gonna starve? How about some food?!"

"I gave you dinner, didn't I? See, right there?"

Hama pointed to an overturned tray at the man's feet, the contents of which were scattered about. Though Hama had made this meal just for him, the man had thrown it away.

"I'm supposed to eat that? Make it again!"

"Sorry, but I don't have time. I'll be leaving soon, so you'll have to cool your heels for a bit."

The man was speechless for a moment. Then he opened his mouth and yelled, "You abandoning your post? Don't screw with me, tax leech!"

Unable to take the stench of alcohol on the man's breath, Hama turned his back on him.

"Bloodsuckers' dog! You're human, and yet you side with these monsters!"

Hama's footsteps stopped. He turned around slowly and stared into the man's face. Under his steady gaze, the man shrank back.

"That shopkeeper you struck… she could have torn your head off single-handedly if she chose to. Do you know why she didn't?" Hama's voice was eerily quiet, but his eyes never broke from the man's.

"Why the hell should I care?" the man hung his head and mumbled.

"Well, think it over until I get back."

And with that, Hama turned and strode away.

His destination was about a five-minute walk from the substation. It was an inconspicuous building that looked like a storehouse, with a pair of double doors at the front.

Hama quietly opened the door.

On the other side of the door was a cozy hall, with ten rows of pews neatly lined up, their backs to Hama. All of the pews from the first row to about halfway back were overflowing with people. Quieting his footsteps, Hama entered the hall and sat down at the edge of the nearest pew.

At the head of the hall stood a large altar. Above the altar hung a symbol that was usually viewed as anti-vampire in books and movies—a cross with the crucified figure of Jesus Christ.

In front of the altar, a Fangless man and woman, both of whom appeared to be Chinese, stood opposite a powerfully-built vampire who wore white ceremonial vestments over his long black robe. The male Fangless held a girl, about three years old, in his arms.

The priest-like vampire dipped a hand reminiscent of a large spider into a stoup of holy water and scooped up a handful. His ears, spread wide and twitching like wings, were visible even to Hama from his distant seat.

"I confer this baptism in the name of the Father, the Son, and the Holy Ghost."

The vampire said this with a husky voice as he poured water on the girl's head. As the water touched her head, the girl suddenly burst into tears from the shock.

Hama had barely made it in time for the climax of the baptism ceremony.

He was in a chapel for the Fangless. The previous head of the Tepes royal family, Queen Lucretia, had established a church in the town surrounding the castle as a place for young vampires who didn't wish to abandon their religious beliefs. Queen Mina, following in her mother's footsteps, set up a similar establishment within the Bund. In a departure from the traditional interior design, this building's plans included elements from Islamic mosques and Jewish synagogues.

The priest spoke the girl's baptismal name and the attendees erupted into applause.

Hama watched quietly from his corner as the participants encircled the family of three and they all exited the church. They likely had no idea that Hama was even there, but Hama's satisfaction showed plainly on his face, seen or unseen.

At last the priest noted that Hama was the only one remaining in the chapel. He walked over to greet him.

Seen up close, the priest's appearance was quite eccentric. His head was a monstrous, asymmetric blend of a human's and a moth's, and he had bony fingers that looked like they could completely encircle Hama's head like the talons of an eagle.

These features, which had marked him upon becoming a vampire, forever set him apart as other than human.

However, the priest's most surprising feature could only be seen by those who looked at him more intensely—his black eyes overflowed with kindness. He cared for children deeply, and he willingly reached out to the needy ones whose parents had abandoned them. Playing soccer with children while in his cassock had made him a famous landmark of the neighborhood.

The more gossipy children referred to him as "Father Diablo." The priest knew and accepted this, finding amusement in the contradictory nickname. When meeting frightened children for the first time, he would give them a toy or a balloon while reassuring them, "It's all right, just call me Father Diablo. Don't forget, now."

"I was sure you would join us today," the priest said.

"You see through everything, Father Diablo." Hama gave a bitter smile.

Hama had very little downtime, but when he did have a free moment to spare, he would sometimes spend it in the chapel. He would grab the furthest seat back and watch attentively the weddings and children's baptisms held there. The fact that he was not acquainted with any of the brides, grooms, or children was irrelevant.

Today, however, he had determined that no matter how busy he was, he would attend this particular baptism.

Hama had a connection to the girl who was baptized today.

A vampire fleeing the Li Clan had requested asylum with House Tepes. Hama teamed up with Beowulf to try and protect the man, but a pursuer killed him in the middle of battle. The man had sacrificed his life to protect his little girl. Queen Mina allowed the orphaned child to live in the Bund, and connected her with a Fangless couple.

Her new parents were both Christians born in Hong Kong. They had become vagrants when Kowloon City was demolished, but immigrated to the Bund. Hama had wanted to bear witness as the girl welcomed this new turning point in her life.

"I have someone I want to introduce you to," Father Diablo said. "When I told him you would come today, he waited and said he wanted to meet you, no matter what."

From the shadows of the altar a familiar figure stepped.

It was the man in the black yacht parka from the market.

When the man pushed back his hood, the worn-out face of a middle-aged Native American man appeared.

"I've seen you before," Hama said. "I've known many vampires over the years, but this is a first, to meet a Navajo vampire like you."

Even though he'd only seen him once and from a distance, Hama sensed something—a presence—from his birthplace.

The man in the yacht parka drew close to Hama, and Father Diablo nonchalantly left Hama's side and disappeared from the hall.

The man identified himself as Brandon Yestewa.

"I knew your father," Yestewa began, with no small talk or preface. "I also knew your mother."

"Therefore you knew me as well?"

Hama's expression hardened. If Yestewa knew his parents, it would mean that he was among those who had denounced Hama's Japanese-born mother as an "outsider" and thrown stones at her.

"When I left the Navajo Nation, you were still a baby. But from the first time I laid eyes on you, I knew you were their child."

Working as an informant on the many Native Americans who lived on the reservation, Yestewa also had a weakness for drinking and gambling. Eventually his greed became so great that he broke into a house and killed the entire family of four living within it. When he tried to run to Phoenix, he was bitten by a vampire.

While evading pursuit by both the police and the FBI, Yestewa became entangled with the hierarchy of Clan Rozenman, which held dominion over North America. Used as a sacrificial pawn time and time again, he grew tired of having others play games with his life, and used his remaining free will to make a move on his own and cross the Pacific Ocean, arriving at the Vampire Bund.

"The priest tells me you're a member of the Japanese police force. If so, I have something to ask of you."

With Hama left speechless, Yestewa went ahead and made his demand. "...I want to turn myself in."

Hama crossed his arms and gazed into Yestewa's face.

"The state of Arizona has capital punishment. If you do this, you'll most likely get the death penalty."

"That's why I want to turn myself in."

"So... you want to die?"

Just as humans envied vampire immortality, there were certainly instances when vampires envied human mortality. At times, the dread of life continuing forever outweighed the fear of life being cut short. That inclination was especially strong with vampires who had little pleasure in their rotten lives.

"If you want to die, then just go above ground tomorrow morning. The sun will take care of you," Hama said bluntly. Thinking of the circumstances of his mother's tragic death, he had no interest in honoring this man's request.

"That's what the priest said as well." Yestewa lowered his

eyes and said softly.

"Your life's path as a human has already closed, but you still have the option to die as a human. Is what you mean?"

Hama looked in the direction where Father Diablo had departed.

"...Did seeing me make you homesick?" Hama asked quietly.

Yestewa hung his head without smiling. It was probably because he was considering what Hama felt at the mention of their birthplace.

"The FBI's in an uproar. A fugitive becoming a vampire and then surrendering is entirely unprecedented."

Hama and Gotoh were sitting with a coffee table between them. After Hama took Brandon Yestewa to the Metropolitan Police Department, he went to speak with Gotoh of the Special District Office and bring her up to speed.

Gotoh knew about Hama's homeland. She didn't offer any facile comments like, "I know how Yestewa feels." She just expressed her gratitude to Hama with, "Thanks for your hard work."

"But you know," Gotoh flipped through Hama's duty log. "This journal's as light as ever. You have plenty of free time, I assume."

Hama shrugged. "On the contrary. Only someone with a lot of free time could write a long journal."

"Still, I like reading what you do have time to write.

But why is your dinner menu attached? Surely that isn't related to your duties?"

"It's just a reminder. I have a large repertoire, so I take great pains to remember what I've eaten and when."

Hama—who had always loved cooking—saw his range of meals increase quite a bit since taking up the post at the Special District station. The Fangless who came to the station for assistance would show their gratitude by teaching Hama recipes, often the simple hometown dishes they used to make when they were human.

Suddenly, Gotoh's cell phone rang.

"What was that?!" At the alarmed tone of Goto's voice, Hama instinctively jumped to his feet.

With the cell phone still pressed to her ear, Gotoh got up and returned to her desk, rummaging through the scattered documents on her desktop.

It seemed like it might be a long phone call.

Hama took a paper sack from his bag and softly set it on the table. Inside the sack was his newest concoction— date palm scones. He had learned the recipe from an Indian Fangless, and after a great deal of trial and error, he had finally arrived at a result that satisfied him.

Anytime he had a late meeting with Gotoh, Hama always brought her something for dinner. She would never say anything remotely resembling thanks, nor tell Hama what she thought about his offerings, but at least she always ate them.

On the other side of the desk, Gotoh's conversation was

heating up.

"Don't give me excuses! As the liaison with the Ministry of Health, Labor and Welfare, you are vital. So what are we supposed to do if you back down?"

Hama watched Gotoh's struggles intently for a bit, but finally, with a bitter smile, he headed for the door.

He opened the door and left wordlessly, and Gotoh showed no sign of having noticed.

There were no pedestrians to be found on the road in front of the Special District Office, and passing cars were few and far between. Even so, several of the office buildings still had lights kindled. It looked as though the bureaucrats of Kasumigaseki were staying up late so as not to fall behind the vampires.

Hama looked at his watch, precisely at the moment where the date changed.

By the time he returned the Bund, it would be nearing the climax of the vampires' night.

Hama suddenly remembered the man he had left locked up in the holding cell.

Perhaps, if the prisoner had sobered up, Hama would make him another meal.

Hama's hair fluttered in the night wind, and he began to walk casually in the direction of Hibiya Park.

End

Dance in the Vampire Bund

A FINE AND
PRIVATE PLACE

STORY
Gemma

ILLUSTRATION
Nozomu Tamaki

There were two infirmaries on the school grounds, one aboveground and the other underground. One infirmary smelled of disinfectants and laundry, while the other smelled of tea and dusty old books.

"Well, Kamimura-kun, Her Highness said this: 'From now on, there will be no differences of nationality or race. Your only identity shall be "vampire".' Even though most of the Fangless are foreigners, your connection to them is stronger than you think. They'll definitely accept you if you talk to them.

"If you can't figure out what to say, ask them what Stigma used to taste like. They'll definitely want to talk about that."

As she watched the well-behaved boy with the black hair and glasses bow and leave the room, Ms. Brussel sighed in satisfaction, stretched her bowed back and flexed her shoulders.

She removed a pack of Stigma from the refrigerator and considered whether to drink it straight from the packet or pour it into a cup. Finally deciding to use a cup, she turned towards the dish cupboard and noticed a female student standing in the hallway.

"Oh, I'm sorry! Please come in."

The student entered the infirmary nervously at Ms. Brussel's beckoning. Her chestnut hair was tied loosely on one side of her head, and her tie was loose around the collar of her shirt. The girl was slightly flashy in appearance, which was rare for the school's students. Her eyes, framed by long lashes, showed unease and wariness as her gaze darted back and forth. It was something that was quite common to students who visited the room for the first time.

"Miss Aihara Mai, yes? Pleased to meet you."

The girl twitched. She probably didn't expect Ms. Brussel to know her name.

"I'm good at remembering people's names." Ms. Brussel tried a playful, gentle smile as she quickly prepared tea for the girl. She took care to show her teeth so that the girl could see that she had no fangs.

"You've come to visit many times, beginning last month, right? Here, please sit."

"……"

The female student looked at her as though trying to decide whether or not to take the proffered chair. She finally turned on her heel and ran out the door.

"Oh my."

Ms. Brussel sighed lightly and watched her depart. It happened fairly often. While most of the students at the school had goodwill towards vampires, there were still people like her who retained their wariness. Ms. Brussel did not think that they should try to change that attitude through force.

Even so, she had thought that it would be most effective to approach that kind of girl directly, but it seemed that she had misread the student. Ms. Brussel removed the small spectacles perched on her nose, cleaned them with her handkerchief, and then slowly poured Stigma into her abandoned cup.

There were various rules and facilities unique to this school, the only school in the world that vampires could legally attend. One of these was the second infirmary responsible for the health care of vampires. Ms. Rosemary Brussel was in charge of the second infirmary, and she was the only vampire whose job was recognized by human society.

Health care was not so difficult for the students' physical bodies. Vampire bodies were strong and subject to fewer sicknesses than humans. There were even jokes that the disease most dangerous to vampires was tooth decay. No, the true concern for vampires was mental health.

It was more difficult for vampires to control their emotions to begin with, and they tended to be more unstable. In addition, since this was a school, there were many vampires who were young both in appearance and in actual age. Ms. Brussel's first responsibility was to prevent their self-destructive tendencies and to encourage their healthy development as students.

Many students would visit her before class, during lunch break, after class, or in the middle of the night. There were kids who were unfamiliar with the Fangless community and uncertain about whether or not they should remove their fangs, and there were kids frustrated at being unable to envision their future as a vampire. Ms. Brussel listened carefully to each of their stories. Sometimes she gave them advice. Sometimes she talked it out with them. Sometimes she pushed them to act.

When the Bund first opened and actual vampires transferred to the school, there had been a tragedy at the school, and the concerns that the students brought with them were often drastic issues, such as whether to live or die. But more recently, while the students' concerns were still serious, their issues had become slightly more peaceful. The most common complaint over the last month or so had been from the Fangless girls wanting to wear crowns. Crowns were difficult to tell from the real thing for both humans and vampires, so it was prohibited by Bund law to wear them.

"Oh, but I understand. Those kids' teeth were a little strange… when they smiled," said Shindo Yuri as she gulped down a pretzel with the efficiency of a pencil sharpener and sipped at her tea.

"It's a style with some history to it; that's why I think it's so fascinating. But young people these days just aren't up to it."

Ms. Brussel bowed her slender back and sipped at her hot water with a pinch of salt.

"Miss Yuri, you shouldn't pick on them."

"I wouldn't do something like that... Oh yeah, I heard that Aihara came to see you."

"Oh yes, that girl you were talking about... She came and left without saying a word."

"She's that kind of girl; she's hesitant about herself."

Shindo Yuri was human. One of the biggest changes that had occurred recently was that human students had begun to visit Ms. Brussel.

The mental welfare of children bitten by vampires or who had nearly been bitten was Ms. Brussel's specialty and another of her important duties here. The human counselor was not full-time staff, and there were still things that only a vampire knew. Even so, there were few patients willing to discuss the trauma of being bitten by a vampire with another vampire, and so for a long time, none of the human students came to the infirmary. It was only recently that several curious students had come to visit.

"How has your class been recently? Are there any kids who stick out?"

"Nothing serious. Even Uemura-kun, the most depressed of them, has been pretty normal lately," Yuri answered as she finished off the box of pretzels and reached for a tart on another tray. "Do you work on commission?"

"Commission? No. Why do you ask that?"

"I was wondering if you got paid less if nobody used your services."

"No, nothing like that," laughed Ms. Brussel involuntarily. Talking to human children without having to hide her nature was a new experience for her, and she made new discoveries every day. "I'm on salary. Anyway, I think it's good if there are fewer people who are so troubled that they need to come here. I'm like a doctor, after all."

"Ah…"

The bell heralding the beginning of class soon rang, and Shindo Yuri bowed and hurried to class.

It was during lunch break several days later that Aihara Mai appeared at the infirmary again.

"Here, come in."

"……"

Yuri, who came with her, pulled her in by the hand and made her sit. While she stared at Ms. Brussel with her large eyes full of wariness as before, it seemed that she was slightly more relaxed due to the presence of a friend. Even so, she didn't drink the tea that was offered.

Ms. Brussel knew about Aihara Mai. Her parents worked at the municipal finance bureau, and they were associated with managing tax revenue from the Bund. Apparently, she had been forced to attend this school because her parents had to maintain good relations with the Bund; she herself did not really like vampires. Ms. Brussel had heard this from the girl's homeroom teacher. Her previous appearance at the infirmary was the first time that Ms. Brussel had seen her in person, and this was now the second time.

The girl was elegant despite her casual appearance, suggesting that she had been brought up well. Her face was pretty, like a flower in full bloom, and while her large, upward-slanting eyes made her look arrogant, Ms. Brussel thought that she would be cute when she smiled. She was the type of girl other girls admired and boys gossiped about—from a distance.

Yuri, who was sitting next to her, ate at her leisure and poked Mai in the ribs. While Ms. Brussel was grateful for Yuri's support, rushing her patients like that was prohibited. Ms. Brussel did not begin talking; she only watched Aihara Mai with a gentle smile.

"Um…"

Around the time Yuri finished drinking her first cup of tea, Mai finally opened her mouth as she glared up at Ms. Brussel through her eyelashes.

"Do you know someone named Catartoni?"

"Johan Catartoni? In second year?"

Mai's face turned red as she spoke, and Ms. Brussel suddenly understood everything.

"I see, so that's how it is…"

"No! I mean, that's not it."

Mai shook her hands in denial, even though she had not been said anything. While Ms. Brussel thought the girl's panic was cute, she set her lips firmly and kept herself from laughing.

"Can you give me any more details?"

"Details? There aren't any details!" continued Mai, still reeling from embarrassment. "I want to know about some things. It's… it's my parents. Right, my parents! I keep getting told to get along with vampires, and everything is fine, but it's just… I kind of like him… a little."

"You want to get along with vampires because of your parents, so you've picked Johan, right?"

"Yes, yes. That's right!"

"That's a good thing. I'm sure your parents would be happy," smiled Ms. Brussel. "Do you like him?"

"Oh! No, no way! It's just that we're in the same class, and our seats are close by… That's all!" Mai almost yelled out her answer, as she rose up from her chair and flailed her arms in a panic. She peered at Ms. Brussel through her unruly hair.

"There's no way that humans and vampires can fall in love anyway, right? This isn't a manga."

"Yes, they can, but there are a lot of obstacles. It's not something I can encourage."

"What?!"

Mai's face changed, turning suddenly pale. She glanced

at Ms. Brussel, then dropped her gaze to the floor. She rose unsteadily to her feet and hurried out of the infirmary, not meeting Ms. Brussel's gaze. Yuri glared at Ms. Brussel once, as though in accusation, then chased after her.

"Why did you say that to Aihara?" Yuri asked, annoyed, as she stuffed chocolate-covered coffee beans into her mouth after school that day. "She's really depressed. She'd finally worked up the courage to come in and ask for advice."

"I do apologize for upsetting her," sighed Ms. Brussel deeply as she drank hot water from her cup. "But love between humans and the Fangless is really difficult. It often ends with both parties being deeply hurt."

"Aren't you the one who said to interact with them normally?"

"You can be friends with them. Normally, anyway. But love is a little different."

Yuri was still suspicious. "Didn't the previous student council president hook up with a grade-school boy?"

"Those kids weren't Fangless."

"You disappoint me." Yuri's expression turned darker as she toyed with the coffee beans in her hand. "You said prejudice is bad, but aren't you the most prejudiced person of all?"

"……"

Yuri seemed to read something in Ms. Brussel's

expression. "I'm sorry; that was over the line. But please take care of Aihara. She's a good girl."

"Yes, I will think about whether or not there's anything I can do for her."

Yuri did not eat the last coffee bean she was playing with and returned it to the dish before she left.

The next few days were very busy.

While the gap between humans and the Fangless had finally closed, there was something suspicious about the state of the world. In addition, another problem had appeared at school: The relationship between the Fangless, who made up the majority of the vampire students, and the normal Fanged vampires had soured.

Of the several hundred vampires in the combined grade, middle, and high school, the number of vampires who had not had their fangs removed comprised not even ten percent. All of these children had passed rigorous evaluations to ensure that they were not prejudiced against humans or inclined to bite, which also meant that most of them were well-behaved and unassertive.

"That's why we don't think they're looking down on us. Actually, we think it's harder to be them. But I guess we don't really have any fondness for the Fanged when we meet them, no matter what we do," summarized Johan Ali Murat Catartoni as he played with his curly black hair.

What Ms. Brussel did not tell Aihara Mai (or rather, she

had no desire to tell her) was that Johan was also a frequent visitor to the infirmary. He would come to chat before class once every two or three days.

"Even though the previous student council president was one of the Fanged, she was very careful to arrange things so that both sides had their own limits and spaces. But neither she nor Her Highness has been around lately."

He had handsome Arabian features. His back was straight, and the dark-skinned arms visible from below the sleeves of his shirt were lithe and well-muscled, giving the impression that he had been actively involved in some sport when he was human. Even so, he did not make much of an impression at first glance, which was evidence that he was good at making himself not stand out. While most Fangless had that tendency, it was rare for someone to be as good at it as he was. He was probably as invisible as the air in his own class. Ms. Brussel thought that Aihara Mai had pretty good taste.

"They've been meeting by themselves a lot recently. They don't talk to us or their human classmates much."

"Have there been any fights?"

"No, there haven't, but it's been close at times. I'm not sure what will happen if this goes on..."

While his grades were average, he was clever. He observed people carefully, and he was one of Ms. Brussel's best sources of information.

"Do you know who the leader of these meetings is?"

"Hmm." After furrowing his brows several times, he answered, "Andrew Nox. From the third year."

"We have to do something."

As things stood, the current situation was a big problem. She had also heard stories from the Fanged vampires. There were several kids who carefully planned their visits so that they would not encounter each other. But she had to wonder what would happen if they crossed paths.

When the idea first flashed across her mind, she thought it a fancy that wasn't worth serious pursuit, but as she considered it further, she thought that maybe it wasn't such a bad idea after all. As she gave it more thought, she came to the conclusion that this was the best course of action.

And more importantly, one of the things that had led her to this idea was the visit from Aihara Mai. She remembered Yuri's words. Maybe she should really think about whether there was anything she could do. In the unfamiliar environment of the school, perhaps there would be a better choice than Brussel's rusty pessimism.

"Johan, do you know this Andrew person?"

"Well, sort of. We don't really get along."

"Can you try to get along then?"

"Huh?"

"…Therefore, I wanted all of you to try the flavor of the new Stigma. Thank you for your help."

Four boys sat around a table made out of desks moved in from the conference room and pushed together. A makeshift tablecloth draped over the table, giving it a formal atmosphere. The boys' expressions were uneasy.

"Maybe you know of each other, but I'll do introductions. Jogasaki-kun is the student council president. This is third-year student Nox-kun." Ms. Brussel greeted the two boys sitting on the right side of the table. These two were Fanged vampires.

"This is Catartoni-kun, a second-year student, and Sano, of the newspaper club." The two boys on the left bowed their heads. They were both Fangless.

"And this is Shindo-san and Aihara-san, both from the second year."

"Um… may I ask a question?" One of the boys on the right, Andrew Nox, quickly raised his hand. "Those two are human, right?"

"Yes. Aihara-san is the sponsor for today's meeting. Her parents obtained the new Stigma early. And Shindo-san is here to help out."

"Pleased to meet you!"

"Pleased to meet you."

Yuri stood next to Andrew, and Mai was closer to Johan. Both bowed nervously. There were seven glasses on the table filled with scarlet liquid. The six students, sorted into pairs, gazed at each other uneasily.

"I wanted to set up an event to get to know each of

you better, and I asked Yuri-san to help. I also asked her to see if Mai-san would attend, so they're our human representatives."

"Wow, that's a heavy responsibility," Yuri said when she was asked, though she accepted the proposal immediately. "Aihara will definitely come," she added.

"But is that really all right? Even I've noticed that the Fangless and the regular vampires aren't really getting along."

"That's why I've set up the party—to do something about it." Ms. Brussel brushed imaginary dust off of her coat. "But I think it will be all right. There are no vampires who don't have anything to say about Stigma."

And thus, Ms. Brussel's prediction turned out to be correct.

"Ugh, tastes like iron."

"Of course it does; it's blood. Even so, it's a bit easier to drink than the stuff was."

"It has a bit of a sweet taste to it. I don't know what the blood sugar level's like though."

"This is sweet? Really?"

"That's how it tastes to us. But Shindo-san, I'm surprised you came to a party like this."

"Well, I thought it'd be interesting because it's weird."

"That's mean. This is the only thing I've ever drunk."

"Huh. You don't drink blood, Andrew-sempai?"

"Nope. There are actually a lot of people like that."

"Hm. That's kind of disappointing… You're vampires, right?"

"Hey, I'm from Ballymagarry, okay? Do you know what it's like living in an English backwater? If you went around attacking people and sucking their blood, they'd figure it out immediately and catch you."

Andrew Nox was the oldest vampire at the school (although he was still about the same age as a college student), and a classic well-behaved vampire. He not only had solid self-control but also low self-esteem, and thus he came across as an unassertive, modest character. These types of kids retained only their pride and intelligence as a vampire, and were chatty to the point of distraction. It was thanks to him that the room was not completely silent.

Yuri took care to move the conversation along so that there were no gaps. Mai answered what she could and sometimes offered new topics. She paused when Johan joined in, but this was probably normal for her. Jogasaki's personality was similar to Andrew's, and Sano asked questions of everyone without fear, perhaps because he had the excuse of interviewing for the newspaper.

Johan Catartoni had successfully made himself invisible here too. He maintained a neutral position, a skillful attitude that was neither too cheerful nor too depressing. While he appeared to be enjoying the conversation, he made no memorable remarks.

"Hey, Catartoni-kun, are you ambidextrous?"

Although Mai sat next to Johan, she had carefully avoided conversation with him. Suddenly, however, she asked him a direct question in a small voice.

"Why?" Johan's startled reply indicated his surprise.

"When you were playing basketball, you shot the ball with both hands."

"How do you know that?"

"You're conspicuous."

Johan's expression turned stiff. It was definitely the first time he'd been called conspicuous.

"Really?"

"Yeah. So are you ambidextrous?"

"Yeah, I am. What about it?"

"Is it convenient?"

"Eh… But why do you want to know stuff like that?"

"Because I'm interested."

"In ambidexterity?"

"Yeah… Well, no… That's not it."

"Wh-what about being left- or right-handed? A lot of vampires are left-handed because they're weirdos."

At the very moment Mai swallowed, Andrew made an untimely interruption. Everyone glared at him except Johan.

Regardless, it seemed that Ms. Brussel's strategy had worked. The four vampires who had attended the party seemed to become friends, and the number of problems other kids brought to the second infirmary decreased visibly as they smoothed things along.

Johan and Mai appeared to have become somewhat close friends. But what surprised Ms. Brussel was that Yuri and Andrew began dating.

"Well, it seems like I kinda like losers," grinned Yuri as she grabbed some orange chocolates. "And Aihara is concerned with appearances."

"That's not it!" laughed Mai, as she pretended to bonk Yuri on the head.

"What do you like about him, Mai-san?"

"Um…" Mai turned red, but didn't fall into her usual panic. "There's no one specific thing."

"But you didn't like vampires."

"Ah, um… Yeah, that's true. It's not that I disliked them; it's more that they're scary. I still think they're kind of scary," said Mai slowly, as she sorted out her thoughts. "I watched them because they're scary. And when I watched him, I thought he was beautiful. Especially the way he stands, the way he runs, when he's playing sports… But I didn't tell anyone, and when I thought about why, it just happened."

"So it's his looks after all."

"No, that's not it!"

"It seems that he used to do gymnastics," Ms. Brussel said with a laugh. "I think that's why he has such a good body. But we're used to behaving inconspicuously, so Mai-san must have been watching him very carefully to notice that. Maybe you are attracted to appearances."

"Stop it!"

A while after that, Ms. Brussel discovered that Mai and Johan had begun dating as well. She gave them her heartfelt blessings the first time they visited the infirmary together.

One week later, she heard that Yuri had been bitten by Andrew and turned into a vampire.

"Yuri-san, you…"

Ms. Brussel was speechless when she saw Yuri, who showed off her well-shaped fangs with an expression like a child who'd been caught playing pranks.

It was at times like this when she felt the limitations of her career. She could not do anything unless the students visited her infirmary of their own accord, and being Fangless, she couldn't even do family visits.

"I didn't think Andrew was a boy who would randomly bite people."

Andrew Nox had immediately been suspended and ordered to stay at home.

"I asked him to."

She had seemed to be a carefree but sensible girl. Ms. Brussel frowned, pressed a hand to her forehead, and heaved a deep sigh.

"Yuri-san, I'm not going to harp on what that has already happened. But you should think things through more carefully for the sake of your future."

"It's not like I did this lightly, you know. I was prepared in my own way."

"That's not what I mean."

Surprisingly, Yuri was not lying. It seemed that she had made all sorts of preparations for becoming a vampire, including moving. She had remembered the content of Ms. Brussel's special class on "If You Became a Vampire," and she had even managed to convince her parents.

"They cried on me. But can Andy not be suspended anymore?"

"Unfortunately, that's not possible. For you, either."

"Huh?"

"Didn't I tell you this? According to the rules, you need to leave the school and be re-evaluated for enrollment."

An investigation was required to see if there had been any dangerous personality changes when she became a new vampire.

"Okay…"

"Well, I think you'll be fine, Yuri-san. I'll work hard to make sure that you can return to school around the same time as Andrew-kun, so please bear with it."

Two weeks later, Yuri passed the compatibility test and returned to school. To everyone's surprise, she broke up with Andrew several days later.

"Andrew-kun's depressed."

"I feel bad, but our relationship has cooled down. I guess I just don't know what I saw in him."

Yuri unapologetically chewed on some pretzels. Even if she couldn't taste them, it seemed that she liked the texture of the pretzels against her teeth and their saltiness.

"Aren't you going to say something about young people these days, or ask why I didn't think about it more, or something like that?"

"This is a matter of personal feelings, particularly for people like us; there's nothing I can say about that."

Luckily, it seemed that Yuri's friendship with Mai had remained intact, and the two of them often came to visit the infirmary together. It seemed that being around her friend and her boyfriend—both vampires now—had fixed some of her dislike of vampires.

"I've started talking to my parents about school recently. They had avoided talking about it before for my sake, but they were happy when I started talking to them."

Ms. Brussel listened warmly as Mai talked happily about her experience.

On the other hand, her work was getting busy. The homeroom teachers responsible for both Yuri's class—where one of the students had become a vampire—and Andrew's class—where one of the students had bitten someone—were tired and depressed. They had to provide care to the students in question and their parents while still teaching their classes.

There was one other thing that Ms. Brussel was worried about. Compared to Mai, Johan's behavior was becoming increasingly strange.

"It's been awhile. How are you feeling?"

"Well… yeah, I'm okay."

It had been a long time since Johan had visited the infirmary, but his response was stuttering, and unlike him, he glanced nervously around the room. He resembled Mai on her first visit.

"Are you doing well with Mai?"

It was unnoticeable unless she was looking for it, but she saw Johan slightly shrink in on himself. She had hit the mark.

It seemed that the problem she had dreaded had finally come to pass. Ms. Brussel took a deep breath and looked straight into Johan's eyes.

"You're worried because you want to bite Mai-san."

This time, it was obvious that Johan shrank away from her. Ms. Brussel placed her hands on his arms in a forgiving gesture. "It's fine. Wanting your beloved to become yours is a natural response."

It was also the biggest obstacle in the love between a Fangless and a human.

A vampire's love included possessiveness that far outstripped a human's. As far as Ms. Brussel knew, the only cases in which love between a vampire and a human had a happy ending was when the former bit the latter and turned them into a vampire. The Fangless suffered more in relationships precisely because they could not do that.

"But you have friends—human friends, vampire friends. These friends are a power that no Fangless has ever had before, so please speak with them. Maybe they will find a way for you."

Ms. Brussel didn't say anything more. While she didn't think she had cured Johan's problems, his expression indicated that he understood, and he thanked her.

She had a bad premonition, but even with her long years of experience, Ms. Brussel could not tell what it was.

One day, Yuri did not come to the infirmary at noon.

Even though she was a frequent visitor, she didn't come every day, so it was not strange that she didn't appear. However, Ms. Brussel had prepared pretzels because she felt that Yuri would come, and that instinct of hers was often correct. Usually, it meant that something bad had happened when Ms. Brussel's instincts proved to be wrong. She locked up the infirmary immediately and headed towards the second-year classrooms.

Yuri and Johan were in the classroom. Even though it was lunch break, they did not take out their Stigma; instead, they were talking to each other about something. It appeared that Johan was questioning Shindo aggressively. Their classmates watched from afar, as it was probably not an attitude he displayed normally. As she looked around the classroom, Ms. Brussel noticed that Mai was not present.

The atmosphere within the classroom grew restless as she entered. Yuri turned pale when she noticed Ms. Brussel's arrival.

"Do you know where Mai-san is?"

"I'm asking Shindo that."

"I already said I didn't know…"

"Yuri-san." Ms. Brussel grabbed the frightened Yuri by the shoulder, and turned the girl to face her.

"I really don't know! I… yesterday… we…"

Ms. Brussel understood everything when she saw the girl's expression. She took them both by the hand and led them out of the room. She released their hands only after they had arrived in a deserted hallway.

"Yuri-san, you bit Mai-san, didn't you?"

Johan's eyes widened in shock. Yuri's face turned expressionless, and the color faded from her eyes. It was the state of a vampire who had completely lost their emotional balance.

It lasted only for an instant. Then Shindo Yuri began to cry, large tears falling from her eyes.

"I… I… Aihara begged me to do it, no matter what… so…"

Ms. Brussel ground her teeth. She had focused her attention on Johan and forgotten all about Mai. That was unacceptable for a counselor.

"Don't be afraid; I'm not blaming you. Mai-san asked

you to, right? She wanted to become a vampire for Johan's sake."

"That's…" Johan was speechless.

"Then what happened? After you bit her and Mai woke up?"

"She seemed frightened. We were at school, and she said she wanted to be alone, so I went home."

"This happened yesterday, right?" As she saw Yuri nod, Ms. Brussel brought out her cell phone. "Do either of you know where Mai-san could be within the school grounds?"

She called the Aihara residence, but there was no answer. Her parents were at work, and Mai had probably not returned home. She could not go outside during the day, and since she had not made the necessary arrangements, she could not go to the Bund either. It was most likely that she was still somewhere in the school.

Ms. Brussel put her arms gently around the shoulders of the two youths and announced, "I will talk to the homeroom teacher for you, but we must find Mai before the end of the day. If you know anyone else who is friendly with Mai, ask them. I think you know this already, but we're racing against time now."

In the end, it was Johan who found her. He remembered Mai mentioning that she liked the rusty smell of the old sociology materials classroom halfway underground.

Mai was hidden behind a steel cabinet. She screamed

and retreated when she saw Johan approach. By the time Ms. Brussel and Yuri arrived, they saw Johan standing there looking completely helpless and Mai hugging herself and crying.

When Johan Catartoni came to the infirmary again after a long, long time, it was after school in the depths of autumn.

"How are you doing? You seem a bit thinner."

"No, there hasn't been much change."

Nothing had changed. He gave her his usual—or rather his former—generic smile, intended to make himself inconspicuous. As was her custom with Fangless students, Ms. Brussel prepared hot water with a pinch of salt and some biscuits and waited for her visitor to speak.

"It's gotten cooler."

"I'm relieved that the days are getting shorter."

Their small talk eventually faded to silence. The cycle continued several times.

"Did you hear that Andrew and Shindo got back together?"

"Oh, really?"

"After Shindo got her fangs removed, her preferences changed again. Fickle girl…"

"You shouldn't say that."

"…So about Aihara…"

Johan fidgeted with the cup of hot water in his hands.

After giving the vaccine to Mai and reversing her

vampirism, Ms. Brussel had counseled her.

"I saw things completely different from before," said Mai weakly, as she stared at the table, trying to avoid seeing Ms. Brussel. "When I came to, it was as if Shindo had become a completely different person. She was strong and scary, a person I couldn't resist."

The absolute obedience of vampires towards their masters could not be put into words, and it was unique to vampires. They were unable to refuse commands from their master, of course, but sensitive vampires would feel a strong sense of submission every day, even if they were given no commands. It was like background noise, and was easily ignored once the person became accustomed to it, but the shock was strong when the vampire was first turned, and there were some who became mentally ill because of it.

"Do all vampires see the world like this? You? Johan?" Mai covered her face with her hands. "I can't do this. It's… It's not human."

"Yes. Vampires are not humans, no matter how close we are to them." In the end, that was the only place she could return to. Ms. Brussel hid her deep disappointment and even deeper guilt, then said in a gentle, smooth and clear voice, "Mai-san, what you felt was not wrong."

Instead of answering, Mai sniffled repeatedly.

"So it's all right," continued Ms. Brussel. "This is all right. Take some time and let your feelings settle down."

She could not say anything else. As Mai left, she hesitated

a moment and then touched her lightly on the shoulder as a sign of encouragement. She felt Mai tremble slightly at the contact, but the girl didn't jump away or push back. She tried to convince herself that it was enough.

"You know that she came back to our class."

"Yes." It was Ms. Brussel who argued that Mai should be in the same class when the discussion came up about transferring her to a different class when she returned to school.

"She seemed to be avoiding me, so I didn't seek her out."

"……"

Johan's expression was unreadable as he stared into his cup with his head lowered. Then he suddenly, he looked up and grinned mischievously at her.

"I got an email from her last night. She said she wanted to go out again, together, the four of us."

Ms. Brussel was speechless for a while, then overwhelmed by many different thoughts. She pressed her hand to her lips and exclaimed, "Oh! Oh my! Is that so? My goodness, that's great. That's really great. Really…"

"But are there any places where humans, the Fangless, and the Fanged can go and have fun together?"

"If that's the problem, I'll tell you of a place I know."

There were two infirmaries on school grounds, one aboveground and the other underground. One infirmary smelled of disinfectants and laundry, while the other smelled of tea and dusty old books. And sometimes, the sound of bright laughter could be heard from the second infirmary.

End

ANDREW   YURI   JOHAN   MAI

THE MOONLIT CLASS-ROOM

STORY
**Gemma &
Tikurakuran**

ILLUSTRATION
**Nozomu
Tamaki**

MS.
BRUSSEL

RYOHEI   CLARI-SSA

CHAPTER 1

When Johan entered the classroom on Monday morning, Karatsu Hirotake wasn't there. The warning bell rang, homeroom came and went, but even after first period had started, he still hadn't appeared.

This was a problem. Not only did Karatsu sit directly in front of Johan, he was one of only a handful of students taller than he was. If Karatsu wasn't there, he had to slump down even more than ever to avoid being seen. He probably also needed to watch his behavior in Modern Japanese class to keep from standing out too badly.

Not standing out if he could avoid it… Aside from just staying alive, that was Johan Ali Murat Catartoni's greatest personal principle. A typical Fangless had no choice but to live a passive life, but in Johan's case, that lifestyle fit him so well, it could even be called his life philosophy.

Johan hated attracting attention and standing out. Positive or negative, the attention that got him was equally annoying. Grades that were neither enviable nor laughable, a presence that was neither praised nor mocked, that was what Johan wanted; in classes, sports, and extracurricular activities, Johan took great pains to stick as close to that philosophy as possible.

"Hey, you hear anything about what they're gonna do about math class?" Kameoka, who sat behind him, whispered during first period.

"Since Sakamoto-sensei isn't here, won't Kamo-sensei come?" Johan answered as softly and expressionlessly as he could.

"Kamo-chan's been out with a cold since yesterday."

"Really? Wonder if it'll be self-study then."

"That'd be nice."

Kameoka had a thick neck, a bull-like body, and a hoarse voice that sounded like his throat was constantly sore, even when he whispered. The instructor's eyes flicked up from the lecture platform, so Johan quickly returned his face to his notes. Given the lack of further interruption, the middle-aged world history teacher returned to his explanation of the colonization policy of France under the Bismarck system. Known for keeping a rigid structure in class, lately he didn't bother to raise his droll voice. Students were probably pleased at the change in policy; surveying the classroom with a sidelong glance, Johan definitely thought so.

It made it that much easier to avoid standing out.

Karatsu's seat in front of Johan was empty. The seat in front of that one was empty as well. In other words, there was no one between Johan and the blackboard. Behind him was Kameoka, next to him was a girl, but the boy who should have been sitting on his other side wasn't there.

Currently, about a quarter of the students in class 2-D were absent, and had been gone for an extended amount of time, or had dropped out altogether. And it wasn't just this class, either, but throughout all of the school.

One week earlier, all the private rail companies had suspended service to and from the metropolitan area to other prefectures after sunset. Johan thought this must have been the last straw. Since that day, the number of students coming to school dwindled conspicuously.

Before that, several things had happened that could have been considered omens. From the Mayor of Tokyo's speech, to the founding of the Anti-Vampire Subjugation Force Metropolitan Police Division, it was no longer possible to look the other way. With the amending of laws, such as the Anti-Subversive Activities Act and the laws regarding nightlife, it seemed like one needed to live with a heightened awareness of one's own actions and their potential consequences. However, most Tokyo citizens possessing common sense and decorum thought that these things didn't have any impact on them, so they put it out of their minds and continued living their lives as usual.

However, that sense of ease was destroyed when transportation facilities like the railways were stopped. Though no objections arose from outside of Tokyo, the city populace was quite shocked. Regardless of their common sense, or the way they lived their lives, it was the first time they had become known simply as "humans who live in the land of vampires." Johan could easily imagine how far that fear and suspicion traveled outside of the Bund. He also imagined that the rest of the world had turned away from him, his brethren, and his ancestors.

Fortunately, the situation on school grounds hadn't gotten that bad. Fangless vampires like Johan and fanged vampires alike could still attend classes and continue interacting with human friends, such as Kameoka, without any hostility. Humans who knew through experience that there were all sorts of vampires had a grounded worldview that couldn't be shaken by wild rumors. When Kameoka had spoken to him earlier, Johan had responded to him without even considering whether his schoolmate was human or vampire.

However, even the school was reaching its limits. At lunch, while sucking on a Stigma pack, Johan noticed a group of girls in the opposite corner, sitting around their boxed lunches, looking over at him every now and then. They should have been used to the sight of him satisfying his hunger with the dark red liquid that looked so much like human blood, but clearly it still bothered them. He thought it might have been better if the Stigma came in an opaque aluminum pack, like the ones store-bought jelly came in. The government never bothered to think of sensible things like that.

Since many students objected to the drinking of blood, it used to be normal for the Fangless, out of respect for others, to gather on the roof or in the courtyard where there were no other eyes and have their lunch there. But lately, they couldn't do that. According to the current student council president, all students were expected to have lunch in the classroom with their peers as much as possible.

The intent had been for humans and vampires living alongside each other to deepen their sense of mutual understanding, but Johan wasn't sure what would result from this recent unpleasantness. There were only two other Fangless left in class 2-D, but one ignored the rules and had gone out for his lunch, while the other one was suspended. Alone under the humans' gaze and with no other options, Johan quickly finished his lunch and hastily crushed up the container. He then pulled out a manga magazine. Finally at ease, the girls chattered in an easier tone.

Still, if Johan approached those girls, they would give a shallow smile and speak to him. However, there were students from other classes who would obviously avoid him while passing in the hallway. Despite the serious situation in the high school, he had heard there were many students in the middle school who had so many absences, they were on the verge of being kicked out, and the elementary students were already gone.

"Johan-kun, got a minute?"

It was almost the end of lunch. Looking up, Johan saw

Shindo Yuri and Aihara Mai standing side by side, with fake smiles spreading across their faces.

"Do you know someone named Petresk in third year?"

"Stefan Petresk?"

Shindo was another Fangless in class D, while Aihara was a human. Shindo had an earthy, subtle quality to her looks, while Aihara was a beauty with striking facial features; the contrast was eye-catching. The two girls were both involved with activities in their own class, so it made sense for them to be out together during lunch.

"What's he like?"

"He's an ordinary guy. He's Romanian, but he's not any sort of nobility or anything. He's in the Art Club, and his family runs an art supply store, or so I heard."

"He's a Fangless, right?"

"Yeah."

Shindo and Aihara exchanged a pointed glance. Johan suddenly had a vaguely bad feeling.

"Could you introduce us?"

"Me?"

His premonition was on the mark. Shindo put her hands together mischievously. She hadn't had her fangs out for more than half a year, so she was a lot more aggressive than most Fangless. Despite their similar status, Johan didn't really like her.

Of course he knew Stefan Petresk. There were just under a hundred Fangless registered in the high school. They all naturally gravitated together; within the school, they created their own organization and they would periodically hold meetings and share information.

"What do you need my help for? You've met him at meetings, haven't you, Shindo?"

"I'm still new, so I don't really know anyone too well. If you introduce me, Johan-kun, I'm sure things'll go smoother."

He could imagine their conversation, even without asking. The two girls had long been obsessed with the idea of improving human-vampire relations. They couldn't just stand by and watch things getting worse day-by-day at the school. Mediating fights, setting up meetings over tea—they were like diplomats. Their friendship with both humans and Fangless gave them considerable persuasive abilities, and the fact that the atmosphere in class D had relaxed quite a bit was thanks in large part to their continuing efforts.

Johan had heard they had expanded their efforts to other classes with limited success, but he had no idea they had moved on to other grades. That was probably why they were out during lunch.

"If he's a third year, why don't you get Andrew to do it?"

"No way. He's no help at all," Shindo shrugged.

"We've heard that Stefan is arguing with human students, but we want to get his side of the story. Can you help us?" Aihara sat down in the seat in front of Johan and looked directly into his eyes.

Johan, while he applauded their efforts, had no interest in getting involved. Sticking his neck into other peoples' problems was one thing he avoided more than anything. Even so, it was hard to refuse Aihara's direct plea for help. At a loss for how to respond, he heard a voice from the window seat on the opposite side of the room.

One of the girls who'd been staring at Johan during lunch was covering her face with her hands and crying; she had been the one looking at him the most. One of the girls sitting next to her put a hand on her shoulder. She shrugged it off, shrinking down and rounding her shoulders like she was sinking further into her sorrow.

Aihara stood up and walked over to the two girls. She spoke quietly, stroking the sobbing girl's shoulders as if trying to soothe her. Johan suspected that the ability to take action at times like this, to move impulsively and voluntarily, was probably why she was adored so much.

Just as Aihara had finally succeeded in calming the girl, the teacher in charge of fifth period entered, and the girl drew back and burst into tears again.

After class, Johan headed for the underground infirmary. He decided to go and see Ms. Brussel for the first time in a while.

Walking down the first floor hallway, he saw a boy he recognized. He was by a window, stepping into the brilliant slanting rays of the winter late afternoon sun that pooled on the floor, and soaking up the light. Even without seeing his face, Johan knew exactly who it was.

"Andrew, what are you doing?"

Andrew Knox looked over his shoulder at Johan, grinning broadly. "Waiting on Yuri."

Andrew was a third-year, and one of the few fang-bearing vampires in the school. He was Shindo's master, and at the same time, her boyfriend. He lacked in scruples, but he was one of Johan's few friends.

"You wanna try this? It's a surprisingly good feeling—so warm."

"Nah, that's tacky."

All of the windows in the school had polarized glass that blocked UV rays, so that if the vampires were hit by sunlight, they wouldn't be hurt. Even so, very few vampires would willingly expose themselves to the sunbeams. It was a masochistic hobby, like stabbing a knife between your fingers and getting a kick out of the possibility of getting cut. Although Andrew was good with others, with an easy-going personality that was rare among vampires, the root of his identity gave him the sense of being twisted; it was probably actually a normal feeling for a vampire.

Johan raised an eyebrow at the sight of a triangular badge sparkling on the lapel of Andrew's blazer.

"You're wearing *that*?"

"It's the rules."

Vampire students who hadn't had their fangs removed

had to wear "Vampire Badges." This was another new rule from the student council president who had taken office this month.

"Besides, I don't care—I'd be glad to show these babies to anyone who asks," Andrew said playfully, and grinned, curling back his lips and baring his fangs.

"Knock it off. Shindo hates it when you do that."

Johan had no idea what purpose the badges actually served, other than to cause needless tension. He understood if the intent was to wipe away the human students' unease, but the things the student council did lately seemed only to run counter to their goals.

"Well, with things as they are, you can't just yield at every opportunity."

"That's true, but…"

They spotted Shindo Yuri walking towards them from the other side of the hall, swinging her arms.

"See ya." Johan bowed and walked away.

"Try not to overdo it."

That was what Ms. Brussel said, after listening to him asking her for advice—or just complain—with a bright smile on her face the whole time. She was school nurse, counselor, and social worker all in one.

"I know Aihara is doing her best, so maybe I should just cooperate."

"What Mai-san is doing is a splendid thing," Ms. Brussel

nodded emphatically. "But if you get pulled in by someone else's splendid actions, it doesn't necessarily mean something good will come of it, especially for someone like you with their own style. I think you should think carefully about what *you* want to do."

"Huh."

The underground infirmary was a place he used to visit once or twice a week, but visitors had dramatically increased due to the recent changes. No matter when he stopped by, it was crowded. At the worst times, people stood in lines that stretched out into the hallway, so he had cut back on his visits.

"Stop by once in awhile."

He certainly wanted to accept this invitation, but a month had gone by since his last visit. Looking at Ms. Brussel, he could tell she was foregoing sleep in order to keep working with all of the students who visited her now. Without showing a hint of the fatigue she had to be feeling, she smiled while pouring boiling water and serving up pretzels on a plate.

"Sensei, I'm sorry, but do you have a—Oh!"

A face suddenly peeked in from the hallway. It was Aihara. Johan jumped up in surprise.

When Aihara recognized Johan, she made an uneasy face. Only Ms. Brussel remained calm, saying, "Oh, what good timing! Since Johan-kun is also here, why don't we continue our previous discussion?"

"Huh?"

Casting a sidelong glance at the perplexed Johan, Ms. Brussel beckoned Aihara to the table, cheerfully readying the teapot.

"Isn't it better for you not to overdo it?"

"Cooperating without overdoing it, now that's important," Ms. Brussel answered nonchalantly. "If you keep your feelings steady, no matter how many stories you hear, you can let them pass without becoming slow to judgment. I'm sure you in particular will be fine."

Uncertain whether he was being flattered or taken for a ride, Johan looked at Aihara, sitting across from him. She seemed uneasy, lowering her eyes to the table.

Johan and Aihara had dated about six months ago. A Fangless-human couple was rare, but although Ms. Brussel had cheered them on, in the end they broke up anyway. There were many reasons, but to sum it up, they couldn't overcome the fact that he was a Fangless and she was a human.

With the passage of time, they were able to return to a state one might call friendship, but Johan had no interest in taking it any further. He assumed Aihara probably felt the same. They hadn't been alone like this since their breakup.

"...What was all that about, at lunch?" Unable to bear it, Johan broached the subject.

"Huh?"

"During lunch break. Those girls. Was it a fight or something?"

"Oh, that wasn't a fight. Umm..." Fumbling for a moment

over whether or not she was supposed to talk about it, Aihara let her eyes wander. Finally, she sat up in her chair.

"Toyoguchi apparently has a problem with vampires." Toyoguchi was the girl who had been crying. Johan had never really talked to her, but he always got the feeling that she was putting up a wall between them.

"Toyoguchi's parents… They work in construction. They were involved in building the Bund, and they're on good terms with many of the Fangless. With good people like them, there's no reason to worry even with the current atmosphere in Tokyo, or at least that's what people are saying. I suppose I feel the same…"

It felt weird, and a little forced, but Johan smiled a little at her words.

"Apparently that's stressing out Toyoguchi. She said she got in a fight with her parents. She even said she doesn't want to go to school."

"Uh-huh. So?"

Trying to force understanding, rather than simply clearing up a misunderstanding, would be cruel. Ms. Brussel, who had already heard of the situation, patted the teapot, her head lowered.

"What'll she do now?"

"I think she would be better off taking a break from school," Aihara answered without hesitation. "If she comes to school every day the way she is now, there's no possibility she can get along with you guys. It would definitely be better for her to have some space."

"And her parents?"

"They're going to meet and talk with me. I came here to finalize my plan." Aihara looked at Ms. Brussel and smiled softly.

Johan suddenly realized that she was moving on. Successes and failures, even her memories of Johan—all were being absorbed, like nutrients she needed to grow and mature.

She had the confidence to grow and change. It was something that human youths could do, but that Johan most likely could never do again.

"I'll help you talk to Stefan."

"Really?! Thanks!" Aihara's face immediately brightened. He thought once again how beautiful she was.

"Good luck with your plan."

With those words, Johan left the infirmary.

Friday morning, Toyoguchi's seat in the classroom was empty.

As if in exchange, Karatsu Hirotake was back in his normal seat in front of Johan.

"Morning," said Johan.

Karatsu's face was pale, and he didn't reply. Kameoka shyly tugged on Johan's sleeve.

"He says his whole family tried to move." Pulling Johan over to the corner of the classroom, Kameoka lowered his voice.

"But they were turned away from the place they moved to, so they came back."

"Did he come from Tokyo?"

"That's definitely gotta be the case."

When Johan returned to his seat, Karatsu pivoted around, pale as a ghost. The self-deprecating smile spread on his face to become a bizarre caricature.

"Good to make your acquaintance again."

Muttering, he turned to face forward again. Johan fished for something to say to Karatsu's back, but he came up empty.

CHAPTER 2

The image of classroom 3-A reflected in Clarissa's eyes was grey. Ever since she had enrolled in this school, everything had become grey in her eyes. The atmosphere in this classroom, where she attended class every day, seemed so dry and dull.

Class 3-A had one fanged vampire student and four Fangless students; there was a surprisingly high number of vampires enrolled in third year. But according to Clarissa's recollections of the past month, they hadn't been conversing happily with the humans at all.

A boy called Komiyama sat next to her. He always sat alone with his head buried in his notes, muttering over the teacher's words or any other unrelated repetitive talk.

Despite the fact that they had been in the same class for almost a year, this boy—she couldn't remember his first name—had been recommended to his first choice private university within the city, but half a month ago, his qualifying test scores had been rejected. Ever since, he spent his days as an empty husk.

It wasn't just Komiyama. Probably by now, there wasn't one student in Class A with any hopes of a career path after graduation. With the National Center exam over as well, Class A contained nothing but students with high grades and rejected applications.

Colleges throughout the country had simultaneously begun deferring applications from this school's students—if not outright declining them—at almost the same time as the night trains stopped running. If things calmed down, another admissions exam would be given, but for now, colleges preferred to focus on other qualified applicants, or so said the politely-worded rejection letters; other colleges flat-out announced that "students of a certain race" were forbidden to enroll. No matter the wording, the reason behind it was the same—they didn't want students who had consorted with vampires to be seen on their college campuses. Students like Komiyama who still came to class every day were one thing, but there was a disappointingly high number of students who had stopped coming to school at all.

Serves you right. You knew what you were getting into, after all.

She had no sympathy for them. None at all.

Clarissa Pieri had two secrets she had never told anyone at school. One of those was that she hated vampires so much, she could die.

"Hey, what year are you? Can I talk to you for a second?"

"Did anything unusual happen today?"

"How do you feel about going to this school? Have you and your parents talked about it?"

One step past the school gate, numerous cameras and microphones chased after her.

This was typical. For several weeks now, journalists had been prowling outside of the school's grounds non-stop. It became intolerable, with students having to walk to and from school in groups, but the journalists showed no signs of giving up and kept chasing after them. The elementary and middle schools were on leave at the time, but as the journalists grew more persistent and aggressive, there was a rumor that parents were pulling their kids out of the school. Clarissa subconsciously made a fist in her pocket, but upon realizing it, she took a deep breath and relaxed. She became irritated at the littlest of things; daily life at this horrible school made the days feel so long.

Once they were a certain distance from the school, the journalists would break off to pursue their next target. Students would walk huddled together to the nearest bus station, then part with their classmates and head off to their separate homes. By the time Clarissa climbed the stairs to her apartment, it was dark.

Before touching the doorknob, she glanced at the floor before the door, the surrounding area, and the ventilation fan. No sign of intruders.

She opened the door and went inside, turning on the light.

She inspected the dreary 6-tatami apartment with its minimal furniture from corner to corner, cleaning as she went.

As she continued, she plunged her hand into the trap door at the back of her desk drawer, removing a small Sig Sauer P232 handgun. Inside the sofa was a recurved 150-pound crossbow. At the bottom of the bathroom hamper were C4 plastic explosives. And on the wall, not a weapon as much as a confirmation of her inner state, was a small, silver cross.

Disassembling, inspecting, cleaning, and finally reassembling the weapons into their normal, seasoned condition, ready to fire. The smell of gun oil was what finally made Clarissa feel like she was at home.

This was the second secret she was keeping. Clarissa Pieri was a professional vampire hunter.

In the morning, Clarissa arrived at school earlier than anyone else. After walking a lap around the school grounds, she would take a different route each day to her classroom.

The people around her would explain it as simply her habit. Which was no lie. The shrubbery by the staff lounge, numerous trees and fences, the tool shed, the social sciences reference room, and the emergency stairs: these were places where the security cameras couldn't reach, places perfect for sniping, places where one could escape, and places where one could hide a weapon. Keeping an eye on those places, she would periodically walk around them, ensuring that there had been no unexpected changes.

Being a Japanese high school, the security here was at a relatively high level. The area around the principal's office was particularly tight, even more so during the visits by Mina Tepes, principal and director of the school. However, even that was nothing compared to the vigilance and defense paid for the protection of high-ranking vampires.

It had been a little under a year since Clarissa started attending this school, and her investigation and preparations were coming to end. This school was like her garden. She was confident that she could kill anyone, anywhere in the school. She would destroy them all, erase any evidence of the deed, and then vanish without a single witness spotting her.

Even so...

Even so...

The orders to start her mission had not yet come.

There was no sign that they would be coming any time soon, either. The organization that Clarissa was affiliated with had sent her to this school one year earlier. It went without saying that her mission was to kill the leader of the vampires, Mina Tepes. But during the time that Clarissa spent living the life of a normal student in order to blend into her new environment, the situation had changed. Mina Tepes and the Three Great Clans who encircled her had come into open confrontation.

It was decided by the higher-ups that in accordance with the strange mechanics of this mysterious society of darkness—one that Clarissa didn't understand and didn't care to understand—the ongoing conflict between Mina and the Three Great Clans, particularly the Rozenmann Clan, should remain under careful supervision. They informed Clarissa, who was considered on the fringe of these matters, of this decision last summer.

Since then, Clarissa continued her student activities while deep in this empty mission—to observe and report. Having endured strict training from a young age and been raised as a Hunter, to be exposed to her prey and age-old enemies in such large numbers—all of whom she could kill easily on her own—and to be forced to play the role of typical student and schoolmate chum to these monsters was a true Hell for her.

But it would be over soon. As a third-year, she would be graduating in just two months. Since she could no longer remain at the school without raising suspicion, Clarissa's mission would be aborted and surveillance would be handled by someone else.

Mina Tepes had not shown herself at school since the fall of last year. At first, it was because she had switched places with an imposter; then no, she was the real deal, and the other one was the imposter. The question of which one was the real Mina Tepes spread all over, eclipsing any focus on assassinating Mina Tepes at the school.

Clarissa didn't know what type of mission they would assign to her next, but surely it couldn't be any more aggravating than this. With that in mind, she looked forward to the upcoming graduation, hopeful about her next phase in life.

To look at Clarissa, one would see nothing but intense pleasure. Having accepted the danger of surrounding herself with vampires, she smiled with a willing spirit.

Though the atmosphere at the school was becoming tenser by the day, it felt good to see that the world was returning to its senses. There were many students acting as friends to the vampires—such complacency would lead to punishment—but there were a small number of students with a flagrant animosity for vampires as well. Since it would blow her cover, Clarissa couldn't go near those people openly, but on the inside she was cheering them on.

Finishing her patrol and just barely making it into the classroom before the start of class, she found Komiyama talking with Stefan Petresk.

"Hey, what are you doing after high school? Have you decided where you're headed?"

"I guess…"

It was the usual morning scene. Stefan Petresk was one of Class A's four Fangless students. For a Caucasian, he had a small, slender build; his large nose and his drooping eyes gave him a distinctive appearance. Because he was said to have been born in Transylvania, his ostentatious appearance was unsurprising.

"Oh? Going to college? Getting a job?"

"I'll keep studying within the Bund. I want to study water supply and get my qualifications."

This wasn't the kind of conversation to have with vampires. Petresk clearly missed Komiyama's ill-will, and answered him honestly. The fact that it was getting on Komiyama's nerves showed in his increasingly shrill voice.

"Hey, vampires have it pretty sweet, don't they? They don't have to do anything, and they're still guaranteed to get fed."

The human and Fangless students, as well as the sole vampire student with fangs, were all very obviously averting their eyes. There was no one to defuse the situation. This wasn't just a case of bullying—this was a warp caused by the strain on relations between vampires and humans, played out by Komiyama and Petresk, and everyone knew it.

"Kuze-kun, aren't you going to stop them? The teacher's coming soon… this could get ugly."

One girl among the group approached a boy two seats in front of Clarissa and spoke to him in a hushed voice. The boy, Kuze, twisted his head, giving the girl an unsympathetic glance.

"Do it yourself."

At the words he spit out at her, the girl looked as if she would cry. Another girl who appeared to be a friend rushed in, grabbed her arm, and led her away. As she went, she shot Kuze a sharp glance. In defiance, he avoided her gaze, resting his chin in his hands once more as he looked out the window.

Kuze Ryohei. Clarissa's classmate.

As a friend of Mina Tepes' servant, Kaburagi Akira, he'd been marked first. He didn't call attention to himself, but he possessed intelligence along with power. Bearing an animosity toward vampires, he had never been terribly outgoing, but since last year when Mina Tepes and Kaburagi stopped coming to school, he started avoiding other people altogether. Judging him to be no use, Clarissa removed him from her list of "Persons of Interest."

It seemed like he had no interest in humans or vampires. He wasn't averting his eyes in disgust from Komyema and Petrask like the other students were—rather, he appeared to have shut them out from the start, and sat glaring fiercely out the window. It was hard to know what he was thinking from his expression.

As she found herself staring at his profile without meaning to, the bell rang and the homeroom teacher came in. Komiyama reluctantly returned to his seat and the environment in the room finally relaxed.

At lunchtime, Clarissa finished eating quickly, then went for a stroll around the school to find a suitable place to enjoy some reading. Despite the small number of students, the grounds were quite large, with several gardens throughout that contained benches and gazebos, making it easy to be alone. It was like an aristocrat's idea of a leisure palace, built by vampires. While walking in the halls, pondering if she should go out onto the roof to enjoy the nice weather, someone called to her from behind.

"Hey, Pieri-sempai."

Turning around, she saw a girl with chestnut hair and a sense of fashion surprisingly gaudy for this school grinning at her.

"I'm Aihara from second year."

"I know. You're famous."

She knew Aihara Mai. She was a strange second-year student—hanging out with the Fangless, sticking her nose into arguments, and constantly trying to mediate between vampires and humans.

"Oh, then this should be easy," Aihara brightened, "Pieri-sempai…"

"Clarissa is fine."

"Clarissa-sempai, you're in class 3-A, right? You have four Fangless and one regular vampire in your class?"

"Yeah."

"We'd like to have a drinking party with some of the class members. It'll be the day after tomorrow, after school. Can you make it?"

"A 'drinking party'?"

Clarissa couldn't believe her ears. Even if the school was fairly untraditional, drinking alcohol would definitely raise hackles as a breech of morality.

"Uh, it's a Stigma tasting party… You know, the stuff that vampires drink. Don't you want to try it and see what it tastes like?"

"Uhhh…" As she grasped the situation, a murderous intent welled up in Clarissa's throat. She just barely choked it down without allowing her face to betray her.

She's not joking. She's trying to make me drink that fake blood!

"Why me?"

"It's because you're so beautiful, Sempai. If *you* come, we should be able to lure in even more people," Aihara answered without a hint of shame.

"Sorry, but I've got plans I can't get out of that day."

"Oh, really?" Then, without looking discouraged at all, she said, "We're gonna do it a lot, so how about I let you know when the next one is? When you have a chance, please come."

"…Okay."

Aihara gave a bow, then trotted off.

There were students like Komiyama who channeled their frustrations into animosity against others, and then there were those like Aihara Mai. Characters like Kuze were hard enough to read, but Clarissa couldn't make heads or tails of what Aihara was thinking. How many people in her class had accepted an invitation to these "drinking parties"?

As soon as Aihara disappeared from sight, Clarissa dug her nails into her palm, then loosened her fist and took a breath.

Clarissa had no idea how Aihara's "drinking party" went,

but three days passed and there was no change in the class atmosphere.

Or rather, one could say it had worsened. Komiyama had goaded Petresk into another argument. Petresk—due to his gentle nature as a Fangless—showed no resistance, so the ill will between the two gradually escalated.

"Komiyama-san, that's enough."

It was after school that day. A homeroom teacher who knew about the situation with Komiyama had been turning a blind eye to his many outbursts, but it had reached a point where he could no longer do so. Something had to be said. When the teacher finally made a move to stop him, Komiyama fixed his eyes on the man. With a sneer, he said, "I know about it. That cross you keep in your pocket."

The teacher's face stiffened in shock.

"These guys are scary, aren't they? You push yourself, even if you don't wanna be here, but since it's your job, you gotta teach these bastards. It sucks. It would be better if they didn't exist."

"Komiyama-san…"

He shook off the teacher's hands and approached Petresk. The pale-faced Petresk looked back and forth between Komiyama and the teacher. Even after he was grabbed by the lapels and shaken, he didn't move, not even once.

"You… you little…"

Komiyama's thin neck swelled as if his words had caught in his throat.

Clarissa couldn't understand the meaning of the words he spat out next, but it was clearly some excessively obscene Japanese slang. It was obvious Petresk didn't understand either, but the hatred and hostility rolled up in those words got through loud and clear. The light disappeared from Petresk's eyes, leaving them hollow like dark caves.

This is bad.

Clarissa rose slightly, preparing to get into position.

Those eyes were vampire eyes, ones that were lost to reason, controlled only by impulse. There was no telling what Petresk would do.

Should I put on end to this?

To watch silently as a vampire killed a human was something her Hunter's pride would not allow. But she couldn't recklessly make a move while all of their classmates were watching. In her moment of hesitation, Komiyama raised his fist. Petresk grabbed his chest.

Huh?

Before Clarissa could react, Komiyama's 175cm body went flying through the air like a cannonball, straight at her.

She quickly caught him and spun him around, breaking up the force with which he had been launched, and slammed him to the ground, avoiding injury to either of them. There was no time left to hesitate; Clarissa had to deal with Petresk, but as she rose to her feet, someone else was moving even faster.

It was Kuze Ryohei.

Kuze took off his coat, nimbly wrapping it around his left hand as he rushed Petresk. With no concern for the menacing stance the reasonless Petresk had taken, Kuze shoved his jacket-wrapped fist into Petresk's mouth.

"…!"

Petresk's movements stopped. Kuze slapped his face two or three times, and the light returned to his empty eyes.

"Calm down. You're just making yourself look like an idiot."

"Ah…"

Having pulled Kuze's fist from his mouth, the pale Petresk crumbled to his knees. Tears spilled down his face.

"Sensei, crosses have no meaning to vampires. Surely they emphasized that in Orientation, didn't they?"

"Yes, I understand. I know that. I'm sorry. I'm so sorry, everyone."

Kuze passed the teacher, still bobbing his head up and down in confusion and babbling words of apology, and headed for Clarissa.

"Are you hurt? That was pretty impressive, just now."

"……"

Dumbfounded, she nodded silently.

For vampires, biting was an act of feeding, sex, and other things. At the moment they bite, vampires are at their most defenseless.

To be risk being bitten was, in the anti-vampire battle, an important chance to open a breach in an opponent's defenses.

Because it was biting that made vampires so frightening, purposefully allowing oneself to be bitten took courage. Even if the opponent were a Fangless, such an act required wisdom and bravery.

"You're the amazing one. Where did you learn those skills?" she asked, quickly letting out her astonishment.

His concerned expression returned to its normal, unsociable state.

"I researched it. I was afraid of vampires, so I learned how to protect myself."

"Amazing," Clarissa said from her heart. Bearing the fear of an unknown monster, having the wisdom to find ways to cope, and then the courage to put it into practice... And he was a mere human. "No use"? What an unbelievable misjudgment.

"You must be proud, being able to pull off something like that."

Kuze, as if exposing the greatest shame of his life, wrinkled up his face and looked to the side, as though he was wringing the notion out of his body.

The next day, there was no sign of Stefan Petresk.

Aside from that, nothing changed. Komiyama had sunk himself into the trench that had formed between humans and vampires. The homeroom teacher carried on with class, pretending not to notice. Whether or not he still carried the cross in his pocket, Clarissa did not know.

For her part, Clarissa also continued her idle daily life, waiting for graduation. But there was one thing that had changed.

"Good morning."

"Hey."

Kuze Ryohei had begun exchanging morning greetings with her.

Just greetings, nothing more. He sat two seats ahead, back to his silent, slovenly self, slouching in his seat. Clarissa stared at his back.

This boy surely hated vampires. So why did he seem to be embarrassed over having skillfully suppressed his classmate? He was a type of person Clarissa had never seen, with a way of thinking she couldn't understand. Him and Aihara both.

In the little time remaining before graduation, observing people like them might prove useful.

The 3-A reflected in Clarissa's eyes was grey, but the back of his crimson blazer bore the faintest hint of color.

CHAPTER 3

"Prom?"

"Yeah. The executive committee is starting it up."

Having finished her lunchtime Stigma pack quickly, Yuri munched on pretzels as she spoke.

"Aihara, why don't you join the committee?"

"Huh? Why me?"

Stuffing her face with teriyaki chicken, Aihara Mai grimaced. Yuri had always been the type to impulsively assign people to jobs.

Having finished his Stigma pack around the same time as Yuri, Johan was now staring at the two girls. He asked, with a puzzled expression, "What's a prom?"

"We did it half a year ago, right?"

"No, we didn't. Remember, half a year ago was *that* time."

"Oh yeah, you're right…"

Once it was pointed out, they all remembered. Around this time last year, the Vampire Bund had collapsed into mayhem. With the foreign vampires attacking, all of the vampires had taken a leave of absence from school at the same time, regardless of whether or not they had fangs. Some of those students never returned to school, and some people, such as Mai, had not yet heard the details.

"Prom is a type of graduation party, held shortly before the ceremony. Our prom is a bit different, since we have food stalls and extracurricular exhibits."

"So, like a cultural festival?"

"Pretty much. It's like we're having two cultural festivals in a year."

"Our school has a lot of events," Yuri cut in. "At the end, in the auditorium at night, the graduating students hold a dance party. Who will pair with whom becomes a battle."

"Hmm…" Johan made a face that could have meant he did or didn't understand. His face never showed what he was thinking.

"Usually, the planning starts at the end of the year before, but this year, we lost that time. We thought about skipping it, but we're going for it."

"It's because things are in such a bad shape that we're doing it," explained Yuri. "The teachers think leaving the atmosphere this way is no good."

The students who had taken a leave of absence were gradually returning, day by day. There were also teachers who had taken a leave, which had become a hindrance to classes.

"That's why I want Aihara in on it!"

"Why? I don't have that kind of free time."

"That's fine. Hey, weren't you going to the student council room for lunch?"

At the reminder, Mai and Yuri stared at each other.

"Crap!"

"Excuse me!"

Opening the door to the student council room, she found the president, Jougasaki, comfortably gnawing on some baked goods.

"Oh, welcome." Mai and Jougasaki knew each other, because they'd been in the same class their first year.

"You're alone today. Are the others busy?"

"Just the opposite. I'm the only one with any work, so I'm working overtime. And you? Another social gathering?"

"Yeah. This time we want to get a lot more people, so we were hoping to borrow the Home Economics room next Friday. Here's the application, and here's a sample flyer."

"Umm, yeah, it's available, so you're good there. How many times have you done this? You've held a lot of them, right?"

"They're very important."

Yuri suddenly spoke up. "Hey, Mr. President, those badges... What's up with them? The people with fangs wear those. I haven't heard good things."

"Oh really? They're a hit with the first-years; I've heard a lot of people saying they feel more at ease."

"Really?"

"Not everyone can do what you guys do."

This time, his voice resounded with disdain, and instantly Jougasaki realized he had said too much. Flustered, Mai shifted her focus to the piled documents on the desk, when the words "Kamome-ya" caught her eye.

"Oh, is this 'Kamome-ya,' as in the bakery?" Mai said eagerly, hoping to salvage the conversation by changing the subject.

"Yeah."

Bakery Kamome-ya was an old bakery, situated in a shopping arcade a little away from Mai's house. When Mai's family got a craving for breakfast foods, they would go there to buy a loaf of bread. Even the bread at the school store was supposedly supplied by Kamome-ya.

"What kind of letter would the student council be getting from Kamome-ya?"

"They're saying they want to stop supplying our bread."

"Why?"

Even as she asked, Mai regretted it. The reason was obvious. It was a school of vampires. Reading her expression, Jougasaki nodded.

"We've put out a petition. If you guys stop by the school store, make sure to buy some bread. It's kinda like a reverse boycott."

"We'll keep that in mind. We'll tell our friends, too."

"Thanks. Oh yeah, did you hear? Prom's been delayed, but the executive committee is working on planning it."

"I had heard about that." Relieved that a lighter topic had finally popped up, Mai nodded. "But is it okay to hold that now?"

"No, it's not," Jougasaki said, shrugging and rolling his eyes. "We've got neither the staff nor the time, but the teachers are demanding it. And it has to be a roaring success, no less. I've been forced to head up the committee."

"You were?" Normally, student council presidents weren't supposed to head up any other committees at the same time. But Jougasaki was serious and competent, and it was clear to see why he was handling leftover work by himself during lunch.

"That's rough," Mai said honestly.

Jougasaki shrugged his shoulders again. "It is what it is."

"Well, we'll look forward to hearing from you about getting permission for the Home Economics room."

"Got it. Oh, speaking of which, Aihara-san, you guys visit the third-years, too, right? Do you know Kuze-san from Class A?"

"Umm…" Mai searched her mind.

"He doesn't say much, but he's kind of cool, yanno? They say he was friends with Kaburagi Akira-san." While Mai was still thinking, Shindo had supplied an answer. That's right; she had a feeling she'd heard something about such an upperclassman.

"If you have a chance, can you try asking him to join the executive committee? He's the only one left of the student council's 'Old Boys' who's still coming to school. I want people with experience to take charge, but I keep getting turned down."

"I'll ask, but don't get your hopes up."

"That's fine. Oh and, there's been a lot of fights in Class A recently, so be careful."

Realizing that warning was probably pointed at herself, Aihara felt her unease return.

That morning in homeroom, there had been an information sheet about prom from the homeroom teachers. Not one person in the class was willing to lend a hand, let alone join the committee.

The next day at lunchtime, Mai and Yuri visited the third year classrooms. They were there to hand out fliers for the following week's social gathering.

"Come check us out!"

"We have vampire cuisine!"

They passed out fliers to the students and left papers on the desks of the absent ones. Since extracurricular activities were popular at the school, this kind of grassroots advertising campaign was not rare, but the reactions from the third years were cold.

"Don't put one there; that's my desk."

Some students were quite blunt about it. She recognized the boy's sunken, neurotic face. He was the one who'd started the fight with the Fangless Petresk who had later dropped out—an upperclassman named Komiyama. At that time, they had tried to plan a Stigma-tasting event for him in order to try to improve relations, but since he hadn't come, it had been pretty pointless.

Some time had passed since Mai and the others had expanded their efforts to include all of the grades, but the results of their efforts with the third years had been less than favorable.

According to rumor, almost all colleges had declined applications from the students at their school. Having their future prospects dashed naturally left them with few positive feelings towards vampires, and thinking of what next year might be like for her gave Mai a dim feeling of unease as well. However, when they graduated, they would all go out into the greater world as "humans who had learned alongside vampires." To think that some of them would leave with such negative feelings towards vampires…

Yeah, it's definitely not good.

She couldn't just stand by and do nothing.

The girls recognized a boy sitting by the window, gazing outside and paying them no attention.

"Kuze-sempai!"

He looked back at them with a suspicious gaze. When they held out a flier, he waved it away and averted his eyes once more.

"You used to be on the student council, right?"

She put all her energy into her smile while speaking, but

this time, he didn't even turn towards her. Mai became a bit offended.

"The student council president was wondering if you would kindly join the executive committee. He said experienced student council members were in demand."

She intentionally raised her voice. Surprised, Yuri looked at her.

Kuze scowled. "What does this have to do with you?"

"Nothing at all. But if you have the ability to do something and you don't, it's a waste, right?"

"But isn't it my choice?"

His reply offered her no handholds. Despite having the entire class' attention focused on him, Kuze didn't even tremble.

This was bad.

Mai had an instinctive understanding of people. She was the type that people found trustworthy enough to seek advice from. There were people that one could communicate with, and those that one could not; she had the ability to make that distinction.

But this person has no interest in anything.

"Ah, Kuze? That's a tough one."

When they visited Class B next, Andrew Knox grinned broadly.

"He seems to be entirely closed up. Even when I greeted him, he ignored me."

"That's because you're half-joking when you talk to him. You're always like that."

Though they seemed to be dissatisfied and grumbling all the time, as things stood, Andrew and Yuri were actually getting along well. They were the only vampire-Fangless couple in the school, yet much of the trouble amongst the vampire students had abated thanks to them.

"Speaking of which, have you heard anything about prom among the third years?"

"Well yeah, I'm the class representative."

"Seriously?"

Mai and Yuri's eyes bulged in unison. That said, Andrew's true age made him the eldest at the school, and his time as a vampire was the second longest. It was probably natural that he was expected to serve as a mediator for the vampire students. The student with the longest tenure as a vampire was the third year Anna Evers, but her body was that of a kindergartener, and in addition, she was on extended absence.

"That's what I'm talking about. If you'd take your responsibilities a little more seriously, we'd probably be more effective in doing stuff like handing out fliers."

"I'm doing what I can." Yuri's comment had frustrated Andrew, and it showed on his face. "But there's a limit to how much one chap can change a bad attitude, no matter what we're told from on high. It's the vampires who're in a tough spot now, not humans. They're dependent on us for how things will go from here on."

"Hm…" He was right, and she had nothing to say.

Andrew was definitely not a bad person, but there was a core part of him that could be particularly pessimistic and careless, and Mai couldn't stand that part. Honestly, she thought Yuri couldn't help but be drawn to guys like that.

Then again, if she became a vampire, her taste in men might change, too.

"I'd rather hear about where you two get all this vitality and endless optimism."

"And what's wrong with that, hm?"

Yuri stepped on Andrew's foot, and he laughed. The two of them were clearly in love, and it was a strange thing. Mai had a hard time separating out when Yuri was flirting and when she was seriously mad at him. As she thought about this, Andrew stopped laughing.

"I get why you're doing this, but with society in this state, you could wind up seriously hurt. Shouldn't you try changing people's attitudes a little more gently?"

Once again, left without a comeback, Yuri—standing next to a silent Mai—stepped on Andrew's foot. This time, even Andrew seemed like he understood.

"I know what he said, but I don't think you really need to worry. He's always a giant worrywart, no matter what's going on."

Yuri had said this to be reassuring, but Andrew's words

had a hint of truth to them. Pondering this as they walked, they noticed a girl with slender legs coming down the stairs.

"Clarissa-sempai!"

Clarissa Pieri was the upperclassman who had just come to Class 3-A; she was an American exchange student of Italian descent. With cool, good looks and amazing style, she was mainly popular with the unaffiliated girls. Even so, they had visited Class A many times and rarely seen her there. It seemed like she was always off walking around somewhere.

"We're doing another tasting; please come if you can. We left a flier on your desk."

She was inviting her just in case, but Clarissa had yet to attend even one of the tastings. Mai figured she would just be blown off again, but at least she had tried.

Clarissa peered directly into Mai's face. "Can I ask you something?"

"S-sure."

"Why do you care so much about vampires and humans getting along?"

Mai thought for a bit. "Well, we go to the same school. It's no fun if people hate each other."

"Why?"

"'Why?'" Mai thought again. "Sempai, do you like it better this way?"

"This isn't about me. I want to hear your thoughts. What is your final target, your goal?"

Clarissa had pelted her with answers in fluent Japanese;

this clearly wasn't mere idle talk. Mai crossed her arms, sinking deep into thought.

In the beginning, it had been the girls in their class who had consulted with them, saying they were worried over the bad relations between the Fangless and humans. She remembered that previously, Ms. Brussel had planned the Stigma tastings to promote the friendship between Fangless and fang-bearing vampires, and that it had gone over well with human participants as well. Mimicking those events had had surprisingly good results. Since then, Mai seemed to find herself knee-deep in the troubles of vampires and humans.

While she was gaining experience, she was driven more by an ever-increasing urge to do something; whenever she saw a fire, she wanted to stick her nose into it. Gaining the know-how and determination came from dealing with the situations right in front of her, not necessarily out of some specific creed or belief.

"I don't really have anything like a goal..."

"You wouldn't be doing this if that were true. Aren't you going after mutual understanding or something?"

"Well, that is what we're aiming for. But that kind of understanding is impossible. Even the different vampire clans have different goals."

Clarissa suddenly went blank, leaving Mai surprised. "Did I say something weird?"

"I didn't think you looked at it that way."

"Really? Hmm..."

Mai thought about it for a time, and when she was sure there were only girls around them, she loosened the collar of her shirt. It had almost healed, but on the nape of her neck were two red scars.

"I started to become a vampire. I wanted to do it, but then I got scared and changed back with the vaccine. At that time, I did a lot of thinking."

Even now, she remembered it clearly. The things and people she had gotten used to seeing… in that moment, they took on a different meaning. The feeling that the human world was disappearing from within her left a bottomless feeling of unease and loss.

Mai's family had a mixed-breed dog called Taichi. He was an old dog, turning twelve this year, and he had become attached to Mai's mother, who fed him every day. Perhaps the way Taichi saw her mother was different than the way she saw her. Since then, the thought had crossed her mind constantly. Even now, she was certain that the Clarissa she saw and the Clarissa that Yuri saw, standing right next to her, were two different people.

"If that's really what you think, then why do you keep doing these things?"

"Well, if we can't get people to understand, then what I want to do is… hmm…" Mai twisted her hair around. "Oh yeah, the atmosphere… Well, you know, the atmosphere here is kinda bad. You understand what I mean, right?" She turned to Yuri for help, but she finally gave up and shook her head.

"You mean the mood here has gotten very dangerous."

"Yeah, exactly." Mai said gratefully. "We don't want that. That's why we're doing this."

"But you two aren't the only ones who aren't happy about this dangerous mood. No one else is doing anything, so why is it that you two alone are acting?"

"It isn't just us."

"Huh?"

Though Mai and Yuri were the only ones going to other grades, there were students here and there doing similar things in classes and clubs. Some of them had been influenced by Mai and Yuri, and some were just doing their own thing. Upon hearing that, Clarissa's eyes grew round.

"We only know of twenty or so people. But that's why we have to believe everyone else is thinking the same thing."

"That many... and here I thought you two were a special case."

"Oh well, I'm sure we don't seem like much, compared to the third years," Yuri chimed in. "With entrance exams and all, they can be a lot more serious. Speaking of which, Sempai, what are you doing after graduation?"

"Me? I..." Clarissa found herself pausing for some reason. "When I graduate, I'll go back to America. I'll figure out what I'm doing after that."

"Really? I hope there's no weird discrimination going on over there."

"Yeah... thanks."

The two girls walked off, leaving Clarissa in the shambles of her expectations.

As they walked, Mai thought deeply. She wasn't sure why she had been so startled, but Clarissa's questioning had given Mai a good chance to put her thoughts in order.

"After all, what we're doing isn't that special, is it?"

"What?"

"This. We've been working real hard lately, but somehow it seems like it's become a mindless routine, just another chore. It's not really anything special—everyone else is surely thinking the same thing."

"That's gotta be it," Yuri smiled broadly. Her white teeth, with the canines missing, flashed. "Hey Aihara, since you're the type to get all stuck in your head, maybe we shouldn't move so recklessly."

"You think so?"

"Yup. Like this whole prom thing. You should do it and have some fun with it."

"That's a whole other conversation. Why are you trying to make me do it?"

"Because if you don't, they'll make *me* do it. And you know Johan is good at running from these things as well."

"The truth comes out!"

The next day in homeroom, Aihara Mai stepped up to the prom executive committee.

CHAPTER 4

He knew from the start that it wouldn't go well. That's why, even if the prom executive committee ended in disaster, Andrew Knox wouldn't despair.

"We'd like the theme for this year's prom to be 'Vampires and Humans Coexisting.'"

The head of the executive committee announcing this right at the beginning of the meeting was like a red light, Andrew thought. Nothing good would come of saying that the strong should coexist with those who were essentially their food. Even so, this first meeting was an important chance for the committee members to get to know each other and, though the air was pregnant with unrest, the meeting ended without event.

It wasn't until the second meeting, three days later, when a commotion broke out over the proposal of the "coexistence" theme.

"We should hold it from morning to evening."

"During the event, the Fangless should also wear badges."

"And vampires with fangs should wear faceguards."

In the end, the meeting turned into an increasingly long list of restrictions against vampires. Naturally, the vampire students were strongly opposed.

"How exactly is this 'coexistence'?"

"It's gotta happen. You can't prove that vampires aren't dangerous."

"So this is what you came up with? Isn't that just like saying that an animal in a cage isn't dangerous?"

"Aren't vampires already wearing faceguards in the Bund? It isn't unreasonable."

"That's just for vampires interacting with tourists!"

"Look at how tense things are now. If we don't stress that it's safe, nobody will come."

"Thinking of it like 'it's safe, even if vampires are there' is messed up. We've been safe from the start!"

The meeting ended with a stalemate, and the third meeting saw no progress either.

It was Aihara Mai who summed up the third meeting with some final words.

"Hang on. Why don't you take this idea home with you and think it over? No matter how we personally believe this 'Vampires and Humans Coexisting' theme will come together, try asking your families. There's probably something here that we're not seeing."

"...Okay then, the next meeting will be the day after tomorrow, Friday."

As Jougasaki, now serving dual roles as the student council president and head of the committee, nodded, the mood in the room calmed down. Numerous attendees looked to Aihara, sharing wordless gratitude.

It wasn't just this time. Through all the meetings, when tempers began to clash, she made great efforts to get everything back on track.

She's trying her best, Andrew thought distantly, as though reflecting on someone else's unrelated struggle. The executive committee consisted of one representative from each class, plus several new members hoping to join. The ratio was two humans to every vampire. Since the human students opposing the committee chair's ideas were not few in number, the committee had literally been divided in two.

Since the ratio of vampires was greater among all students, Jougasaki wanted to include their opinion, so he recruited priority members. In this way, the "coexistence" Jougasaki had put forth was not just about saving face. True to form, this was the result the student council president had come up with, a fact that made Andrew's heart grow heavy.

He personally thought that wearing a faceguard was acceptable. Not because it would lead to coexistence, but because there were those who wanted it; and whether or not coexistence would ever be a possibility depended on people like that becoming more comfortable around vampires.

"How did it go, Andrew-san?"

"Did the flow of events change this time?"

Having returned to the classroom, Andrew found himself surrounded by a bustling crowd of students. Among them were several vampires from Class B. As they questioned him, the honest Andrew winced.

To be sure, he was the oldest vampire among the students who had ever laid eyes on Her Highness, with the added benefit of still having his fangs. He was higher up in the hierarchy, and he had no complaints. That being the case, the reason he had wanted to go to school from the start was because that was where other younger vampires were. He himself had not lived thirty years, which meant he was seen as a youngster by vampire society. As a member of an upper crust family, the expectations attached to his behavior and views could be troublesome.

"Jougasaki-kun is terrible, isn't he? Here I thought he was a good and honest guy."

And there were several among the mob who were humans. In Class B, where tensions between humans and vampires had gradually increased, at some point a group of students suddenly drew closer to the vampires.

This didn't necessarily mean a lessening of hostilities; quite the opposite. As a result of intensifying tensions, the whole class, regardless of lineage, divided themselves under the banners of "pro-vampire" and "pro-human." Humans resisting that tendency, or simply taking too long in expressing a preference would result in them being shooed away from the human side, leaving them no choice but to get close to vampires that would accept them.

"Jougasaki is a good chap. Don't talk trash about him."

At Andrew's words, the humans and Fangless alike around him looked displeased. It was a little weird, causing Andrew to smile.

The same thing was happening even in other classes, to varying degrees. According to rumor, similar incidents of thought suppression were developing in human society at large. While passing people in the halls, they would glare as if they had seen a demon. Andrew, who had donned a protective charm and kept his eyes lowered as he walked, happened upon a beautiful girl and inadvertently looked up.

"Hello, Knox-kun."

"Oh, hello."

Clarissa Pieri gave a light bow, then headed down the stairs. The famous beauty of Class A, she interacted with Andrew and the other vampires without showing preference—an ability for which she was famous. A normal student with that attitude would quickly be lumped in with the "Vampire side," but her cool good looks spared her from that fate. As he was ruminating over how good her legs looked stretching down from her skirt, and the finer points of her backside, another student approached him from across the hall. Andrew recognized his unkempt hair and shadowed eyes immediately: Kuze Ryohei, also from Class A.

"Oh, hello."

Giving only a quick scowl in return, Kuze passed by without saying a thing until he was a few steps away.

"You. You haven't seen Pieri from my class, have you? Clarissa Pieri?"

That was a weird question. When Andrew gestured to indicate that she had gone down the stairs, Kuze followed her, without a word of thanks.

Kuze was clearly in the "pro-human" clique, and Clarissa was impartial. Both were popular among the third years, a fact that was clearly acknowledged.

Regardless, having bumped into the two in succession, Andrew's impressions were mismatched. Neither of them were really like their images. Rather, he had a feeling they were quite the opposite.

As he watched them go, Andrew tilted his head, but that was as deep into thought as he went.

The fourth meeting also ended without any progress to show for it. The incident that clinched things happened that day after school.

A first-year girl named Sakuma was attacked by a hoodlum on the way home, and she was seriously injured.

The suspect was not caught. The victim testified that her attacker had read that this school was a "School of Monsters." So the attack might or might not be attributed to anti-vampire vigilante groups.

The school immediately prepared several buses. Ironically,

students from distant places like Saitoma and Tama had stopped coming or withdrew altogether around the same time as the railway stoppage. So picking up and dropping off the remaining students at their homes was not difficult. However, the larger problem would not be solved so easily.

The next day, Andrew could sense that the animosity and rejection in his classmates' glares had doubled. The one they should hate was the assailant who attacked Sakuma; turning their anger on the vampires at their school was absurd. But such thoughts wouldn't pass as logic anymore.

"I can't take it! We should protest."

"Andrew-san, if you told us to, everyone would be with you."

Even among the Fangless, there were those who were saying disturbing things. Their personalities were generally docile; but in such pressing circumstances, it seemed these types would come out of the woodwork.

"If you won't do it, I will. Those Fangless guys will join me, too."

One of the ones saying disturbing things was a boy called Yagou. He had always been a student at the school, but during the Jean Marais Dermaille incident, he had become a vampire. There had been many students in the same situation, but Yagou hadn't had his fangs removed. If he gave the order, surely most of the Fangless of similar origins would follow him.

"Stop that. Nothing will come of it."

"The Living Removed" were vampires like Yagou. In order to continue attending this school as they did before, they were forced to hold onto their memories of feelings from their days as humans. When those who aren't humans try to live among them, they cannot see the line and know when to stop and step back from it. Because they lack a so-called "vampire intuition," in times of peace they had the advantage of getting along more easily with humans, but in circumstances such as this, all it did was backfire.

It won't be long now for this academy, either, Andrew thought as he patted Yagou's shoulders soothingly.

"What's going on with the prom executive committee now?"

They were on the way home from school. While walking through the tunnel connecting the Bund to the mainland, Yuri asked Andrew her question anxiously.

"With what happened on the day of the fourth meeting, information for the fifth meeting hasn't been released yet. Didn't Mai-chan tell you?"

"Aihara's been really down lately and not in much of a mood to talk. Did you hear about the 'vampire eviction' demonstrators?"

"No. What's that?"

"They're a group of people trying to convince the vampires to get off the mainland and out of the school. They've been around for a while, but lately, they've stationing themselves around the front gate and holding demonstrations."

"Those chaps must have a lot of free time on their hands. Even if they keep it up, it's pointless—we don't even use that entrance."

"This isn't funny. The mood in our class is bad enough, and the third-years are even worse."

Things had gotten really bad.

Since the girl's assault, the humans and vampires in Class B hadn't exchanged words that Andrew knew of. It was lucky that so many temporary drop-outs had left their seats empty, for the students sitting next to vampires could freely move to seats further away.

"Well, but everyone's pretty rational. Even though we don't know what people are really thinking, no one's complained to us. I haven't heard any stories of pins in people's shoes or anything like that, either."

"Hey Andy, that face of yours makes it hard to tell whether or not you're joking. Where did you master it?" Yuri raised her eyebrows, speaking in a sharp short voice like a dagger. "You're British. Is everyone in the U.K. that inscrutable?"

"You have to put up a good front, like you can do anything." Andrew gave her a wide smile.

"Oh, cut it out!" Yuri's teeth made a grinding sound. If she'd had fangs, they would have shown. "Don't you know when it's okay to joke around and when it's not? The school's in a bad way here, you understand? Are we even gonna be able to keep living here?"

Andrew's smile disappeared. It seemed his joke had gone too far. He did that often; it was a bad habit. He cleared his throat.

"Yuri, I seriously think humans and vampires are doing fine. I honestly thought this school would fall apart much sooner. You know I'm a fatalist. I don't think vampires and humans can coexist out in the world. As for this school, until relations between here and the mainland completely fall apart, I think it's a place to enjoy our friends. Isn't that what I've always said?"

"Do you really think of it that way?"

"Yes, I do. Going further, I'd say that was Her Highness' idea all along and the reason she created this place."

In reality, since the previous year's commotion with Ivanovic, Her Highness hadn't shown herself at school even once. It was probably her way of saying playtime was over.

Once public opinion started moving, it wouldn't stop. Like water running down a glacier, if the popular opinion gathered enough mass, it wouldn't matter how dim-witted it was. Once it started moving, no matter how many people resist, it could not be slowed or stopped.

But that was fine. It had only been a year, but Andrew had gotten to attend school in a capacity approved by his clan, like a normal human. Taking classes, joining a club, making human acquaintances—even having a girlfriend (even if she shared his blood). His flirting was a top rate performance, truly first class.

Having come to that conclusion, he'd grown to enjoy his fleeting school life. That was his intention.

"This test of trying to force vampires and humans to get along has been going on throughout the world for a long time. Nothing on the scale of the Bund, I'll grant you, but with individuals, families, and villages. And there isn't one example of a time when it went well."

"Do you think what we're doing is also useless? Is that why you won't help us?"

"I'm planning to help you," Andrew smiled bitterly. "I don't think it's meaningless. You've started a variety of things. But as to whether or not you can turn the tide…"

Having said that much, Andrew held his tongue. Yuri was sobbing, shedding large tears. Andrew, having closed himself off to his feelings, did not know what to do, and Yuri left quickly. Other students continued home, passing a dazed and confused Andrew.

"Shindo, you were that girl Sakuma's friend, right?"

It was the next morning.

From outside the class, one could tell that Yuri was down in the dumps, and Mai was equally unresponsive, putting out an air of being difficult to get close to. Johan, who had called on them, sighed and informed Andrew.

"She was close enough to Shindo to follow her and apply here. Even so, when she wanted to write a get-well card, no one would tell her which hospital. When she called the house, the person on the other end hung up without saying a word."

"Are you serious?"

He had done it again. Andrew clutched his head. He had talked too much, and screwed it up, as always. It felt like he had swallowed a big lump of iron.

"What did she say?"

"Different stuff, like about exercise and stuff…"

"Like she wasn't useful. She said something like that, didn't she?"

"…Yeah."

He really did understand. It wasn't necessarily that Yuri and Mai had confidence in what they were doing. They had dealt with feelings of unease—that it might all be meaningless—and still moved forward. He, who had no courage of his own to fight his uncertainty, had gotten in their way.

Yuri would probably get back on her feet. When she began walking on once more, would he still be able to stay by her side? Coward that he was.

"I think I figured one thing out."

"Yeah?"

"It seems I seriously do like Yuri."

When he entered Class B, the cold stares of the "pro-human" clique and the enthusiastic stares of the "pro-vampire" clique always greeted Andrew.

"Hey Yagou-kun, I have a favor to ask."

"What is it?"

"Do you know a first-year girl named Sakuma?"

Yagou tilted his head, but it was the Fangless girl next to him who spoke up. "The girl who was attacked?"

Andrew nodded. "Sayama-san, can you find out where she's hospitalized?"

"Well…" Sayama frowned. "She was attacked by that so-called vigilance corps, right? Even if someone knows where she is, whether they would tell us or not…"

"If you find someone who knows, that's fine; just let me know. I'll go ask them myself."

"It's dangerous." Yagou looked surprised.

"That's fine. I have to do at least this much."

Though he couldn't look at the girl he loved, Andrew continued to think of her in his heart.

CHAPTER 5

"Yo, Shindo!"

"Hey you two, it's been a while!"

Suekichi Akito and Mitsuo Nagisa hadn't changed a bit in the time since she'd last seen them. For the first time in a long while, Shindo Yuri felt like she'd been given a tiny reprieve.

"It's not like we can come freely, not right now. I'm relieved that you don't seem to have changed."

She was happy to hear Nagisa say the same thing.

Nagisa, whose plump face with its close-set features gave the impression of a mild person, had been Yuri's friend since her middle school days. The bright-eyed Suekichi was Nagisa's boyfriend; both were in Class 2-C.

The students temporarily dropping out of school had increased since the incident; the number of students at school had plummeted to almost half of the original count. Due to the decreased student count, several classes had been combined. Because Class D, the class Shindo was in, and the neighboring Class C had their breaks together, Nagisa and Suekichi could stop by for the first time in a while.

There had been one more big change in the past several days.

"Shindo, have you seen *that*?"

"Oh, I've seen it. It's unbelievable. What kind of yakuza hideout is this?"

Under the guise of escorting human students and staff, police officers had strengthened their presence around the perimeter of the school. On both sides of the school gate, standing one by one, about ten meters apart, they were quite a spectacle. Thanks to the police, the "vampire eviction" demonstrators that had taken residence in front of the gate 24/7 had now distanced themselves, however…

"That's really…"

"Yup."

Their true objective wasn't so much to protect the human students as it was to prevent the vampire students from leaving the school grounds. Even if no one said it, everyone was thinking it.

"Did you see those long, narrow pouches they wear on their hips? They have UV flashlights in one side of them."

The boy who had delivered this report with a smug face kept stealing glances at them from his window seat. There were also students passing by the happily babbling Yuri and her friends, making disgusted faces as they went.

Nobody was trying to hide the fissure between the humans and the vampires anymore—the school was divided cleanly in two.

At the student council meeting a few days back, despite the strong objections of the Fangless, all vampires were forced to wear badges on their jackets, and clubs were asked to limit their activities after sunset. Returning the favor, the vampires who had gladly lent their physical strength to take on physical labor and nighttime work now only offered their services to members of the vampire clique. Members of the human clique and the vampire clique rarely spoke to one another. When they walked in the halls, humans walked on the window side and vampires walked on the classroom side. It no longer even seemed strange when violent incidents broke out.

Violent incidents had become common in the city as well. The store next to the cafeteria had pulled down its shutters a while ago. With merchants refusing to deliver goods, the store found itself with nothing to sell.

"That's right, how was Ayaka? You saw her, right?"

Ayaka Sakuma, one year younger, went to the same middle school; the three of them used to hang out together. But Ayaka had been beaten up by the vigilantes a few days earlier, and she had been hospitalized. Yuri, as a vampire, was not allowed to visit her.

"Mm…." Nagisa looked down with a frustrated face. "Her injuries are healing, but naturally, she doesn't want to come back to school. Our parents are telling us we shouldn't attend here anymore, either."

"What?"

Yuri smiled bitterly. Sensing the mood, Nagisa hastily changed the subject.

"That reminds me, Yuri-chan, I heard you've been fighting with your boyfriend. What happened with that?"

"O-oh, that? He apologized."

Over a week after the day of their fight, Andrew had bowed his head deeply and handed her a scrap of paper. Written on the paper was the name and contact information for the hospital where Ayaka was admitted.

"But you know, by that time, I already knew the name of the hospital she was in. I had already researched it on my own. I thought it would have been a love letter or something. Weird…"

"Doesn't that make him a good boyfriend though, trying so hard for you?"

"I guess so."

"But how did you look into it?" Akito asked. "The family was keeping it secret, weren't they?"

"Well, you know that girl Pieri-san in the third year? She said she humbly prostrated them."

"Why? I know Pieri-san, but does she know Ayaka?"

"Who knows?" Yuri shrugged.

"On that note, Shindo, you've been doing some pretty weird things lately. Joining up with Aihara…" Akito said. Nagisa's expression slightly darkened. "Is it all right?"

"What's weird about that? We're doing it the right way."

Mai and Yuri were keeping up their efforts. That being

said, when they held their tastings, nobody came. The best they could do was to occasionally go into other classes and listen to people, trying their best to remember to greet and socialize with students from the human clique.

"Really, I think it's amazing. I thought I might join up, but Class D is pretty chill."

"Ah, there's that too. When it's just us, it's more strained."

"Tell that to Aihara. She'll be really happy!"

"Where is Aihara?" Akito looked around the classroom. Nagisa gave a tug on his sleeve.

"In the infirmary."

"Is she hurt?"

"Oh, no. She's in the underground one."

"Oh, the one with the vampire nurse. Is she all right?" Nagisa's face looked uneasy once more.

"Hm? Right now, that's probably the most peaceful place in this whole school."

After talking for a bit, Yuri nonchalantly got up from her seat.

Leaving the classroom, she stood against the wall by the entrance to the bathroom and stretched her shoulders, taking in a deep breath.

It was true that Mai had gone to the underground infirmary. Yuri had encouraged her to do so. Mai was probably planning on polishing up her strategy from here on, but Yuri had entrusted Ms. Brussel to ease her stress.

Watching Mai's increasing exhaustion and strain had

become painful. Mai was probably feeling responsible in a way she shouldn't for the failure of the executive committee.

Yuri herself was at her limits. Originally, unlike Mai, she didn't have any particular sense of responsibility or duty. In the beginning, she had taken her activities with Mai lightly. Having confidence in her concern for others and her social skills, it hadn't been too much for her up until now.

But now I'm so tired...

Exhaustion weighing heavily on her shoulders, Yuri took one more deep breath.

"Now the third years have combined classes," Mai said, looking around the classroom.

"Can they do classes properly that way?"

At lunchtime, Yuri went to Andrew's classroom, dragging Mai, who was deep in thought on her own, and the thoroughly entrenched Johan along with her.

She hadn't come to the third year classroom in over a week. The atmosphere had become too volatile; her presence could quite easily backfire. If she could just chat lightly like this, she wouldn't get caught up in the stares being thrown her way.

"What they're studying in Class A isn't all that different. Also, the teachers have given up on their entrance exam countermeasures." Andrew shrugged.

"Oh yeah, Mitsuo said that Pieri-sempai knew the hospital's address. Is she a friend of Ayaka?"

"No. They don't seem to be all that close, but she did pay Ayaka a visit."

"Why?"

"I don't know, but…" Andrew made a rare sour face. "I think she really hates vampires."

"Huh? But she's so neutral. She even talks to us sometimes."

"She's faking it. She hates vampires to death, but she doesn't want anyone to know, so she hasn't taken either side. Don't you get that feeling from her?"

"Why doesn't she want anyone to know?"

"Umm… I think it's because she's actually a vampire hunter, sent from the Vatican or something?"

"Are you stupid?"

"No, really. She's Italian."

"Are you stupid?"

"All joking aside," Johan took over the conversation, a rarity for him. "I also feel like there's something abnormal about her. It's kind of scary."

"Hmm. If Johan-kun says so, then it must be true."

"That's so mean! Anyway, if you want to know about Pieri-san, he has all the details. Hey, Kuze! Come here for a second!"

The atmosphere in the classroom swelled. Kuze, sitting by the window, gave them a suspicious look.

He seemed irked that Andrew had repeatedly called on him. He sluggishly stood up and ambled over to them.

Kuze Ryohei was a strange one. Having been close friends with the school's most famous student, Kaburagi Akira, would have been enough to set him apart. As someone who hated vampires, he would normally have been seen as a member of the pro-human clique, but he didn't interact with any of them. He didn't collaborate on the restrictions placed on vampires, but he definitely didn't oppose them either. Seen as a traitor by the human side, and with the vampire side guarded against him, he hid his feelings, spending his days in sullen silence.

It was Kuze to whom Andrew turned and, smiling, said, "Pieri-san has some mystery about her, doesn't she? What's the deal with her?"

"Why are you asking me?"

"Haven't the two of you been hanging out together lately? "……"

Kuze's expression changed. The tone of his voice lowered. "What of it?"

"Nothing. Since I know, I thought I should tell you."

Kuze glared at Andrew, whose smile did not falter, then said in a low, unpleasant voice, "I don't know what she is, and I don't care. But it's just… she's not normal."

"If Kuze says so, then it must really be the case."

"Tch."

With that, Kuze turned his back to them and briskly returned to his seat. Several odd and hostile stares were focused on Andrew from the other students. As he drew in a deep breath, Yuri lightly tapped his back.

"Workin' hard, aren't you?"

"Don't make fun of me."

"Pieri-san hasn't turned in her future planning form yet, has she?"

"I heard that after she graduates, she's returning to America. But who cares about future plans at a time like this?"

"It's been asked that they be handed in to the Board of Education. A lot is being said about us on the outside. It's trivial, but we can't neglect it."

The teachers must have it rough, too, Yuri thought. With circumstances as they were, managing the school was no ordinary challenge. The official homeroom teacher of Nagisa's Class C, Yamazaki-sensei, had been absent for some time, and the head of student life, Daitabashi-sensei, had developed stomach problems due to stress and was a regular patient at the hospital. Teachers such as the veteran Shimizu-sensei, in charge of future planning for the third years, had collapsed due to a stroke. Classes had been combined not only due to the numbers of absent students, but also because the number of absent teachers had increased, and because so many hindrances to school affairs had come up.

"If you run into Pieri-san, could you please tell her that as well?"

"Sure."

Yuri found Clarissa Pieri on the emergency stairs

connecting the walkway with the courtyard.

"Sempai! What a weird place to run into you!"

It wasn't that Yuri had been looking for her. This stairway was a secluded location, and the garden it descended into was a little-known place where people wouldn't randomly drop in. When she didn't want anyone to hear her conversation, or when she simply wanted to be alone, Yuri often used this place.

"Sempai, you know about this place, too? It's nice, isn't it?"

"...I also often like to be alone," Clarissa instinctively made a grimace. She probably wanted to be alone right now. A little flustered, Yuri lowered her head.

"Um, I heard you went to visit Ayaka in the hospital. Thank you very much."

Clarissa's expression softened a bit. "Are you an acquaintance of Sakuma-san?"

"We went to the same middle school. How about you, Sempai? Are you an acquaintance of hers?"

"Not necessarily."

Her hesitant speech, her averted eyes, and a feeling resembling a bad premonition made Yuri remember what she had heard at lunchtime. Since becoming a Fangless and especially since society had fallen into this current state, her ability to sense hostility had become frighteningly good.

She's just not that type.

While thinking this, she couldn't help but ask, "Sempai, is

it true that you hate vampires?"

Instantly, Clarissa's eyes lit up with a perceptive gleam.

"Who told you that?"

"Er, well..." Pressured, Yuri fumbled for words. "It's not so much someone in particular, just a rumor I've been hearing. But since you're talking to me like this, I think it must not be true."

"So, that kind of rumor is spreading..." Clarissa heaved a sigh. After remaining silent for some time, she lifted her head as if she had made a decision and looked Yuri in the eye as she spoke.

"It's probably rude of me to say this, but I'll be straight with you. I don't like vampires. The reason I went to see Sakuma-san is because she was an indirect victim of vampires. I couldn't just let it go."

Clarissa took a step towards Yuri.

"Can I ask you a question as well? Before, Aihara-san said she didn't think vampires and humans could come to an understanding. Do you feel the same?"

"I..." Despite faltering under Clarissa's keen stare, Yuri answered. "I don't think vampires and humans are that different."

"Is that the reason you mediate between humans and vampires?"

"Not exactly." *Mediate? Wow, she knows some difficult Japanese words, doesn't she?* Yuri thought with secret admiration. "In that way, I'm kind of like Aihara. I do it because I don't like the tension."

"Really, even now? I think we've gone way beyond tension, haven't we? Aren't you two still working together to make the atmosphere at school better? Do you think that will be the result?"

"It's a little rough," Yuri smiled bitterly. "To be honest, it's discouraging. I've had times where I think it's just impossible. But I can't quit now."

"So you're just riding your momentum?" Clarissa's pursuit had no leniency. Yuri began to feel irritated.

"Momentum? Well, I suppose. But we have plenty of people who would come to our aid."

"Those people don't want to come to your aid. You understand that, right?"

"I know that!"

Yuri couldn't take it anymore. Her field of vision grew dark, and everything in front of her —except for Clarissa— disappeared from her sight. Clarissa's face showed surprise, and Yuri knew her outburst would be bad, but she couldn't stop it.

"Doesn't it bother you that things are so strained? What if, instead of a fight, it became a massacre? Don't you get it, that it's not right? If we can do something, we should give it a try, don't you think? Is that really so weird?"

As she finished speaking, her field of vision gradually returned. Clarissa's face remained firm, but she took a deep breath and said in a calm voice, "No, it's not weird. Not even a little. That's why I was so surprised."

"……"

Yuri took a deep breath as well and calmed herself.

"Sorry about that. I went too far."

"No, I also said too much. I always thought that vampires were motivated by instinct and passion alone."

"Generally, that seems to be the case. But you won't find that lifelong tenacity among those of our age. People like me just want to live gently."

"Indeed. I have some thinking to do, so please excuse me."

With a bow, Clarissa descended into the courtyard. Though Yuri had actually come here to be alone in the courtyard as well, she didn't feel like following Clarissa.

"Oh yeah, Iwashita-sensei said that you needed to turn in your future plans form!"

Without looking back, Clarissa waved her hand in acknowledgment.

Walking down the hall as she mulled over Clarissa's words, Yuri stopped in front of Class D. There were voices coming from inside.

Since they had combined with Class C, the old classroom that Yuri and the other Class D students had used had become an open classroom, used primarily for storage. While it wasn't strange for people to be in there, Yuri stopped because she recognized the voices.

"It's gotta be tough, but I'm rooting for you."

It was Suekichi's voice. He was originally a member of Class C; what was he doing in Class D? Yuri peered in through the open door.

"I said I'm fine. I can carry it myself."

"I can at least do this much for you."

With his back to Yuri, Suekichi lifted up a big cardboard box. It was the box with the posters and pamphlets that Yuri and Mai had made earlier. And of course, there in a secluded corner of the classroom, separating documents into piles, was Mai.

"I'll be your ally, Aihara. Call on me anytime."

"Oh, okay. Thank you."

So that was what was going on. Yuri realized that Suekichi, who should have had no interest in vampires, was suddenly switching sides not because he had the hots for Yuri, but for Mai instead. Not realizing such a simple thing was pathetic, she thought to herself.

She took several steps back, trying not to make a sound, and when Suekichi came lumbering out with the box in his arms, she smiled and waved as if she had just now been passing by. Suekichi gave a frustrated, awkward smile, but after that, relieved that Mai wasn't looking, he smiled bitterly, so only Yuri could see.

At her current level of physical strength, Yuri could have carried the box just as well as Suekichi, but she decided to cut her friend some slack.

"The last bus home leaves in 20 minutes. You should

hurry… Isn't Mitsuo waiting for you?"

"Ah, oh yeah… Aren't you going home soon, too, Aihara?"

"I still have stuff to do. Thanks for helping out."

Suekichi, with a reluctant face, was pushed for his true intentions by Yuri.

"I'm warning you, don't send any weird signals. I'll tell Mitsuo."

"Whaddya mean, 'weird signals'?" Suekichi's face stiffened and he looked at the ceiling as he answered.

Please don't get me involved in anything else. Yuri gave a heavy sigh that neither Suekichi nor Mai could hear.

CHAPTER 6

How it came to a head was clear, but Jougasaki Masahiro no longer remembers the story that led to that point.

It started in the third year classroom; that was definite. That Jougasaki and some other second years were there was also certain. They had probably gone there in response to the removal of vampire students. A verbal argument breaking out and things going critical was, by now, a daily occurrence; but today in particular, and what course of events had led to this, he could not remember. Usually when things got to the breaking point, one or both sides would retain their logic and prevent the situation from exploding. At least, until now.

As the school's student council president, Jougasaki had intended to fulfill his duties in all earnestness. The previous president, Shinonome Nanami, was a respectable and talented upperclassman. When Queen Mina first marched into the school as both principal and student, Shinonome openly challenged Mina in order to protect the students' autonomy. She became a vampire during the Jean Marais

Dermaille incident, and she was one of the first vampires to receive permission to attend the school off of the island. As a special case, she returned to the school and resumed her seat as student council president.

Naturally, Nanami's polices did a complete reversal once she became a vampire. She went from challenging the Vampire Queen to implementing strong polices to care for the students who'd become vampires during the aforementioned incident, racking her brain for ways to maintain harmony between the human students and the vampires from the Bund, then shifting completely to the vampire clique. In her private life, she was secretly apprenticing as a maid for Queen Mina.

"When I became a vampire, that was the first time I could understand their feelings and just how big Her Highness' heart is." Nanami herself had said that, but the number of students who also felt that way wasn't large.

Ah, so that's what being a vampire is like.

He did not think Shinonome's policies were wrong. Humans and vampires learning together… this school was unique in that regard, so having strong concern for vampires during this introductory period was natural. After she joined the vampire clique, her sense of justice and clarity were still strong, but when she suddenly went on a long-term break, he was proud to be selected as her emergency replacement.

Queen Mina's greatness was something he could understand. He hadn't spoken with her up close more than a handful of times, but he was sure that the contrast between her cute physical appearance and the majesty of her mature mind, as well as her boundless charisma, led the people involved with her to feel a deep sense of respect and affection for her. Or perhaps that was simply the natural leadership of the ruler of the vampires.

The fact that the principal and the student council president were both vampires somewhat biased the situation towards their side, so in order to tip the balance back to the human side, as Shinonome's successor, he was well aware of his obligations.

That was before everything changed.

Jougasaki worried deeply over what the student council president should do and how he should lead the school. It was no joke that he had dropped seven kilos during that time. He consulted with his family for advice, but their response was merely, "You should quit the student council at such a dangerous school." After all, they reasoned, since it was a voluntary activity for the students, one should invest only the minimum amount of work, and entrust other students with the bulk of one's responsibilities, which Jougasaki felt was just cheating.

After thoroughly thinking it over, he sought to return the school back to normal through imposing restrictions on vampire activities. To deal with public opinion, he came up with the best plan he could think of to allow the school to take pride and advocate for itself. This involved having the vampires eat in public places, and making the ones with fangs wear badges.

Many of the human students and teachers alike responded favorably to his plan. The majority of vampire students saw it as unavoidable and willingly complied. Gaining strength from their support, he pushed forward with his policy.

But the atmosphere in the school did not improve. Though the vampire students complied and the human students felt relieved, there was no sign of reconciliation between the two. It was around this time that the vampires began expressing their opposition of the restrictions, but he made light of their objections. He felt that they, who came to school from the Bund, only to go back to it afterwards, couldn't possibly understand anything about being pressured by public opinion.

As affairs within the city grew worse, the search for the cause continued. However, Jougasaki was too serious to let go of his plan. He was determined to push forward on the restrictions. He vaguely realized that he had lost his way, but he could no longer see the crossroads where the turn had taken place.

Jougasaki no longer remembered how, within the dispute, things had become so heated. But those words that would become the spark still remained vivid in his ears. A vampire student named Yagou said to the student council:

"You guys are fine; you can just transfer to another school.

We don't have anything but this school."

Next to Jougasaki, the student council secretary Karatsu stood with the corners of his mouth twitching, and—Jougasaki remembered seeing and thinking this—he knew this would be bad. Karatsu had just transferred out three weeks ago, but then he had transferred back. That was because when it had been discovered that he had gone to this school, the government at his new home had turned his family away.

"Whose…"

Karatsu's whole body was shaking.

"Whose fault do you think it was that I couldn't transfer?"

By the time he realized what was going on, it was too late; Karatsu, who had jumped up, was beating Yagou's face with all his might.

Yagou's eyes quickly darkened as if they had been extinguished, and Jougasaki knew things were about to get even worse. The next moment, Karatsu's body flew backwards past Jougasaki, knocking the teacher's desk over and crashing into the chalkboard.

Amid the billowing chalk dust and debris stood Yagou with both hands thrust out, his body rattling ridiculously. His power had finally manifested itself. He hadn't intended to hurt anyone.

"You—"

Several people jumped in to subdue him, and several members of the student council, now hot under the collar, joined in the fight. The Fangless students tried to stop it and the one or two vampire students with fangs cried out something, but no one could hear.

He remembered thinking that he should stop it. But, equally as clearly, he remembered not saying anything. Whether he was pulled into the fray or jumped in of his own accord remained unclear; he grappled as he was pushed into the maelstrom and someone's hand knocked off his glasses. That was the last thing he remembered clearly.

Later, he had no choice but to rely on his hazy memories, but he did know it proceeded with frightening smoothness.

The attempt to subdue the combatants had instantly turned into a fistfight, involving all of the students in the classroom, then it spilled out into the students in the hall. From there, it spread in the blink of an eye to the whole third floor of the east building.

"Kill them!"

"Run them out!"

Jougasaki and the others leapt out of the classroom with a loud roar, laying hands on any vampire students that caught their eye, immediately charging into the hallway while continuing their assault.

It's because of them.

It's because of them that we ended up like this.

We humans will take this school back with our own hands.

After suppressing so much tension for so long, something

exploded within Jougasaki, and he allowed it to blaze to his heart's content.

Some of them ran away; others couldn't take it and joined in the fray.

"You bastards!"

"Are you callin' us that?"

He didn't understand the words being thrown about, but every time he was struck, he struck back. Jougasaki's blood boiled. Some of the human students cried out and ran; others, their eyes bloodshot, joined in the fight.

Several people brought chairs into the hall to create a barricade. At Jougasaki's instruction, his allies curled their bodies and plowed into the foundation of the barricade with their shoulders. With the foundation unstabilized, on their second charge they used their backs to break through the chairs, jumping off the heads of the concealed vampire students.

One-on-one fighting did not suit the vampires' physical strength, and five-on-one grappling dulled their maneuverability. While everyone's blood was boiling, Jougasaki and his allies stood in a strange place, composed. He stood with a leg raised, about to stomp on a fallen vampire, when someone grabbed that leg and slammed him against the ceiling. He choked for a minute, then as he looked down, he saw that the boy who threw him had been surrounded by several students and was brought down.

One student who'd broken through the classroom window

rolled all the way down the hall. Chasing him was a vampire whose eyes had gone completely black, swinging his arms around like a wild animal, grabbing people one at a time by both legs and tossing them through the window frame. At one point, Jougasaki's troops had swelled to almost a hundred people; from end to end, the hallway was packed with brawling humans and vampires.

"Hey, stop!"

"Calm down!"

"Someone get a teacher!"

They were yelling out meaningless words like worthless, irritating flies. Jougasaki grabbed a chair by both legs and swung it about, scattering people like newly-hatched baby spiders.

He wanted to laugh to his heart's content. In reality, he probably did laugh.

"Get ahold of yourselves!"

That was from a persistent fly who had hung around without running away. He recognized that face. A third-year named Kuze Ryohei.

He remembered that face. Even though he had been in student council, Kuze had done nothing to help. Even though he had habitually said he hated vampires, he had not collaborated on the restrictions. Kuze-sempai was so busy worrying about himself that he couldn't be bothered to help them out. Jougasaki lifted a chair over his head without saying a word, aiming to strike that unkempt brown hair.

"Watch out!"

Someone shouted, just before he took a violent punch to the jaw. When his vision flickered back, Kuze was there, with a female exchange student standing a little bit behind him. Believing that she had defended Kuze and kicked him in the jaw, Jougasaki was seething.

"I'll fucking kill you!"

The legs of the chair had come off at some point, but it was perfect now; it had become sharp and jagged. Jougasaki took a stance, then thrust it towards her face with all of his might. He felt the sensation of tearing through cloth and cutting through flesh. That raw sensation, if only for a moment, brought Jougasaki back to his composure.

"Huh?"

What the chair leg had pierced was not Kuze, nor was it the exchange student.

A small, slight figure was doubled over the end of the chair leg, like a meatball pierced by a toothpick.

On the other side of the swaying soft pink cardigan, the exchange student and Kuze stood with their eyes wide open. A petite, wrinkled face twisted with all its might, the corners of the eyes blurred with tears. The mouth was trying to form a smile, and Jougasaki understood why.

In the end, without ever finishing that smile, Ms. Brussel left behind only that strangely twisted face, crumbling into ash.

CHAPTER 7

The next day, it rained from the morning onward.

When Kuze Ryohei entered the classroom, a desk had been placed next to the podium, decorated with a single daisy. *Oh yeah, that happened here in Class A*, Ryohei thought, as if it were someone else's problem.

Before homeroom, in an announcement to the whole school, the principal gave a short funeral address in Ms. Brussel's honor, then held a moment of silence. When that was over, all of the classes were conducted like normal. Here and there broken window glass lay on the ground, and twisted chairs and desks were strewn about. Along with the bruises on students' faces and bandages on their limbs, these were the only reminders left of yesterday's events.

Standing before the mound of ash that had been once Ms. Brussel, no one moved nor said a thing. In a perfect mirror of how things had begun, the stillness spread like fire, the conflict came to a close. Humans and vampires were equally dumbfounded, surrendering themselves to the despondence that comes after a violent storm passes through.

Finally someone (no one is sure who) began picking up the scattered glass fragments in the hall, righting the fallen desks, and returning the destroyed classroom to its original state. Someone grabbed a plastic bag, and together, everyone scooped the mound of ash into the bag. The first one to start doing that was the hollow-eyed Jougasaki. The last little bit that could not be scooped was swept up with the debris and moved to the incinerator. Someone handed him a mop and, without thinking, Ryohei took it and began scrubbing the floor. During that time, not one person spoke, as if they had all been possessed by something that had descended on them; they completed their tasks quietly.

And after the cleaning was done, everyone silently left the school. How he spent the bus ride home, how he returned to his house, what he did after that—Ryohei no longer remembered.

He slept like a rock, and when he awoke the next morning, his entire body ached. His mother, who had been persistent in telling him to stay home from school since the explosion incident, begged him to stay home this time, her face pale. But he assured her that he was all right and left the house.

In a rare occurrence, it seemed like no one was absent. That is, excluding those who had already stopped coming to school before the previous day's incident.

The gloomy mood that had prevailed until yesterday had

disappeared, replaced with nothing but emptiness. It had been customary for some time for the human clique and the vampire clique to gather at the window side and the hall side, respectively, but today everyone forgot about this and took their original seats. Clearly their opposition had not been resolved, but it was like some foreboding thing that could crush them all, looming in the distance.

Rather than descending into sadness, a sense of surprise prevailed, as if they were all somehow detached from reality. Yagou, Andrew, Clarissa Pieri—they all seemed this way.

At lunchtime, as if they could no longer bear it, a crowd of students came to the classroom. Regardless of year, gender, or family, they silently entered and gathered around the small desk next to the podium. The second-year who often stopped by, Aihara, was there, along with her companion, a Fangless whose name he could not remember. Even Jougasaki and Karatsu were among the crowd. There were those who put their hands together and prayed, those who silently looked up at the ceiling with tears rolling down their cheeks, and those who simply looked at the vase or at the floor and collapsed into tears. The classroom soon became a full house, with people lining up in the hall to get inside. It seemed as if at least half of the population attending the school that day had stuffed themselves into that room.

Ryohei himself had never set foot inside the underground infirmary. But through his classmates' conversations, he had learned what kind of person Ms. Brussel was, and by looking around him today, he could tell just how loved she had been.

The image of her back, clothed in that pink cardigan, crumbling like a sandbag was seared on the inside of his eyelids. It wasn't the first time he had seen a vampire die, but he had never seen it so close up before.

Why did she cover for me?

In his head, he understood. It wasn't that she was protecting Ryohei or Clarissa in particular. No matter who it had been, she wanted to stop the disastrous tragedy of a student killing another student, even if it was in exchange for her own life.

But that was why, more than ever, he wanted to know why it was *him* she'd protected. He increasingly thought it imprudent, and a sense of gloom stood in the way of his feelings of gratitude.

Ryohei could not lay eyes on the desk with its flower that everyone else was gazing at.

The crowd in the hall began to stir from some unseen point. As he wondered what it could be now, he heard someone trying to explain through the noise, waving a cellphone around as they shouted into the classroom.

"The school's gonna be shut down!"

In short, it seemed the Mayor of Tokyo had revoked the school's permit. Ryohei quickly looked it up; several websites had posted the story as breaking news.

"What'll happen to this school?"

"They're not just going to close it right away. They'll at least let us finish out the year, won't they?"

"Then what will we do next year?"

The great sense of unease that had shrouded them reared its head once more.

"Why don't we have a prom?"

The one who had raised his hand and stepped forward was a dark-skinned Fangless boy.

He was surely one of the second years who had come into the class with Aihara. He never really left an impression.

Taken aback or just puzzled, everyone stared at the boy who had walked up to the podium. He cleared his throat once and spoke.

"I'm Johan Catartoni, second year. I don't know how best to say this, but the theme of the prom was 'Humans and Vampires Coexisting,' right?"

In the crowd before him, Johan saw Jougasaki standing in front. Jougasaki hung his head like he wanted to disappear.

"Isn't that what we're doing right now?"

Jougasaki lifted his head in surprise. The faces of the people around him were mystified.

"Right now, we know better than anyone else whether humans and vampires can or can't coexist. How far we can go together and what went wrong."

The crowd heaved. As if he had been pushed, Johan took a step closer to them.

"There's no one else in the world who gets this like we do. Not the bigwigs in the Japanese government, not some hundred-year-old aristocratic vampire family—nobody has the experience of spending their days together like we do. No one can do this but us.

"I loved Ms. Brussel. I loved the office she kept for us. I loved that while drinking Stigma, I could tell her my worries and complaints. I even made my first human friend there.

"I never liked standing out. If there was something worth raising my voice over, I would tell myself that it was something that I should just deal with. But just dealing with it lead to this.

"It's no good. It's too much. So I want to raise my voice."

As if those last words had been wrung out of him, he fell silent.

Nobody said anything. There was neither clapping nor jeering.

Ryohei didn't say anything either. Standing in amazement, he stared at Johan.

Ever since the Vampire Bund had been established in Tokyo Bay, Kuze Ryohei found himself pulled into things.

He should have just been a normal high school student, but somehow he'd ended up at a school where vampires and humans studied together. His blue-collar father had ended up involved with the Bund's construction, and he had been seriously injured in an accident on the worksite. His father was still hospitalized and the family's finances were handled by workman's compensation and sympathy money; in other words, they lived off a vampire pension. Even Ryohei's tuition was exempt. In spite of having his life thrown into sudden disarray by those monsters and spending his time keeping away from them, Ryohei found himself in a position where he couldn't see them as his enemies.

Kaburagi Akira, whom he had thought of as his best friend, was now the vampire queen's manservant. When she tried to lead an opposition as part of her student council duties, the student council president, Shinonome Nanami, became a vampire herself. Even Saegusa Yuki, who had fallen in love with Akira, went to the other side. Because they had been friends with Akira, some of them had been implicated as accomplices, while others had died in an explosion.

Currently, Akira's whereabouts were unknown, Yuki was out of school due to her serious injuries, and Nanami had also disappeared. The humans around him who had gotten heavily involved with vampires had all been stirred up and drifted off somewhere.

I can't take any more.

It's too much.

Kuze Ryohei only hoped for one thing—to never again get involved in anything or to have his life stirred up in any such way, especially anything that involved vampires.

He had closed his heart. He didn't get involved with anyone else, and he spent his days without participating in anything. Yesterday, he had seen the result of that decision.

He had no desire to stop the deepening opposition between vampires and humans, nor did he want to agitate it. If that riot hadn't started right before his eyes, he would have taken refuge and looked the other way.

"We don't have anything but this school."

At Yagou's words, if Karatsu hadn't beaten him in a fit of rage, Ryohei himself probably would have. The human students also probably wouldn't have anything but this school before too long. Without realizing this, the vampires took offense and kept painting themselves as the victims.

But whether he would have killed him was a different story. Ryohei knew what it was like to become the victim of someone else's reckless violence. Understanding their feelings, he couldn't just leave it be, and so he had tried to stop it. This was the result.

I...

Out of despair, up until now Ryohei had decided merely to withdraw further. He had even thought that quitting school would be all right.

But an underclassman who was also in despair had come forward. He had called on them to raise their voices.

Have I ever...

He couldn't take it anymore. He felt the way Johan did, but... Johan was a vampire. To have the same feeling as a vampire... Well then, what was he, as a human, doing?

Have I ever raised my voice?

What should he do?

"All right. Let's do it."

Before he realized it, he had stepped forward and was standing next to Johan.

Things grew even more chaotic from there.

There was a flood of applicants for the rejuvenated prom planning committee. This volunteer activity was once again respected. The school's spirit suddenly became extremely festive. As if the thing haunting them had fallen away, or as if nothing had ever really been there at all, the members of the student council rapidly regained their enthusiasm. Moreover, conscious of the fact that this might be the last celebration their school ever held, they raised their ashen faces.

"To spread only correct information regarding vampires."

At their first meeting, the theme of the prom and the accompanying exhibition was decided. Every class and club, in the face of declining student numbers, followed the planned theme and began revolving their activities around planning. Without anyone apologizing or shaking hands, relations between vampire students and human students returned to normal.

It wasn't all roses, however. The general prom committee had just started the year before. They had already been keeping an impossible schedule, starting in January; now it was already mid-February, meaning they had less than a month until the event.

Ryohei, along with Jougasaki, Andrew, Johan, Aihara, and Shindo, were elected to an administrative committee of six. Their first action was to adjourn to the student council room for half a day, in the hope that they could come up with a solid plan.

"I'd heard things were stalled, but I never imagined that they were this far behind."

Having read the first planning committee's meeting minutes, Ryohei spoke up in surprise.

"And this went on four more times... No matter how you look at it, a prom would have been impossible for you guys."

"There's nothing I can say to that." Jougasaki hung his head with a dejected face. He had talked about quitting the student council and leaving school, but based on Ryohei's and the student council members' opinions, he gave up on that and took his seat again on the administrative committee. Having a strong sense of responsibility to start with, his efforts were extraordinary.

"I'll say this, though: events live and die with their budgets. Whether or not you have money makes a big difference in whether or not you can do the job."

"Right!"

That budget was a problem, as the school's management had suspended their permission and begun preparations to close the school. The city was in a bad state, and the principal had sent no instructions. No school had been chosen to accept the students, so there was no time to approve such trivial things as a budget for a special event. But Ryohei and Jougasaki took a chance, and they succeeded in acquiring the majority of the money that had been pooled for the next school year.

"It really is different when you're working with someone who's experienced." Jougasaki spoke those words from the bottom of his heart.

"This is normal, you know."

Akira had always been at the center of his circle of friends, and when he decided on something, he was the type of guy who wouldn't get distracted or give up. Yuki had always been quiet, but once she became acquainted with Akira, she'd become an unstoppable force of nature. Because he hung around those two so much, Ryohei had become adept at cleaning up other people's messes and managing others.

"You all can do this much at least. You decided to sign up and join; now it's do-or-die time."

"I can't do it! I'll die!" Andrew Knox cried out, but Ryohei cut him off with indifference.

"Just do it! If we don't finish this all up tonight, we can't start assigning tasks tomorrow."

"Can we really carry all this in one night?" Andrew called out once more, pointing to a pile of lumber and steel pipes that would have filled five trucks.

"You said you would do anything."

"Yeah, I know what I said, but—"

Andrew had been the only one to run and hide during

the riot. Embarrassed, he had offered himself up, saying he would do anything, and so he became a candidate for the executive committee.

"Nobody's telling you to do it alone. You can get other vampires to help you. That's why we chose you."

"They're all busy with their own preparations, so it's not like I can call on them."

Regardless of his integrity, or lack thereof in the current situation, and despite being the oldest and most senior student, he still lacked the proper authority to call on help from others.

"Kuze-san, you help, too. This isn't vampire racism, is it?"

"I'm heading off to pull an all-nighter to finish up the fliers, since they're being posted tomorrow morning. Can they do it?"

"Huh?"

"Andrew. I'll help you, so let's hurry up and finish this."

It was Yagou, rolling up his sleeves and tapping Andrew's shoulder. Next to him was Sayama. There were also some students like them who adored Andrew's lack of dignity. Knowing that it couldn't be helped, Andrew picked up some lumber and his face showed a hint of happiness.

"Aha ha, it's good medicine." Shindo Yuri laughed light-heartedly as she spread out her pretzels on the tabletop with brisk movements. "He left me behind, too, that jerk."

"How are the exhibit design submissions going?"

"They're coming along fine." Yuri handed Ryohei the box

of papers she'd been holding under her arm. "The Art Club's exhibit is pretty typical, but still interesting. And the Sports Club keeps asking to do a teahouse."

"Since the Sports Club is basically humans, there's not much else they can do. But spread the word that we need to limit the eating and drinking exhibits as much as possible."

"All right. On that note, the Railroad Research Club wants to borrow the cafeteria kitchen and hold a restaurant."

"The Rail Club? Why?"

"One of their members is a second-year named Frazier, who's a chef and nutritionist. They say she's working to master classic German cooking."

"Hm. That could be interesting. But wasn't there a notice or report about that?"

"Aihara's parents work in the capital, so they looked into it. It sounds like it could develop into something."

"Yuri, when can the Light Music Club start working on the stage? Is it okay to go ahead?" Sakuma Ayaka trotted into the classroom, carrying a stack of papers.

"Tomorrow we'll have all the materials in there to divide them up, but any time after that is okay. Probably the best time would be starting in the evening, the day after tomorrow."

"Okay, I'll go let them know."

"And tell them to talk it over with the Woodwinds Band."

"All right."

As Sakuma turned and padded off, Yuri smiled broadly

after her. "I'm so glad she's coming to school again."

The best thing about the prom preparations was that many of the students who had been out of school came back after hearing what had happened. Even several students from the Bund returned. Some were like Sakuma Ayaka—only recently discharged from the hospital—who had returned to school despite their parents' objections.

"Yeah. I never thought I'd see her again." Mumbling earnestly, Yuri tossed another pretzel in her mouth.

"You know, those don't have any nutrition but they're loaded with calories…"

"Seriously?"

"We finished handing out the fliers!"

Massaging their necks and wrists, Mai and several other girls entered.

"Ah, good. I was nervous about that."

"Thanks for doing it. Nobody tried anything, did they?"

"We were fine. The plan was a success!" Flashing the "OK" symbol with her thumb and finger, Aihara smiled.

One of the biggest problems with putting the prom together was the police squad surrounding the school. As much as they were meant to keep away the "vampire eviction" demonstrators, they were still a disturbing presence. There was also the problem of how the school would handle the media.

"How about we just hand out fliers and invite people right

out front?" Mai suggested. "I think they'll be okay with it since it benefits humans as well; and besides, how can they say no to a bunch of cute, smiling high school girls?"

There were many who said it was too dangerous, but Mai took the initiative and gathered up her friends, picked up the advertisement fliers that Ryohei and Jougasaki had stayed up all night creating, and immediately headed out.

"The police unit was super nice. When we had to go past the demonstrators, they came with us. We were so relieved…" sighed a chubby girl named Mitsuo, removing a sash that read, "Please come, meow!"

"Aihara-san, you're amazing! You walked right over to a bunch of guys holding clubs and said, 'Please join us!'"

"Well, I told you. When you put on your public face, the boldest one's the winner."

"That's pretty funny coming from the guys who hung out so magnificently in our class whenever our mood sucked the most."

Mai and Nagisa laughed at Ryohei's words. After a bit, Nagisa left quickly because her class still had preparations to complete.

"What's your class doing?"

"It was Shindo's idea," Mai answered as she gulped from a water bottle. "We're going to bring in some Fangless who've lived in the Bund for a long time, and have them tell us stories of life long ago. There's even a survivor of Goryokaku."

"Ah, that sounds good. And not a lot of prep-work."

"Only three people have stepped up to help run the show, so we're pretty short-handed," Mai slammed the bottle down violently. "Desperate times call for desperate measures."

"That's too bad. I guess ability takes precedence."

"It's okay," Mai's face was serious. "The publicity takes care of itself, but I don't know what'll happen the day of the event. Will we be safe, picking up our guests and dropping them off?"

"They've got a shuttle bus running from the train station, plus the school buses. They'll probably start coming early in the morning, so you're probably gonna have to stay overnight at the school."

"Ugh!" In contrast with her disgusted voice, Mai was smiling.

"You're happy about that, aren't you?"

"That's because I'm also a student here. I'm seething."

"I have another job for you, since you're in such a good mood." He tossed the USB memory stick from his pocket at Mai.

"Print out the contents of that and make enough copies for each class."

"Ugh!" This time, Mai's face matched the disgust in her voice.

In addition to transporting their guests, there was another problem—purchasing the materials and equipment.

"How was it?"

"No good. Once they figured out we were from this school, they shut us down."

"Gotcha, there are a lot of shops that aren't available to us. This is getting worse by the day."

Karatsu and Suekichi wiped away sweat. They'd been running around the city for half a day, trying to gather materials, but they only wound up with a small amount of leftover stock.

"Looks like going through the Bund is our only option. How's that going, Johan?"

"We've arranged for paint and plywood. Tomorrow, they're going to try and do something about stationary." Johan answered as he confirmed the contents of the computer screen.

Foreseeing that buying materials for the prom would be difficult within the city, he had proposed the idea of arranging everything in the Bund and having the students pick it up in person.

"I'm glad we were at least able to get the steel pipes and the lumber. If we had to carry those from the Bund, people might see them as weapons."

"How old are you?"

"Twenty-three. Also, you said we needed fabric?"

"Yup. The Fashion Club and the café are cosplaying together. They haven't decided on their costumes yet, though, so hold off on the fabric for a little longer."

"If we don't hurry, we may run out of time," Johan drooped over the chair, massaging his forehead.

"It's kinda late to be saying this but…" Karatsu mumbled while removing his coat. "Something was weird about the town. Kinda scary."

"It was like a ghost town, wasn't it? Nobody was out and walking about, and a bunch of the houses had broken windows," Suekichi agreed.

"Up until recently, they were the same as us." Ryohei spoke as he examined the contents of the shopping bag. "Something unexpected happened, and we jumped the rail."

"……"

Kuze, Karatsu and Suekichi all looked at one another, then at Johan, lowering their heads.

"Please stop it," Johan wiped his face like he was embarrassed from the bottom of his heart. "The remaining problem is food. There isn't much coming into the Bund."

"A lot of people are doing food and drinks… What about the businesses that supplied the school store?"

"That's a complete loss," Karatsu shook his head. "Kamome-ya, who handled our bread, wouldn't even answer the phone."

"Isn't there someone here whose family owns a grocer or something?"

"Ishiguro in Class E has one, but he hasn't been coming to school," Suekichi rubbed his forehead.

"Please try and contact him. If luck is on our side, we

might be able to get them to sell us some things. This is the turning point, so we're counting on you."

"Right!" Johan, Karatsu and Suekichi's responses came in perfect unison.

At night, Ryohei walked down the hallway alone.

It was safe to say it was very late, but the lights in the classrooms were still lit and the voices did not cease. With just a week until prom, the number of students staying overnight to continue working was increasing. Ryohei himself hadn't been home since the day before yesterday. His mother had been worried, but when he said, "It's better to stay here and be safe than take my chances walking home alone in the dark," she was satisfied.

As he walked, he opened his mouth wide and yawned. Even though the students called it a sleepover, very little actual sleeping took place. Until that morning, he'd been caught up in managing the prom and assigning the tasks that still needed to be completed. With the plans tucked under his arm, he was now looking for someone in particular.

"Hey, so this is where you were."

After descending the emergency stairs from the second floor walkway, he came to a small courtyard. It was just as Yuri had told him, and there was Clarissa Pieri. He raised his hand as she rose, supple as a cat, from a bench covered in the shadows of surrounding shrubbery.

"Yes...?"

"I heard you weren't helping out at all with your class' preparations. As a member of the executive committee, I thought I should come and say something to you."

"I'm sorry, but I'm not interested. Is that all?"

"Not quite," Ryohei smiled bitterly. "I don't think I ever properly thanked you for what you did during the riot. I owe you my life."

Clarissa looked away. "I didn't do anything. The one who saved you was that... Ms. Brussel."

"You saved me." Watching his footing, Ryohei took a step towards Clarissa. "What's more, Ms. Brussel also saved *you*."

Clarissa's pale face stiffened. Ryohei let his shallow smile slip, and walked around to her, glaring directly into her face.

"Don't want to admit you were saved by a vampire?"

"I don't know what you're talking about."

"I know a bit about people like you. You're not a student, are you."

His first suspicion had come when she caught the flying Komiyama. That skill... Inside of that performance, Ryohei felt a coldness. To her, the human body was nothing but a machine to be honed for destruction—such inhumanely sharpened coldness. At that moment, Ryohei had remembered something.

It wasn't more than a faint connection, but cautiously observing, he became certain of his suspicion. Every day he saw Clarissa nonchalantly check predetermined places within the school, and pretending that her open dislike of vampires didn't exist. As he watched her, his suspicion changed to a certainty.

The same feeling was emitting from her as from Angie and Tatyana.

"……"

Clarissa was until the end a pitiable girl attached to an unjustifiable fate, or so her face said as she stood there, completely still. But at the heart of the gaze she fixed upon him, Ryohei could sense something rising up like an icy razor.

"Well, it doesn't matter either way," Ryohei said, losing all the power in his shoulders and allowing them to slump. "There's all kinds at this school, even some who aren't human. If you participate in the prom, though, no matter what you are, I won't interfere."

Clarissa tightened her lips, then looked at Ryohei. Her irritation showed in the heightened color in her face.

"…Something like a prom isn't going to go over that well."

"You won't know until you see for yourself."

"Those vigilantes are wandering about outside. If they come and launch an attack, it's all over."

"It will be what it will be."

"I have no interest in that stupid commotion. I won't participate."

"You covered for me, didn't you?"

"That has nothing to do with it!"

"And I hear you went to see Sakuma in the hospital."

"…That's entirely different."

"When Aihara and the others were handing out fliers the other day, you secretly protected them—I watched you do it."

Clarissa's cheeks glowed red in the evening light. Ryohei smirked.

"I'll say it as many times as I have to. I don't think this event will go over well," Clarissa said after a long pause.

"Go ahead and say it. I don't think all of it will go well, either."

"…I'll only do what I can."

"That's what we're all doing."

"And I won't help out with the 'Sister Café.'"

"Tell that to your class representative."

Looking at her bright red face, Ryohei guffawed. He laughed so hard, tears formed in the corners of his eyes. It had been a long time since he had laughed like this.

"I'll let the your class reps know that you'll help out with the prom in your own way."

"Hmph."

Ryohei wiped away a tear and turned his back to Clarissa, leaving the courtyard.

Moonlight shone in long slanting beams through the windows, framing the hallway in white. Feeling strangely at peace, Ryohei walked the path to the meeting room. Even at times like this, more work was piling up by the hour. When he got back, he'd probably be yelled at by Jougasaki.

Looking up from the window, he saw that the moon stood brightly in the sky, not quite round enough to be full.

Mai looked at the watch adorning her petite wrist.

7:28. Almost time for the rendezvous.

The watch's round face and leather belt trembled; it was cold. As the underground entrance, surrounded by cold concrete, was meant for vampire use only, the HVAC unit wasn't working at all. Mai, who didn't normally commute from the Bund, continued to wait in this unfamiliar place, enduring the cold.

She was waiting on the three guests that Class 2-D had invited from the Bund.

Class D's presentation was "Living History, Secret Stories: HISTORIE." Attached to a title that sounded awfully familiar was the explanatory subtitle: "Vampires With Long Lives Share Their Knowledge and Experiences With Us." In other words, they would gather around vampires who had personally experienced famous events beyond the confines of history books, in a sort of tea party.

The people selected as guests were, as much as possible, connections of the Fangless, whom they sought out and wholeheartedly persuaded.

From within the dark tunnel that stretched out from the Bund, she began hearing soft footsteps. She saw the shadow of a small figure.

Straining to see, Mai stared at the shadow and, without thinking, took a step back.

From the shadowed entrance emerged a samurai with his hair in a topknot.

He wore zouri, and hakama paired with a kimono displaying his family crest, and a pair of daishou was sheathed at his hip. The topknot on his head was not a wig; it was real. But, without a trace of foolishness, his dark, rustic face suited him well.

The samurai opened his stubborn-looking upturned mouth. "I am Sakaguchi Junnosuke. Might you be here to escort me?"

"Ah, yes, yes. That's right. Welcome."

Mai's eyes dropped to the list she was holding, hastily nodding. And then, she gathered her courage and asked a question.

"Um… do you always dress that way?"

"Do not speak such foolishness. This is the first I have donned a topknot since I was bitten. As you requested stories of long ago, I decided to match my garments to the occasion."

"So, that topknot…"

"Yes, it was a great deal of trouble," Sakaguchi stroked his smoothly-shaved forehead. "I have found the Bund lacking in people who can do Japanese hairstyles. When I had them shave my forehead, they almost gave me a crew cut."

According to the list, Sakaguchi was part of the Denshuu

Unit of the army during the Bakumatsu portion of the Edo period. As a member of the shogunate army, he participated in the Battle of Toba-Fushimi, and during the Battle of Hakodate he fought alongside Hijikata Toshizo. Clearly, he was chosen to appeal to the Bakamatsu fans.

As Aihara exchanged greetings anew with Sakaguchi, they could hear the clanging of a bell from within the tunnel.

Out of the tunnel came a strange bicycle, with a large front wheel that was over one meter in diameter. The back wheel, in contrast, was not more than 30 centimeters in diameter. It was an antique bicycle, one that could have rolled out of a 19th century European photo.

Pedaling the bicycle was a Caucasian gentleman, wearing a top hat and a sleek tailcoat without a single wrinkle.

The gentleman stopped his bicycle in front of Mai and Sakaguchi, dismounting with elegant movements, and stretched his back. He was a tall man, nearly two heads taller than Mai. Pushing up the edge of his top hat with his hand, he turned to Mai and gave an affected smile.

"Bonjour, mademoiselle."

"Bonjour, Monsieur Duran," Mai greeted him in faltering French.

The second guest, Emil Duran, was a 19th century construction engineer. He was a member of the Eiffel Tower steel frame construction division, and in 1889, he had participated in the construction of the Eiffel Tower.

Are they all going to be a bunch of cosplayers...?

Without giving voice to her thoughts, Mai introduced Sakaguchi and Duran.

"Oh, you're a Frenchman are you? I know some French as well. Our military training was done in French. *Attention! Salut! Arrêt!*" Sakaguchi called out in a thick voice.

"Oh, splendid!" Duran clapped generously.

Leaving the pair, who had become a two-man comedy show, Mai turned towards the tunnel to wait for the remaining person.

He was already there.

He was a slender gentleman, past middle age, dressed in an understated modern suit. Using a stick, he slowly walked towards Mai and the others, and it was evident that his right foot dragged slightly.

Mai changed her impression of the gentleman as he drew closer to her. He wasn't past middle age; he was somewhere around forty. He exuded a sort of dignity that belied his outward appearance. With the exception of Queen Mina and her secretary, Vera, this was the first time she had seen a vampire who had such a vast gap between their physical age and their outward appearance.

He was Count Julius Bancroft. After the rebellion of the Three Great Clans around four hundred years ago, when Queen Mina was hidden in the Ottoman Empire, he guarded her as a member of the Imperial Guard. He had served as a senior vassal to the Tepes family, but for some reason, he'd had his fangs removed two hundred years ago, and was relieved of his duties.

There weren't many in the Bund who had lived longer than Count Bancroft. When his name came up, the thought that such a major figure might come to the school and the prom caused quite an uproar.

The one who had arranged for his presence was the currently absent Anna Evers. She didn't know the particulars, but Anna had a friend who was a former novelist, and that friend had introduced her to Bancroft.

"Thank you so much for coming," Mai greeted him nervously. "Bancroft... sama, everyone's really looking forward to hearing your stories."

His status being so far removed from her own, Mai was struggling with what title to use to address him.

"I'm afraid they're nothing but an old-timer's tales," Bancroft smiled apologetically. "I thought I might speak of my friendship with William Shakespeare."

As she stood in front of their three guests and began to guide them, she stifled a chuckle.

Finally, the cool one is here!

Andrew sat in a chair that had been left in the corner of the classroom, staring through the polarized glass window at the front gate of the school. They had spent the last night preparing without sleep or breaks, and they had finally finished just in time for the main event.

Outside the front gate, the demonstrators began gathering

their troops with the first light of dawn. Today, on the day of the prom, their numbers far exceeded anything they had shown in previous days.

Resting his chin on the windowsill, Andrew muttered in a flat voice, "It's probably freezing. I can't believe they're going to this much trouble this early."

The police unit, holding their own with the demonstrators, had also drastically increased their numbers. The Tokyo Metropolitan Police Department had pushed for them to stop the prom a second time, because a call to attack the prom had been posted on the internet.

The leading internet bulletin board, 3-Channel's Vampire board, had turned into a den of groundless rumors and hate speech until a week ago, when it was taken offline for "server maintenance." On social media sites, the spread of false rumors and harassment by individuals saw a severe increase.

The Tokyo Metropolitan Police Department had come a mere step away from suspending the prom, but the teachers at the school fiercely resisted. They did not want the hard work of the students who had banded together and strove to make this prom a success to go to waste.

In the end, TMPD's massive deployment of police officers was a preventative measure. However, in the event that any trouble started during the prom itself, they had promised to close down the entire event immediately.

"I wonder if they're going to attack," Yagou called from behind.

"Who knows?" Andrew answered listlessly. "As far as they're concerned, this school is finished. No matter how tough they try to make themselves look online, I wonder if they have the guts to march in here and start something with us."

"All we've done is plan for the prom; we aren't prepared for a fight at all."

"Sure we are."

"Huh?"

"The prom itself is the fight, which is only fitting."

Yagou stepped back and stared at Andrew appraisingly.

"What?" Andrew grimaced.

"It's not like you to talk like that."

"Shut up."

The clock hanging on the classroom wall read 8:15.

"It is now one hour until the ten o'clock opening. I repeat, please refrain from filming or interviewing our attendees. In exchange, as a general rule, you are free to interview students. However, if the content of the interview is found to be inappropriate by the executive committee, the interview will be halted."

Yuri raised her voice to the ten or so men and women sitting before her. It was a briefing prior to the event regarding mass media coverage. Yuri, who had been placed in charge of public relations for the executive committee, had almost single-handedly taken care of the flood of mass media.

There were over two hundred applications to cover the prom on the day of the event. A TV station had even requested full coverage from the preparation stage, but naturally, they were declined. In the end, representatives were chosen by lottery from newspapers, television, magazines, internet media, and freelancers.

Media coverage had never been allowed within the Bund. The only one who had ever covered the shopping district or residential district, bustling at night with vampires, was a freelance writer who had tried to become a vampire himself. For all mass media organizations, this prom was the first chance to cover "a place where vampires go about their daily lives."

"The prom's venue will be from the front entrance to the left side of the first and second floors, as well as the auditorium. The rest of the school is off-limits. Please consult the school map that was distributed for more information."

"Can I ask a question?" A woman from the television reporters' group raised her hand. It was a reporter whose face Yuri recognized. She was wearing a turtleneck sweater, clearly for protection against more than just the cold.

"Go ahead," Yuri urged her on.

"Earlier, you said you would halt any inappropriate interviews, but could you specify what exactly would be 'inappropriate'?"

"I can answer that easily," Yuri said, cracking a smile.

"Any interview where our students are not treated like normal high school students."

The reporter tilted her head. "…I don't get your meaning."

"All of you want to cover the vampire students more than anything, right? Vampires are different from normal humans, so you want to ask them about different things. But could you please try to put those thoughts aside for today? Right now, in this school, there isn't one student who isn't normal. Whether they are human or vampire is irrelevant—we are all high school students. A lot has happened here, but we're finally able to see past it. At least in this school, we vampires aren't out of place."

"I disagree. Vampires are not normal. To say so would be just like comparing a child coming home from overseas to a foreigner living in Japan; it's apples and oranges," the reporter's voice hinted at her passion. "You know what Tokyo is becoming right now, don't you? Humans and vampires cooperating to hold an exhibition is—I don't know how else to say this—not normal. We all came here to cover this not-so-normal event."

The other journalists could only nod their heads in agreement.

"I understand," Yuri's smile did not fade. "Well then, please allow me to change our meeting's venue and I will gladly explain. Please, right this way."

Yuri led the reporters to the auditorium.

Onstage, the Light Music Club's rock band was rehearsing.

The song they were working on was the nostalgia-filled classic by The Blue Diamonds, "Jounetsu no Bara."

I don't know if there's something like eternity, or if the flow of time will continue on…

The vocalist was hopping around the narrow stage passionately, as if this were a real performance. The guitarist and bassist, undeterred, also came forward, trying to add appeal to their performance. Behind them, with sweat flying all around, the drummer relentlessly beat time on the snare. In contrast, the more subdued presence of the keyboardist coolly kept the rhythm.

Unchanging despite the passing time, could there be such a thing?

As she gestured to the students on stage, Yuri said, "One Fangless and one fang-bearing vampire are part of that five-member band. Can you tell which ones they are?"

The journalists looked at one another.

"How about you?" Yuri pressed the female reporter for an answer.

The reporter remained silent and shrugged helplessly.

"The drummer is Fangless, and the bass player is the fang-bearing vampire."

Yuri's face suddenly became serious.

"All right, one more question. Within that group, which one is the abnormal high school student?"

The reporters' only reply was a deep silence.

Yuri's smile returned and she bowed deeply.

"Thank you for your understanding. We look forward to your cooperation today."

9:59.

Jougasaki's voice flowed out from the speakers throughout the school.

"This is the head of the prom's executive committee, Jougasaki. Due to the time, I have no intentions of making a long speech. You all banded together, overcame a lot of challenges, and now we've finally arrived. All you third years, make some wonderful memories along with us, with no regrets!" Jougasaki could be heard taking a deep breath. "At this time, the 20XX Rokujo Academy Prom has now begun!"

Jougasaki's announcement was covered up by the ringing of the ten o'clock bell and the raucous applause erupting from every classroom.

"The shuttle bus is here!"

Karatsu's voice rang out like it was calling for someone, and several students came bustling down to the front entrance at the school's front gate. An armband wrapped around his right arm read "Guide."

A shuttle bus had been arranged to run between the campus and the nearest train station for attendees coming to the prom from the outside. The idea was not to incite the demonstrators, who were gathering in increasing numbers. If the attendees had to walk out in front of the demonstrators, the overexcited demonstrators were very likely to cause a violent incident.

The large bus, having crossed the main gate and entered the school's grounds, slowly rounded the traffic circle and arrived at the main entrance. The parking spot for the bus was specifically chosen to keep the boarding and disembarking passengers out of view of the demonstrators.

With a hiss of released air, the bus door opened.

Their faces bright, the students took their positions.

No one got off the bus.

When Karatsu peered into the bus, no one was on board.

"Don't worry about it; I thought this might happen. The second one is coming soon!" Karatsu reassured the disappointed students as they saw the bus off.

However, upon realizing that both the second and third buses were empty, even Karatsu's confidence began to falter.

"It's only been fifteen minutes since it started. How many hours are left...?"

"Umm..."

Suddenly someone called out to them. Karatsu and the others turned to see a young couple, about college age, standing there.

"We'd like to see the prom. Is this where we enter?"

The boy was holding one of the fliers Mai had passed out to the demonstrators.

Karatsu looked to the main gate and saw more and more people ready to enter, awaiting approval.

"Okay, now bringing two people in!"

Karatsu's voice was so loud the students standing next to him instinctively covered their ears.

As the day went on, the shuttle bus ridership began to pick up as well. The majority were the students' family members and friends, but among them were also those who came out of genuine interest. Disgusted by baseless rumors, they wanted to learn about the vampires, or to see if vampires and humans truly had a chance to coexist, which was just the result the executive committee had hoped for.

The one thing uniting all the visitors was the feeling that this was just a typical school festival. The Science Club presented their research on the man-made blood Stigma, while Class 3-B did an exhibit explaining the history of House Tepes, and then there was Class 2-D's tea with the long-lived vampires—it was an event designed around vampires. However, the majority of the prom could have been found at any other school cultural festival, such as performances by the humanities clubs and food stands.

The reporters who had been literally chomping at the bit seemed to have lost their momentum as well. Yuri wasn't worried, though. Until they had started living in the Bund, Fangless youngsters took for granted how precious a "typical school life" was. She'd had no sense of it until she became one of the Fangless.

The preliminary media briefing had been tight, but in reality, when the journalists interviewed the vampire students, they discussed their differences in lifestyle and the gaps between clans without concern; the media was able to gather the information they'd really hoped for without any problems.

While she was watching the female reporter, who was at the Science Club's exhibit reluctantly taste-testing some Stigma, Ayaka popped her head in and waved Yuri over.

"What's going on?"

When Yuri stepped out into the hall, there was a couple standing behind Ayaka who appeared to be about middle-aged.

"Yuri, these are my parents."

"I'm Ayaka's father. Thank you for always looking after our daughter."

Yuri was speechless, and she silently bowed to the two in return.

"We came to apologize to you today," Ayaka's father said. "We apologized to Nagisa-san earlier. Please forgive us for any pain we caused you."

"No, that's... I... not being able to go visit her in the end..."

"When Ayaka returned to school, we had a big fight," her

mother said, smiling bitterly. "With an angry face I've never seen before, she told me, 'At least come to the prom. If you don't like what you see, you can pull me out of school.'"

"Yes, that's what our daughter said," her father agreed. "After that, we had several conversations with vampire students. It seems our fear was misplaced."

"Yuri-san…" Ayaka's mother took one step forward and took Yuri's hand.

"Please continue to be friends with Ayaka. And when the day comes that you all can walk about freely, please come visit our home. We will always welcome you."

Yuri stood stiffly upright, unable to say a word. Tears traveled down her cheeks.

"Oh, Yuri… here," Ayaka handed her a handkerchief.

As she dabbed her eyes with the handkerchief, Yuri finally came to a realization.

We weren't wrong.

In her mind, Yuri saw Ms. Brussel's calm smile.

Ryohei went to a table. Instead of a proper lunch, he chewed on taiyaki cakes. Around him, his classmates were bustling about in nun costumes, taking orders and waiting tables.

Out of nowhere, a paper cup filled with coffee was placed in front of him.

"Here, it's on the house."

Ryohei lifted his head to see class representative Satomi

Elrange wearing a business-like smile. Satomi was one of Class 3-A's "vampire trio," and she was the one behind the Sister Café.

Ryohei muttered his thanks and drank the coffee in one gulp.

"It's a huge success."

Even though it was lunchtime, it was still surprising that almost all tables in the classroom were full. The design didn't have anything in particular to do with vampires, but a maid café probably had a similar vibe.

"Where's Clarissa? I don't see her anywhere," Ryohei said.

"Dunno. We managed to get her into a nun costume, but as soon as the prom started, she disappeared."

So she did wear it after all. Without realizing it, Ryohei's face broke into a grin.

"Well, she's probably not used to serving customers."

"My biggest fear is that if a rude customer shows up and gives us a hard time, she'd probably break his arm in one blow."

"You said it."

As they smiled at each other, a loud sound like that of a fight broke out outside. It was followed by a girl's scream.

The students and visitors inside of the classroom looked around with puzzled faces.

Without a word, Ryohei left his table and burst into the hallway.

Attendees, some looking like they wanted to cry, were rushing down the hall and away from the classroom two doors down. It was definitely the site of the Art Club's exhibit.

Ryohei broke into a dash and sped to that classroom.

The classroom was in a state of panic.

In the center of the room, like an island, several desks were turned over. The sculptures that had been on top were scattered about on the floor.

Near the blackboard, a young male attendee was lying down and being attended to by a member of the Art Club. Fortunately, he appeared to be conscious. Nearby, a boy around the same age was standing back, clutching a tote bag and looking over at the boy on the floor with a worried face.

In the back of the classroom, several vampire students had surrounded and pinned one student. The other student, lying on the floor, didn't stir even once.

It was Stefan Petrosk.

And then Ryohei began to understand.

"What happened?" Ryohei asked a girl standing nearby.

"S-S..." the girl was so frightened, her teeth were chattering. "Stefan-sempai suddenly attacked him..."

"That's not true, Kuze-sempai," Kameoka, an Art Club member, spoke up. "The guy made fun of Stefan-sempai's paintings. 'Why are they all pictures of the night? Don't get cocky and think that a vampire could ever be an artist.' Stuff like that."

Ryohei looked at Stefan's artwork, lined up against the wall.

All of them were landscapes in watercolor. As vampires couldn't leave the building in the daytime to sketch a picture, of course they were only pictures of the night. But looking at the pictures one by one—a sky where the stars appeared to be falling, the night sky on a rainy day, the evening star, and so on—the motif varied, and they were all skillful and distinctive paintings.

Ryohei approached the boy with the tote bag. "I'm Kuze from the prom executive committee. I apologize for all of this. Are you injured?"

"No, I'm all right," the boy with the tote bag was very apologetic. "I'm sorry; he was a real jerk. The stuff he said would make anyone mad."

"He probably hit his head. I'll take him to the infirmary right away. He'll be attended by a human, so please don't worry."

Ryohei gave instructions to the surrounding students, having them take the fallen boy to the infirmary on a makeshift stretcher. After that, as a member of the executive committee, he announced the shutdown of the Art Club exhibit and took Stefan to a separate room to calm him down. He also remembered to follow up with the attendees who had witnessed the incident.

Luckily, the boy Stefan had grabbed didn't sustain any serious injuries, and he admitted that he was wrong to insult

Stefan. And so, as not to make a bad situation even worse, they agreed to leave.

Having heard the whole story, Jougasaki felt a surge of relief. It was a shame that the Art Club's exhibit was closed down, but he wanted to do anything they could to prevent it from affecting the rest of the prom.

Even if the trouble at the Art Club exhibit didn't leave a trace, even if the demonstrators didn't burst through the gate, with one hour to go until close, the tension inside the meeting place slowly grew.

General admission to the prom was planned to end at 4:00. It was earlier than typical school festivals usually ended, but as public transportation stopped when the sun went down, it was a step taken to secure the attendees' safe commute home. Afterwards, a dance party for students only would be held in the auditorium, and at the end of that, the curtain would fall on the prom altogether.

In Class 2-D's room, the tea with long-lived vampires continued at a leisurely pace. Within the classroom, three people would encircle each guest vampire, taking turns lending their ears to stories of long ago.

The Bakumatsu fans who had taken to Sakaguchi were fervently listening to tales of Hijikata Toshizo and Enomoto Takeaki—raw testimonial of his experiences as one who had experienced the Battle of Toba-Fushimi firsthand.

Duran, keeping pace with Sakaguchi, was popular in his

own right. Ironically, rather than secret stories of the Eiffel Tower, as had been requested by the executive committee, gossip from 19th century French high society and stylish French jokes proved to be more popular.

Bancroft's table was filled with girls from the Literature Club for almost the entire day, listening intently to his stories. There were also elderly people who wrote down his stories as if they were scholars, without letting one word slip by. Among the journalists was one reporter who had locked on to him and fired questions at him, one after another.

Johan, who had recently gotten into Shiba Ryoutarou, was sitting in the corner of Sakaguchi's group, listening to his stories of the distant past.

Personally, he thought this type of passive setup suited his personality best. No presentations to deliver to the attendees, no need to put in a lot of effort serving food and drink to their customers.

For prom to end uneventfully like this would be the best thing. Not having found a partner for the dance party was disappointing, but it was what it was.

Sakaguchi suddenly fell silent. Despite being surrounded by students, he drew back and in one beat, his face tightened. It was a fitting face for a samurai.

At the next table, Bancroft had also ceased speaking. His spine stiffened and he looked in Sakaguchi's direction.

"You sense it too?" Bancroft asked, returning Sakaguchi's look.

"Yes," Sakaguchi nodded. "The air has become strange outside of this building."

The sound of footsteps indicated people running in the hall. One, two—they were increasing.

Johan had a bad feeling about this.

"Those bastards in the vigilante group are fighting with the police unit!"

The first one to break the news to Jougasaki was Karatsu.

"What? I thought I heard earlier that they were planning to go home."

"Look at this." Karatsu opened a laptop and placed it in front of Jougasaki.

"This is why they're making such a fuss."

It was an internet video sharing site.

Within the chaos of the shaky footage, a boy wearing a school uniform launched himself at another boy, the moment where he shoved the other boy away with all his strength clearly displayed. The video cut out right in the middle of the confusion, amidst thumping sounds and screams.

"This was the incident in the Art Club," Karatsu said. "Someone filmed it, put it online, and the demonstrators saw it."

"Who would do that?"

"The boy that was with him," a different voice answered the question.

Ryohei entered the committee room with Kameoka in tow.

"He probably stuffed a camera in that tote bag he was carrying. Stefan was set up."

"But what would be their point in doing this?" Jougasaki still couldn't believe it.

"The guy who uploaded the video left a comment. Here, take a look."

Urged on by Karatsu, Jougasaki looked at the screen once more. Above the video, this was written in the comment field:

It was an unprovoked attack! A member of the prom committee said "He'll be taken care of in the infirmary" and ran off with him. I don't know where he is now! Please save my friend!!

"What a pack of lies!" Kameoka was stunned.

"They want to shut down this prom at all costs," Ryohei said grimly.

"But to go this far…" Jougasaki was at a loss for words.

"Including the media people, we have about sixty or seventy guests left. If we send them home, they'll be caught up in this whole mess." Karatsu's face was pale. "And even if we do try to send them home, we may get rushed by the vigilantes—we won't escape unscathed."

"What do we do, committee chair?" Ryohei asked Jougasaki.

Ryohei's eyes said, *You decide.*

All of his comrades surrounding him were focused

intently on him.

Jougasaki looked at his program sitting on the desk. After opening it over and over again, it had gotten crumpled and covered in writing and labels.

Was it really acceptable to allow the prom that the entire student body had put their blood, sweat and tears into to end like this? Was there no way to see it through until the end?

Jougasaki clenched both fists.

"…Close everything down. The safety of our attendees and students takes priority."

Ryohei nodded.

The other students nodded in unison; Yuka and Nagisa broke into tears.

"Does Yuri know about the commotion outside?" Ryohei asked Karatsu.

"No, I don't think she does yet."

"Tell her right away. We have to explain it to the media people as well."

Suekichi immediately left to search for Yuri.

"But what will we do? If they get into the school, we can't fight them," Kameoka pressed Ryohei for an answer.

"And if the police won't hold them back…" Yuka said, discouraged.

"Their numbers are too large," Karatsu shook his head. "When I last checked, they were already one-on-one with the police. They're probably closing in on the school gate by now."

"Let's evacuate the attendees into the underground entrance. From there, there's only one route, so they'll be easier to protect and we won't easily be taken by amateurs," Ryohei said.

Ryohei hadn't stopped thinking of Clarissa's words—if the vigilantes break through, then it's over. Therefore, during preparation, he had sought out a suitable evacuation spot for the worst case scenario.

"Committee chair, make a school-wide evacuation announcement. Try to word it in a way that doesn't start a panic," Ryohei said to Jougasaki. "We have no choice but to deal with the vigilantes ourselves."

"When you say 'deal with,' what do you…?" Jougasaki asked with a stiff expression.

"If you want mochi, you go to the mochi shop. Let's borrow the knowledge of a military strategist."

"A strategist?"

Each of the guests in Class 2-D had different reactions.

"So you are requesting that we 'lend our knowledge' instead of 'lending a hand'?" Sakaguchi agreed with the other responses. "You want to protect your own school. I respect that."

"I do not care for fighting," was Duran's answer. "Simply use the counterattack defense systems put in place for Her Highness Queen Mina."

"It's not like we can use weapons to wound or kill,"

Ryohei argued. "We don't want casualties on either side."

Bancroft merely sat upright with his eyes closed.

"We're out of time. We simply want to protect our school. Please help us."

A heavy silence overtook the classroom. Even Mai and the journalists who had been left behind were holding their breath, awaiting the outcome.

"...Five hundred years," Bancroft mumbled to no one in particular, his eyes still closed. "I've lived five hundred years, and I had grown exhausted of meetings and farewells alike."

Bancroft decisively opened his eyes and slowly rose from his chair.

"Today, I met you all and for the first time in many years, my blood boiled."

Sakaguchi vigorously threw off his haori, and begin nimbly tying up his sleeves with his sash.

Duran took a deep breath and casually took off his tailcoat, removed his necktie, and set them on the table.

"Fetch us a map of the school," Sakaguchi said.

"Also, a tape measure." Next to hop on board was Duran.

"And give us five minutes," Bancroft's eyes overflowed with the pride of the man who had guarded Queen Mina over two hundred years ago from the might of the Three Great Clans.

Just as Ryohei took a deep breath in relief, Suekichi burst into the room with a completely different expression.

"Sempai! It's Jougasaki!"

The vigilantes had already rushed the gate. The police had been struggling to make them leave, but the crowd just grew and became more packed, crushing people up against one another. Some people in the crowd violently shook the one bus sitting outside the school gate. The driver was nowhere to be seen.

"Where have you taken that youth?"

"Planning to increase your numbers and invade Tokyo?"

"Get out of Japan, vampires!"

The heated crowd swarmed the flawless gate door, shaking it violently. The gate was higher than the ones found at other schools, so they couldn't climb over, but as they shook it back and forth, it looked as though they could push it in.

Jougasaki had faced the mob alone.

There were only a few meters between them and the gate. The hatred and fear that the vigilantes spread was so thick, it seemed as if you could touch it if you extended your hand in front of you.

Any impulses that Jougasaki had about running back into the school building had been twisted out of him. As both the committee head and the student council president, he would do what he had to do.

"Everyone!" Trying not to lose to their headwind-like bellowing, Jougasaki raised his voice with all his might. "I am the prom committee chair, Jougasaki. I will explain it all to you!"

"That asshole's the boss of the vampires," someone jeered in response.

"This has nothing to do with vampires! As a representative for the prom, I have come to resolve any misunderstanding between everyone."

"Misunderstanding?! Where in that video is there a 'misunderstanding'?"

"Return the boy you abducted!"

"Quiet down and I'll explain. That video was shot at the Art Club's exhibit, and yes, the fight it showed did happen."

The vigilantes lost their tempers.

"So you admit the boy was attacked!"

"Showing your true colors now, aren't you? Vampire bastards!"

"The boy was unharmed. He received a medical exam in the infirmary and was sent home. He is no longer in the school."

"Because you took him to the Bund!"

"Show us proof that he made it home safe!"

In other words, prove that the devil exists. There was no way to win such an endless argument.

"We cannot present any evidence that he went home," Jougasaki said without hesitation. "But we have other evidence. Is the one who shot the video out there? If you're worried about your friend, then surely you're here. Please let us talk to you! If you do, we can clear up this misunderstanding quickly!"

The vigilantes winced a bit. Somehow, they had seen the video online, yet it seemed none of them had directly confirmed with the one who had taken the video.

Ryohei and the others watched the exchange from the front entrance.

"He's nuts..." Suekichi mumbled.

Ryohei shook his head. "Trying to reason with people like that is pointless. They'll think they're being mocked and get even more upset."

"You're saying this won't work?"

Ryohei nodded. He took out his phone and called Karatsu, who was stationed in the security office.

"Karatsu, when I give you the signal, close the shutter over the front entrance. Leave your phone connected."

Ryohei returned his phone to his pocket and looked around at the other students.

"Okay, let's go get our committee chair."

At that moment, a voice rang out.

"Wait!" It was Mai. "Just wait... a little longer..."

Mai, whose sense of responsibility was so strong, understood Jougasaki's feelings so much it hurt. Although he should have been afraid, he believed that this was his job and so, he faced them. She wanted to let him do as much as he could.

"I really do understand your concerns, everyone. That's why..."

About to press for answers, Jougasaki's voice suddenly paused.

Among the vigilantes was the owner of Kamome-ya.

Glaring with bloodshot eyes, the owner's mouth was crooked and he was speaking ill of Jougasaki.

The school, already facing plenty of prejudice since day one, had once had Kamome-ya supplying their bread without any comment. Now the owner was standing on the front lines of the mob that wanted to shut down the prom.

Were relations between vampires and humans this broken?

He understood that truth in his head, but this was the first time he had ever felt it from the bottom of his heart.

Jougasaki felt as if his legs had literally crumbled beneath him.

Flying with deadly aim, a rock hit Jougasaki right in the forehead.

Jougasaki grabbed his head and staggered. Blood dripped through the cracks in his fingers.

The vigilantes saw blood, and they got excited. They began throwing rocks en masse.

"It's no use! Let's go!"

Ryohei and the others leapt out of the entrance and rushed towards Jougasaki.

"Look! There's a huge pack of vampires!"

"They've come to refresh their troops!"

"We'll never let you turn us!"

As if vampires would come running outside in broad daylight. The vigilantes had left their sense of logic so far behind, they couldn't even grasp this.

The hands rattling the gate door increased in their violence and finally, they knocked one of the hinges out of place.

The gate door caved to the pressure from the mob, and it started to bend inward.

As Ryohei and the others dealt with the stones raining down on them, they lifted up Jougasaki and ran back to the building with all their strength.

"Karatsu! Close the shutter!" Ryohei called.

Almost in sync with Ryohei's voice, the gate door fell down.

As the vigilantes released a barbaric yell, they burst onto the premises.

Ryohei and the others dashed into the building, out of breath. They ran through the entrance with its rows of shoe lockers, heading for the left side and the prom meeting area.

The front line of the vigilantes burst into the entrance, pursuing Ryohei and the others. The shutter was almost halfway down, but it wasn't enough to stop them.

We're going to be caught.

Just as Ryohei thought this, a black shadow appeared out of nowhere and blocked the path before the vigilantes.

It was Clarissa, wearing the Sister Café nun's robes.

Without thinking about it, she stomped like she was standing on a bellows and confronted the now stalled frontline with a noble face.

"Your prey is vampires, right?"

Clarissa opened her mouth wide, showing off shimmering fangs that should not have been there.

"If I'm what you're hunting for, then try your hand against me, pathetic humans!"

Clarissa's long black robes flapped like a large bird as she ran off to the right.

"It's a vampire!"

"It's a girl!"

"Kill her!"

They seemed to forget that Ryohei and the others even existed. Switching targets, the avalanche of vigilantes rumbled off to the right after Clarissa.

"That girl…" Ryohei muttered.

"Let's get moving!" Suekichi called.

As they picked up Jougasaki and started to run once more, the deep rumble of an engine broke through their ears.

On the other side of the grid-patterned shutter, which had already fallen about one meter, the front of the shuttle bus appeared.

"No way," Suekichi muttered.

Ryohei and the others could tell what was coming next, so they ran towards the prom meeting area without looking back.

The sound of the engine swelled even further, and the shuttle bus broke through the shutter and leapt into the entrance. As it plowed over the shoe lockers, it pushed on without stopping to the interior hallway. The torn bumper, dragging shutter debris, scraped the steel-made shoe lockers with a terrible, metallic squeal.

The bus finally stopped when it hit the wall that formed the end of a T-shaped intersection.

Several people rushed in through the gap in the shutter. Most of them went to the right after Clarissa, but some of them saw Ryohei and the others and went to the left, after them.

In the hallway in front of the entrance to the prom meeting area, desks were stacked in a barricade that blocked the hall almost to the ceiling.

"Hurry, hurry!"

At the bottom right corner of the barricade, there was an opening about the size of a desk where Yagou stuck his head through, beckoning Ryohei and the others.

One by one they climbed in, escaping to the other side.

The barricade was three desks thick.

The first of the vigilantes that had followed Ryohei and the others thrust his head in, but Yagou crammed a desk into the hole and pushed the rioter out. He slid two more desks into the crack, tying wire around the innermost desks to finish off the barricade.

The rioters grasped onto the barricade and shook it repeatedly, but the stacked desks barely swayed.

The students who had rescued Jougasaki collapsed in exhaustion.

"Please treat the committee chair's wounds," Ryohei barely managed to say between gasps.

In the hallway, all of the vampire students had built a second barricade. They moved the desks at a tempo above what humans could do; the barricade was built at a fevered pitch that was reminiscent of a video with dropped frames.

"Duran-san planned it on the fly for us." Yagou showed Ryohei the paper with the plan drawn on it. "We didn't just stack them up. There are plenty other tricks."

As the rioters shook the barricade, the first row of desks broke off, and twelve desks fell on them like a wall.

"The barricade is buying us time," Yagou said. "While it's delaying the rioters, we should prepare ourselves."

Ryohei stared at the other side of the barricade, in the direction Clarissa had run off.

Clarissa zipped down the hall alone. There were many people chasing after her, several of them right on her heels. So as not to completely lose them, she was regulating her speed, preserving some distance.

A rope hung from one wall of the hallway. Clarissa pulled out a knife and cut the rope as she ran by.

A volleyball net fell gently from the ceiling, covering the heads of several people running at the front of her pursuers.

"Aaaah!"

Several of the runners that had been caught in the net collapsed. Several more tripped on the fallen men and fell themselves.

Without losing speed, Clarissa rounded the corner. She jumped at the point where she turned, leaping two meters and landing on the other side.

The rioters pursuing her rounded the corner and suddenly pitched forward, slamming into the floor. 30 centimeters off the floor, several strands of piano wire were strung across the hall.

Clarissa had been going around the sections of the building outside the prom's meeting place in clandestine, building a homemade trap zone.

Just as she had told Ryohei, she did not think this event would go well. But just because she said that didn't mean she planned to do nothing about it.

It wasn't that she was moved by some particular emotion like friendship or duty. Without making a distinction between humans and vampires, she had no patience for those who justified their violent impulses in the name of law and order.

The ugliness of their amateur mob violence made her self-aware, and it threw her own sophisticated brand of violence into stark contrast. She would lead as many of them as she could around by the nose, even if that meant breaking more than one of those noses.

Clarissa dashed up the stairs and hid herself in the shadow of the dance floor.

Her pursuers appeared on the floor before her, and climbed the stairs to give chase. When she decided they had climbed high enough, she released several hard baseballs all at once.

Losing their footing on the balls, the men let out idiotic yelps and tumbled down the stairs all the way to the previous landing.

Clarissa had to laugh. This wasn't some slapstick comedy from 50 years ago, but for them to attack the school so sloppily...

However, the number of pursuers had steadily increased, climbing the stairs with enough vigor to fill them up. The small number of baseballs that she had dropped was equivalent to throwing water on a burnt stone.

Clarissa quickly climbed to the second floor, sprinting down the hall. At that moment, she stepped on something and lost her balance.

It was a ball someone behind her had thrown.

Her legs weakened and the rioter behind her closed the distance.

The man in the front line tried to grab her shoulder. Looking over her shoulder, Clarissa sent an elbow strike to the man's nose. As blood erupted from his nose, he toppled over.

In no time, Clarissa struck her next pursuer with the palm of her hand. His eardrum ruptured and he writhed in violent pain.

Clarissa fought on, making liberal use of eye gauges and kicks to the groin. She efficiently stole their will to fight with every blow.

But she quickly went from being superior to being outnumbered. Clarissa was cornered at a window. She was completely surrounded by them, with no gaps. Their eyes swirled with a fear of vampires and a hatred of this girl who had toyed with them.

Getting through unscathed was going to be difficult.

At the moment, she was preparing for the worst—

"Clarissa!" Suddenly a voice came from directly above her. At the same time, a long-handled mop came sailing in through the open window behind her.

In possession of a weapon, she turned for a furious counterattack.

She struck at their throats with the blunt end of the mop, pushing up their chins with the metal fitting holding the cloth in place, and knocked them back with a side strike to their heads, one after the other.

"I'll lend you a hand."

It was Ryohei who leapt in through the window.

What am I saying? I have no hand-to-hand combat knowledge! Ryohei thought, then suddenly grabbed Clarissa around the waist.

"Hey, what are you…?"

Just like that, Ryohei gave Clarissa a shove out the window.

Glancing back at the dumbfounded vigilantes, Ryohei put his foot on the windowsill and leapt outside.

Clarissa landed with skillful agility, while Ryobei fell to the ground at her side.

"That hurt!" Nursing his leg, Ryohei grabbed Clarissa's hand.

"Let's go!"

Raining jeers down on them from the second floor, the vigilantes nevertheless jumped down, though they seemed to be hindered by a lack of courage.

Ryohei and Clarissa hid in the shade of a shed near the school building.

Ryohei rubbed his ankle, which seemed to be lightly sprained.

"Damn, guess I can't do it like him after all," Ryohei said in a soft voice.

"Hm?" Clarissa made a puzzled face.

"It's nothing," Ryohei shook his head.

"By the way, when did you become a vampire?"

Clarissa opened her mouth wide and stuck her hand in. She pulled out the fake fangs she had used to fool the vigilantes and threw them into the bushes.

"Since you went that far for us, I'll let you off the hook for skipping out on the Sister Café," Ryohei said jokingly.

A vampire hunter rescuing vampires by pretending to be a vampire—that wouldn't even make it as the punchline to some terrible joke. After all this time, Clarissa was contending with self-loathing.

"After I helped you get away, why did you do something so dangerous?"

"I knew you'd been setting traps," Ryohei said readily. "Even though you were coming to school every day, you didn't participate in the preparations for prom. I think anyone would wonder what you were up to."

"……"

"If you're gonna do us the favor of protecting the prom, why don't we protect it together? That way, our chances of success will increase, I think."

The sound of glass breaking could be heard from somewhere.

Clarissa and Ryohei cautiously poked their heads out, trying not to be seen.

There were tons of people crowded around the outside of the school building, attempting to break the polarized glass windows. Some threw concrete blocks, others repeatedly beat at the windows with bars.

"This is bad. At this rate, the barricade'll be pointless," Ryohei's face clouded over.

"Die, vampires!"

"It's crumbling! Push harder!"

The barricade was at the path to the underground entrance; it could be called the last line of defense. With that last barrier between them, the students fought back against the rioters.

It could be said that the students fought a good fight. They took Sakaguchi and Bancroft's advice. They capitalized on having the home team advantage and toyed with the rioters, guerilla warfare style. They made good use of everything from fire extinguishers to cleaning supplies, even vegetable oil and flour. They were able to fight while causing as little injury as possible to their opponents.

However, with no reinforcements coming in from the outside, it was only a matter of time until they were overwhelmed. The multi-layered barricade had been effective in buying them time, in accordance with Duran's plan, but now the rioters were barging in through destroyed windows, and the students were left with no other methods for defense.

The more powerful vampires, male and female alike, held up the last barricade together. The area just beyond the barricade was teeming with rioters who had literally lost themselves in the moment. Their vulgar shouts tormented the students, physically and emotionally.

Despite being in a dangerous, almost life-or-death situation, Andrew fell into a strange mood. He usually took a casual view of things, having come to avoid thinking of things too seriously. But now, here he was, standing at the forefront and trying to defend the prom. He usually would have said, "I'm not that type of guy!" and been the first one to run and hide.

Casually glancing next to him, his eyes met Johan, who was also pushing against the barricade. Johan—who hated standing out—would have usually thoroughly avoided a situation like this as well.

Wondering what normal was anyway, Andrew reflected that putting one's life on the line was the kind of thing that would change a human; and apparently, it would change a vampire as well.

He must have been thinking the same thing, because Johan smiled sheepishly.

Just then, Andrew's cellphone rang. It was *Yellow Submarine*, a melody completely unfit for the current situation. Without the luxury of being able to lift even one hand from the barricade, he had no choice but to let it ring.

Almost in sync with Andrew's ringtone, Johan's cellphone also rang. Before they realized it, the cellphones of Yagou, Yuri, Satomi, and every other student in the area began to ring.

Yagou, who found this very odd, used his body to hold up the barricade as he freed a hand and opened his cellphone.

It was an email message. The sender was unknown.

The message was only one line:

In ten seconds, all of you need to get down and cover your eyes and ears.

Yagou showed Andrew and the others the the message.

The color drained out of Andrew's face. Thinking quickly, he called to his friends.

"Everyone, get back! Do as the message says!"

"But if we leave the barricade, it will—" Johan started to say.

"It's fine! Just do it! Now!"

All of the students removed their hands from the barricade at once.

The barricade, having lost its support, began to crumble. Through the cracks in the dislodged desks, they glimpsed the sweat-drenched faces of people who had lost their hold on sanity.

Andrew and the others got back from the barricade as fast as possible and threw themselves to the ground. They covered their ears with both hands and shut their eyes tight.

The next moment, a blinding flash and a deafening roar completely filled the hall.

Even though the message had warned him and he'd prepared for it, the dizzying light still penetrated Andrew's eyelids, and the sound of the explosion pierced through his palms to his eardrums.

Beyond the ringing in his ears, he could hear the cries of agony and strained breathing of the rioters.

There was a sound interlaced with their cries that he couldn't quite make out. It was the sound of heavy footsteps, like military boots. And it wasn't just one or two people.

Then came the sound of something heavy hitting the floor,

the sound of something heavy and soft being thrown down, the sound of pained moaning—all of these various sounds blending amongst their surroundings.

Had someone come to save them?

Andrew tried to lift his head to find out.

"Keep your head down!"

The man's sharp voice echoed, and Andrew lay back down, confused.

One pair of heavy footsteps drew closer to Andrew. The footsteps stopped at his side, and he felt a large gloved hand softly pat his head.

"You did well. Hang on for one more day."

It was the same voice as the sharp one from earlier, but gentler. Without waiting for a reply from Andrew, the stranger ran far away.

Before he realized it, the mass of heavy footsteps had disappeared.

As Andrew gradually lifted his head, his eyes met Johan and Yuri, both of whom were also still down.

Andrew and the others stood up and looked across the wreckage of their barricade.

The rioters, who had been frothing with mindless rage until only a short time ago, were lying still in the hallway like tuna at a fish market. Not one of them was left without their hands tied behind their backs. Closer inspection revealed that their thumbs were bound together with plastic ties.

All of the students just stood and stared dumbfoundedly.

The realization that they had actually escaped critical danger had yet to dawn on them. They didn't even have the energy to say anything.

Andrew leaned wearily against the wall, sliding into a sitting position on the floor. Absently staring at the ceiling, he brooded over the man's parting words.

The next day, he would learn the meaning of those words.

In the end, the head of the police unit still couldn't grasp what had happened.

They had been struggling to suppress the vigilantes and demonstrators who had become rioters charging the school, when several Humvees appeared, chasing away much of the mob. With the appearance of some kind of special forces, carrying equipment that the police weren't used to seeing, they got out of their Humvees. At which point, he thought they had entered the building, but first, they got into a skirmish with those rioting on the school grounds and sent them running.

The vigilantes and demonstrators suddenly came to their senses, as if they realized that their opportunity for destruction had passed. By this time, the sun had already begun to set. If they didn't get to the nearest train station soon, they would lose their only way home and end up having to deal with sleeping outside on the school grounds. As they watched, the demonstrators' numbers dwindled.

As the police unit head stood in astonishment at this sudden change in an extreme situation, a strong man who appeared to be this group's leader, but whose identity he could not confirm, approached him.

"Twenty-two rioters have been restrained within the grounds. You can arrest them for illegal trespassing, interfering with official duties, property damage, and assault," the man's voice was muffled beneath his face mask.

"J-just wait a second. Who in the hell are you guys? If you're affiliated with the police, you should first state your name and title."

"I'm your subordinate," the man had said.

"Wh-what?"

"All of us are your subordinates," the man repeated calmly. "In order to protect the students, you sent us in and we subdued and apprehended the rioters, who were involved in criminal activity."

The police unit head couldn't think of even one response.

"This was all to your credit." The face mask blocked the cop from reading the man's expression. He began to walk off, then leaned in to whisper into the officer's ear. "Let's just leave it at that. You will definitely thank us."

There was the sudden sound of an explosion, then everything lit up.

When the commanding officer looked up at the sky, he saw that fireworks were being set off from the roof of the school, one after the other. In the prom plan, submitted prior to the event, there was a description of these fireworks, which were to be set off after sunset. The sun hadn't gone down yet, but out of desperation, the students had set them off ahead of schedule.

Turning back to the man in the face mask, the commanding officer realized that he was gone. As he looked around, perplexed, all of the Humvees started up at once and pulled away in a straight line.

The police officer could only watch them leave in silence.

Ryohei was looking for someone. With everything returning to normal, there was someone he wanted to hear from. He found them through the advice of numerous people he passed in the hall.

A fire had been set in the Art Club's exhibition room, resulting in the sprinklers going off and soaking everything in the room. The artwork on display by the club's members had been soaked to the point of ruination.

Stefan Petresk was in the classroom, darkened by the setting sun, sitting on a chair he had set amid the water, staring at the wall.

All of his pictures hung on the wall before him, soaked so badly that the paint had begun to run.

"Stefan." When Ryohei called to him from the entrance, he turned his head slightly, but did not face Ryohei.

Ryohei stepped into the puddle-covered room, and sat down in a chair beside Stefan.

"My dad loved painting," Stefan said while still looking at the wall, "I've heard the Fangless village where he was raised got along well with humans, and that the artist who taught him was a human."

Ryohei remained quiet. He thought this was a time for listening rather than speaking.

"But their relationship with the humans soured over something small, and they were taken advantage of by Ivanovic's Fangless hunters..." Stefan's words came out in a rush. "The only ones who got away were my dad and my grandmother. Of my father's hundreds of paintings, he couldn't even grab one to take with him..."

Stefan stood up and approached the wall. He stretched out his hand towards his paintings, and one by one, began violently ripping them off the wall.

"After that, my dad never painted again." Stefan finally turned to face Ryohei, "So, what should I do?"

Stefan had opened his heart to Ryohei and revealed the big wound within. Ryohei would need to find a way to move past that wound and get close to him.

"Ahh..."

Stepping on fragments of glass, Andrew limped along and breathed a sigh.

"This place is terrible as well. They really messed it up..."

It was late at night.

The inside of the auditorium looked like the aftermath of a storm. Glass was broken, the blackout curtains were torn off, and the paneling on the wall was torn off in places. The iron pipe scaffolding used for lighting during live shows was torn down, and was taking up the center of the room. Since musical performances had been going on when the attack started, trash and plastic bottles from the live show were scattered about. The room was lit only by the moon shining through the windows, where only the frames remained, making it seem like an eerily quiet piece of art.

"Stop complaining and clean up." As if on cue, Yuri handed him a broom. Next to her, Mai was briskly sweeping up glass.

"Oh, can't it wait until tomorrow?"

"You know exactly why it can't. Besides, there isn't much left."

Almost the entire school yard, all of the areas of the school building open for the event, and even areas that were supposed to be off-limits to attendees had all been completely laid to waste by the rioters. Though there were still over 30 minutes left before the official close time, the prom had already been shut down. The dance party, the crowning event meant to cap off the prom, had to be abandoned. They had to explain the situation to the police and get the attendees from the infirmary onto the shuttle bus and to the train station.

Even so, there were no students here who thought of the prom as a failure. Despite the disruption, not one person had died, and they had managed to keep the number of injuries surprisingly low. Some of the attendees even shook hands with the vampire students when they left.

Surely, that wasn't meaningless. Surely some change had

been made, even if it was as small as a flower bud. Even the most pessimistic students assured themselves of that.

They were already weary from the long, sleepless nights of getting ready for the prom. With the attack by the rioters piled on top of the latent tension that day, their energy and physical strength were reaching their limits. Some students held bitter memories that they couldn't wipe away. Even so, their hearts were light. Saying the things they should say, doing the things they should do, and protecting what they should protect. They were brimming with a strange sense of fulfillment, with strength in their eyes and smiles on their lips.

"Done at last."

Ryohei put the mop aside and took a breath. There were no curtains nor glass in the windows, and the wings of the stage were still in a state of disrepair, but at least the floors of the auditorium were, for the most part, back to normal.

"Thanks for your hard work today."

"Good work."

Everyone said it, but no one went home. They were having a hard time leaving.

Then music began to flow from one side of the speakers installed around the stage. Somehow, the wiring seemed to be working again. Someone had gone into the broadcasting room, and put on Cleopatra's *Yes, This Party's Goin' Right*.

"I don't believe it."

"A dance party? Now?!"

The students scattered throughout the auditorium began moving to the music. It was contagious, and before they knew it, one by one they started to dance.

"Hey, don't play the music too loud. Someone else might bust in here."

As jokes intermingled with the shouting, Ryohei shook his head in disbelief and looked around. Clarissa, who had helped with the auditorium cleanup to everyone's surprise, stared at the dancing students in amazement.

Somehow, Ryohei made his way to Clarissa.

"Hey, wanna dance?"

Clarissa looked away for a moment. Then she shrugged and took Ryohei's outstretched hand.

Let's get together
Spread the love around
It'll be the night to remember...

As to be expected of an American, Clarissa had some impressive club dance moves. For Ryohei's part, he didn't know much about dancing, so he mimicked her movements and vaguely swayed his body, but to the casual observer, they seemed good together.

Andrew grabbed Yuri's wrist, and Johan took Mai's hand, and they danced happily, if awkwardly, together. Jougasaki timidly offered Satomi his hand, and she accepted it with a smile.

Those who were dancing together wouldn't necessarily stay together. They might be pulled apart by fate, or separated by mountains. Some of them simply got tired of each other, and ended their relationships. Some of them would never see one another again after graduation. And, unmistakably, there were those who—against their wishes— would be inseparably connected throughout their lives.

There were countless reasons to separate. There were countless reasons to join together. It was the same for humans and vampires alike.

If, for example, Mai and Johan continued to be good friends throughout their lives, that did not lead to humans and vampires coexisting. Likewise, if they went their separate ways, that wasn't evidence itself of humans and vampires being incapable of living together.

"I didn't really find an answer, after all."

"An answer to what?" Clarissa asked as she danced.

"Whether or not vampires and humans can coexist."

"I've been thinking that over," Clarissa smiled coldly. Her hazel eyes took the moonlight and reflected it back as a piercing clear light.

"I think that question has been around since before we humans first spoke words. It's not like a couple of high school kids taking a stab at it would find an answer so easily to a question that has been unanswerable for tens of thousands of years."

"No kidding," Ryohei laughed. Then his face became

serious and he asked, "So what are you, really?"

Clarissa gave him a light smile.

"I'm your classmate, and the one who protected the prom along with you. Is there anything else you need to know?"

Without giving an answer, Ryohei silently extended his hand. Clarissa took it and performed an amazing turn.

Are you watching, Akira? Are you seeing this, Yuki?

This time, I've surpassed you. I'll graduate one step ahead of you and wait for you up ahead.

So hurry and come back. Come back, graduate properly, and catch up with us.

"…Along with Queen Mina."

"Hm?" Clarissa made a strange face.

"Oh, nothing."

In the sky, the moon.

On the ground, human and vampire children.

As the pale light shone on them, they danced. Until the moon sank down in the western sky, they continued to dance.

One day…

The tunnel leading from the Bund entrance was jam-packed with students walking to the school.

The youths, all lively chatter as they walked, ranged from elementary school children to high school students. Then again, as they were all vampires, their outer appearances and true ages did not necessarily match up.

As she walked, blending in with the children, she was absorbed in deep emotion. To think that the day would come when she would step out of that tunnel and be able to attend the school once more... she could hardly believe it. If she had heard seven years ago that she would be able to do so, she probably would have laughed it off as some kind of joke.

The state of affairs surrounding vampires had changed greatly since the events of that prom day. The day after prom, a city-wide vampire hunt was held by vigilantes throughout Tokyo, but most of it was thwarted by Beowulf. At the same time, the "real" Mina Tepes returned to the Bund, and it came to light that the one reigning over the Bund up to that point had been an imposter.

She wondered if it hadn't been the forces of Beowulf who had rescued them at the prom. The clothes worn by the mysterious men, glimpsed when she lifted her head to observe them, looked identical to those worn by the members of Beowulf they saw later.

It wasn't just the Bund that had changed, but human society, too.

All of the media that came to the prom reported their findings following the resolution of the Vampire Pandemic. They highlighted the vampire students putting themselves out there, trying to protect the human attendees with all of their might.

After that, the Japanese government demonstrated a more harmonious attitude towards vampires, and the state of affairs surrounding the Vampire Bund quickly improved. When it came to peaceful coexistence between humans and vampires, Japan was the clear world leader. The fact that this school was still standing was the best proof of that.

Having arrived at the school, she took the elevator to the first floor, walking down the hall to her new job.

She could see through the polarized glass that the truck for Kamome-ya was parked in the front yard, making a delivery. It was obvious to her that the owner of Kamome-ya had aged quite a bit. He was cheerfully exchanging greetings with the students walking to school aboveground.

Finally, she reached a room with "Infirmary" written on the doorplate. She hung a plate with her own name written on it under the doorplate and went inside.

When she had been a student, there had been two separate infirmaries—one for human use and an underground one for vampire use. Now they had been combined into a single infirmary on the first floor, aboveground.

It was probably another result of the prom that there was no longer a need to divide them up.

The first thing she pulled from her bag was a small picture frame. In the picture was a slight, older woman holding a coffee cup and smiling warmly.

Brussel-sensei, how is the infirmary, after all these years?

She placed the picture on the windowsill where it would get sunlight. What Brussel-sensei had given to this school, she now needed to pass on to the next generation.

There was a soft knock at the door.

"Come in." At her invitation, one of the ladies from the office poked her head in.

"Shindo-sensei, the principal is calling for you."

"All right, I'm on my way," Yuri responded courteously. As her first duty as the new school nurse, she would go and meet the principal.

True, she never dreamed this would be how she would reunite with the principal. Surely they could build a good working relationship.

Everything would go well; Yuri's chest swelled with that conviction.

The sunlight shining in through the polarized glass illuminated her future as well.

End

DOUJINSHI CHRONICLE

FEVER DREAM

Release Date: August 16, 2009 (Comic Market 76)

Title Origin: The title of George R. R. Martin's 1982 vampire novel. It refers to the dreams brought on by a fever.

DOUJINSHI CONTENTS:

Short Manga: (untitled) by Nozomu Tamaki
A big commotion, with Mina and the other characters celebrating the upcoming anime.

Short Story: "Night and Darkness" by Tikurakuran
A mysterious girl and a giant wolf appear before a Nazi war criminal on the run.

Short Story: "Death of a Salaryman" by Gemma
An ordinary man becomes a vampire in an accident and takes part in strange human experiments.

Trivia Collection: "The Devil is in the Details"
An explanation of the origins of the many quotations and homages that appear in the series.

PRODUCTION NOTES:

Nozomu Tamaki
Our commemorative first issue. At the time, I had no idea I'd be publishing ten whole issues (ha ha). Partially because it was the first, I filled the manga with inside jokes; it was my first and only time doing that.

Ever since *Tokimeki Tonight* (Heartthrob Tonight, a manga from 1982), beautiful young vampire girls have been thought of as wearing nothing but a cape. In this manga, too, the queen remains undressed, but the "nothing but a cape" look was prohibited for the anime. Director Shinbō had already done it in *Tsukuyomi: Moon Phase*, so his opinion was that *Bund* didn't need that kind of gimmick. But it really did feel like something was missing, so I figured, "Okay, I'll do it in a doujinshi (ha ha)." Of course, the character designer, Konno-san, overturned the ban and drew the look a lot.

Tikurakuran
I've always liked history, so I thought of a story that involved real-world history. The main character of this story later becomes the director of the Bergamasque Laboratory. A former Nazi, he is completely unrepentant about his wartime misdeeds, and Mina-hime approves.

My intent was to express that Mina was never a "good guy," and that vampires have a different value system than humans. The basis of this story came from an exchange in the manga between Mina-hime and an elderly man, who call each other "Fräulein Mephistopheles" and "Doctor Faust" respectively.

The title came from *Yoru to Kiri* (Night and Fog), the Japanese title of Viktor Frankl's book *Man's Search for Meaning*, about his experience in a Nazi concentration camp. Many of the chapter titles in the manga are taken from other works, so I followed suit for all of my short stories.

Gemma
It was towards the end of 2007 that Tamaki-sensei came to me and said, "Hey, wanna write a *Bund* story?" I wracked my brain and came up with a list of traits that had not been seen in the Bund up to that point—not a cool old guy, but rather a pathetic middle-aged man, fat, who regrets becoming a vampire. I decided to write a character with all those traits.

The title I came up with was apparently too dull, so Tamaki-sensei came up with a title based on the play *Death of a Salesman*.

THEY THIRST

Release Date: December 31, 2009 (Comic Market 77)

Title Origin: The title of Robert McCammon's 1981 vampire novel.

DOUJINSHI CONTENTS:

Short Manga: (untitled) by Nozomu Tamaki
A short story serving as a sort of introduction to the anime, depicting Mina and Akira's first encounter.

Short Story: "Lies & Silence" by Tikurakuran
The secret feud between House Tepes and Counselor Ryuu over a man who escaped from the Li Clan.

Short Story: "Of Endless Silence and Rest" by Gemma
What does Fate have in store for a vampire who requests a fang extraction from the Bund's chief dentist?

Hidden Character Design Collection:
"From the Depths of the Dark Cradle"
A few design points not referenced in the main story, such as the living habits of werewolves.

PRODUCTION NOTES:

Nozomu Tamaki
    I tried drawing a more complete version of the first (second?) chance encounter between Akira and Her Majesty, which only shows up as a brief flashback in the main manga. The anime writer Yoshino-san praised the line "Does your tummy hurt?" as perfect for expressing everything about Akira. I still remember fondly how I said, "But it's from *Future Boy Conan*," and he paused for a second, then shouted, "I wasted my compliment!" (Ha ha!)

Tikurakuran
    I had so much fun writing the action scenes for my last story that this time, I filled it with action. On the other hand, I also put a lot of energy into Mina-hime and Counselor Ryuu's friendly bargaining.
    Around this time, Gemma-kun's character Harvey had made an appearance in the main manga, and that spurred me to create Counselor Ryuu. But I got too greedy when designing him, and he became a really big character—the kind that's not so easy to write. I stole the idea for Ryuu's mind control powers from Dan Simmons' vampire novel *Carrion Comfort*. It's really good, so if you come across it, you should definitely read it.
    I got the title from the Japanese title of David Martin's 1990 suspense novel, *Lie to Me*.

Gemma
    It looked like I would be allowed to write these stories for a while, so I thought I'd make characters that would be easy to reuse, and I came up with Saji-sensei. I ended up using him again and again, far beyond what I'd ever planned, and he even made an appearance in the main manga—such unexpected good fortune that I suspect I've used up all my luck.
    I got the title from the inscription on the grave of Ferdinand Cheval, an eccentric Frenchman from the late 19th century: "Tomb of silence and endless rest."

SAVE THE LAST DANCE FOR ME

Release Date: April 29, 2010 (COMIC 1[STAR]4)

Title Origin: The title of The Drifters' hit song, "Save the Last Dance for Me."

DOUJINSHI CONTENTS:

Short Manga: (untitled) by Nozomu Tamaki
The story of the anime original character Mei Ren up until she meets the impostor queen.

Short Story: "S.A.G.A's Cooking Classroom" by Gemma
A collection of stories about the four boys undergoing the Ceremony of Trials and their attempts at cooking.

Short Story: "A Flag Full of Stars" by Tikurakuran
In the 16th century, the chief vassals of House Tepes have their final battle against the three branch families.

Four-Panel Manga: "Good Luck, Akira-kun!!" by Masayuki Fujiwara

PRODUCTION NOTES:

Nozomu Tamaki

I drew this while mourning the loss of Mei Ren, whose time in the world ended with the anime. I tried drawing the fruit drop candies she's always sucking on.

I remember Kobayashi Yū-san, the actress who voiced her, putting a lot of effort into Mei Ren because it was her first time playing that type of villainous character. When this doujinshi was released, a writer acquaintance of mine told me, "Kobayashi-san found out about it, and she really wants to read it," so I gave him a copy for her. I wish I could have found out how she liked it.

Gemma

The unusual names that appear in this work all have the same source as those of Graham and the others, the *Hamidashikko* series. Ronald was a friend of Graham's adoptive father; Eve Horn is Angie's biological mother, who is also an actress; Elvarje is Sanin's pet horse; the "meal to satisfy me" is the name of the meal Angie made in Part One of the series; and the title is from another part of the story, *G.A.S.M.'s Cooking Classroom*. Oh how I wish I could've put in more *Hamidashikko* references...

Tikurakuran

This is my favorite of all the short stories I've written. I wanted to write about the Old Codgers back in the day when they were active in the uprising of the three branch families, but the story ended up having a different main character. Furthermore, I made a point of omitting the key parts—Lucrezia's death and Mina-hime's escape. I figured Tamaki-sensei would put them in the main manga someday.

Bad Ischl is a place that appears in *Carrion Comfort* (mentioned above). Incidentally, the strategy that Mina uses to infiltrate the Bund towards the end of the manga is the same tactic used in this story by Alphonse the First. It might be interesting to look at this as a message from Mina-hime to Alphonse. The delegation that Lorenzo talks about in the end is the Tenshō Embassy.

For the title, I really liked the linguistic feel of the title of the *Star Trek* novel *A Flag Full of Stars*, so I tried doing my own version.

LOST IN THE VAMPIRE BUND

Release Date: August 1, 2010 (Comic Market 78)

Title Origin: From the 1979 song "Lost in Hollywood" by the British hard rock band Rainbow. Literally, it means "unable to find your way in the Vampire Bund," but metaphorically, it can mean "engrossed in the Vampire Bund."

DOUJINSHI CONTENTS:

Short Manga: (untitled) by Nozomu Tamaki
While she sleeps, Mina-hime dreams of being high-school aged and flirting with Akira.

Short Story: "Time to Hunt" by Tikurakuran
A female vampire is ordered to smuggle human blood.

Short Story: "The Sun Beyond the Window" by Gemma
Saji-sensei uncovers the mystery behind a vampire girl's death at her high school.

Four-Panel Manga: "Good Luck, Akira-kun!!" by Masayuki Fujiwara

Trivia Collection: "The Devil is in the Details"

PRODUCTION NOTES:

Nozomu Tamaki
    I drew this manga because I wanted to see seventeen-year-old Mina and adult Akira again. The bikini she wears in the short is the same one she's wearing on the cover. The situation is that Mina is held unconscious by nanomachines, and Fake Mina is spying on her dreams.
    It's explained in a roundabout way in the main manga, but the reason the Impostor is able to copy Mina so perfectly is that the nanomachines have transmitted all of Mina's memories—including these dreams—to the Impostor, and she has seen them all with her own eyes.

Tikurakuran
    The concept for this story came from the bows and arrows of the Mughal Empire, which I saw on the History Channel. I combined this idea with a vampire psycho killer. The 3-chan bit at the beginning of the story is my attempt at portraying human society's reaction to vampires.
    There's some Librarian bait casually mixed in with the comments on the screen. Gemma-kun and Fujiwara-sensei helped me to come up with subjects for the 50 threads—some serious, some totally ridiculous.
    I relied entirely on Gemma-kun for the image processing. I played with a lot of things for this story, so please look carefully. For the Librarian's appearance, I imagined the actor Patrick McGoohan playing him.
    The title is from Stephen Hunter's 1998 novel of the same name.

Gemma
    As I wrote in the doujinshi's afterword, my motive for writing this story was my shock and joy that Saji-sensei appeared in the main manga.
    Tikurakuran-san follows the naming pattern of the manga, and he always names stories after foreign novels and movies. I'm not educated enough for that, so this title is original.

BLOOD MUSIC

Release Date: December 31, 2010 (Comic Market 79)

Title Origin: From the title of Greg Bear's 1985 science fiction novel, *Blood Music*.

DOUJINSHI CONTENTS:

Short Manga: "Friends ~A Few Rumors About Him~" by Nozomu Tamaki
Childhood friends and classmates talk about their impressions of Kaburagi Akira.

Short Story: "Apples from a Tree" by Gemma
The 80-year strife between a vampire mother and child as history makes sport of them.

Short Story: "The Manchurian Candidate" by Tikurakuran
The Li Clan's connection to the 1970 attempted coup in China.

Four-Panel Manga: "Good Luck, Akira-kun!!" by Masayuki Fujiwara

Trivia Collection: "The Devil is in the Details"

PRODUCTION NOTES:

Nozomu Tamaki

I wanted to reaffirm what kind of a guy this Akira kid is. As we listen to all his friends, we can see that after a certain point in time, their impressions of him change significantly. I don't think that's too unusual in adolescence, although it's probably not as drastic as it is with Akira. The key here is that it's done in an interview format, and Akira himself does not make an appearance (ha ha). Since we get answers from Yuki, who is still in bed and cannot talk, I guess this takes place between volumes 12 and 13.

Tikurakuran

Aside from Counselor Ryuu's presence and the battle at Zhongnanhai, the events leading up to the Lin Biao Incident are historical fact. It was fun figuring out how to fit the fictional parts into an established course of events. Also, the geography of Beijing and the layout of the Chinese-Japanese embassy are exactly as they are in real life. This time we got to use our real-world knowledge.

Even though I created them, I was starting to think that Counselor Ryuu's mind control powers were a little too invincible, so for this story, I smashed them to pieces. In the end, Ryuu has "an idea"—that's me making puppy dog eyes at Tamaki-sensei, as if to say, "It would be really nice if this could be foreshadowing for something that happens in the manga." Also, the girl in the photo is Min-Mei.

The title comes from the American film, *The Manchurian Candidate*. It refers to the Li Clan's Manchurian customs, and Ryuu's plan to have Mao Zedong assassinated and succeeded by Lin Biao.

Gemma

Tikurakuran-san writes stories that combine history and various time periods so well I thought I'd give it a try. As for the result, I couldn't say.

I got the title from the English idiom, "The apple never falls far from the tree," which is similar in meaning to the Japanese idiom, "A frog's child will be a frog." The first printing had the title completely misprinted, and I still remember how depressed Tamaki-sensei was about that.

LET THE RIGHT ONE IN

Release Date: August 14, 2011 (Comic Market 80)

Title Origin: From the English title of the 2004 Swedish vampire novel, *Let the Right One In*. It's based on the tradition that a vampire cannot come inside until invited. The novel was adapted into a Swedish film in 2008, and an American remake (*Let Me In*) was filmed in 2010.

DOUJINSHI CONTENTS:

Short Story: "The World of Dance in the Vampire Bund: Building the Bund & School Life" by Nozomu Tamaki
An introduction to some unused concepts and to school life at the academy founded by Mina.

Short Story: "Les Enfants Terrible" by Tikurakuran
The siblings Jiji, Clara, and Anna find themselves in a dire predicament with Harvey.

Short Story: "Hematologie du Gout" by Gemma
A vampire on an endless quest for delicious blood searches for human blood.

Four-Panel Manga: "Good Luck, Akira-kun!!" by Masayuki Fujiwara

PRODUCTION NOTES:

Nozomu Tamaki
This work ended up with a strange flavor—not really any behind-the-scenes information or reminiscences here. I like it fairly well. I had come up with many school-related ideas, but I couldn't find a chance to draw most of them, so I wrote them all down here. Some of the material I reveal here was used in a collaborative novel for this issue.

Tikurakuran
My own child was growing up, and that's part of why I thought of writing a story featuring "child" characters like Jiji and Harvey. When creating Harvey's bodyguard, I thought it would be fun if the bodyguard was a child too, and so Mack was born.
Harvey and Mack live independently of the vampire hierarchy, so theirs isn't the usual master-servant relationship; they built up a sort of father-son relationship that has them almost equals. The song the three siblings sing is one that my child loved at that age, "Anpanman Gymnastics."
Furthermore, this work has several references to Gemma-kun's "Hematologie du Gout." If you have some time, I encourage you to look for them. The title is from French poet Jean Cocteau's 1929 novel of the same name.

Gemma
Lazzaro Spallanzani is a biologist who lived in the 18th century. Of the names listed by the protagonist, Caravaggio is a 16th century Italian painter; Lord Ruthven is the protagonist of John Polidori's "The Vampyre"; and Ms. Dieudonné is the protagonist of Kim Newman's *Anno Dracula*. Laurentis is an original character. *Bergamasque* is a piano suite by Debussy, a reference to a region in Italy. The title, of course, is from Brillat-Savarin's famous work La *Physiologie du Goût*.
I will never forget that Tamaki-sensei's wife was at the booth that summer, and she gave us frozen towels. It felt so good I could have died.

NO DIFFERENT FLESH

Release Date: December 31, 2011 (Comic Market 81)

Title Origin: The title of Zenna Henderson's 1966 science fiction novel, *No Different Flesh*.

DOUJINSHI CONTENTS:

Short Story: "No Different Flesh" by Tikurakuran, Gemma, and Nozomu Tamaki

A tale of people who fight the conspiracy surrounding the artificial blood, Stigma, tracing the history of House Tepes from the 17th century to the present day. All the original characters from past short stories make an appearance in this one. It is composed of three parts, with the prologue and epilogue manga drawn by Nozomu Tamaki.

Four-Panel Manga: "Good Luck, Akira-kun!!"
by Masayuki Fujiwara

PRODUCTION NOTES:

Nozomu Tamaki

Tikurakuran and Gemma said they were going to collaborate on a story, so I thought I could make my manga part of that story, too. As a result, I ended up drawing more pages than I've ever done before. They worked so hard writing this story, and then I stole the spotlight by giving Mina such a good line in the epilogue. Sorry.

Incidentally, the fake Wikipedia article and the vampire jokes printed at the beginning of the book were my creations.

Tikurakuran

This collaboration started when Gemma-kun and I had the idea to put all of the original characters we had created into one story. I was deeply touched to see the two-page character sheet that Tamaki-sensei drew for us. Because of the characters' concepts, it became a story spanning 400 years. I'm a little sad that we weren't able to include really good foreshadowing in the 17th century arc.

The story doesn't take place in Japan, so when Cunningham was showing movies in Part Two, I decided to translate the original English titles instead of using the Japanese movie titles. *Itaria-jin no Shigoto (The Italian Job)* and *Kuroi Nichiyōbi (Black Sunday)* are my translations of the Japanese titles of *Mini-Mini Daisakusen (The Italian Job)* and *Burakku Sandee (Black Sunday)*.

The reason watching the movies puts the Director in such a bad mood is that he's a former Nazi, and he hates Israelis (Jews).

Incidentally, for this Comic Market, Tamaki-sensei's daughter came to help out. While our product is marketed at everyone, we were in the men's section, so having a high school girl selling at our booth was a pretty bold move. Around this time, Tamaki-sensei could no longer hide his growing family-man persona.

Gemma

Tikurakuran-san and I met each other when Tamaki-sensei hosted a relay novel on his website. So it was a piece of cake to write something together… or it should have been, but this was the hardest story we ever wrote.

Incidentally, the writing was divided like so: Tikurakuran wrote Part One; Gemma wrote Part Two; and in Part Three, Tikurakuran wrote the Connie parts, and Gemma wrote the Mack parts. Well, that was the plan, but I was running behind, so I had Tikurakuran help me.

TWEET OF BEEHIVE

Release Date: May 5, 2012 (COMITIA 100)

Title Origin: From the original title of the 1979 Spanish film, *Spirit of the Beehive*. Because the subject matter is Twitter, we changed it to "Tweet of…"

DOUJINSHI CONTENTS:

Short Story: (untitled) by Nozomu Tamaki
Mina-hime starts using Twitter and answers fan-submitted questions.

Short Story: "Dog Day Afternoon" by Tikurakuran
After coming to Japan, the Wolf Boys hit the town to pick up girls.

Short Story: "Ever After" by Gemma
The story leading up to Jiji and his sisters being adopted by fellow Fangless.

Four-Panel Manga: "Good Luck, Akira-kun!!" by Masayuki Fujiwara

PRODUCTION NOTES:

Nozomu Tamaki
I drew this manga with the idea that Mina had started using Twitter. The questions were all real questions from my Twitter followers and fans. I got a ton of questions, which made it a lot of fun, and it made me really happy. I think there were even a couple of questions from international fans.

As I took on Mina-hime's persona to answer these questions, I think I started to know what it feels like to masquerade as someone else, like a *nekama*—a guy who pretends to be a girl online (ha ha). It's more fun than you'd think.

Tikurakuran
It wasn't until after the doujinshi had gone to print that I realized I had given my story the same title as Chapter 41 of the *Bund* manga. If I get a chance, I want to change it to "The Wolf Boys go to the Capital."

At first, I planned to do an epic historical piece, but I didn't have the time to finish it, so I thought I'd try my hand at light comedy (which was a big challenge). I used all kinds of tricks to bump up the page count.

There's almost nothing about the Wolf Boys' private lives in the main manga, so I had Tamaki-sensei tell me all about them as I wrote this story. There's still room to play with these characters, so I might put them in another story in the future.

Gemma
Desmond's last name is Evers, which I got from African-American civil rights activist Medgar Evers. I took almost all of Desmond's history from Evers's life. In contrast, I gave his wife a pretty weak history. After I wrote it, Tamaki-sensei said, "Actually, in my character concepts, I had her a veteran nurse who had studied under Florence Nightingale, but since you've already written it, let's go with that."

I'm sorry; the title is another original.

PAVANE POUR L'INFANTE VIVANTE

Release Date: August 12, 2012 (Comic Market 82)

Title Origin: From composer Maurice Ravel's 1899 piano piece *Pavane Pour une Infante Défunte (Pavane for a Dead Princess)*.

DOUJINSHI CONTENTS:

Short Story: "Kiss x Kiss" by Nozomu Tamaki
After the fake queen leaves, Akira and Mina spend some quiet time together.

Short Story: "Bund no Chūzai-san (Bund Policeman)" by Tikurakuran
The daily challenges faced by Inspector Hama, the only human police officer in the Bund.

Short Story: "A Fine and Private Place" by Gemma
A vampire and human struggle over their interracial love in high school.

Four-Panel Manga: "Good Luck, Akira-kun!!" by Masayuki Fujiwara

PRODUCTION NOTES:

Nozomu Tamaki

The setting here is that Part One is over, and everything has calmed down. I came up with the idea when I was live-tweeting the anime and I wrote, "In the manga, Akira's first kiss was stolen by a transformed Mina-hime in volume one."

I've always wanted to write about it. I really wanted to put it in the main manga, but it would have been too much of a stretch to fit it into the chronology. The line "I don't remember it!" is really good, if I do say so myself (ha ha).

Tikurakuran

This story is the first time I ran out of time and gave up. Originally, it was going to be in three parts, and there was supposed to be an action-packed second act where Hama used thermography to find the abducted humans—who are the opposite of the police's vampire hunters—and save them after a fight. I had to break my self-imposed unwritten rule of at least one intense action scene per story.

There are references to past gaiden stories scattered throughout the story, so if you have all of the doujinshi, see if you can find them. I was really happy when my original bit character the demon priest was used soon after in "The Memories of Sledgehammer."

Any Kansai native aged forty or older will remember *Hana no Chūzai-san (Flower Policeman)*, which is where I got the title.

Gemma

Mina and Akira, Nanami and Yuzuru—in the manga, all the human and vampire couples are deeply in love, so in this story, I wanted to show that not all of these relationships work out so well.

The title is from title of Ellery Queen's novel *A Fine and Private Place*.

...MUST COME TO AN END

Release Date: December 29, 2012 (Comic Market 83)

Title Origin: From the phrase "All good things must come to an end," penned by Geoffrey Chaucer in his poem titled "Troilus and Criseyde."

DOUJINSHI CONTENTS:

Short Story: (untitled) by Nozomu Tamaki
Epilogue set after volume 14. Mina-hime bestows Chimie with the 'Kiss of the Rose.'

Short Story: "The Moonlit Classroom" by
Tikurakuran & Gemma
The students of Mina-hime's private school—humans, Fangless and vampires—join together to hold their prom, while the hysteria of Tokyo's vampire pandemic rages on around them.

Commentary: "Dance in the Vampire Bund Doujinshi Chronicle"

Trivia Collection: "The Devil is in the Details: Complete Version"

Four-Panel Manga: "Good Luck, Akira-kun!!" by Masayuki Fujiwara

PRODUCTION NOTES:

To commemorate the publication of *Dance in the Vampire Bund Vol. 14*, which drew "Part 1" of the Bund Saga to a close, Circle Tamakiya released the "...Must Come To An End" doujinshi. The 100-page book marked the tenth consecutive issue of Circle Tamakiya's official *Dance in the Vampire Bund* doujinshi and included the preceding "Doujinshi Chronicle" section you just read, which revealed lots of fun trivia, tidbits that didn't make it into the short stories, and production secrets about "Part 1" of the series that couldn't be revealed until now.

Thank you so much for reading and we'll see back in the *Bund*verse for the start of *Dance in the Vampire Bund II: Scarlet Order*!

ダンスインザヴァンバイアバンドTVアニメ放映記念同人誌

THEY THIRST

環屋

ダンスインザヴァンバイアバンドアニメ化記念同人誌

FEVER DREAM

環屋

ダンスインザヴァンバイアバンド アニメ終了記念同人誌

SAVE THE LAST DANCE FOR ME

環屋

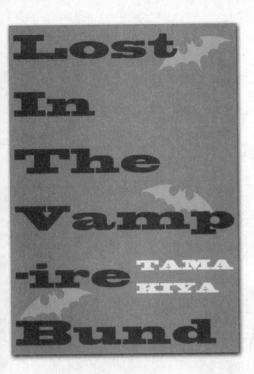

Lost In The Vamp -ire Bund

TAMA KIYA

BLOOD MUSIC

TAMAKIYA

TAMAKIYA

LET THE RIGHT ONE IN

No Different Flesh

tamakiya

Pavane pour
l'infante vivante
〜生ける王女のためのパヴァーヌ〜

環屋

Pavane pour
l'infante vivante
〜生ける王女のためのパヴァーヌ〜

Tamakiya

Dance in the Vampire Bund